BELFAST
400 PEOPLE, PLACE AND HISTORY

EDITED BY S.J. CONNOLLY

Queen's University
Belfast

BELFAST 400
PEOPLE, PLACE AND HISTORY

EDITED BY S.J. CONNOLLY

LIVERPOOL
UNIVERSITY PRESS

First published 2012 by
Liverpool University Press
4 Cambridge Street
Liverpool
L69 7ZU

Copyright © 2012 Liverpool University Press

The authors' rights have been asserted in
accordance with the Copyright, Designs and
Patents Act 1988.

All rights reserved. No part of this book may
be reproduced, stored in a retrieval system,
or transmitted, in any form or by any means,
electronic, mechanical, photocopying,
recording, or otherwise, without the prior
written permission of the publisher.

British Library Cataloguing-in-Publication data

A British Library CIP record is available

ISBN 978-1-84631-635-7 softback

ISBN 978-1-84631-634-0 cased

ISBN 978-1-84631-636-4 cased with slip case

Typeset by Alan Ward @
www.axisgraphicdesign.co.uk

Set in Jannon by Stormtype and FS Elliot by
Typesmith

Printed and bound on FSC accedited stock by
Gutenberg Press Ltd, Malta

Front cover image: Belfast Views, Wellington
Place © Paul Lindsay / Scenic Ireland.

Back cover image: Photo by Michael Walsh,
www.pushfotografik.com

Endpapers: A Birds-Eye View of Belfast 1883.
Image courtesy of Belfast City Council.

Contents

Preface

The immediate occasion for this book is the 400th anniversary of the granting in 1613 of a royal charter to the newly established town of Belfast. It is an anniversary that fits all too easily into one version of history. It emphasizes the town's origins as an instrument of the plantation whereby James I and his ministers sought to transform what had been the last stronghold of Gaelic Ireland into a British and Protestant colony: indeed the charter was one of several granted, not to bolster a new urban network, but to create constituencies that could be counted on to return Protestant MPs to a forthcoming Irish parliament. From this it is easy to move on to Belfast's subsequent role as one prominent theatre in the prolonged political conflict arising from that episode of conquest and dispossession.

None of this background is ignored in the pages that follow. At the same time the impetus behind the book is a strong sense, shared by all the contributors, that there is a great deal more to the history of Belfast than a zero-sum contest for possession between mutually hostile groups defined exclusively by their religious and political allegiance. Archaeological investigation reveals a history, stretching back millennia before King James's charter, of human interaction with a rich but challenging environment. There is fragmentary but tantalizing evidence of a medieval Belfast, whose fortunes rose and fell with those of the first English settlement in Ulster. The seventeenth-century plantation town may have begun as a minor outpost, overshadowed by Carrickfergus to the north, but a little over a century later, Belfast was one of Ireland's most important ports. By the late eighteenth century it was also an Irish example of what has been called 'the urban renaissance', developing as a centre of polite manners, cultural refinement and intellectual enquiry. It is no accident that it was in Belfast that the United Irishmen launched their doomed but visionary attempt to escape from the narrow confines of Ireland's ethnic and religious conflicts, hoping instead to realize the vision of progress and liberation held out by the Enlightenment on one hand, and by the American and French revolutions on the other.

If the achievements of eighteenth-century Belfast are today less clearly remembered than they should be, it is largely because they have been overshadowed by the truly extraordinary developments that took place after 1800, as a medium-sized port and commercial centre expanded to become a manufacturing powerhouse. At the beginning of the twentieth century, when Britain was just ceasing to be the world's largest industrial economy and its empire covered a quarter of the globe, Belfast was the United Kingdom's eighth largest city. In terms of its signature products, linen and ocean-going liners, it was a centre of world importance. The late Victorian and Edwardian architecture of the city centre is a monument to the spirit of confident self-assertion and civic pride fostered by this spectacular economic success. Yet the physical infrastructure of that success, the mills and other factory buildings, the forest of chimneys that once greeted the approaching traveller, even the shipyards, have largely disappeared. Where they survive it is as isolated pieces of 'heritage', as a once proud centre of large-scale manufacturing seeks to create for itself a new, post-industrial identity. Largely vanished also, through massive schemes of urban redevelopment, are the long streets of small terraced dwellings constructed during Belfast's industrial heyday, and with them, to a large extent, the tight-knit working-class communities they once housed.

The history of Belfast is long, complex and many-layered. Alongside the cappucino bars and call centres of the contemporary city there are still visible remnants of the industrial giant that was for a time Ireland's largest urban centre. Behind them again, less visible but still recoverable, are the traces of older phases of development: the Atlantic port, the plantation town, the succession of tower-houses and castles erected to defend a strategic ford, with the communities that grew up around them. The chapters that follow try to recover something of the experience of the men and women who lived and worked in all of these different Belfasts.

S.J. Connolly
February 2012

Acknowledgements

The idea of a new history of Belfast was first suggested by Anthony Cond of Liverpool University Press, and I am most grateful to him and his colleagues for their assistance throughout the book's production. In particular Alison Welsby has undertaken the challenging task of coordinating the different elements of the finished work, and has displayed admirable calm and patience throughout.

The book is published with financial support from Belfast City Council and Queen's University, Belfast. At a time when the city faces so many important decisions about its future, it is gratifying to see these two key institutions come together to support a work of this kind. My research for the project was funded by a Leverhulme Trust Research Project Grant, and I am most grateful to the Trust for its open-minded willingness thus to support a venture into a largely new field of research by an academic in late career. The project grant also made possible the employment as research officer of Dr Gillian McIntosh, who took responsibility for coordinating the work of the contributors and for research on the visual images. Parts of the volume also draw on earlier research carried out by myself and Dr Dominic Bryan for the Economic and Social Research Council project 'Identities and Social Action', supported by ESRC grant RES-148-25-0054.

For assistance in obtaining copies of images for the volume I am grateful to Dr Eileen Black, Mr Ben Crothers (Naughton Gallery, Queen's University) and Dr Joseph McBrinn (University of Ulster). Robert Heslip has also been of great assistance, both in his professional role as Heritage Officer for Belfast City Council and in a personal capacity, for his knowledgeable advice on a range of historical issues.

In my work on Belfast I have been fortunate in learning from four of my doctoral students, Dr Paul Harron, Dr Alice Johnston, Dr Jonathan Wright and, at an earlier stage, Dr Catherine Hirst. I was also fortunate to have had, as my own supervisor long ago, a pioneer of the historical study of Belfast, the late Professor Tony Hepburn. It is one of my great regrets that I became seriously interested in the city and its history too late to benefit more fully from his knowledge and insight. Finally, my thanks as always to Mavis Bracegirdle, this time for her tolerance as a total outsider lays hands on the history of her native city.

Other contributors to the volume have also asked for their thanks to be recorded. Ruairí Ó Baoill would like to thank Dr Philip Macdonald and Professor Sean Connolly for reading over earlier drafts of his chapter and making useful suggestions for its improvement. Thanks also to Gahan and Long Ltd for permission to use the image reproduced on page 74. Philip Macdonald is grateful to Siobhan Stevenson (National Museums Northern Ireland), Robert Heslip (Belfast City Council), Colin Dunlop and Stephen Gilmore (Northern Archaeological Consultancy Ltd), Audrey Gahan (Gahan and Long Archaeological Services Ltd), Ruairí Ó Baoill, Audrey Horning and Colm Donnelly (Queen's University, Belfast) and Nick Brannon. Gillian McIntosh would like to thank Tom Clyde, Robert Corbett, Maura Cronin, John Curran, Patsy Horton, Diarmuid Kennedy, Pamela Linden, Joseph McBrinn, Leanne McCormick, Ian Montgomery, Michelle O'Riordan, Diane Urquhart, and the staffs of Belfast Central Library, the Linenhall Library, the Public Record Office of Northern Ireland, National Museums of Northern Ireland, the National Museum of Ireland, the National Library of Ireland and Special Collections, Queen's University, Belfast. Stephen Royle gratefully acknowledges a Small Research Grant from the British Academy, and would like to thank Dr Edwin Aiken, now a lecturer in Geography at Bristol, for his contribution as post-doctoral research assistant.

S.J. Connolly
Belfast, July 2012

Abbreviations

Benn, *Belfast* (1823) [George Benn], *The History of the Town of Belfast, with an Accurate Account of its Former and Present State* (Belfast: A. Mackay, 1823)

Benn, *Belfast* (1877) George Benn, *A History of the Town of Belfast from the Earliest Times to the Close of the Eighteenth Century* (Belfast: Marcus Ward, 1877)

BNL *Belfast News Letter*

BPP British Parliamentary Papers

NAI National Archives of Ireland, Dublin

PRONI Public Record Office of Northern Ireland, Belfast

UJA *Ulster Journal of Archaeology*

List of Tables

Selected Maps

Imagining Belfast

S.J. Connolly and Gillian McIntosh

Do not you think Belfast ought not to have been built where it is?

Well, it is perhaps a crotchet of my own that there are parts of the town that it would be better had not been built upon, but one cannot help what has been done.

You think Belfast ought not to have been built where it is?

I think it would have been better if the streets had not been built sometimes under high-water mark.

[...]

The wisest thing the Corporation could have done would have been to knock down the town altogether?

No; but I say that people certainly show an improved knowledge about those things, for they are not taking the land.[1]

These extraordinary exchanges, during an enquiry in 1859 into the affairs of the municipal borough of Belfast, had a specific context. Robert Young, a rising young architect who was to become one of the leading figures in the development of the nineteenth-century town, was justifying his opposition to a controversial recent initiative: the construction in the mid-1840s of Victoria Street and Corporation Street, laid out as broad new thoroughfares designed to carry traffic crossing the new Queen's Bridge from County Down away from the congested town centre. He believed that the council should instead have widened the existing Rosemary Street. By trying to push him into declaring that the town should not have been built at all, or at least not on its existing site, the council's lawyer was clearly seeking to discredit Young's evidence. Yet his repetitive hectoring touched on a real point. Belfast's success as an urban centre, about to enter its most dramatic phase just as these exchanges took place, was achieved in the face of a remarkably unpromising natural environment. To put it another way: there were indeed good reasons to question why Belfast, built where it was, should have prospered as it did.

Young's arguments in 1859 focused on the problem of building a town on low-lying, waterlogged land. As evidence he pointed to the subsidence

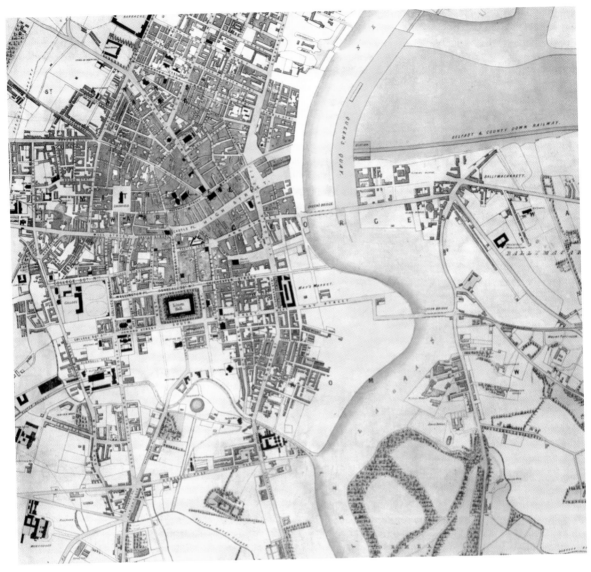

affecting the first buildings erected on the new Victoria Street. Seventy-five years earlier the White Linen Hall, intended as the showpiece of the rapidly growing late eighteenth-century town, had suffered embarrassingly from the same problem, as had the exclusive new housing development in nearby Donegall Place.[2] And indeed, the need for adequate foundations was to continue into the twenty-first century to demand heroic counter-measures on the part of builders. Poor natural drainage was also one reason for the long delay in equipping the Victorian town with a proper system for sewage disposal. But there were also other problems. Belfast Lough provided a sheltered haven for shipping, with the valley of the River Lagan as a convenient corridor extending deep into a fertile countryside. As a port on the shores of this lough, on the other hand, Belfast was initially unpromising. Its harbour

This detail from James O'Hagan's map of Belfast in 1848 clearly illustrates the town council's first major exercise in urban planning. Victoria Street, driven through a former waterfront slum, carries traffic crossing the recently completed Queen's Bridge from County Down away from the town centre and towards the markets, now relocated from the centre to a new site on the periphery of the built-up area.

Photograph © National Museums Northern Ireland. Collection Ulster Museum. IA 1848.

was a silted-up expanse of shallow water, eventually to be made suitable for ocean-going shipping, and for a shipbuilding industry specializing in large vessels, only through massive engineering works. In addition Belfast would develop as a successful centre of heavy industry in a region that had no significant deposits of iron ore or coal, and at a time when other Irish towns were experiencing industrial decline and demographic stagnation. In all of these respects Belfast in its heyday seemed, to many, a miracle of human achievement against the environmental odds.

This image of a town created from almost nothing encouraged a distinctive perspective on Belfast's past. One by-product of the growth of civic pride that characterized the provincial cities of Victorian Britain was the publication of substantial and celebratory local histories. In Manchester Town Hall, for example, a series of murals by the artist Ford Madox Brown began with the building of a Roman fort at Mancenion in AD 80. The inhabitants of nineteenth-century Belfast were not indifferent to history in general. When the British Association for the Advancement of Science visited the town in 1852, the arrangements for their reception included an elaborate display of ogham stones, Irish manuscripts and other antiquities put together by Robert Shipboy McAdam and his brother James, proprietors of the Soho Iron Foundry. The launch the following year of the *Ulster Journal of Archaeology*, edited by Robert Shipboy McAdam, was further evidence of a commitment to the serious study of the past. The history of Belfast itself, however, aroused less enthusiasm. James Adair Pilson, the first local author to take up the task of publicizing the town's achievements, entitled his work a *History of the Rise and Progress of Belfast* (1846). What he produced, however, was primarily an enthusiastic description of the contemporary town. The 'history', just ten pages long, opened with the observation that Belfast was 'comparatively a modern town', with 'no claim to ecclesiastical antiquity, or monkish patronage, for its foundation'.[3] The *Belfast News Letter*, commenting in 1888 on the town's promotion to city status, turned the absence of a lengthy past into a positive virtue: 'Our history is modern, neither encumbered by legends, nor disfigured by tragical invectives. Belfast greatness began within living memory.'[4] Later still, in 1948, a locally born poet offered his own irreverent paraphrase: 'This jewel that houses our hopes and our fears / Was knocked up from the swamp in the past hundred years.'[5]

This sense of pursuing an elusive goal influenced even those few who did devote themselves to the study of Belfast's history. George Benn (1801–82), son of a brewer and landowner, began the short account he published in 1823 by noting that there was no town in Ireland 'which has advanced to eminence with equal rapidity, or which has been so little distinguished in the ancient history of Ireland, and so much in the modern'.[6] His much more substantial *A History of the Town of Belfast*, written more than half a century later, began on the same note: 'Belfast, as a town, has no ancient history.' A colleague, himself an antiquarian and archivist, wrote to congratulate Benn on his achievement: 'I think you have managed to do an almost impossible thing, namely to create a history for an unhistoric town.'[7]

To a large extent, no doubt, this disavowal of a historic past was no more than a pragmatic response to the thinness of the documentary record and the absence of significant architectural remains. Ideology, however, may also have played a part. As Belfast emerged as the capital of Irish Unionism, a degree of historical amnesia was one response to the embarrassments presented by the events of the 1780s and 1790s, when the same town was the birthplace of a United Irish movement committed to the establishment of an independent Irish republic. There were also the obvious attractions of suggesting that Belfast's economic growth had come about after, and as a direct result of, the union of Great Britain and Ireland in 1800. In 1841 Henry Cooke, the leading Presbyterian clergyman of his day, concluded a lengthy oration against the repeal of the Act of Union with an appeal to local pride:

> Before the union, Belfast was a village; now it ranks with the cities of the earth. Before the union it had a few coasting craft, and a few American and West Indian ships – and that open bay, which now embraces the navies of every land, was but a desert of useless water. The centre of our town was studded with thatched cottages, where now stands one of the fairest temples to the genius of industry and commerce. Our merchants, then unknown, are now welcomed in every land […] In one word more I have done with my argument. Look at Belfast, and be a Repealer – if you can.[8]

All this, as will be clear from Chapter 5 below, was a grotesque misrepresentation of the actual state of development that Belfast had reached by the late eighteenth century. But Cooke's vivid imagery appears to have taken root. A full three decades later the *Belfast News Letter* precisely echoed his language, contrasting the population of 174,000 revealed in the census of 1871 with the supposed situation a century earlier, when 'Belfast was not much more than a fishing village, with a population of about 9,000.'[9]

The task of a new urban history of Belfast is thus to steer a course between extremes, avoiding both the exuberant inventions of Manchester Town Hall and the wilful amnesia of the Revd Henry Cooke. Such a narrative must begin with the history of human settlement in the general area of the Lagan estuary, extending over several millennia, and now gradually coming to light through the piecemeal work of archaeologists. It must trace the development of a settlement at Belfast itself, from the glimpses that occur in the early and medieval records to the fuller account that can be constructed of the early modern and eighteenth-century town. At the same time it must do justice to the extraordinary transformation that did indeed take place in the nineteenth

George Benn (1801–82), pioneering historian of Belfast as portrayed by Richard Hooke. Hooke (1820–1908), originally a carpenter and partly self-taught, established himself from the 1840s as Belfast's leading portraitist, catering to the aspirations of the merchants and professional men of the expanding industrial town.

Photograph © National Museums Northern Ireland. Collection Ulster Museum. BELUM.U2341.

century, as Belfast became one of the great industrial centres of the United Kingdom. Throughout it must take account, not just of the changing character of Belfast itself, but of the very different ways in which those who have lived there imagined themselves and the town that was their home.

Table 1: Population of Belfast, 1757–2001

	Town/City	Outer Suburbs
1757	8,549	
1791	18,320	
1821	37,277	
1831	53,287	
1841	75,308	
1851	97,784	
1861	119,393	
1871	174,412	
1881	208,122	
1891	255,950	
1901	349,180	48,329
1911	386,947	52,295
1926	415,151	58,716
1937	438,086	68,088
1951	443,671	103,976
1961	415,856	162,570
1971	362,082	240,309
1991	236,116	244,435
2001	232,319	265,541

Source: 1757, 1791: Raymond Gillespie and S.A. Royle, *Irish Historic Towns Atlas – No. 12: Belfast to 1840* (Dublin: Royal Irish Academy, 2003), p. 10 (contemporary estimates); 1821–1901: W.E. Vaughan and A.J. Fitzpatrick, *Irish Historical Statistics: Population 1821–1971* (Dublin: Royal Irish Academy, 1978), pp. 36–37, 47; 1901–2001: F.W. Boal and S.A. Royle, *Enduring City: Belfast in the Twentieth Century* (Belfast: Blackstaff Press, 2006), p. 82.

Beginnings

The importance of geography, both positive and negative, was evident from the very earliest times. Ireland's oldest urban centres, such as Dublin and Waterford, could trace their origins back to Viking settlements established around the year 900. Before that some already had an existence as significant monastic sites. Belfast's continuous history as a town, by contrast, went back no further than the early seventeenth century. Even in the much longer history of human settlement along the east Ulster coast, the site, low-lying and waterlogged, had few attractions. Instead, as the archaeological record makes clear, the earliest inhabitants of the district made their homes where the more affluent suburbanites do today: on the higher ground of the Malone ridge, the Castlereagh hills, or the lower slopes of the Antrim plateau. Traces of these settlements were visible to the inhabitants of the early modern and nineteenth-century town: the Giant's Ring to the south; McArt's Fort, on a height above the town, where Theobald Wolfe Tone climbed on a last excursion with his radical friends before leaving for exile in America; the dugout canoe uncovered in 1868. Others, as Ruairí Ó Baoill outlines in the following chapter, have been brought to light by systematic modern excavation, making it possible to build up a picture of human settlement in the surrounding landscape, extending back to perhaps 4000 BC.

At the same time that water diminished Belfast's prospects as a place to live, it also gave the site its enduring significance. Over time changes in river and sea levels, along with the gradual build-up of a sandbank, created a natural crossing point over the broad, meandering waters of the Lagan estuary. The strategic importance of this ford may well account for the location of the

Belfast in its physical setting, at the head of the Lagan valley and the mouth of Belfast Lough, with what was initially the more important stronghold of Carrickfergus to the north. Of the lesser rivers shown, the Farset and Blackstaff were used extensively for industrial purposes, before being culverted over in the late nineteenth century. The Milewater was for a time part of the town's water supply, feeding into extensive waterworks constructed in 1842, but was redeveloped from the 1870s as a public park.

Map by Stephen Ramsay Cartography.

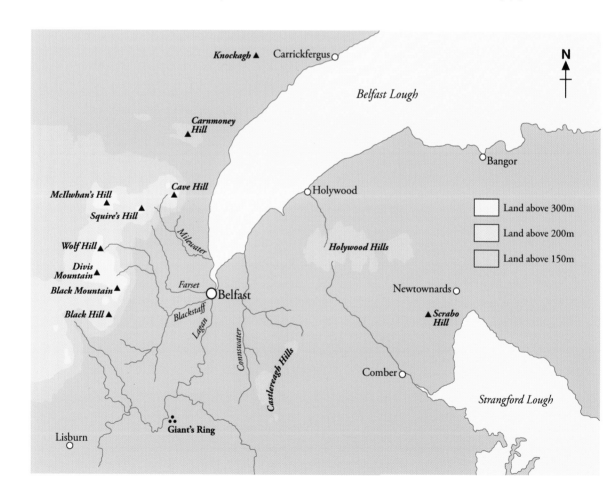

The Long Bridge, completed between 1680 and c.1685 and spanning the broad shallows of the undrained river, confirmed the central importance to Belfast's development of this long-established crossing point on the Lagan. J.W. Carey's nostalgic portrait was completed in 1903, more than fifty years after the crumbling seventeenth-century structure was replaced by the Queen's Bridge.

Reproduced with the kind permission of Belfast City Council.

battle of 668 whose terse mention in the annals provides the starting point for Philip Macdonald's account in Chapter 3. It was certainly the central reason for subsequent settlement on the site. It was not until the 1680s, with the construction of the Long Bridge, that the ford became redundant. By this time military advantage was becoming less important and commercial traffic more so. But the 21 arches of the new bridge, the largest structure of its kind in Ireland, testified to the extent to which Belfast's fortunes remained inextricably bound up with the river crossing.

Ireland's second major phase of urbanization began with the English settlement of the twelfth century, and this time Belfast was part of the process. The settlement on the Lagan began as no more than one of a system of defensive mottes in the hinterland of the main castle and settlement at Carrickfergus. Its first name, *Le Ford*, highlights once again the importance of the river crossing. The written record offers little more than tantalizing occasional references to a castle and a church. The archaeological evidence, examined in detail in Chapters 2 and 3 below, hints at the possibility of something more substantial – as for example with what may be the remains of a waterfront structure found beneath the current Victoria Square.[10] But investigation is still at an early stage. Neither type of source, moreover, tells us anything about the people who spent all or part of their lives as residents of this first Belfast. Evidence from other, better-documented urban centres suggests a multi-layered picture. The passage and periodic enforcement of bye-laws denying persons of Gaelic Irish language, dress and name the right to participate in town life, or excluding them entirely from urban centres, testify to a desire to preserve the towns as centres of English culture. Yet in practice the need to trade with a Gaelic hinterland, and to recruit new inhabitants for centres whose living conditions ensured that deaths consistently exceeded births, brought about a constant interchange across ethnic lines. East Ulster towns were smaller than their counterparts in Munster and Leinster, and lay on the outer fringes of the English colony. But a stray reference in 1333 to an

Irishman holding land in return for rent and the provision of labour at hay making suggests that in Belfast, too, pragmatic considerations ensured that settler and native did not live wholly separate lives.[11]

Belfast was one of the high-water marks of English settlement in Ireland. After 1300, military reversals and the collapse of population following the devastating plague known as the Black Death (1348) meant that the colony contracted. Carrickfergus, along with some east coast towns such as Ardglass and Greencastle, survived as outposts of the lordship, in sporadic contact with Dublin by sea. Belfast, on the other hand, passed into the hands of the local branch of the O'Neills. Occasional references to a castle on the site being besieged or captured testify to the continued strategic importance of the river crossing. When the earl of Essex, in 1573, set out ambitious plans for a colony in east Ulster, he identified Belfast as 'a place meet for a corporate town, armed with all commodities, as a principal haven, wood and good ground, standing also upon a border, and a place of great importance for service'.[12] However, these plans did not survive his death in 1576. Instead the story of Belfast as an urban centre, in suspension from some point in the late fourteenth century, does not resume until after 1600, in the very different context created by the Ulster plantation.

Over the next two centuries the history of the re-established town was to move in time with the rhythms of a much wider world. In Great Britain necessarily imprecise estimates suggest that the proportion of the population living in towns rose from well under 8 per cent in 1600 to perhaps 30 per cent in 1700 and to 40 per cent by 1801.[13] Ireland remained consistently poorer and less urban. But there, too, there were periods of commercial expansion in the 1620s and 1630s, and during 1660–85. From the mid-1740s the country enjoyed a longer and more dramatic boom. Rising demand for Irish agricultural produce, first from across the Atlantic, then in industrializing Britain, along with the runaway growth of linen manufacturing, made possible the rise of Dublin as an elegant European capital and of Cork as a great Atlantic port. Belfast remained smaller than both, but it nevertheless moved steadily up the Irish urban hierarchy. Its progress in the first half of the seventeenth century was modest. John Milton's dismissal in 1649 of 'a barbarous nook of Ireland' was a snarl of political and ethnic contempt rather than an informed economic judgement. But Belfast in 1640 was in fact a town of only 400–500 inhabitants, a third of the population of the plantation showpiece at Derry. By the 1690s, on the other hand, it was being spoken of as the most important town in Ulster. This was primarily on the basis of rising exports of beef and butter. By the mid-1720s, with the added commercial weight conferred by an expanding linen trade, it was Ireland's third busiest port, and possibly its sixth largest town.[14]

'A barbarous nook'

John Milton's celebrated dismissal of Belfast highlights the complex shifts of allegiance that took place in the town during the British and Irish civil wars of 1641–53. Following the rising in arms of the Ulster Irish in October 1641, British settlers in Antrim and Down mobilized in their own defence. In Belfast they were commanded by Arthur Chichester (1606–75), nephew of the town's founder and later first earl of Donegall. At this stage Irish Protestants, menaced by the forces of the Confederate Catholics, were generally reluctant to be drawn into the civil war between king and parliament that had begun in England. Instead they accepted the leadership of the king's lord lieutenant, the duke of Ormond, who controlled Dublin. The Belfast force also cooperated with the army that the Scottish government, also at this stage neutral in the struggle between king and parliament, had sent to Ulster to protect settlers there. By 1643, however, Scotland had joined the war on the side of parliament. By this time too, many Irish Protestants were coming to see the English parliament as a more reliable (and better resourced) ally than the king. Chichester sought to hold Belfast for Charles I but was betrayed by his own soldiers, who opened the gates to the Scots and aligned themselves with the English parliament.

The execution on 30 January 1649 of Charles I changed everything. The Scots were already disillusioned with their radical English allies following disputes over the shape of a future religious settlement. They now protested angrily at the execution by an English parliament of a monarch who was also king of Scotland, and who had recently negotiated a new alliance with his Scottish subjects. The presbytery of Belfast joined in the general condemnation of 'an act so horrible, as no history, divine or human, hath laid a precedent of the like'. Milton, in reply, poured scorn on 'a generation of highland thieves and redshanks' permitted 'by the courtesy of England' to establish themselves in 'a barbarous nook of Ireland'.[1] Harsh words were followed by military action, as the Ulster Scots took up arms against the English parliament, for a time even entering into an alliance with the Confederate Catholics. Indeed the only recorded siege of Belfast was by an English army in October 1649, ending after three or four days with the surrender of the town and the temporary expulsion of its Scottish inhabitants.

1   [John Milton], *Articles of Peace Made and Concluded with the Irish Rebels and Papists [...] and a Representation of the Scotch Presbytery at Belfast in Ireland, Upon all which are Added Observations* (London, 1649), pp. 42–43, 60, 64–65.

In the late eighteenth and early nineteenth centuries the development of Belfast once again followed a broader pattern. The traditional view was that British towns remained chaotic and backward until municipal reform in 1835 replaced their archaic corporate institutions with elected councils. Modern research, however, suggests that it was only only in the 1830s and 1840s that the leading provincial towns began to lose ground in the face of increasing pressures. Before that most coped well with the first stages of industrialization and population growth. Local Acts of Parliament provided ad hoc solutions to the worst urban problems, creating Paving Boards and similar bodies to undertake tasks, such as organizing the lighting and cleaning of streets, that the old corporations were unable or unwilling to undertake. Civic pride inspired new building projects and the development of cultural institutions. Rising prosperity enhanced the role of towns as centres of consumption and sociability.[15] The experience of Belfast was very similar. In the mid-eighteenth century it went through a period of stagnation, due mainly to the incapacity of the fourth earl of Donegall. From the 1760s, however, it enjoyed a spectacular renaissance, reflected in the construction of new streets and public buildings, the establishment of charities and public bodies, and the creation of new social amenities. A Police Act in 1800 provided, not just for the eventual creation of a new system of law enforcement, but for a much improved system of local government.[16]

Subsequent rebuilding was to obliterate the greater part of the improved late Georgian town that thus came into existence. Instead its image is preserved in a phrase. Belfast in the late eighteenth and early nineteenth centuries was supposedly 'the northern Athens'. The label has provided a useful shorthand for historians seeking to define this distinctive period when Belfast was already a rapidly growing town but not yet a fully developed industrial centre. It has also served as an implied critique of the Belfast of the Victorian era and after, seen as having lost its earlier cultural and intellectual distinction in the pursuit of industrial wealth.

At this point, however, it becomes necessary to look more closely at the contemporary rhetoric from which the phrase is taken. The notion of Belfast as a second Athens has been traced back to a prologue spoken in the town's theatre in 1793, predicting that 'old time shall yet, with glad surprise / See in Belfast a second Athens rise'. The author of the piece, Hugh George Macklin, was later to achieve prominence as advocate general of Bombay. In 1795, however, he was a 24-year-old lawyer whose extravagance in speech had led his Trinity College contemporaries to nickname him Hugo Grotius Bragadaccio.[17] The much more widespread use of the term 'northern Athens' over the next few decades, equally, should not be taken altogether seriously. The real 'northern Athens' was of course Edinburgh, but the same language was used elsewhere

Donegall Place, Donegall Square and the area immediately adjacent were initially developed as a residential district, allowing wealthy residents to withdraw a short distance from the increasingly congested central area. From the mid-nineteenth century these private houses were replaced by the offices and warehouses of the expanding commercial centre. Numbers 7–11 Chichester Street, a terrace of four-storey houses dating from 1804, is an isolated survival of Belfast's lost Georgian architecture.

Photograph © Sean Connolly.

Donegall Place with the Linen Hall at its head. The trees and railings testify to the street's former status as an elite residential quarter. By this time, however, the expansion of the town's commercial centre meant that shopkeepers and merchants were invading the area, while affluent residents moved on to more peripheral locations such as College Square. Detail from James O'Hagan's map of Belfast in 1848.

Photograph © National Museums Northern Ireland. Collection Ulster Museum. IA 1848.

with little discrimination. In the early 1840s the opening of new assembly rooms in the local inn led a local newspaper to proclaim that the small town of Leominster had become 'the Athens of Herefordshire'. Later in the century Aberdare gloried in its reputation as 'Athen Cymru', the Athens of Wales.[18]

Did the claims of Belfast to Athenian status have any firmer foundation? There is undoubted evidence of a quickening of intellectual life in the late eighteenth and nineteenth centuries. On closer examination, however, much of this activity appears to have involved the same rather narrow circle of individuals who came together in a range of literary societies, educational institutions and publishing ventures.[19] In 1813 a correspondent in the *Belfast Monthly Magazine* published his scathing estimation of the tastes of the wider urban community:

> At present, in many companies, if by any chance the conversation should be turned to any object above the fashions, the weather, or the unimportant occurrences of the day, a large proportion of the company become dumb […] and the person who is hardy enough to introduce a literary subject has it all to himself.[20]

Here it may be necessary to allow for the assumed superiority of a self-appointed elite. Yet such comments, at the very time that the concept of a northern Athens was taking hold, remain a warning against taking exuberant contemporary rhetoric at face value.

Alongside this possibly misleading image of a late Georgian cultural efflorescence which the Victorian city was to fail to sustain sits another, even more potent, legend of a glorious past betrayed. This is the idea of radical

Belfast, the original home of the United Irishmen, which after 1798 supposedly succumbed to the forces of religious prejudice and economic self-interest, becoming instead a centre of bigotry and reaction. Here, even more clearly, the notion of a sudden break between the late eighteenth-century town and its nineteenth-century successor must be treated with caution. There was strong support in Belfast for the American War of Independence, for the campaigns of the Volunteers for free trade, legislative independence and parliamentary reform, and for the ideals of the early French Revolution. The United Irishmen, however, were from the start a radical minority, seeking to influence a much larger body of reformist opinion. Hence it is hardly surprising that, as events moved towards a military confrontation, many who were by no means admirers of the established order should have given their support to the government. Figures such as the Presbyterian minister William Bruce and the newspaper proprietor William Joy could sincerely claim that their loyalism in 1798 had in no way been a betrayal of their reformist principles.[21]

In considering the subsequent development of attitudes to Belfast's radical past, it is important to distinguish two strands within the legacy of the United Irishmen. By the 1840s it was clear that Belfast Protestants no longer supported any form of Irish self-government. Their change of heart was in part a response to the fears aroused by the new style of Catholic mass politics developed by O'Connell. There was also the growing sense, so powerfully articulated by Henry Cooke in 1841, that Belfast's prosperity was inextricably linked to the Act of Union. Even here, however, it is worth noting the appearance in 1848 of a shadowy Protestant repeal association. A commitment to political reform, meanwhile, was another matter. Throughout the early decades of the nineteenth century there was continued support in Belfast for the curbing of patronage, the widening of the electoral franchise, Catholic emancipation, the ending of the slave trade and other reformist causes. Even in 1835 the town's Conservative MP, James Emerson Tennent, addressing a meeting in Dublin, clearly felt that its liberal political record required a carefully worded defence:

> whatever political character may have been attached to Belfast by persons at a distance, from a recollection of the prominent part which it had once unfortunately taken in some of the most painful events in our history, its inhabitants had given abundant proof, during the last few years, that however impatient they might be of the existence of abuses, and however anxious for the rooting out of every grievance, they were still warmly attached to, and uniformly actuated by, those sound and constitutional principles which were at once protective of the prerogative of the crown and the most extended liberty of the people.[22]

In a more positive spirit, George Benn, in 1823, followed his account of the rise and defeat of the United Irishmen with an assurance that 'the spirit of political opposition which has so long distinguished the town of Belfast [...] has by no means evaporated', and that it retained 'the name of the most independent and public spirited town in the kingdom'.[23]

These words, written by a young man of 22, can be contrasted with those of the much older George Benn who in 1877 completed the full version of his history of Belfast. At this point Belfast still had a Liberal party, but the wider political environment had been transformed. Parliamentary reform in 1832 and 1867, along with the secret ballot, had opened the way to a popular and participatory, if not yet wholly democratic, electoral system. Meanwhile the Church of Ireland had been disestablished; civil service reforms had allowed merit to supersede political connections as the basis of official appointments; the criminal law had become more humane; the press was free of censorship; and there were the beginnings of land reform. In all of these ways the major grievances that had inspired the radicals of the late eighteenth and early nineteenth centuries no longer existed. It was against this background that Benn rounded off another neutral, factual account of the 1790s with the somewhat cryptic sentence: 'The spirit and enthusiasm of those distant days have long died out in the meaning of the last century.'[24]

The final stage in the redefinition of the legacy of the 1790s was visible in Belfast's response to the celebrations held throughout Ireland on the centenary of the insurrection in 1898. By this time the Home Rule crisis of 1885–86 had given local politics a sharper adversarial edge. A large commemorative procession, making its way from Smithfield to Hannahstown, came under sustained attack from a hostile Protestant crowd. How far the hostility of the attackers arose from any close knowledge of the events of 1798, and how far from a more direct response to the green banners and other nationalist symbols carried by the marchers, remains unclear. In fact the crowd quickly lost interest in the nationalist marchers, and instead engaged in several days of attacks on the police, the religiously mixed Royal Irish Constabulary whose replacement of the local town police in 1864 was still bitterly resented. The political leaders of Belfast loyalism, however, were explicit in their condemnation of the events of a century earlier. In a public letter the grand master and grand secretary of the Orange Grand Lodge of Belfast denounced the rebellion as 'an armed insurrection [...] characterised by a series of most foul and cowardly murders and massacres of innocent men and women whose only offence was their Protestantism'.[25] Some, notably the small group of Protestant nationalists such as Alice Milligan and F.J. Biggar, remained true to the historical reality, invoking the names of Henry Joy McCracken and other local leaders. On the other hand the Catholic nationalist processionists who made their way to Hannahstown were content to subsume Ulster's 1798 into a pan-Irish movement, marching as they did behind a mounted figure representing Robert Emmet to music that proclaimed them to be the boys of Wexford. In other words, while the descendants of the original United Irishmen rejected all connection with their memory, their local ideological heirs built their commemoration around events that had taken place more than 200 miles away. Historical amnesia, in Belfast, had two faces.

Workshop of the World

The changes that took place in Belfast across the nineteenth century were by any standard dramatic. Claims for the precise extent of Belfast's industrial primacy cannot always be taken at face value. One account, in 1913, noted that 'Belfast claims to have the "largest in the world" in no fewer than five different classes of industrial establishment: the largest shipyard, the largest linen mill, the largest mineral water factory, the largest tobacco factory, and the largest rope-walk', before adding shrewdly that such assertions were not always open to rigorous statistical verification.[26] But Belfast's position in the urban hierarchy had nevertheless changed dramatically. In 1800 it was just outside the 20 largest towns in the new United Kingdom. By the eve of the First World War it was the UK's eighth largest city, with a population that had risen from just below 20,000 in 1800 to 387,000 in 1911.

Observers in the first half of the nineteenth century were already aware that Belfast's industrial development set it apart from other Irish towns. To the Scot Henry Inglis, writing in 1834, its mills and factories, with their 'scores of tall chimneys and their clouds of utilitarian smoke, remind one of Manchester, Glasgow and Leeds'.[27] Anna and Samuel Hall, nine years later, were equally impressed by 'the most flourishing town of Ireland, and second in prosperity to few of the commercial or manufacturing towns of England'.[28] These flattering comparisons, however, related to the growth of a single industry, linen. The successful application of water and steam power to flax spinning, coming just at the time when Irish cotton was struggling to compete with larger English and Scottish producers, had given factory-based manufacturing a new lease of life. However, the experience of the second half of the century was to show that linen, a luxury product, was highly vulnerable to fluctuations in the global economy. By this time also, Belfast faced growing competition from low-cost producers in eastern Europe. Textile production, in any case, was a low-wage industry employing a largely female labour force. A Belfast in which the spinning and weaving of linen had remained the main economic activity would not have been Belfast. Instead the likelihood is that it would have resembled late nineteenth- and twentieth-century Derry: a factory town, but one plagued by high male unemployment and poor overall living standards.

What happened instead was that a second stage of industrialization, built around heavy engineering, and more particularly shipbuilding, secured Belfast's position as one of the industrial giants of the late Victorian and Edwardian United Kingdom. The history of shipbuilding can be traced back to the 1790s. At that stage, however, Belfast was only one of several Irish shipbuilding centres. As late as 1866, in fact, Belfast accounted for 3,717 tons of new shipping, rather less than half the Irish total of 8,096, while Waterford launched a respectable 2,370 tons and Dublin 1,170.[29] It was only during the 1870s that Belfast became the one Irish shipbuilding port of any significance. And it was only in the 1890s and 1900s that its two yards, Harland and Wolff and Workman, Clark & Co., moved into the first rank of United Kingdom producers.

The rapid flowering of shipbuilding in a region without local supplies of coal and iron was to give rise to much later speculation as to the hidden secret, most commonly assumed to be some exceptional talent for entrepreneurial innovation, behind Belfast's success. However, the *Belfast News Letter*, writing in 1862, before Belfast shipbuilding had yet escaped a purely Irish competitive context, offered a prescient account of the town's natural advantages:

> from its proximity to the best and cheapest iron and coal markets both of England and Scotland, and the abundance of cheap labour obtainable, this trade only requires to receive proper encouragement and facilities to take the precedence in those branches over all the other towns of Ireland.[30]

Modern studies confirm that Harland and Wolff did in fact make more use than other yards of unskilled labour, which in Belfast was abundant and cheap. At the same time the town's good-quality housing, and the employment for female members of the household provided by its linen mills, allowed it to attract specialized skilled workers where needed. There were also definite advantages, at a time of rapid technological innovation, to being a latecomer. In the 1880s Belfast's output remained a fraction of that of the Clyde – 35,000 tons in 1888, compared to 280,000 tons. But already by 1883 the American consul reported that 'Belfast, a modern shipbuilding port, is the Clyde's keenest competitor in fine passenger boats'.[31]

Finally there was, as the *Belfast News Letter* had noted, the town's easier access, compared to other Irish towns, to the leading British centres of heavy engineering. Only a narrow strip of water separated Belfast, with its much-improved harbour facilities and abundant waterside space, from the increasingly overcrowded shipyards of the Clyde and the Mersey. Back and forth across it passed raw materials, technical expertise and human capital, creating what was for practical purposes a single region of advanced industrial production.

Urban growth and industrial expansion confronted the people of Belfast with a whole new series of challenges and opportunities. The worst consequences were felt in working-class residential areas. Some of the poorest inhabitants of the town continued to live, as in the eighteenth century, in courts and alleys behind the main streets, where rising numbers added to already chronic problems of overcrowding and the lack of basic amenities such as water and sanitation. In the new residential districts that had grown up to the north and west, and across the river at Ballymacarrett, conditions were also often desperate. Whole rows of houses had been erected back to back, with water provided from a few communal pumps and no provision even for shared privies. Similar conditions existed in other industrial towns. Indeed observers noted that Belfast had no equivalent to the notorious tenements found in Dublin and in Scottish towns, or to the cellar dwellings found in English cities. But the consequences of overcrowding and a lack of basic sanitation were nevertheless apparent. Recurrent outbreaks of epidemic disease – cholera in 1831–32 and 1848–49, typhus in 1847 – spread with terrifying rapidity. Even in normal years the other diseases of poverty and overcrowding gave Belfast the highest death rate in Ireland. Pioneering research by the noted physician and philanthropist Andrew Malcolm, published in 1856, publicized the terrible human cost of Belfast's conquest of the world market for linen, as respiratory diseases caused by breathing in sharp-edged dust particles and working in the hot, damp conditions required by wet spinning condemned generations of millworkers to years of misery and a premature death.[32]

Even outside the lanes and streets of the working-class districts, industrial growth brought with it a marked deterioration in the urban environment. The inhabitants of the late eighteenth-century port and commercial centre, responding to contemporary notions of politeness and improvement, and guided by an absentee but interventionist and economically powerful proprietor, had managed to combine physical expansion with architectural grace, both in the new streets and in public buildings such as the Assembly Rooms and Poor House. By contrast the great wave of further building that took place after 1800 in what was now increasingly a factory town was more utilitarian in style. This may have been particularly the case in the fever of speculative building unleashed by the mass leasing of the Donegall estate in 1822. Inglis, despite his admiration for Belfast's industrious appearance and the absence of beggars, commented harshly on the 'liny hungry look of the modern streets of Belfast […] streets and rows present unbroken lines of buildings, uniform in height, and unrelieved by the least architectural ornament'. Around 1840 the architect Robert Young, arriving in Glasgow as a student, was struck by its monumental architecture, and years later recalled his feelings of 'pain and humiliation thinking of the poor, shabby, mean brick and plaster of my native town'.[33]

The plainness of Belfast's architecture was matched by the prevailing social atmosphere. The novelist William Thackeray, visiting in 1842, commented on 'the great activity and homely, unpretending bustle' to be seen on the principal streets. 'The men have a business look, too, and one sees very few flaunting dandies, as in Dublin.'[34] The town's own principal newspaper, in 1851, went further:

In the cloud which constantly overhangs the peaceful valley in which it nestles, and in the tall chimney-stalks which, in every quarter of the noisy town, shoot up from the dark masses of sombre buildings, [the visitor] sees unmistakeable evidence of ceaseless activity and profitable perseverance; while, in the anxious faces and hurried motions of the persons whom he observes hastening along the crowded thoroughfare, he discovers indications which convince him that he is among a people who fully appreciate the advantages of economising time, and devoting the most earnest attention to business.[35]

This was the authentic voice of the early Victorian era, where smoke was a sign of progress and labour the only virtue. These were the values that had helped transform Great Britain into the most advanced economy in the world. So it is hardly surprising that Belfast, an increasingly significant part of that transformation, had also made them its own. At the same time there is also a hint here of the price paid for industrial progress, in terms not just of environmental degradation but of a driven, even neurotic, culture.

Samuel Smiles

Samuel Smiles (1812–1904) was a leading spokesman for the core values of the Victorian age. In a series of widely read books, commencing with *Self-Help* (1855), he preached the virtues of thrift, industry and self-discipline as the key to both individual success and general social improvement. Not surprisingly, he found much in Belfast to approve of. In *Men of Invention and Industry* (1884) he wrote of the city's 'wonderfully rapid rise [...] originating in the enterprise of individuals, and developed by the earnest and anxious industry of the inhabitants of Ulster'. Its success, he argued, proved that what the rest of Ireland needed to better its condition was not changes in its laws, or better natural resources, but simply 'energy and industry'.[1]

Smiles's interest in Belfast had a personal basis. His son William was director of the Belfast ropeworks, and Smiles's visits to the city brought him into contact with leading industrialists such as Gustav Wolff and Edward Harland. Harland, at Smiles's invitation, contributed an autobiographical chapter to *Men of Invention and Industry*. In 1884 Smiles noted approvingly that a strike at the ropeworks had ended with the men returning to work for a reduced wage. Three years later he attended a shareholders' meeting where the management announced a dividend of 7 per cent for the half year. Afterwards they retired to the directors' private room, where Smiles took a glass of sherry while the directors had 'half ones'.[2]

William Smiles's son Sir Walter sat as a Unionist MP in the Westminster parliament, representing County Down and later North Down from 1945 until 1953, when he was drowned with 132 others in the sinking of the *Princess Victoria* ferry off the County Down coast.

1   Samuel Smiles, *Men of Invention and Industry* (London: John Murray, 1884), ch. 10.
2   Smiles to Janet Hartree, 7 April 1844, 6 August 1887 (West Yorkshire Archive Service, Leeds, WYL/A/1/175, 197).

Already by the time of the *News Letter*'s comments, however, there were signs that this utilitarian culture was beginning to be undermined by new aspirations for the development of the town and its presentation to the outside world. By the late 1840s residents themselves had begun to express misgivings about the contrast between Belfast's rising economic importance and its continued lack of impressive buildings. There was particular outrage at the rundown state of the customs house, and at the inadequacy of the post office, run from the ground floor of an ordinary house.[36] Even as these complaints multiplied, the first steps were being taken towards a transformation of the town's appearance. The newly created municipal council's first major venture into town planning, the laying out of Victoria Street, was completed by 1849. Early problems of subsidence, and delays in the filling in of vacant lots, seemed to bear out Robert Young's dismissal of the project, but over time what had been a waterside slum district became the site for an array of prestigious commercial properties. The erection of new market houses at one end of the new thoroughfare freed the town centre of nuisances such as the pork market that had regularly closed the whole of Waring Street to other traffic. Railway termini at York Road and

As elsewhere, the railway, symbol of the new age of technological achievement, inspired some of the finest marriages of commercial function and architectural style. The terminus of the Belfast and Northern Counties Railway at York Road, completed in 1848, underwent major expansion during the 1890s. R.J. Welch's photograph of c.1900, from an advertisement for the attached hotel, depicts an unnaturally clean and uncluttered streetscape, but does full justice to the scale and elegance of the new complex. The horse-drawn trams would be replaced by electric vehicles from 1905.

© National Museums Northern Ireland. Collection Ulster Museum. BELUM.Y.W.10.21.270.

183

The Queen's College, opened in 1849, was one of three institutions created as an alternative to the Anglican-dominated Trinity College, Dublin. The choice of Belfast was determined less by the town's economic pre-eminence than by denominational politics. Catholics lobbied hard for the ancient ecclesiastical centre of Armagh, but the government bowed to the demand for a clearly Presbyterian college to balance those in Catholic-dominated Galway and Cork. Charles Lanyon's illustration of his design includes a number of ornamental details omitted from the building as finally erected.

From the Collection of Queen's University Belfast.

The transfer to Belfast of the County Antrim assizes, traditionally held in Carrickfergus, gave Charles Lanyon a further opportunity to consolidate his position as the premier architect of the expanding town. The new prison (1846) and court house (1850), facing one another across the Crumlin Road, provided a visible symbol of authority in the heart of the unruly working-class residential quarter of west Belfast. The neoclassical elegance of the court house is evident even in its current sad state of decay.

Photograph © Stephen A. Royle.

the new Dublin Road (now Great Victoria Street) combined visible symbols of modernity with architectural elegance. The York Road terminus, in particular, boasted an elaborate Tuscan façade by Charles Lanyon, the rising star of local architecture. In the next few years Lanyon completed four other major projects: the grim mass of the Crumlin Road gaol (1846) and the more elegant court house directly opposite (1850), and to the south of the city, in the alternative Tudor gothic style, the Queen's College and the Deaf and Dumb Institute.

Over the next two decades the completion of the Harbour Office (1852–54), the Custom House (1854–57) and the Town Hall (1869–71) put an end to complaints about the shabbiness of the town's public buildings. Private enterprise too made its contribution to the new urban landscape. Some of the most striking projects were located on Donegall Square, from which the remorseless spread of the town's commercial centre had by now driven the original genteel inhabitants to seek new homes in the suburban perimeter. The new offices and warehouses that took the place of their earlier town houses, however, were not merely functional buildings. Instead they combined the representation of commercial confidence with the expression of a new civic pride. A row of busts lining the first floor of the warehouse erected for the Jaffé brothers in 1862 proclaimed the harmony of art and commerce. Peel and Cobden, the apostles of free trade, with Watt and Stephenson, the pioneers of steam power, sat alongside Shakespeare and Michaelangelo, Schiller and Homer. As in other cities of the period the preferred architectural style for both public and private building was that of the Italian Renaissance, thus looking back to a previous period when culture and commerce had worked together to create a great urban civilization.

The Harbour Commissioners' Offices (1854). The Ballast Office on Donegall Quay, home to the town's Harbour Commissioners, was demolished to make way for Charles Lanyon's Italianate Custom House (1857). Its replacement, designed by the Harbour Engineer George Smith (1792–1869) rather than by a professional architect, is a worthy companion to Lanyon's celebrated building, and the two together give striking expression to the new sense of civic ambition that had come to characterize the expanding town.

Image supplied courtesy of Belfast Harbour Commissioners.

The transition from the 'hungry liny look' criticized by Inglis to the Italianate elegance of the public and commercial architecture of the 1850s and 1860s testified to the growing awareness of Belfast's rising status as an industrial centre. As early as 1847 the *News Letter* demanded to know why Belfast, 'the acknowledged metropolis of Ulster, distinguished as it is by its literature, its mercantile and its commercial enterprise, the seat of two colleges, and returning two members to the imperial parliament', should not be a city.[37] The year before had seen the publication of Pilson's *History of the Rise and Progress of Belfast*, sketchy in its treatment of history, but in other respects a classic of what in the United States was to become known as 'boosterism', the extravagant promotion of a particular town or city. Another significant publication, thirteen years later, provided a somewhat more ambiguous reflection of the town's self-image. *The Provincialisms of Belfast and the Surrounding Districts Pointed out and Corrected*, published in 1860 by David Patterson, a teacher at the town's Deaf and Dumb Institute, was an earnest manual of self-improvement. 'Now that the continually increasing importance of our town has already brought us into communication and intercourse with most parts of the world', readers were told, phrases and expressions that had once been acceptable were no longer so: 'it behoves us to look a little more sharply to our Ps and Qs'. There followed a catalogue of mispronunciations ('wake' for 'weak', 'beg' for 'bag'), grammatical errors such as the misuse of past participles ('I seen him') and non-standard words such as *oxtther* for armpit and *throughother* for confused. Readers were urged to note the errors they found in their own speech, and to practise the correct form daily until it took over from the familiar but incorrect version.[38]

ULSTER RAILWAY TERMINUS.

The Ulster Railway terminus on Great Victoria Street. The first section of the Ulster Railway, running from Belfast to Lisburn, opened in 1839. The link to Dublin was completed in 1852. A second line, from a terminus at York Road to Ballymena and subsequently Derry, was begun in 1848 and completed in 1860. A third line, from east of the river to Holywood and beyond, also commenced operation in 1848. Detail from James O'Hagan's map of Belfast in 1848.

Photograph © National Museums Northern Ireland. Collection Ulster Museum. IA 1848.

By the 1860s the transformation of the late Georgian residential quarter into an extension of the town's commercial heart was well advanced. The three-storey warehouse – more properly a showroom – opened in 1862 by the Jaffé brothers, linen manufacturers, is notable for the busts of leading figures in science, art and commerce that line the exterior.

City Hall & Bar Red © Chris Hill, Scenic Ireland.

The same mixture of confidence and uncertainty reflected in Patterson's volume was evident in the response to invitations to put Belfast itself on display to a wider world. News that the town was to be included in Queen Victoria's first visit to Ireland in August 1849 initially aroused some nervous diffidence. Belfast, one local newspaper admitted, 'has little of architectural ornament', so that the most it had to exhibit was 'a busy, industrious and independent population'.[39] In the event the visit came to be seen as a great success, commemorated in the naming of Victoria Street, Queen's Square and Albert Square. The large area of reclaimed land created by the recent harbour excavations, formerly Dargan's Island but now redesignated Queen's Island, was for several years the site of a commemorative fete.[40] In 1852 the town's successful application to host the annual conference of the British Association for the Advancement of Science, defeating rival bids from Hull, Leeds and Brighton, was likewise seen as a major triumph.

Belfast was also represented at London's Great Exhibition of 1851, contributing 63 of the 300 Irish items on display in the Crystal Palace. Its contribution of £581 towards the cost of the Exhibition was small compared to the sums of over £2,000 raised by Leeds, Manchester and Glasgow, but comfortably exceeded the £406 raised by what was still the much larger city of Dublin. The exhibition was well publicized in Belfast, with regular newspaper reports, lectures, and a preview of paintings intended for display there.[41] As in other towns a Travelling Club set up for the occasion organized cheap excursions to facilitate visitors to the Exhibition.[42] But the experience of this first exposure to the wider world was not altogether a happy one. There were complaints about the expense associated with the exhibition, and of visitors to London having been 'fleeced'.[43] There were also charges of 'unfair treatment', possibly referring to criticisms that Irish linen – despite the award of a medal to the Royal Flax Improvement Society – 'lacked an aesthetic dimension'.[44] These resentments carried over into a rather grudging and limited participation in the Paris exhibition of 1855.[45] Industrial exhibitions, however, were an important part of nineteenth-century commercial culture, seen as an opportunity both to celebrate economic achievement and to boost it still further by self-advertisement and the dissemination of ideas and expertise. By the time of the Paris exhibition of 1867 Belfast was ready to participate more enthusiastically. The Chamber of Commerce organized the display of linen (a 14-foot high showpiece), and all the major linen houses represented the 'Northern capital'.[46] Belfast linen merchants were also strongly represented at the Philadelphia Centennial Exhibition in 1876, while the town's leading printer, Marcus Ward & Company, executed the cover of the British catalogue, 'a handsome emblematic design in low tones'.[47]

The fashion for industrial exhibitions also spread to Ireland. Belfast firms, disgruntled by their London experience, displayed limited enthusiasm for the

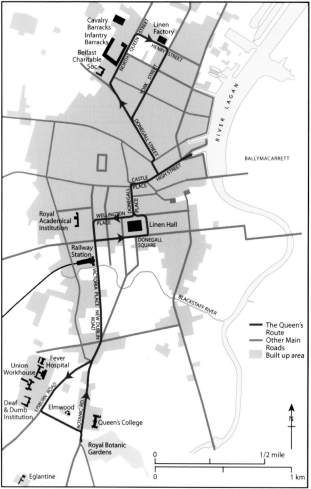

Map labels:
Cavalry Barracks
Infantry Barracks
Belfast Charitable Soc.
Linen Factory
NORTH QUEEN STREET
HENRY STREET
YORK STREET
DONEGALL STREET
RIVER LAGAN
BALLYMACARRETT
CASTLE PLACE
HIGH STREET
DONEGALL PLACE
WELLINGTON PLACE
Linen Hall
DONEGALL SQUARE
Royal Academical Institution
Railway Station
VICTORIA PLACE
NEW DUBLIN ROAD
BLACKSTAFF RIVER
Fever Hospital
Union Workhouse
LISBURN ROAD
Deaf & Dumb Institution
Elmwood
BOTANIC RD
Queen's College
Royal Botanic Gardens
Eglantine

The Queen's Route
Other Main Roads
Built up area

0 — 1/2 mile
0 — 1 km
N

Queen Victoria's one-day visit to Belfast on 11 August 1849 was a significant boost to the self-esteem of its citizens. Her progress through the town provides a snapshot of a rapidly changing urban landscape. The first stage took the royal procession through the traditional urban centre, High Street, and then into the more recently created elite quarter of Donegall Place. After pausing at the Linen Hall, centre of the town's premier industry, the queen's party moved on to areas of more recent development, passing the new railway station on what is now Great Victoria Street to visit the Botanic Gardens and the newly opened Queen's College, before doubling back to pass Mulholland's Mill on the edge of the industrial district north of the town centre. The Queen's party did not venture into the main working-class residential district to the west. The *Belfast News Letter* lamented that this meant that they missed two other sights of the rising town, the Crumlin Road court house and gaol.

Courtesy of Queen's University, Belfast, Cartographic Department.

Cork exhibition of 1852, but responded more wholeheartedly to the Dublin exhibition of the following year.[48] The Royal Flax Improvement Society again took charge of showcasing the town's signature product, but there were also specimens of textile and other machinery manufactured in the town, as well as of more traditional craftsmanship by coachbuilders, a pianoforte maker, and workers in stone and marble. Two firms, Murphy and Corry, presented early examples of what was to become a significant, though often overlooked, Belfast industry, aerated waters.[49] Subsequent participation in events dedicated to Irish industry was complicated by political divisions. In 1882 Belfast delegates withdrew from the planning of a forthcoming National Exhibition when some organizers, responding in part to the arrest of Parnell and other nationalist leaders, declined to invite the queen to act as patron of the event. In 1887 and 1888, however, the town's businessmen took a full part in industrial exhibitions at Manchester and Glasgow, in Irish sections organized through the Royal Dublin Society. Belfast products also appeared in the Irish section at the St

Jennymount Mill, off York Road, established in 1856. The major extension carried out in 1891 by John Lanyon, son of the celebrated architect Charles, created an imposing building in the style of an Italian palazzo, another example of the marriage of functionality and style, commerce and culture, that characterized the town's industrial heyday.

Photograph © Sean Connolly.

Louis World Fair in 1904. But on this occasion the official handbook gave its acknowledgement of the Ulster linen industry a distinctly nationalist slant:

> On the other hand, the linen manufacture, for which the Irish climate and other conditions offered advantages not shared by Great Britain, was encouraged by bounties and special tariff regulations, no British manufacturer being likely to be injured by Irish competition in linen goods. The result of this policy, carried over several generations, was not only to develop the linen and to destroy or enfeeble the woollen and other industries; it also had a still more important social and moral effect. It raised up in the North a population habituated to industry, a fertile soil for any further industrial growths of any description, while it killed, for the time being, not only the industries, but also the industrial spirit of the South.[50]

In 1894, meanwhile, Belfast had organized its own Arts and Industrial Exhibition. There was optimistic talk of a larger, international exhibition to follow, but organizers, anxious about the financial commitment, had to admit that Belfast, located where it was, could not hope to attract the audiences seen in Manchester and Glasgow.[51]

At the same time that Belfast adjusted to its new status as an industrial centre, the older notion of a northern Athens remained a part of local rhetoric. By this time, however, the phrase was even more clearly a cliché, employed in the interests of elegant variation. The *News Letter*, for example, reported in 1877 that Belfast, as was often the case in 'the northern Athens', had largely escaped a recent violent storm.[52] The local bookseller William McComb, writing in

The buildings of the Queen's College, redesignated Queen's University in 1908, are now seen as one of the jewels of the city's Victorian architecture, but in fact they took shape over a long period. The Hamilton tower, topping the front entrance and named after the Revd Thomas Hamilton, president of the college from 1889 to 1908, was added in 1907, as part of extensive additions that completed the north side of what became the quadrangle. It was never well regarded, and was removed in 1922.

Courtesy of the National Library of Ireland.

1861, clung gamely to the traditional use of the phrase: 'it is more than half a century since Belfast was first classically named "the Northern Athens" from the distinction which it had gained, even then, in the cultivation of polite literature'.[53] Others, however, poured scorn on any such claim. The anti-establishment *Ulsterman*, in 1856, went so far as to suggest that the term had from the start been intended sarcastically.

> But our townspeople, with a mingling of Irish vanity and Scotch obtuseness to a joke, took the satire as a compliment, and adopted the name 'Athens of Ireland' – though Heaven knows our crowded manufacturing town, with its neglected lower class and hideously uneducated upper class, has no more claim to such a title than degraded Wolverhampton has to be called the Paris of England.[54]

In 1892 a speaker at the Queen's College Literary and Scientific Society attempted to bring the definition into line with common usage, arguing that Belfast could, 'on social, commercial and political grounds', claim the title of 'northern Athens'. An opponent, however, responded that the title could properly belong only to 'a home of art and culture', with the clear implication that Belfast did not come into this category.[55]

Was this rejection of any claim to cultural distinction justified? James M'Cosh, Professor of Logic and Metaphysics at the Queen's College, testifying before a parliamentary committee in 1858, admitted that few of his students came from the town's mercantile and manufacturing elite. Instead 'a very large number are satisfied with what they receive in the Belfast Academy and the Belfast Academical Institution, since at the age of thirteen, fourteen or fifteen

S.F. Lynn's statue of Henry
Cooke, erected at the
junction of College Square
East and Wellington Place
in 1876, replaced an earlier
monument to the earl of
Belfast. Cooke (1788–1868),
a vigorous upholder of
theological orthodoxy
within the Synod of Ulster,
campaigned vigorously to end
the traditional association
between Presbyterianism and
political Liberalism, arguing
instead that Protestants of
all denominations should
unite against the rising threat
of Catholic nationalism.
The Liberal *Northern Whig*,
protesting at the placement
in a central thoroughfare
of so divisive a figure, wrote
derisively of 'anthems
drummed in Sandy Row / Oft
echoing in those ears of brass'.
Photograph © Sean Connolly.

boys enter business. This is the case with the sons of persons who have ten, twenty and thirty thousand pounds.'[56] At the same time Victorian Belfast was not by any means a cultural or intellectual desert. The Linen Hall Library and the Natural History and Philosophical Society remained active throughout the nineteenth century and beyond. An Art Society founded in 1836 had collapsed two years later, and a first School of Design, opened in 1849, closed in 1855. However, a new School of Art appeared in 1870, and the free public library established on the newly constructed Royal Avenue in 1888 included an art gallery under a specialist curator.[57] Meanwhile the completion in 1862 of the Ulster Hall provided a first-class venue for musical events. Concerts were, for several reasons, the central cultural activity of the Victorian British middle classes. At a time when the theatre remained suspect to many on moral and religious grounds, performances of classical and sacred music combined culture and sociability, in a setting theoretically open to all but in practice rendered exclusive by cost and dress codes. Hence it is no surprise that it was in this cultural area that Belfast particularly shone. A survey in 1913 concluded that the Belfast Philharmonic Society, established in 1874 through the amalgamation of two earlier bodies, represented 'a standard […] which is not attained, or even approached, elsewhere in Ireland, including Dublin'.[58]

The Politics of Representation

At the same time that Victorian urban elites looked to concert halls and literary societies to bolster their sense of civic pride, they also looked to sculpture for statues and monuments to add dignity and style to the streets and squares of their remodelled town centres. Here, however, Belfast's uncertain relationship to its own history inhibited development. In 1862 John Clarke, who had served as the town's second mayor, suggested that 'every stranger, in visiting our town, must be struck with the very few public monuments and memorials we have of the past'.[59] At this time Belfast had in fact only one public statue, erected in Wellington Place in 1855 to commemorate the earl of Belfast, eldest son of Lord Donegall, who had died two years earlier of scarlet fever contracted during a visit to Naples. The statue – commonly known as 'the black man' owing to the dark patina of the bronze – memorialized the town's leading family, but was primarily a tribute to Belfast himself, who had actively promoted both cultural development and social improvement. Fourteen years later the memorial to Prince Albert at the bottom of High Street provided a new focal point for what was then still the town centre.

Two further additions proved more controversial. In 1874 the statue of the earl of Belfast was found to be deteriorating in its exposed open-air site, and was moved indoors to the new town hall.[60] Its replacement was a statue of Henry Cooke, a Presbyterian church leader of undeniable distinction,

but noted also for his vigorous advocacy of Protestant unity against what he presented as the menacing forces of Catholicism and Irish nationalism. The president of the Queen's College, also a Presbyterian clergyman but one of firmly Liberal allegiances, had already refused an application to place the statue in the grounds of the college, and the appropriation of the earl of Belfast's place at the centre of a main thoroughfare gave rise to some complaint.[61] However, the issue was partly defused when the town's most prominent Catholic businessman, the baker Bernard Hughes, spoke publicly in favour of the statue.[62] No such magnanimity was on offer two decades later, when the lord mayor unveiled the statue erected at Carlisle Circus to another Presbyterian clergyman, the prominent anti-Catholic controversialist Hugh Hanna. By now Belfast was a city polarized by the issue of Home Rule. Hanna's statue was paid for by public subscription, but clearly had the backing of the lord mayor and corporation. The *Irish News*, on the other hand, saw the unveiling as 'one of those periodical demonstrations of Orangeism and religious bigotry' with which Belfast was 'unhappily only too familiar'.[63]

In comparison with these inauspicious beginnings, the years before the First World War reveal what looks like a sudden enthusiasm for public statuary. The change seems to have been inspired by the erection of the City Hall, creating a new space in the grounds around it that demanded appropriate furnishings. The first statue, of Sir Edward Harland, former lord mayor and joint head of the shipyard on which the city's world-wide reputation largely depended, was unveiled in June 1903. A month later Edward VII unveiled a statue of Queen Victoria in front of the still-unfinished building, and in October 1905 the

The statue of Queen Victoria, unveiled in 1903. Her incongruous position, blocking the view of the grandiose front entrance of the City Hall, led the *Irish Builder* to joke irreverently that the queen appeared to be stepping out of a mausoleum that was not to her liking.
Courtesy of the National Library of Ireland.

The unveiling in 1906 of the monument to the marquess of Dufferin and Ava, part of Belfast's belated acquisition of an appropriate suite of public sculpture.
Courtesy of the National Library of Ireland.

commander-in-chief unveiled a memorial to men of the Royal Irish Rifles who had died in the Boer War. There followed statues of three more former lord mayors, Sir James Haslett (1909), Sir Daniel Dixon (1910) and Robert McMordie (1919).[64] There was also an elaborate memorial to the marquess of Dufferin and Ava, an imperial potentate of genuine distinction, who had served as governor general of Canada and viceroy of India, but whose direct connection with Belfast was confined to his brief leadership of the town's Liberals in the general elections of 1865 and 1868. A memorial to those lost on the *Titanic*, completed in 1920, originally stood in the roadway before the City Hall, before being moved into the grounds in the late 1950s. In 1929 there followed a Cenotaph to commemorate the dead of the First World War. Belatedly, and within the confines of a single, now rather crowded civic space, Belfast had at last acquired the political identity expressed in stone that it had earlier lacked.

The first decade of the twentieth century saw two other attempts to give artistic expression to a civic identity. In 1903 the council commissioned the artist J.W. Carey to produce a series of murals for the Ulster Hall, recently taken into municipal ownership. The result was a series of images depicting an imagined eighteenth- and nineteenth-century Belfast.[65] Shipbuilding was represented by a reconstruction of William Ritchie's pioneering boatyard of the 1790s, linen by a view of the White Linen Hall picturesquely shrouded in snow. The historical scenes were mainly from the eighteenth century: the blockade of the Lough by the French privateer Thurot in 1760, a Volunteer parade in High Street in 1793, the Malone turnpike and the beginnings of the coach road to Dublin in a pre-railway 1830. The one nod to a more distant past, a portrait of Corby MacGilmore, a fifteenth-century chieftain based in a stronghold on Cave Hill, drew on a fictional source, the recently published story by local author Samuel Ferguson. The overall impression was of an exercise in sentimental antiquarianism: a Belfast in its industrial heyday looking back, through a prism of nostalgia, to the earlier, less sophisticated world of its youth.

A second venture had greater promise, but ended less happily. In 1905, as the City Hall neared completion, the artist Robert Ponsonby Staples proposed a series of murals for the new municipal centre illustrating the city's industries. With encouragement from Brumwell Thomas, architect of the City Hall, the lord mayor Sir Daniel Dixon and private patrons, Staples went on to produce triptychs depicting shipbuilding and linen manufacture. His aim, as he explained in the *Northern Whig* newspaper in 1909, was to reflect the realities of contemporary working-class life.

> My idea was, and still would be, to execute a series of panels illustrative of all the leading industries of this city, so full of such activities […] It is to the poor working people of Belfast to whom I hope and believe the works I have done will appeal now and hereafter, to show them that scenes torn from the grime and toil

of their daily life, may be made beautiful; the thousands of the Island, who, when they and their friends pass through the City Hall, will appreciate the great hulk of the steel-clad ship they have pieced together; or the riveter in his tawny jacket, the skilled mechanic, fitting with utmost care the multitudinous blades of a turbine, with the companion picture of a holiday group starting down the lough. Then a group of York Street spinning girls, with bare arms and feet on the wet tiles of the damp rooms, with a dainty doffing mistress supervising them, shows well beside a panoramic view of Belfast with men and women flax-pulling. These are simple everyday things, but I know the interest they have evoked, and [they] may be of more permanent value than a complete series of vermillion-coated aldermen and mayors.[66]

The final barbed remark referred to the tradition of commissioning civic portraits, which Belfast City Council had enthusiastically adopted since the 1870s.[67] It may also have been directed at the group portrait of the council, *The Proclamation of Edward VII in Belfast*, 1901, by Taylor and MacKenzie, which although incomplete had already been displayed in the City Hall at its opening ceremony. In any event, all this was in sharp contrast to Carey's sentimental antiquarianism. And ultimately, Staples' paintings were rejected by the city council. It is possible that his known support for Home Rule made him and his work unacceptable. Alternatively the civic elite may have looked with less favour on depictions of the city's docks and mills in the aftermath of the bitter industrial disputes of 1905–07. But whatever the reason a significant opportunity had been lost to give visual expression to Belfast's moment as a great industrial centre.

A Mature Industrial City

Belfast became a city in 1888. (The promotion of its mayor to lord mayor came four years later, in 1892.)[68] The privy council's decision to create a city overturned the precedent that only towns containing an Anglican cathedral could enjoy this status; Belfast's elevation thus opened the way to city status for Birmingham and other centres of industrial importance but a limited historical past. The news was announced by the lord lieutenant when he visited in October 1888 to open the free library erected on the town's new showpiece, Royal Avenue. Driven through the old Hercules Street and a tangle of surrounding side streets, the broad new thoroughfare, lined with shops and offices, was primarily intended to clear a bottleneck obstructing traffic in the direction of York Road railway station. But its construction also transformed the town's topography. Belfast had grown up around the east–west axis created by Waring Street and High Street. In 1869, as the veteran journalist Frankfort Moore later recalled, the newly constructed Albert Clock was regarded as the centre of the town.[69] Now, however, that centre shifted decisively, to Donegall

Previous spread: A group portrait of Belfast City Council, members of their families and other prominent citizens, attending the reading of the proclamation of Edward VII in January 1901. The image it presents is a distinctly idealized one. Contemporary descriptions suggest that in reality this attempt at civic ritual degenerated into near shambles. The pressure from the crowd was so great that the 220-strong military guard of honour had to unfix their bayonets to avoid possible injury, and were eventually able to escape the crush only by climbing on to the platform. One observer compared the affair to the devastating riots of summer 1886. By contrast the official painting, commenced by Ernest E. Taylor (1863–1907) and completed after his death by William MacKenzie, concentrates on offering recognizable individual portrayals of the civic worthies gathered round the lord mayor, Sir Daniel Dixon.

Reproduced with the kind permission of Belfast City Council. Photograph © Bryan Rutledge.

Sir Robert Ponsonby Staples (1853–1943) at work on his ill-received painting. For the task of providing the Belfast establishment of the early twentieth century with an artistic representation of their city's identity, Staples, a Protestant Home Ruler known as the 'barefoot baronet' because of his belief that leather shoes harmfully cut people off from the earth's magnetism, represented a singularly unfortunate choice.

Photograph © National Museums Northern Ireland. Collection Ulster Museum. BELUM.Y4838.

Square and the extended north–south corridor of Donegall Place and the new Royal Avenue. The strict specifications contained in the building leases for Royal Avenue created a spectacular boulevard, with buildings constructed in a variety of styles but rising to four or five storeys to reach the stipulated cornice height. Over the next three decades the southern end of the new centre was redeveloped on the same new scale. Department stores for Robinson and Cleaver (1888) and Anderson and McAuley (1899) on Donegall Place, office blocks such as Ocean Buildings (1902) and the Scottish Provident Institution (1902) on Donegall Square, dwarfed the elegant warehouses of the 1860s and 1870s. The completion in 1906 of the new City Hall, replacing the Linen Hall at the centre of Donegall Square, confirmed the monumental quality of the new town centre.

The construction of Royal Avenue had a second significance. Hercules Street and the surrounding side streets had been a mixed district of shops, small businesses and residential properties. Royal Avenue, by contrast, was a street of offices and retail outlets. Over the next few years a programme of clearance in the surviving courts and entries removed the last residential neighbourhoods from the city centre. Belfast thus completed the classic

Royal Avenue, laid out in 1880–81, was the single most important public improvement project of the second half of the century. Its completion was an expensive but self-financing enterprise, the costs being covered by the fees charged for building leases on the new boulevard. Moreover, by resorting to a local Act of Parliament rather than existing improvement legislation, the council evaded any obligation to rehouse the several hundred persons made homeless by the destruction of the working-class district around the former Hercules Street. Against this, however, must be put the erection on the new street of the Free Public Library, which also became the home of the Belfast Natural History and Philosophical Society's museum and of an art gallery.

Courtesy of the National Library of Ireland.

The Scottish Provident Institution building (1897–1902), designed by the firm of Young and Mackenzie, represents the third phase of the development of Donegall Square, as the elegant warehouses such as the Jaffé brothers' premises (p. 33), themselves erected on the ruins of genteel Georgian residences, were in turn displaced by huge monuments to the wealth and self-confidence of the late Victorian and Edwardian city.

Photograph © Chris Hill, Scenic Ireland.

transition from early modern to modern urban centre. In 1750 its wealthiest citizens had lived in the town centre, surrounded by a ring of poor cottages on its outskirts. A century and a half later the relationship between wealth and space had been reversed. Beyond what was now an uninhabited centre of shops and offices, the working classes were housed in an inner circle of residential districts to the north, west and east, the lowest-paid in simple kitchen houses, the better-off in larger dwellings with a parlour or extra bedrooms. The middle classes, on the other hand, resided in the increasingly built-up suburbs of the Malone ridge, the Antrim Road or the east shore of Belfast Lough, where what had once been small and medium-sized demesnes surrounding gentlemen's residences had been sold off one by one to provide sites for rows of detached and semi-detached houses. The wealthy, meanwhile, lived further out still, in country houses beyond the reach of suburbia.

Suburbanization had been made possible by public transport. A network of trams, initially horse drawn but from 1905 electrified, along with the railways extending to the south, north and east, carried commuters and shoppers back into the city centre. This transformed urban space, with its broad pavements and bright lighting – initially gas but from 1895 electricity – was by now the site, not just for business, but for sociability and consumption. Offices sat

Sydenham, as depicted by Nicholas Joseph Crowley in 1864, showing the eastern shore of Belfast Lough, before the commencement of extensive suburban development, as a landscape of fields and scattered villas.

Image supplied courtesy of Belfast Harbour Commissioners.

The Sicilian marble staircase of Robinson and Cleaver's department store (1888) was part of the arrival in Belfast of a whole new retail culture in which brightly lit interiors and elaborate displays conveyed the image of consumption as a pleasure rather than a necessity.

Courtesy of the National Library of Ireland.

Electric lighting first came to Belfast through the small generators installed in department stores and other premises from the 1880s. The municipal supply commenced in 1898 with the opening of the new electricity station on East Street Bridge on 18 October 1898, symbolically chosen as the same day on which the foundation stone for the new City Hall was laid. However, it was the massive increase in capacity required by the electrification of the tramway system in 1905 that brought prices within the reach of most domestic consumers.

Photograph © National Museums Northern Ireland. Collection Ulster Folk & Transport Museum. HOYFM. WAG.3166

The beginnings of suburbanization. The area immediately south of the White Linen Hall, low lying and flood prone, proved unattractive to upper- and middle-class residents seeking to escape from an increasingly crowded town centre. Instead suburban building commenced where the rising ground of the Malone ridge provided a more attractive location, further enhanced by the siting there of the Queen's College. The Crescent, built by James Corry in 1846–52, was a particularly ambitious development, clearly modelled on John Wood's design, half a century earlier, for the Royal Crescent at Bath. Detail from James O'Hagan's map of Belfast in 1848.

Photograph © National Museums Northern Ireland. Collection Ulster Museum. IA 1848.

side by side with restaurants and cafés, as well as a new generation of brightly lit and spacious public houses, replacing the cramped, gloomy drinking dens of an earlier era. Alongside the varied amusements offered by the Ulster Hall, there were now music halls – the Alhambra (1873), the Olympia Palace (1891), the Empire Theatre of Varieties (1894) – as well as a revived Theatre Royal, reopened in new premises after a fire in 1881, and the newer Grand Opera House (1895). Shopping had also been transformed. Thomas Gaffikin, describing the High Street of his youth in the 1820s, recalled 'low fronts and small windows of little panes […] protected, or rather encumbered, with strong iron railings on the outside'.[70] These were premises that one entered to make a predetermined purchase. By contrast the new department stores, such as Robinson and Cleaver and Anderson and McAuley, with their brightly lit interiors, spacious aisles and profusion of artfully displayed goods (ticketed to avoid the embarrassment of having to ask for a price and then not buy), were temples to the new culture of consumption, positively inviting the casual browser and the passer by. Where earlier observers had compared Belfast to Manchester or Leeds, *The Times* in 1913 looked further afield: 'Castle Place, with its width, its broad shop fronts, its endless procession of electric cars, and the business like air of the crowded pavements, might well be the centre of some such city as Philadelphia or Chicago.'[71]

The City as a Stage

Alongside Belfast's new role as a city of consumption as well as production, self-indulgence as well as labour, important changes were taking place in the political context. As the demand for Home Rule gained ground in the late nineteenth century, Unionist spokesmen responded by insisting on the distinctive identity within Ireland of their Ulster heartland. Belfast, already set apart by its industrial success, now became the capital designate of a putative separate region. The organizers of the Ulster Unionist Convention of 1892, summoned to protest against the second Home Rule Bill, opted for the respectable surroundings of suburban south Belfast, where 12,000 delegates assembled at specially erected wooden pavilions – decorated with images of harps, shamrocks and mottos in Irish – at Stranmillis. The more extended mobilization of 1911–14, on the other hand, laid claim to the city centre and appropriated some of its most significant buildings. The mass signing of the Solemn League and Covenant commenced at the City Hall. Unionist leaders walked there from the Ulster Hall, following a service conducted jointly by the Church of Ireland, Methodist and Presbyterian churches. The lord mayor, Robert McMordie, and the Unionist members of the corporation in their civic robes met them in front of Queen Victoria's statue.[72] They signed the pledge under the dome of the City Hall, on a table covered with the Union

Jack, an image immortalized in one of the brass reliefs that decorate the statue of Edward Carson erected at Stormont in 1933. The *Irish News* noted, among other complaints, that the headquarters of the municipal administration had been transformed into 'the sacred temple of Toryism and Orangeism'.[73] Meanwhile the old Town Hall acted as a signing venue for Covenanters who had missed the Ulster Day event, as Unionist headquarters and as the home of the Ulster Volunteer Force between 1913 and 1914. The Ulster Hall also served as the venue for several Covenant-related events – not least the dramatic eve of signing rally – while the Municipal Technical College (1907) later provided premises for the Ulster Volunteer Force's bakery. Later in 1919 the decision of the Belfast authorities to hold their Peace Day independently of the armistice celebrations not only of Dublin, but also of London, confirmed their sense of separateness.[74]

With the Government of Ireland Act (1920) and the partition of Ireland, Belfast became, in a legal as well as a symbolic sense, the capital city of Unionist Ulster. The new state was inaugurated by King George V in June 1921 and the City Hall briefly became its parliament building. For the outside world the significance of the brief inauguration ceremony lay in George V's appeal to 'all Irishmen to stretch out the hand of forbearance and conciliation, to forgive and forget', a signal of the British government's progression towards a settlement with southern nationalism. For Belfast, however, the visit itself was an event of central importance. As the open-top royal carriage drove through the city, the streets were lined by thousands of observers, 'an avenue of cheering and delighted citizens'.[75] The City Hall – 'the architectural symbol

The City Hall and the monumental architecture of Donegall Square provide a background to the crowds assembled to sign the Solemn League and Covenant on 28 September 1912.

Photograph © National Museums Northern Ireland. Collection Ulster Museum. BELUM.Y.W.10.21.127.

of the progress and greatness of Belfast' – was vital to the ceremony.[76] All the local newspapers were impressed with the occasion, although the *Irish News*, generally supportive of the royal visit, observed that the newly recruited Ulster Special Constabulary, widely seen as an aggressively Protestant force, had been incongruously occupied in washing offensive graffiti about the pope from some of Belfast's walls.[77] In addition to the crowds that thronged the city centre, spectators took advantage of the slopes of Cave Hill and Bellevue to watch the arrival and departure of the royal flotilla, while the banks of the harbour were lined with flag- and handkerchief-waving supporters.

The king's visit was also notable for having been made against the wishes of his advisors, who believed that it exposed him to unnecessary danger. According to Lady Craig's diary: 'The King said to J. when he was saying goodbye in the yacht, "I can't tell you how glad I am I came, but you know my entourage were very much against it". J replied, "Sir, you are surrounded by pessimists, we are all optimists over here."'[78] The concern of the royal advisors was understandable. Ten days before the visit seven people died in fighting in the city, while the day after the parliament's inauguration the IRA blew up the train carrying the king's escort, the 10th Hussars, back to Dublin, killing four men and 80 horses. In the years 1920–24 453 people died as a result of communal violence, and the city was under continuous curfew between July 1920 and December 1924. The death toll, reflecting the belief on both sides that what was at stake was a stark choice between two radically different political futures, dwarfed even the most serious sectarian clashes of the preceding century, and was not to be matched again until the early 1970s.

The arrival of King George V and Queen Mary for the opening of the first Ulster parliament, on 22 June 1921, marks the beginning of a new phase in Belfast's history, as the political and administrative capital of Northern Ireland.

Reproduced with the kind permission of the *Belfast Telegraph*.

Belfast was now home to Northern Ireland's new government. After its initial sessions in Belfast City Hall, the state's parliament sat for a decade in the Presbyterian Assembly's College on Botanic Avenue. Government departments were scattered throughout the city centre; the Department of Labour was housed in Ormeau Avenue, the Department of Finance in Donegall Square West, and the Department of Education, for a time, in the Presbyterian Assembly College. By 1932 the construction of the new parliament building at Stormont in east Belfast was completed. Lord Craigavon believed it would 'stand on its base of granite from the Mountains of Mourne, as a symbol of the link between Great Britain and Northern Ireland'.[79] That Unionists invested so much significance in a building was unsurprising. From the impressive wooden pavilion that housed the 1892 Ulster Unionist Convention in south Belfast, they had progressed through the opulent Belfast City Hall, to another striking granite and marble edifice: 'The beautiful white buildings, as yet unstained by the smoke or rain of generations, towered in their impressive dignity, and if anything looked more stately for their baptismal day.'[80]

The City in Decline

At the same time that Belfast embarked on its new role as a capital city, it began to lose the industrial pre-eminence long associated with its name. The reasons lay outside the city itself. Shipbuilding suffered from a contraction of demand, as the volume of world trade recovered only slowly after the First World War, then slumped again during the Great Depression of the 1930s. Meanwhile linen, an expensive textile requiring careful maintenance at a time when domestic servants were becoming a luxury, was losing ground in world markets to cheaper, more convenient fabrics. In both sectors Belfast firms in fact performed creditably, maintaining or even increasing their share of world and UK production. The Belfast Harbour Commissioners also displayed enterprise, embarking on an extensive programme of improvements that prepared the way for the one industrial success story of the period, the establishment in 1937 of the Short and Harland aircraft factory. But the simultaneous contraction of demand for the city's two staple manufactures was disastrous. Between December 1931 and May 1934 no ships were launched from Queen's Island, while the number of shipyard workers fell from 10,428 in 1930 to 1,554 in 1932. Thereafter Harland and Wolff recovered somewhat, but Workman, Clark, burdened by loans taken out before the crash, went into liquidation in 1935. Meanwhile the number employed in Northern Ireland's linen industry fell by more than a quarter between 1924 and 1935. The experience of industrial decline was not uniform. Other industries – the ropeworks, Gallaher's tobacco – were less affected by the problems of the world economy, and there was, as elsewhere in the United Kingdom, some growth in retail, the service industries and public employment. This helps to explain why the 1920s and 1930s, years of recession and mass unemployment, were also the period that saw the spread of the cinema, the wireless and, among the more affluent, the motor car. For the one in four of Belfast's working population who remained unemployed for much of the 1930s, however, this visible evidence of the growth of a consumer society can only have added to their sense of deprivation and exclusion.

Industrial decline had political consequences. In a celebrated episode in October and November 1932 unemployed workers from Catholic and Protestant districts joined in mass protests against the inadequate relief offered to the unemployed by the Belfast Poor Law Guardians. But economic uncertainty and deprivation also exacerbated sectarian conflict. Tension built up steadily from 1931, reaching a peak in the riots arising from the Twelfth of July parades in 1935. There were ten deaths as well as widespread evictions and workplace expulsions. Writing a decade later the poet Louis MacNeice explained how this violence gave an additional layer of separateness to Belfast:

> As recently as 1935 there were serious shootings and burnings in Belfast between Protestant and Catholics (NB the political alignment in the country is all but identical with the religious alignment) [...] The fact remains that Northern Ireland has in our time had more experience of political violence than England, Scotland, or Wales. This is why her policemen, unlike those in the other three territories, always carry arms when on duty.[81]

It was this period of unrest that saw a 'peace wall', the first but not the last to be built in the city, erected in Belfast's Sailortown.[82]

Belfast's problems in the interwar period were intensified by the poor quality of local administration. By the early twentieth century tightening central government control had begun to deprive Britain's urban centres of their administrative autonomy, and with it of the dynamism and enterprise that had characterized the cities of the Victorian era. In Belfast the problem was exacerbated as the politics of partition stifled other forms of debate. An enquiry in 1928, set up following the discovery of serious corruption in the Housing Department, uncovered massive deficiencies. Some, such as the excessive range of business dealt with by the whole council rather than by committees or officials, reflected the failure of administrative structures to keep pace with the increased volume and complexity of business. The council, the report noted, was attempting to manage a city along lines suitable to the running of a village. But there was also evidence of the complacency and corruption encouraged by prolonged one-party rule: appointments by patronage rather than on merit, and serious deficiencies in the provisions for tendering and accounting. The closed nature of urban government was summed up in the person of the wealthy businessman Sir Crawford McCullagh. Implicated in the housing scandal, he briefly lost his council seat in 1925 but returned two years later and went on to serve as lord mayor continuously from 1931 until 1942, and again from 1943 to 1946.[83]

For the citizens of Belfast the failings of municipal government were initially most evident in the poor provision for public health, reflected in high levels of maternal and infant mortality and in deaths from tuberculosis and pneumonia. Incompetence and complacency had further lethal consequences in April and May 1941, when German bombing raids found the city horrendously ill-prepared. Emma Duffin, a nurse, found the scenes of carnage she witnessed more terrible even than those she had seen during the First World War:

> With tangled hair, staring eyes, clutching hands, contorted limbs, their grey-green faces covered with dust, they lay, bundled into the coffins, half-shrouded in rugs or blankets, or an occasional sheet, still wearing their dirty, torn twisted garments. Death should be dignified, peaceful; Hitler had made even death grotesque! I felt outraged, I should have felt sympathy, grief, but instead feelings of repulsion and disgust assailed me.[84]

The war years also saw a second financial scandal, this time involving the purchase of a site for a tuberculosis sanatorium at Whiteabbey. In an explicit

A photograph of an unnamed residential street, published in 1955 to illustrate a newspaper article on unemployment in Belfast. The bleak and dilapidated vista, testimony to the long-standing inadequacy of corporation housing policy, must be set alongside Patricia Craig's affectionate tribute to the 'old Belfast' of her youth (see p. 53).

Photograph © Bert Hardy / Picture Post / Getty Images.

condemnation of the council, the Northern Ireland parliament introduced legislation to place the affairs of the city in the hands of commissioners appointed by the government.

The death toll of the blitz apart, the war years were good to Belfast. Employment rose in shipbuilding and engineering, and wages improved significantly. American troops brought extra spending power, as well as a touch of glamour (and a perceived threat to the virtue of local women).[85] Post-war reconstruction, and even more the demands of the Korean War, permitted local manufacturers a last hurrah. In the late 1940s a traveller arriving in Belfast by rail from the south still entered what was visibly a major industrial centre, where on his left 'the lofty mill buildings and groves of tall chimneys climb up the mountain almost to the summit'.[86] By the mid-1950s, however, the pattern of decline resumed. Between 1958 and 1964 a third of linen plants closed and 45 per cent of workers lost their jobs. Shipbuilding's free-fall began in 1964; from that point Harland and Wolff made a loss every year. Like many cities in the United Kingdom, Belfast was experiencing de-industrialization, a development exacerbated and altered for the worst by the 'Troubles'. But it was still a city capable of inspiring affection. And equally, it was a city that many of its citizens had affection for. The critic Patricia Craig, writing in 2007, looked back nostalgically on the Belfast of the late 1950s:

> the city I grew up in was immeasurably more dense and physically integrated than the Belfast of today [...] That old Belfast wrapped itself around you like the comforter specially procured for Baby Bunting in the nursery rhyme. It led you by the hand down its pungent entries and alleyways, along sedate three-storey, red-brick terraces, up the sidestreets of Stranmillis and into la-di-dah Malone, through the fields at the back of the Falls Park where rough boys roamed with their dogs, past churches and flour mills and factories and primary schools, deeper and deeper into the throughother enchantments of Smithfield and the spirited byways of the Falls [...] As an inhabitant of Belfast, you started out with a lot of affirmative possibilities which might lead you in one direction or another, as the city activated your conformist or dissenting tendencies.[87]

Image and Memory

In 1932 Sir Robert Baird, proprietor of the *Belfast Telegraph*, presented Belfast Corporation with a painting that he had commissioned from the artist William Conor. *Ulster Past and Present* depicted a line of warriors with cloaks, shields and spears marching towards a centrally placed dolmen, while beyond it industrial workers in shawls and flat caps passed under the shadow of a shipyard crane, against a background of factory chimneys. At first sight this was a striking challenge to the short-term perspective on Belfast's origins proclaimed by Henry Cooke in 1841 and implicitly accepted by Carey and others. By this time,

William Conor's *Ulster Past and Present* (1932), the distant Irish past and the Ulster industrial present brought together at last, though in a context in which the rupture between them was greater than ever.

Image supplied courtesy of Joseph McBrinn and published with the kind permission of the Estate of William Conor.

Ulster Past and Present (1932), detail.

Photograph © National Museums Northern Ireland. Collection Ulster Museum. BELUM.U1934. Reproduced with the kind permission of the Estate of William Conor.

however, several decades of Unionist writing had established the notion that early historic Ulster had already been a separate region, defending itself against the incursions of the Gaelic south. In this new perspective it became acceptable to show the world of Cú Chulainn as metamorphosing over time into that of Harland and Wolff.

A second significant feature of Conor's painting is that this successful marriage of the ancient past and the industrial present was achieved just at the time when that present too was about to pass into history. As Belfast's industrial pre-eminence began to fade, its place in the developing iconography of the new Northern Ireland became less certain. Friezes commissioned by the government for the British Empire Exhibition in 1924, and the Glasgow Empire Exhibition in 1938, included representations of shipbuilding, linen and tobacco.[88] But these sat beside images of rural and seaside Ulster, intended to promote Northern Ireland as a holiday destination. The guides produced from 1927 by the Ulster Tourist Development Association likewise depicted a rural pastoral idyll, offering golf and an unspoilt landscape to potential visitors. Belfast as a significant port was also one of the principal features of the Ulster Tourist Development Agency's *Ulster* guides in the 1930s: 'Belfast is Ulster's ocean gateway.'[89] In tourist and advertising posters there was little, apart from varieties in the depiction of the landscape, to distinguish images of Northern Ireland from those of the Irish Free State. There were few illustrations of Belfast per se, and even fewer references to its industrial character. Where such images emerge or are hinted at,

The launch in 1935 of the *Duke of York*, built by Harland and Wolff and intended for the Belfast–Heysham ferry route, as depicted by Norman Wilkinson (1878–1971), a British painter specializing in maritime scenes. The clean lines and bright primary colours reflect the painting's origin as an image commissioned for a poster advertising the London, Midland and Scottish Railway.

Reproduced with the kind permission of the National Railway Museum and the Science and Society Picture Library (NRM/ SSPL).

LAUNCH of T.S.S. DUKE of YORK
QUEEN'S ISLAND, BELFAST
painted by Norman Wilkinson R.I.

LMS

as in Norman Wilkinson's portrayal of industrial Belfast's busy port, they were sanitized depictions of a harbour in which no one seemed to work.

Alongside such cosmetic images, one further visual representation of the city stands out. This was John Luke's mural for the City Hall, commissioned to mark the Festival of Britain in 1951.[90] Luke had earlier contributed Belfast-inspired images to the 1938 exhibition, offering highly stylized depictions of men and women engaged in industrial work. His 1951 mural had the same consciously artificial quality, allowing him through a representation of the distant past to remind the viewer of those industries that had until recently made Belfast great. He himself claimed that he had begun by thinking of the linen industry, and from that had passed on to the granting of the town's first charter in 1613.[91] The finished mural thus has at its centre the figure of Sir Arthur Chichester, reading the charter to an audience of townspeople beneath a clearly recognizable Cave Hill. The emblems of later development, a spinning wheel and a partially completed wooden ship, are placed on either side. A foreshortened history thus links Belfast's nineteenth- and twentieth-century industrial growth to its plantation origins more than two centuries earlier. The Elizabethan military costumes of the central figures also link the town's origins to the world of Sir Francis Drake and the foundation of the first British Empire. From another point of view, the poet John Hewitt, writing thirty years later, felt that the 'simple, rather sober, admittedly static' style of the painting was also part of its appeal as a depiction of Belfast, 'for we are not a mercurial, Mediterranean people'.[92]

In 1961 Luke received another commission: to create a mural for the then Belfast Institute of Further and Higher Education (BIFHE) at Millfield (now Belfast Metropolitan College). This time what he chose to depict was an industrial, technologically advancing city. Part of the mural, for instance, represented the structure of an atom, while the dominant foreground image was of a large piston turbine, and cranes, new bridges and liners filled the landscape. Particular images, such as shipbuilding and the presence of Belfast's workers, echoed Luke's City Hall mural. In the new work, however, these were not principally manual workers (who have a ghostly presence as unfinished builders) but architects and technicians overseeing machines. The rope making and flax spinning depicted in the City Hall were replaced by the construction industry – the skeleton of scaffolding frames one side of the mural – and transport (there is an early image of Concorde, as well as an incomplete Ulster bus). The City Hall provided a distant backdrop but was dwarfed by a skyscraper. In 1951 the City Hall mural looked to the past, and Belfast's foundation story. The BIFHE mural, in progress throughout the 1960s, was future orientated, speaking to viewers of a modern age. It was the piece of art that dominated the rest of Luke's life, but was left unfinished at the time of his death in 1975. Its fate in some ways mirrored that of the city, whose development ground to a halt in the face of civil unrest.[93]

If traditional artists made only sporadic attempts to depict the changing

John Luke's mural showing Sir Arthur Chichester reading the town's newly granted charter to an assembly of inhabitants in 1613, created for Belfast City Hall to mark the Festival of Britain in 1951. It was the latest and perhaps the most successful in a succession of efforts to create a visual representation of the city's convoluted relationship to its own past.

Photograph © Chris Hill, Scenic Ireland. Reproduced with the kind permission of Belfast City Council.

Belfast of the post-war years, new media had meanwhile become available. The BBC established a station in Belfast in 1924; given the limits of its transmission range, its listeners were largely the population of Greater Belfast. Radio was hugely popular in the city. By 1945 Northern Ireland had 150,000 licence holders, as well as an unknown number of unlicensed sets. By 1955 the number of licences had risen to 220,000. It is perhaps in broadcasting that Belfast popularly articulated its gritty urban character in the interwar and post-war period. BBC Northern Ireland produced and broadcast some seventy kitchen comedy dramas in the 1930s, many reflecting a Belfast identity through dialect. The post-war embracing of a new regionalist policy meant employing more staff from Northern Ireland in an organization dominated by English and Scottish personnel. Following the war Andrew Stewart, its director, instructed his staff to cultivate their own garden. This allowed for the commissioning and broadcast in 1948 of Joseph Tomelty's radio drama *The McCooeys*, depicting a Belfast family and set in a terrace 'kitchen house'. Carefully neither Protestant nor Catholic but distinctly reflecting urban Belfast, it ran successfully for seven years. Also of note was the poet W.R. Rodgers' portrait of his childhood in Belfast, broadcast in 1955 as *The Return Room*, 'probably one of the finest feature programmes devised in Northern Ireland after the war'.[94] Through it Rodgers described his puritan upbringing: 'Gay goes up and grim comes down. The Puritan pepper and salt, if it looked like granite tasted like drama. It had two sides to it. Everything in Belfast had two sides.'[95] In literary fiction Brian Moore's *Judith Hearne* (1955) offered a vivid depiction of post-war Belfast as a deeply provincial city locked in gloomy stasis. (Moore himself had emigrated to Canada in 1948.) But it was left to a later generation of Belfast writers, emerging in the 1980s and 90s, to articulate the city's experience in the 1960s and after, and indeed to establish Belfast as 'a place of contemporary urban experience' in fiction.[96]

The City and the Troubles

Belfast city centre became a no-go area in the 1970s, an urban doughnut whose citizens had retreated to the periphery, driven not only by violence but by the availability of new housing. Between 1971 and 1991 the population of the area within the city boundary fell from 400,000 to 281,000. Belfast had scarcely been affected by the IRA campaign from 1956 to 1962, which was largely a rural affair, but the new phase of violence began as an urban phenomenon. Rioting in the summer of 1969 and the Protestant invasion of the lower Falls and the Ardoyne led to huge population displacement, with 3,500 people moving from their homes as a direct result. The British army was back on Belfast's streets and the city was one cockpit of a destructive cycle of terrorism and repression. In the first four years of the 'Troubles' a minimum of 8,000 families in the Greater Belfast area, and perhaps up to twice that number, were driven to leave their homes, an enforced movement of population without parallel in Europe since the Second World War.[97] Between 1969 and 1977 more than a thousand people were killed in Belfast, and there were 2,280 explosions. The image, and reality, of Belfast being presented to the world was increasingly ugly.

Bombings, shootings, the forced movement of large numbers of families, the destruction of businesses and lives, all became fodder for global television and newspaper audiences. Retrospectively, efforts to commemorate the jubilee of the state – 'Ulster '71' – through an exhibition and tourist events appear doomed from the start.[98] Neither local nor state government was working. In March 1972 Stormont was suspended and Northern Ireland came under direct rule from Westminster. As a result of the Macrory Committee's (1970–73) recommendations Belfast Corporation was radically restructured; housing had already been transferred to the Northern Ireland Housing Trust (later the Housing Executive). Now district councils were established to deal with minor services, while regional authorities became responsible for services such as roads, sewerage and education. From 1973 the city council was elected by proportional representation. Though still dominated by Unionists, it now included both the Ulster Unionist Party and their rivals in the Democratic Unionist Party, members of the nationalist Social Democratic and Labour Party, the non-sectarian Alliance Party, the Workers' Party and Sinn Féin. But the municipal administrative system it controlled had been reduced to being responsible for 'bins, bogs and burials'.[99]

By the early 1970s Belfast was no longer a capital city, no longer a municipal centre of any significance, and no longer an industrial or commercial powerhouse. Ironically, the one area of growth in terms of jobs during the 'Troubles' was the public sector; in 1985 there were 346,000 service jobs, of which no fewer than 207,000 were in the public employment.[100] There was a familiarity to the trends emerging from the city; in the 1920s and 30s Belfast had experienced rioting, population displacement, the destruction of property and the presence of the army on its streets. These markers of civil unrest were apparent again in the late 1960s. Few, however, could have predicted that it would take thirty years for these 'Troubles' to be resolved.

Commemorations and the City

> Those waving hills – that chequered plain, –
> Thanks to thy stars, thou Queen of Towns,
> Confirmed success thy labour crowns.
>
> from Mary Lowry, *The Story of Belfast* (1913)

1913 marked the tercentenary of the granting of Belfast's town charter; there were no civic commemorative events. As the *Belfast News Letter* explained:

> But for the menace of Home Rule, which the great majority of the people of Belfast regard as a peril to the future welfare of the city, we should all be engaged just now in making public celebration of the Tercentenary which falls due on Sunday.

Debates about the city and national politics were played out in the pages of its popular press. In its editorial the *News Letter* repeated the argument of a city without a history: 'beyond the history of its growth', 'our city cannot boast of its connection with the storied past of Ireland'.[101] The *Irish News* noted the 'uncelebrated Tercentenary' through a lukewarm review of Mary Lowry's *The Story of Belfast*, arguing that Belfast and Ireland would 'move on more rapidly' when both were 'self-governed and free'.[102] In its tercentenary editorial it reminded its readers: 'A city is not a country, and its people are not a nation; even proud Venice in its palmiest days could not wholly separate itself from Italy, though its people fought other Italians with dour and grim persistence for several centuries.'[103] The paper devoted more than a full page to recording 'chapters of the city's story which, in all probability, will not be mentioned to the same extent elsewhere'. It drew attention to noteworthy national figures connected to the city: the poet and antiquarian Sir Samuel Ferguson, the dramatist James Sheridan Knowles, Nationalist MPs Joseph Devlin and Thomas Sexton, the United Irishman Henry Joy McCracken, and the Young Irelander Charles Gavan Duffy. The Church of Ireland Dean of Belfast preached a special tercentenary sermon with a sombre tone. Reflecting on the achievements of the city, he reminded his audience of how much more could have been attained had the citizens of Belfast been 'more righteous, more sober, more pure'. In relation to the ongoing Home

Rule crisis, he advised that his congregation 'distinguish between the error we resist and the individuals who hold that error'.[104]

By the time of the city's 350th anniversary, in 1963, the political climate was less menacing. On the other hand Belfast's days of industrial greatness were all too clearly behind it. The lord mayor, Martin Wallace, addressing the committee responsible for organizing commemorative events, acknowledged the economic difficulties, but went on to invoke Saint Paul. It was their duty, he suggested, to 'make people realise that it is, on the whole, "no mean city", but a place of which we are very proud'.[105] In his foreword to the official commemorative guide to events he returned, further restricting the scope of the coming anniversary, to the theme of a limited history. Belfast was essentially 'a creation of the nineteenth century' and could not 'rival the romantic history of such great cities as London or Edinburgh'. Nevertheless, he continued gamely, 'if our past is rather less colourful in some respects it is certainly not lacking in purpose and achievement'.[106] And his conclusion struck a similar tone:

> No one knows what the future may hold, but I feel that we cannot do better than echo those great words of Abraham Lincoln when he said – 'With malice toward none; with charity to all; with firmness in the right, as God gives us to see the right, let us strive on to finish the work we are in.'[107]

From this rather downbeat starting point, the city went on to organize a miscellaneous selection of commemorative events, all worthy in their own right, but revealing in their lack of a unifying central theme. An historical exhibition in the Ulster Museum focused on the familiar areas of civic, architectural and industrial development, along with social 'enlightenment and public services'. An early suggestion that the display should include a section representing Protestantism in Belfast was quietly dropped; instead there were 'portraits of local worthies from the early sovereigns'.[108] Another exhibition, in the City Hall, was devoted to trade and industry. There was also a series of arts events, a bus tour of the shipyards, a military display, band recitals, a fireworks show and a lecture on the history of Belfast by Professor Estyn Evans of Queen's University. The Lord Mayor's Show was on the theme '350 years of progress', and Princess Margaret visited the City Hall on 7 June, unveiling a plaque to mark the anniversary.[109] Separate religious services took place in St Anne's Cathedral and in St Mary's Catholic church in Chapel Lane. The *Irish News* seized the opportunity to juxtapose its report of the St Mary's event with news that John F. Kennedy, about to visit the Republic of Ireland, had rejected an invitation from Prime Minister Terence O'Neill to include the northern state in his itinerary.[110]

The Belfast that celebrated its 350th anniversary thus displayed none of the exuberance of the city that had opened its magnificent new City Hall just over half a century earlier, or even of the rising town that had been so flattered to receive a day-long visit from Queen Victoria in 1849. Yet it retained a distinctive

Today and yesterday (1967), by the Belfast cartoonist Rowel Friers (1920–98), captures the city on the cusp of an evolution. Friers juxtaposes the ubiquitous urban working-class terrace with a modern office block, acknowledging Belfast's ambitions to progress from old-fashioned industrial city to modern commercial centre.

Published with permission from BBC Northern Ireland Archives and by kind permission of the Rowel Friers Trust.

identity, shaped in part by its industrial background, in part by the landscape in which it stood. The latter aspect in particular was captured in the short history of Belfast written for the occasion by John A. Young, the city solicitor:

> And so today the crowded streets grow more crowded, the teeming traffic multiplies, development intensifies; tall chimneys belch forth their aura of pall; aesthetic values struggle, not always in vain, to combat the torrent of mercantile realities, unemployment mars the labour front; concert-hall and theatre valiantly strive to make their impact against the ubiquity of television; and above all the surge and the maelstrom broods, guardian-like and sombre, the dark and the green mountain shapes, the stony starkness of Divis, the gentle slopes that are the Hills of Castlereagh, and the placid outlines of 'Napoleon's Nose' – 'the glorious face of the sleeper that slumbers above Belfast'.[11]

The next fifty years were to bring changes more drastic than anything Young or his readers could have imagined. These were to be driven in part by revived or resurfacing political animosities, in part by the impact on an already struggling city of new and destructive economic trends. In the aftermath of that dual process of transformation a new anniversary provides the opportunity once again to take stock. The future is no clearer than it was in 1963. This time, however, we are better placed, through the new research reflected in the chapters that follow, to connect the city of the present day to the full extent and complexity of a unique and compelling history. By doing so, moreover, we can ensure that whatever comes next is faced by an urban society that has at least a better understanding of itself and of the forces that have made it what it is.

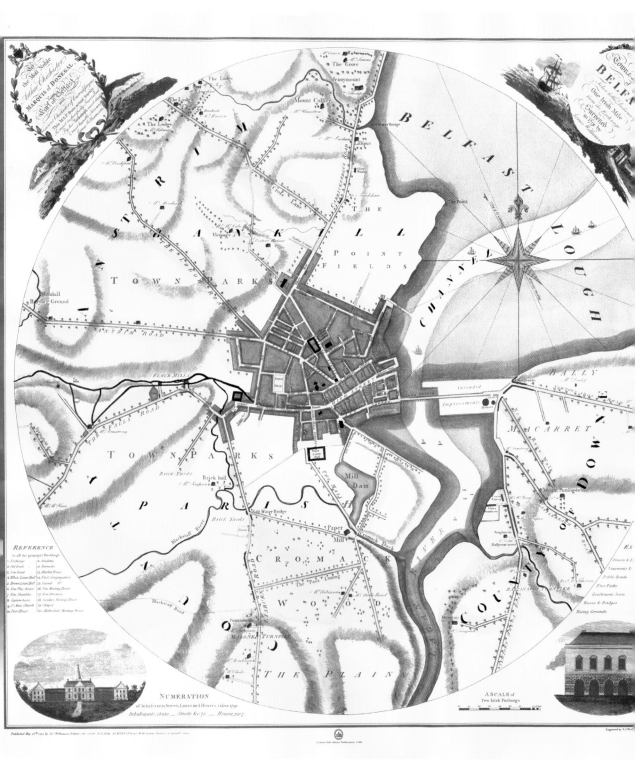

A Linen Hall Library Publication, 1988

2 Beneath Our Feet:
The Archaeological Record

Ruairí Ó Baoill

There are at least 9,000 years of archaeological settlement in the hills and
high ground around Belfast and almost 800 years of nucleated settlement in
what might be termed historic Belfast. This chapter presents an overview of
archaeological sites located in and around Belfast, along with a summary of the
main discoveries from the more than one hundred excavations that have been
carried out in the city. As such, it is a summary account of our knowledge of
the archaeology of Belfast as it currently stands. This body of information will
increase as more pieces of the story are uncovered through new excavations
and analysis of material from previous investigations. Until 2011 no single book
had been written that specifically dealt with the large amount of material that
exists concerning Belfast's archaeological heritage.[1] The quality and quantity
of information that has been acquired since the first licensed archaeological
excavation took place in the historic core of Belfast in 1983 is now a substantial
resource for the study of the city's history. Archaeology can no longer be
regarded as the poor relation of the disciplines engaged with by those
researching the heritage and history of settlement at Belfast.

The Prehistoric Archaeology of Belfast

The setting of Belfast has always had an important effect on the nature of the
settlement that has evolved there. Belfast is surrounded to the north-west by
the Belfast hills (the southern end of the Antrim basalt plateau), to the west
by the well-drained glacial deposits of the Malone ridge, and to the south by
the Holywood and Castlereagh hills. These geological features have created a
basin within which the later nucleated settlement developed. To the north and
north-east of Belfast is Belfast Lough. Within the low-lying Belfast basin, in
what we now regard as Belfast city centre, run three rivers, the Farset, Blackstaff
(Owenvarragh) and Lagan. Although only one of these rivers is still visible,
they have always, through the sediment they have deposited and the episodes
of flooding that they were liable to, had an effect on the type of settlement

that evolved in the city centre. At the same time the natural resources they provided would have been very attractive to prehistoric peoples, and there is archaeological evidence from the coasts and high ground around Belfast of settlers exploiting the available resources from the earliest times of human occupation in Ireland.

The Mesolithic Period (c.8000 BC–c.4000 BC)

The earliest people came to Ireland in the eighth millennium BC (the Mesolithic or Middle Stone Age period). They lived a semi-nomadic lifestyle, using base camps from which they went out hunting, fishing and gathering whatever fruit and berries were in season. To date, the best-preserved archaeological evidence for a Mesolithic settlement comes from Mount Sandel near Coleraine in County Londonderry.[2] Here, the remains of a circular hut and storage pits containing hazel nut and wild apple seeds as well as the bones of wild pig, hare, birds, eels and trout have been uncovered. No such Mesolithic settlement site has yet been discovered at Belfast. Because the organic nature of the materials used in this period, such as wood and animal hides, means that they rarely survive, much of the archaeological evidence of the Mesolithic peoples in Ireland comes in the form of non-perishable artefacts, especially their flint tools. These flint tools were sometimes used in conjunction with wooden shafts or handles as arrows and spears for hunting, harpoons for fishing and axes for clearing vegetation and shaping wood. Other flint tools were fashioned for use in the hand, such as a variety of scrapers for preparing animal hides and cutting notches and perforations in organic materials, and burins for working antler and animal bones. The most common artefact, found on sites dating to the Later Mesolithic period (c.5500–c.4000 BC), is the leaf-shaped flint blade used as a spearhead or knife and known by archaeologists as a 'Bann flake' (or more properly 'butt-trimmed flake') because of the large number that have been found along the River Bann.

The evidence for Mesolithic settlement in Belfast comes from a variety of places. Mesolithic flints, including axes, have been found near the Ormeau Bridge, reflecting the exploitation of the River Lagan's resources such as fish and reeds, and at Old Forge and the Malone Road up on the Malone ridge, showing that the importance of this location was recognized from the earliest times. More evidence comes from two sites close to the George Best Belfast City Airport, where evidence for Mesolithic occupation and both flint and chert tools was uncovered. Other flint artefacts were found in material deposited on the shoreline, north of Holywood town, after the construction of a sea wall there. More recently, in spring 2011, a group of flint artefacts that may date to the Late Mesolithic were recovered by Professor Emeritus Mike Baillie from beneath the roots of a tree that had fallen over, close to the entrance to Ormeau Park.

The Mesolithic peoples would have found abundant resources in the area around Belfast. They could catch fish and shellfish in the rivers that flowed into the Belfast basin and in Belfast Lough. Much of the high ground and hills would have been covered in trees and vegetation that supplied both wood for huts and tools and berries, fruits and nuts to supplement the meat and fish diet. Mammals such as wild boar and hare could be hunted for food and hides, and birds were also caught and eaten.

In the Early Mesolithic (c.8000–c.5500 BC) increased sea levels probably restricted activity to the hills and coastline along the higher ground to the south of what is now the city centre. The small Mesolithic population may have amounted to only a few extended families and the lives of Belfast's first settlers must have been governed by what plants, animals and seafood were available at various seasons of the year.

The Neolithic (c.4000 BC–c.2500 BC)

The major change in material culture and economy occurred in the Neolithic (New Stone Age) period, some 6,000 years ago. The exact nature of the change, bringing with it new technology and a lifestyle radically different to that practised in the Mesolithic, remains unclear. The archaeological evidence of changes in culture and technology that occurred in the Neolithic and in the following period, the Bronze Age, suggest that there was probably some movement of people, but the evidence of movements of whole populations is more ambiguous. The Neolithic peoples lived in permanent settlements. They grew crops, such as barley and wheat, and managed the landscape through tree clearance to give themselves space for their settlements and agricultural activities. They kept domesticated animals, such as cattle, sheep, pigs and goats, all species new to Ireland at this time, and they made clay pottery vessels for storage, cooking and burial rituals.

The tools that the Neolithic peoples used were markedly different to those of the Mesolithic period. These included arrowheads and javelins for hunting, high-quality axes (very often made from a stone known as porcellanite, mined from Tievebulliagh and Brockley, Rathlin Island), and grinding stones for processing the cereals they had grown. But it is in the stone memorials that they put up to their dead that the Neolithic peoples left their most lasting mark. These Neolithic monuments are the earliest visible evidence for prehistoric people in Belfast. The picture they paint is of an increased, vibrant population – perhaps in the hundreds – marking out territory, living under leaders who were able to organize numbers of people in the erection of their monuments, and possessing a complex set of religious beliefs.

To date, no Neolithic house has been uncovered in Belfast. Evidence from elsewhere in Ireland suggests that in the Early Neolithic the houses would have been rectangular or sub-rectangular in plan, but that by the end of the period people were living in circular-shaped dwellings. The houses would have been constructed of wood and clay or sod, organic materials that decay over time and now leave no traces above ground. As with the Mesolithic, however, traces of Neolithic settlements survive through the evidence of non-perishable material such as flint, stone and pottery. As in the case of the Mesolithic, Neolithic settlement has been found predominantly on the high, well-drained areas around Belfast, such as the slopes of the Belfast hills and on the Malone ridge.

The Malone ridge has, for millennia, been one of the most desirable places for people to settle in Belfast. The ridge stretches back from the Ormeau Bridge, close to the mouth of the River Lagan, southwards to the Giant's Ring at Ballynahatty. The modern Lisburn Road follows the line of the ridge. There is evidence of people living here from the time of the earliest settlers at Belfast. Part of the attraction is that the well-drained glacial deposits of the Malone ridge meant that water seeped away, protecting the foundations of the wooden-founded houses of the early settlers. Another attraction is that the southern end of the Malone ridge opens up on to the fertile Lagan valley, a hinterland very important to the eventual development of urban settlement at Belfast. At this southern end other ridges of sandy deposits emanate to the east and west that were clearly early routeways. Finally, close to Ballynahatty and Shaw's Bridge was located what was at this time the lowest fording point of the River Lagan. This was before the falling sea level resulted in the development of the sandbank close to the modern Queen's Bridge that from medieval times onwards encouraged people to settle in what is now the site of Belfast city centre.

The importance of the Malone ridge is highlighted in the location of Belfast's best-known prehistoric site, the Giant's Ring within the Ballynahatty complex of archaeological monuments. The earliest monument is a Neolithic passage tomb, now much decayed. The tomb type gets its name from the fact that it comprises a stone-lined passage leading to a main chamber, which may be sub-divided with smaller chambers set off a central area. Both the passage and chambers are surrounded by a kerb of stones and were covered by a mound of earth and stones. The Ballynahatty tomb was later enclosed by a large circular earthen henge (ritual enclosure), 200 metres in diameter, with a bank that survives up to 4 metres in height, with the passage tomb in the centre of the circle. The henge has been dated by archaeologists to the Later Neolithic period. The scale of the henge monument implies that whoever had it constructed had access to large amounts of manpower and the authority to organize and execute this huge architectural task, which is still impressively visible in the landscape. Within the henge, the passage tomb may have been the focus of a ritual or religious activity and the space within the henge means that very many people would have been able to observe this taking place. Whether the actual ritual was open to participation by everyone in the community is, however, unlikely, given the evidence for the beginning of stratified society in the Neolithic.

Barrie Hartwell of Queen's University directed ten seasons of archaeological excavations at the Ballynahatty complex in the 1990s and these uncovered the remains of a large double wooden enclosure in a field to the north of the Giant's Ring, marked out by huge postholes that the now-rotted posts would have stood in.[3] The inner enclosure was associated with other internal structures, again marked out by posts. These were interpreted as a temple where the dead were left out to be ritually de-fleshed (a process known as excarnation). These structures were dated to the Later Neolithic period. At some point around 2500 BC the timber complex, which had stood for as long as one hundred years, appears to have been deliberately burnt down and destroyed, possibly as part of a ritual action to put the temple out of use.

Passage tombs were the largest and most dramatic of the megalithic (large stone) tombs of the Irish Neolithic, the best-known examples being those at Newgrange in County Meath. The commonest type of Neolithic tomb found in the northern half of Ireland, however, is the court tomb. These monuments typically take the form of a chambered gallery that contained interments, which was covered by a trapezoidal-shaped cairn of stones and earth that opened at one end on to a semi-circular forecourt. Such a tomb, known locally as the Hanging Thorn Cairn, was excavated on McIlwhans Hill, west of Cave Hill, in 1937 and sherds of Neolithic pottery were uncovered within it.[4] Another type of Neolithic tomb, known as a portal tomb because the upright stones (orthostats) holding up the large capstone that covers this type of monument give the impression of a door, stands at Greengraves near Dundonald. It is known locally as the Kempe Stones. The remains of three other Neolithic tombs, all of uncertain type, are located on Wolf Hill.

Even if the houses where they lived have not yet been discovered, there is thus much archaeological evidence of Neolithic activity at Belfast. This comprises, in addition to the tombs, the remains of tools and domestic pottery.

Two clay pots recovered from I.J. Herring's 1937 excavation at the Neolithic court tomb known as the Hanging Thorn Cairn, McIlwhan's Hill, Ballyutoag, Ligoniel.
Photograph © National Museums Northern Ireland. Collection Ulster Museum. MMCK11.

An occupation site, consisting of a variety of flint tools and pottery, was discovered in the grounds of Tyrone House, off the Malone Road.[5] Another site where Neolithic pottery and flint was recorded was on the south-facing slope of Squire's Hill in upper Ballysillan. Unsurprisingly, a large amount of the evidence for Neolithic activity at Belfast comes from the area of the Malone ridge. Finds include polished stone and porcellanite axes, scrapers, flint blades and other flint flakes. Beyond the Malone ridge, polished stone axes have been found at Ardoyne, Fortwilliam and Ekenhead in north Belfast and near the Queen's Bridge (and the River Lagan) in what is now central Belfast. On the higher ground of the Belfast hills three Neolithic flint-working sites, where tools were fashioned or completed, have been found at Ballymurphy and on Black Mountain.

The best-known collection of artefacts from Neolithic Belfast is the internationally important group of porcellanite axes known as the Malone Hoard, now on display in the Ulster Museum. Found in around 1872 at Danesfort, Malone Road, the hoard consists of 18 large polished porcellanite

The Malone Hoard group. Made out of porcellanite, this group of beautifully crafted symbolic or ritual tools comprises some of the finest objects known from the Irish Neolithic.
Photograph © National Museums Northern Ireland. Collection Ulster Museum.

axes and one chisel. The axes are too large to have been practical tools and are clearly of symbolic or ritual purpose. They indicate that the owner (and commissioner) of this impressive collection was a person of wealth, power and status.

The Bronze Age (c.2500–c.500 BC)

It was in the third millennium BC that the peoples of Ireland first started producing metal tools, jewellery and weapons. The ability to work metal, the result of the development of a prehistoric mining industry and the invention of smelting, and the working of bronze (an alloy of copper and tin) illustrate a more obvious display of wealth and division within prehistoric society. The people who mined the copper and tin could probably not have afforded the jewellery and weapons that these ores were turned into. New pottery forms were introduced in the Bronze Age, especially a type called Beaker, named after the shape of the vessels. The development of new technology, and the increasing production of desirable objects of wealth which needed to be protected, appears to have led to a more warlike and militaristic society in Ireland, especially in the Late Bronze Age (c.1200 BC–c.500 BC).

The Bronze Age is the first period for which we have archaeological evidence of prehistoric houses at Belfast. In 1982 an enclosed hut circle was excavated in Ballyutoag townland on McIlwhans Hill.[6] The circular house was roughly 8 metres in diameter and showed two phases of occupation. Radiocarbon dates from the site suggest that people were living there in the Late Bronze Age, perhaps between 1050 BC and 750 BC. Another Bronze Age circular house was excavated at Ballyregan, Castlereagh, in 2004. The house was nearly 7 metres in diameter and two pits close to the house contained pottery from the Late Bronze Age.

New megalithic monument types were also erected by the Bronze Age peoples of Ireland. These included stone circles (though these may have begun in the Late Neolithic period), wedge tombs (megalithic tombs in the shape of a wedge), stone cairns, cist burials (in which individuals were buried in stone-lined graves, with some cists containing multiple burials) and standing stones. Very often the monuments are built in prominent positions on hills that have fine views across the nearby landscape. The new monument types may reflect the development of new ritual and burial rites. Towards the end of the Bronze Age in Ireland ritual or tribal (royal) centres, such as Clogher, County Tyrone, start to appear in the landscape.

Bronze Age burial cairns are located on the summit of a hill close to Divis Mountain and also on Black Mountain. A long cist was recorded at Derriaghy in 1837. The potential wealth of archaeological sites that may still exist in the Belfast hills, but have as yet been unrecorded, has been recognized by archaeologists, and surveys by both the National Trust and the Ulster

Archaeological Society are currently identifying and recording many new monuments. Standing stones also survive in the Belfast area. These include the well-known Long Stone at Ballybeen, Dundonald. This was excavated in 1983 along with an adjacent ring ditch that contained a Late Bronze Age cremation burial.[7] Other standing stones can be found on the top of Divis Mountain at Ballygomartin and at Ballynahatty, part of the religious complex there.

Bronze Age pots have been recovered from a variety of locations around Belfast, including Kilmakee, Ballylesson and Danesfort, on the Malone ridge. Early Bronze Age pottery and worked flints were also found at a site near the George Best Belfast City Airport. In addition a number of discoveries of high-quality objects illustrate the richness of Bronze Age society in the neighbourhood of Belfast. In 1993 a Late Bronze Age gold dress-fastener was discovered in a gully, possibly a sunken path, on Cave Hill. Whether the dress-fastener had been hidden or lost there is unknown. A leaf-shaped Bronze Age sword was uncovered from near the Queen's Bridge in the centre of Belfast. In prehistoric times in Ireland, rivers were often associated with deities and the sword may have been ritually deposited by someone important both as an offering to the deity, perhaps as part of a ceremony, and as an ostentatious act to show that the person was of such wealth that they could afford to spare such a precious object. In 1868 a dugout canoe was found close to the Albert Bridge in east Belfast, showing the importance of water transport both for travel and for exploiting the resources of the nearby rivers.

The best-known Bronze Age site at Belfast is the Giant's Ring complex at Ballynahatty. West of the Neolithic henge and passage tomb, later tombs such as cist burials, ring barrows and a standing stone indicate continuity of religious activity over several millennia at the site. It may be that all this religious and ritual activity at Ballynahatty, at the end of the Malone ridge and so close to the vital River Lagan, marked it out as a special place of the dead in the Neolithic and Bronze Age.

Within the last decade new archaeological evidence has started to come to light relating to a second important prehistoric religious landscape at Belfast

Bronze Age gold jewellery found at Belfast. The large cup-ended dress-fastener on the right was found on Cave Hill in 1993. The group of three small artefacts on the left (reproduced at a larger scale to show detail) are (a) at top left, a sleeve-fastener (without discs) which would have functioned a bit like cuff-links and (b) top right and bottom, two artefacts known as 'hair rings' or 'ring money', probably used to adorn the hair of some notable person. The delicate incised decoration on the sleeve-fastener and the top hair ring shows the skill of Bronze Age artists.

Photographs © National Museums Northern Ireland. Collection Ulster Museum. MMCK18, MMCK23.

that may be on a par with Ballynahatty. At Carrowreagh, east of Dundonald, a henge enclosure has been excavated, in whose ditch were discovered pottery and flint arrowheads, along with 11 circular enclosures or ring ditches and a Bronze Age cremation. Two standing stones are also in close proximity. The Carrowreagh complex appears to date to the Late Neolithic or Early Bronze Age. The prominent location of the complex, overlooking what is now the Newtownards Road, probably an ancient route between Belfast and the Ards, and with panoramic views across the Belfast mountains and both the Craigantlet and Castlereagh hills, mark it out as a major archaeological site.

The Iron Age (c.500 BC–c.AD 500)

New metalworking technology was again introduced to Ireland in the period following the Bronze Age. As yet there have been no definitely identified Iron Age sites at Belfast. The well-known and much-visited monument called McArt's Fort, a fortified promontory jutting out from the eastern side of Cave Hill that overlooks Belfast, may be such a site, but without scientific archaeological excavation this remains unproven, and it may possibly be Late Bronze Age. The promontory is oval-shaped, and most of its sides drop steeply 50 metres down to the slopes of the hill. However, at the western side of the fort, where the neck of the promontory joins Cave Hill, there is a large ditch roughly 8 metres wide and 3 metres deep protecting access to the promontory. Such promontory forts are traditionally dated to the prehistoric period. The function of McArt's Fort and what type of buildings originally lay on the promontory is an enigma that only future archaeological investigation will solve.

The Early Christian Archaeology of Belfast

Unfortunately for archaeologists and historians, the prehistoric peoples of Ireland were not literate and so have not left us any written descriptions of themselves. To find out about them we rely on the archaeological study of the places where they lived and were buried, the material culture that they left behind and the monuments they erected. The coming of Christianity to Ireland in the fifth century AD and the literacy that accompanied it, which led to the recording of significant people, places and events, gives us another important strand of information that helps fill out the story. From this period onwards we have both an archaeological and a documentary record. It is during the Early Christian period (c.500–c.1200) that Belfast is first mentioned in written texts, in the mid-660s AD.[8] As Belfast emerged into historic times we know that the people living there were Christian and that they spoke Irish. Nearly all of the townland names around Belfast are derived from Irish and very often these are descriptive names. Thus the name Stranmillis derives from the Irish 'An Struthán Milis' or 'the sweet stream', describing that part of the River Lagan above the Ormeau Bridge where the waters stopped being tidal (and salty) and were now safe to drink.

The economy of Early Christian Ireland was firmly based on agriculture, with cattle being the principal form of currency and status for individuals. People lived in dispersed settlements, in raths or ringforts, farms that were enclosed by anything up to three circular banks and ditches. Some settlements were unenclosed but these are difficult to identify above ground. Raths or ringforts are the most numerous of all monument types in Ireland and many still survive around Belfast. Stone-lined subterranean tunnels known as souterrains, used both for storage and as a place of refuge during times of danger, are often associated with these settlements. This monument type gives its name to the unglazed, fired-clay cooking ware called Souterrain Ware that is usually found on Early Christian-period sites in eastern Ulster. One such souterrain was investigated at Seaview allotments off Fortwilliam Park, north Belfast, in the 1930s. Other souterrains have been recorded at Ballymagarry, Black Mountain, and at Ligoniel on Wolf Hill.

To facilitate the growing population in the Early Christian period, there appears to have been deliberate forest clearance on the slopes of the Belfast hills and around twenty raths are located along the 600-foot (180-metre) contour line between Black Mountain and Cave Hill. On the other side of Belfast, another group can be found on the Castlereagh hills between the 400–500-foot (120–150-metre) contours. Many of these raths appear to be on the line of new routeways that developed during the Early Christian period and that emanated from the newly formed sandbank that allowed the crossing of the River Lagan at its junction with the River Farset. The old prehistoric crossing point at the southern end of the Malone ridge, close to the modern Shaw's Bridge, seems to have declined in importance as a result.

A rath at Shaneen Park, Ballyaghagan, in north Belfast was excavated in 1948 and 1950.[9] The rath had an external ditch and a souterrain in the interior. Among the artefacts retrieved were sherds of Souterrain Ware pottery, a fragment of a shale bracelet, a bronze ring pin and buckle, other metal artefacts, a hone stone for sharpening tools and fragments of a wooden bucket. Interestingly, other artefacts found at the rath show it to have been re-occupied in the thirteenth or fourteenth centuries at the time when the Anglo-Normans had founded the first nucleated settlement at Belfast.

Several dozen raths are recorded as having existed in other parts of Belfast. These include sites at Ballymurphy, Ballygomartin, Glencairn, Ballysillan, Kilmakee and Derriaghy. The Malone ridge also still appears to have been a choice location for settlement in the Early Christian period. Destroyed raths are noted as having been located at Danesfort, Malone Demesne, in what are now the grounds of Stranmillis University College, and at Old Forge/ Malone Upper.

At least one large Early Christian settlement, comprising a series of enclosures and at least 23 circular houses, has been excavated at Ballyutoag townland in the Belfast hills.[10] Souterrain Ware pottery, flints for lighting fires, the stem of a bronze dress pin and a fragment of a shale (lignite) bracelet were among the finds. It is uncertain whether the settlement was used for booleying (transhumance), the seasonal movement of cattle between different pasture lands, or whether the settlement was a permanent establishment. If it was permanent, it is estimated that it may have held as many as 100 people. It is possible that other such settlements in the hills around Belfast are waiting to be discovered.

Although this period is called the Early Christian period, our evidence for churches at Belfast is quite slight. The church and graveyard at Shankill, located at what is now Shankill Park, may have been the most important at this time. The name Shankill comes from the Irish *seanchill* meaning 'old church', which may reflect its antiquity. An unpublished excavation in the churchyard that took place in 1959 uncovered Souterrain Ware pottery and evidence of metalworking, all finds consistent with an Early Christian church. The bullaun stone (a large stone with a circular depression in the centre like a font) that currently stands outside St Matthew's church, a short distance up the Shankill Road from Shankill Park, is said to have come originally from Shankill graveyard. Such stones are traditionally associated with early church sites across Ireland. The modern Shankill Road reflects one of the early routeways from the ford across the River Lagan in central Belfast and again might suggest that the church here was set up on one of the most important approaches to the ford. It would appear that the Chapel of the Ford, discussed below, later took over as the parish church of the Anglo-Norman settlement at Belfast.

Another type of monument dating to this period has also been discovered at Belfast. Two horizontal mills, wooden water-driven structures to facilitate millstones that ground corn for breadmaking, have been uncovered. The first was found at Dover Street, off the Shankill Road, in 1876. The second was uncovered at McGladery's brickworks on the Springfield Road in 1930. Both monuments show that the rivers that ran into Belfast have been exploited by settlers for at least one thousand years, if not longer.

The Medieval Archaeology of Belfast

With the medieval period (c.1200–c.1600) and the coming of the Anglo-Normans to Belfast we have evidence, for the first time, of a nucleated settlement that is recognizable as the forerunner of the modern city. The site and context of the medieval settlement at Belfast is described and discussed in more detail by Philip Macdonald in Chapter 3, and it is not proposed to replicate much of the currently known historical documentation for this.

The medieval settlement at Belfast falls into two distinct phases, though how quickly the second period followed the first is still uncertain.

The first phase of nucleated settlement at Belfast occurs with the coming of the Anglo-Normans to Ulster in the late twelfth century. Carrickfergus was the principal centre of the Anglo-Norman earldom and Belfast was established as a satellite manor and borough town. The first reference to a building in Belfast dates to 1262, when a castle is noted. The second phase of medieval settlement, this time a Gaelic one, was ushered in when the area around Belfast came under the control of the O'Neills of Clandeboye in the fifteenth century. There are references to an O'Neill castle in Belfast, as well as to their principal castle, located at Castlereagh, in both Irish and English records of the fifteenth and sixteenth centuries.

In archaeological terms there is evidence for medieval activity in the centre of Belfast in both the early and late medieval periods. During the re-culverting of High Street in the 1860s, a lead-alloy brooch of twelfth- or thirteenth-century date was uncovered. During building works in 1854–55 and 1922 between Castle Place and Corn Market three skeletons were dug up. One of these was carbon dated to the fifteenth century.[11] Excavations under the Woolworth's and Burton building on High Street in 2003 uncovered a curving medieval gully, possibly a property boundary, and sherds of Medieval Coarse Pottery (the Ulster unglazed pottery tradition of the medieval period).[12] In late 2004/early 2005, during excavations under the Kitchen Bar in Victoria Square, an earthen clay bank protected by a post-and-wattle breakwater fence was uncovered. A sherd of glazed medieval pottery of thirteenth- or fourteenth-century date was found in association with the bank and it has

Tantalizing traces of medieval Belfast? Excavations in 2004–05 on the site of the new Victoria Square retail development uncovered what appeared to be the remains of a waterfront, comprising a clay bank and a fence of 16 posts interwoven with strands of wattling. A single sherd of medieval pottery found in association with the feature may date it to the medieval period. See also below, p. 119.

Photograph © Gahan and Long Ltd.

been suggested that this structure may possibly have been the remains of some sort of quayside or wharf for boats docking or unloading from the Farset or Blackstaff rivers.

Beyond the centre of Belfast there are substantial remains of Anglo-Norman earthen fortifications known as mottes, probably constructed in the late twelfth or early thirteenth centuries, which run in a protective line from Holywood in the east, westwards through Dundonald, meeting the River Lagan at Edenderry and continuing beyond.[13] Surviving mottes in the greater Belfast area include those at Dunmurry, Edenderry, Belvoir Park, Breda, Shandon Park, Knock and Dundonald. Given the unsuitability of the alluvial deposits that covered the centre of the Belfast basin, it is unlikely that an effective earthen fortification could have been constructed from this material. It may be that the Anglo-Norman castle in Belfast was a square earthwork like the one that survives at Ekenhead off the North Circular Road in north Belfast.[14] This site has never been excavated and the date of its construction has not been determined. However, it may have been an outlying centre to the main Anglo-Norman manor/borough settlement at Belfast.

One of the interesting aspects of the Anglo-Normans in Ulster is the level to which they interacted with the local Irish. A David O'Coltaran is mentioned in 1333 as having supplied labour instead of rent by helping to bring in the harvest at Belfast. Not only is this evidence of acculturation between the two groups, but the man also has the honour of being the first local person whose name we know. Further evidence of this accommodation might also be seen at the rath at Shaneen Park, not far from the Ekenhead square earthwork and discussed earlier in this chapter. The archaeological evidence from the rath, a specifically Irish type of architectural construction, suggests that it was re-occupied in the Anglo-Norman period and glazed medieval pottery and other medieval artefacts were found there. Whether the new occupants were Irish tenants of the Anglo-Normans with access to Anglo-Norman goods or Norman colonists themselves, it shows a potentially greater inter-mixing at Belfast than the written records usually suggest.

There is one enigmatic monument, located in the grounds of Castle High School off Fortwilliam Park and close to an Early Christian souterrain described above, which may be a late medieval fort. Known as Fortwilliam earthwork, the monument is lozenge-shaped with projecting bastions to the north-east and south-west. The fort is substantially intact although heavily overgrown. Located on a ridge with excellent views from the site in all directions, but particularly over the old shore road running from Carrickfergus to Belfast, the plan of the fort suggests that it might have been constructed in the late Elizabethan period or the very early seventeenth century, but at present this cannot be verified. No excavations have taken place at the site and the exact date of the earthwork is uncertain.

The Clandeboye O'Neill stone inauguration chair, now on display in the Ulster Museum. The inauguration stone, used for the coronation of new chiefs, was located in or near the principal Clandeboye O'Neill tower-house at Castlereagh. It was removed around 1750 and reused as a seat in the Belfast Butter Market until 1829. The inauguration chair then spent time in houses in Belfast and County Sligo before being obtained by the Belfast Museum, precursor to the Ulster Museum, in 1898. The O'Neill tower-house at Castlereagh survived into the nineteenth century and is portrayed on a Downshire estate map of 1803. No above-ground remains of the castle now survive. The other Clandeboye O'Neill tower-house, at Belfast, was substantially demolished and incorporated into the grand fortified Jacobean house erected by Sir Arthur Chichester in the early seventeenth century, in the area around modern Castle Lane/Callendar Street.

Photograph © National Museums Northern Ireland. Collection Ulster Museum. BELUM.A305.1911.

Although the principal buildings of both the Anglo-Norman and the later medieval Clandeboye O'Neill settlements have not yet been discovered, this situation may one day change. Most of the early buildings (with the exception of the tower-house) were presumably built of wood, sod and other organic materials that easily decay, leaving no record above ground. However, given that excavations in Belfast have shown that there are still deep archaeological strata surviving in the city centre, targeted excavation may mean that at some later stage we may actually uncover the remains of these important early buildings and be able to determine a more accurate layout of the two medieval settlements that once were at Belfast.

The Archaeology of Seventeenth- and Eighteenth-century Belfast

In the early seventeenth century Arthur Chichester re-founded the third version of Belfast to be located in what we know now as the city centre. The main axis of his new town was, again, High Street, with a fortified house, known as the Castle, in the area of Castle Lane/Castle Place and a church, rebuilt in 1622, at the end of High Street, on the probable location of the medieval Chapel of the Ford. It is unfortunate that, unlike Carrickfergus, there are no early maps that help us to track the evolution of Belfast from medieval manor and late medieval Clandeboye O'Neill settlement to plantation town. Belfast was first mapped in detail by Thomas Phillips in 1685, some seventy years after Chichester re-established the town. We do, however, have a written description of the town in 1611 when the Plantation Commissioners visited:

> We came to Bealfast where we found many masons, bricklayers and other laborers aworke, who had taken downe the ruynes [ruins] of the decayed Castle there almoste to the valte [vault] of the Sellers [cellars] and had likewise layde the foundation of a bricke house [for Chichester] 50 foote longe which is to be adjoyned to the sayd castle by a stayrcase of bricke which is to be 14 foot square.
>
> The house to be made 20 foot wyde and two Storeys and a halfe high. The Castle is to be buylte two Stories above the Sellers, all the Roomes thereof to be valted and platformes to be made thereon. The Stayrcase to be made 10 foote higher than the Castle, about which Castle and House there is a stronge Bawne almost finished, which is flankered with foure half Bulwarkes. The foundacion of the wall and bulwarke to the height of the water table is made with stoane, and the reste, being in alle 12 foote high above the ground, is made with brick. The Bawne is to be compassed [surrounded] with a lardge and deep ditche or moate, which will always stande full of water.
>
> The Castle will defend the Passage over the Foorde [ford] at Bealfast between the Upper and Lower Clandeboye, and likewise the Bridge over the Owynvarra [or Blackstaff river] between Malon[e] and Bealfast. This work is in so good forwardnes that it is lyke [likely] to be finished by the mydle of next somer [summer].[15]

The description of the 'ruins of the decayed castle' with its 'valte and Sellers' almost certainly describes the demolition and partial reuse of the late medieval Clandeboye O'Neill tower-house, thus locating its original position as somewhere in the area of Castle Lane/Callendar Street. The first ever licensed archaeological excavation in the centre of Belfast, carried out in 1983 by Nick Brannon of the Northern Ireland Environment Service, after the demolition of the Brands and Norman shop at the junction of Castle Lane and Callendar Street, failed to find direct evidence of any of the three castles. Although sherds of Early Christian Souterrain Ware, Medieval Ulster Coarse Pottery and fragments of seventeenth-century North Devon and German Stoneware pottery were found in deposits, as well as rubbish pits and a ditch, nothing attributable to any of the castle structures came to light.[16] Another excavation, at 10–16 High Street, carried out in 2005, uncovered two early walls that were interpreted as relating to the 'Old Shambles Gate', illustrated on the 1685 map as part of the gardens associated with the seventeenth-century castle.

The 1685 map, although some seventy years later, gives further evidence about the layout of the new town. The town centre was based on the banks of the River Farset with houses portrayed as narrow terraces, one or two storeys high, with slate or tile roofs and with long back gardens running off behind the terraces. A mill and millpond is shown at Millfield as well as the house and gardens occupied by the Chichesters. An interesting sub-circular bawn-type of

Thomas Phillips's 1685 bird's-eye view of Belfast. This first detailed map of Belfast was drawn up more than 400 years after the Anglo-Norman settlement, 200 years after the Clandeboye O'Neills took control of the place, and 70 years after Sir Arthur Chichester re-founded the third version of Belfast. In the half-century before Phillips's map was produced, sections of the town's defensive ditch, created in the 1640s, had been filled in and he was not able to accurately record it all. However, archaeological excavations in 2001 uncovered a section of this 'missing' ditch at Gordon Street, close to the location of the seventeenth-century Strand Gate into the town. Among the features portrayed on the 1685 map are the principal buildings of

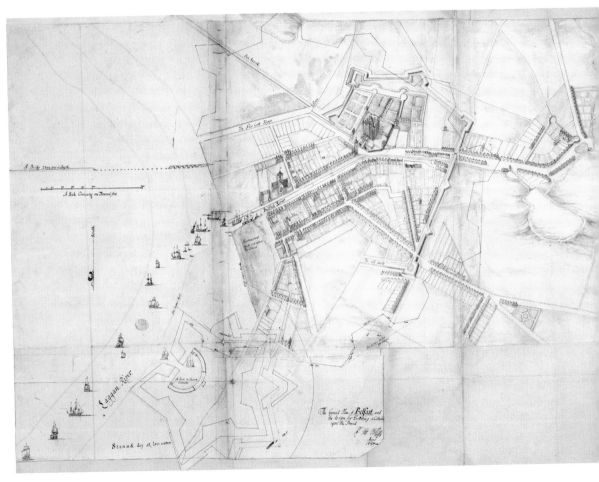

seventeenth-century Belfast – the castle and gardens, the market house, the corporation church (replaced in 1811–16 by St George's on High Street), the town defences, the terraces of red-brick houses that made up the streets of the town and the mill at Millfield. One of the major changes to previous town layouts was that planned streets now extended further north, into the area now called Cathedral Quarter.

© The British Library Board (Maps.K.Top.51,37).

fortification is shown in the area of Townsend Street, beyond the seventeenth-century town boundaries. This building, which possibly lies beneath the car park of a school, has never been properly identified or investigated, and its date remains uncertain.

One of the major developments of the seventeenth-century town from that of the earlier medieval settlements is that it occupied areas of land on the northern side of the River Farset, in what is now Cathedral Quarter. On the 1685 map what are now called Waring Street, North Street and Royal Avenue are all shown with terraces of houses and back gardens. Archaeological excavations around Cathedral Quarter have shown that the ground north of the River Farset (modern High Street) was mostly undeveloped in the medieval period and one of the defining features of Chichester's Belfast was that this area was laid out and built upon, while at the same time the town was extended across the River Lagan into what is now east Belfast. The core of the seventeenth-century town was still initially bounded to the east by the shoreline, modern Victoria Street, but from the end of that century there were determined attempts to reclaim and improve this part of the town.

Excavations at Waring Street have uncovered the foundations of some of the seventeenth-century houses.[17] An excavation directed in advance of the construction of the Potthouse bar at the corner of Waring Street and Hill Street uncovered evidence of property boundaries laid out by the seventeenth-century surveyors, running back from Waring Street below the red-brick terraces that fronted on to it. Among the thousands of sherds of seventeenth- and eighteenth-century ceramics retrieved, mostly English wares, was just one sherd of Medieval Ulster Coarse Pottery, reinforcing the picture that this part of Belfast did not lie within the boundaries of either of the two medieval settlements. The attraction of building on higher, drier ground can be seen from the archaeological evidence from the 2003 excavation under the Woolworth's and Burton building on High Street (already discussed in the medieval section of this chapter), where episodes of post-medieval flooding were identified in the strata uncovered. Interestingly, further east along High Street, an excavation carried out in 1984 in advance of the construction of the In-Shops car park showed no evidence of flooding in the seventeenth- and eighteenth-century structures and strata uncovered.

Although Arthur Chichester walled Carrickfergus between 1608 and 1615,[18] Belfast was given no such defences. It was not until the 1640s and the decade of warfare that took place in Ireland between 1641 and 1653 that fortifications were regarded as necessary. The construction of the defences was begun in 1642 and when finished constituted a ditch with internal bank, a maximum of ten bastions (projecting outworks) and three gates (the Mill Gate at modern Castle Street, the North Gate at modern North Street and the Strand Gate near the old seventeenth-century shoreline close to the junction

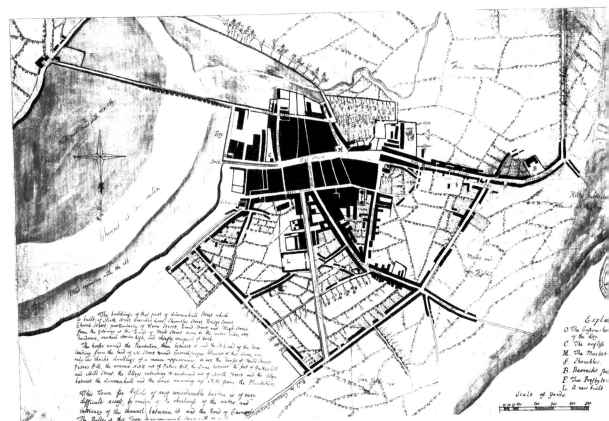

of modern Gordon Street and Victoria Street). By the time that Thomas Phillips drew up his map of Belfast in 1685, sections of the town's defensive ditch had already been filled in, less than fifty years after it had been built. Phillips seems to have been unable accurately to record the full circuit of the town defences, so there are blanks on the map. The line of the ditch is totally absent from the 1757 map of Belfast, though sections of it may have survived until the late eighteenth century.[19]

Happily, three sections of the mid-seventeenth-century defences have been uncovered through archaeological excavation. In 1990, on the north-western side of Donegall Street, where Writers' Square is now located, the ditch was found to be 3 metres wide and 1 metre deep, though heavily truncated by later activity on the site. Seventeenth-century animal bones, ceramics, glass, clay pipes and leather shoes were recovered from the ditch. It has been estimated that a 60-metre stretch of the ditch still lies undisturbed under the site that could be investigated in the future. In 2001, at Gordon Street, a second section of the defences was uncovered. Here the ditch was found to be 2–3 metres wide. Seventeenth- and eighteenth-century pottery and cattle horns and cores were recovered from the ditch. The cattle bone may have been a by-product of the tanning industry, which is known to have been carried out at nearby Waring

Map of Belfast prepared for the Donegall estate in 1757. Plans for a new phase of urban development began under the fourth earl, but were brought to fruition only after his successor came of age in 1761. Some of the details shown may thus be aspirational. What is clear, however, is that by this time, less than a century after Phillips's map, virtually all above-ground evidence of Chichester's Belfast castle and gardens, and of the mid-seventeenth-century town defences, are gone.

Reproduced with the kind permission of the Linen Hall Library.

The handwritten note accompanying the map provides an important snapshot of the urban landscape on the eve of the fifth earl's improvements:
    'The buildings of that part of Linenhall Street [later Donegall Street] which is built,

of North Street, Hercules
Lane, Shambles Street, Bridge
Street [later Ann Street],
Church Street; particularly of,
Wern [Waring] Street, Broad
Street [later Bridge Street]
and High Street from the
gateway at the end of Mill
Street down to the water tide,
are handsome, several stories
high, and chiefly composed of
brick.

'The houses named the
Plantation, them betwixt it
and the N[orth] E[ast] end
of the lane leading from
the head of N[orth] Street
toward Carrickfergus, likewise
of that Lane, are only low
thatched dwellings of a mean
appearance; so are the houses
of Mill Street, Peter's Hill, the
avenue N[orth] N[orth] W[est]
out of Peter's Hill, the Lane
betwixt the foot of Peter's
Hill and Mill Street, the alleys
extending N[orth] eastward
out of North Street, and
the Alley betwix the Linnen
Hall and the Lane running
up N[orth] W[est] from the
Plantation.'

Following spread detail:
James Williamson's 1791
map of Belfast. This portrays
Belfast on the cusp of
the Industrial Revolution.
Among the buildings
shown on the map are
the Downshire Pottery,
Ravenhill Road (marked as
'China Manufactory'), and
the Smylie and Edwards
glasshouses (marked as 'Glass
Houses') in Short Strand.
Both of these sites have been
archaeologically investigated
in the last two decades.

Full map page 62.

Reproduced with the kind
permission of the Linen Hall
Library.

Street in the seventeenth century. During an excavation on Queen Street in
2005, a 19-metre stretch of the town ditch was investigated. It was found to be
7.5 metres wide and 0.9 metres deep.

At Church Street in 2000, excavations found evidence of the disposal
of butchered bones and domestic rubbish along with metalworking in the
seventeenth and eighteenth centuries.[20] The site lay just within the boundaries
of the mid-seventeenth-century ditch and the discoveries made there suggest
that at this time there was no pressure in this part of the town to expand
beyond those limits.

One of the most important buildings in seventeenth-century Belfast was
established at the end of the century. This was the Belfast *Potthouse* (pottery),
which produced highly decorated, high-quality tin-glazed earthenware
(otherwise known as Delft) vessels using Carrickfergus white clay.[21] The pottery
was in operation from c.1697 to c.1725, when it ran into financial difficulty
and closed. The excavation carried out in advance of the construction of the
Potthouse bar uncovered the red-brick terrace where the potters were living
and thousands of fragmentary sherds of material fired in the kilns. However,
the pottery building itself remains elusive, possibly marked on the 1757 map
of Belfast, sitting back from Waring Street, but not yet precisely located. Many
of the excavations that have taken place in Cathedral Quarter in the last two
decades have uncovered deeply stratified dumps of material from the kilns,
but it is only in recent years that complete vessels have come to light. The
Potthouse is so important because it is an early pointer to the industrial and
manufacturing future for which Belfast would become renowned.

The two oldest standing buildings that survive in Belfast city centre were
built in the second half of the eighteenth century. The Assembly Rooms, at the
bottom of Donegall Street, was begun in 1769 as an arcaded market house.[22] A
second floor was erected in 1776 to be used as assembly rooms. The building
was much altered in 1845 and 1895. The other, and more substantially original,
building is nearby and of a similar date. Clifton House, also known as the
Charitable Institution or the Poor House, was built between 1771 and 1774 and
now stands at the corner of Clifton Street and North Queen Street.[23] When first
constructed it stood at the end of a country lane. This is perhaps the reason that
Belfast does not appear to many of its citizens to have any long history. With
Belfast castle having burnt down in 1708, the town defences no longer visible
by 1757, and the castle gardens swallowed up by new building in the 1790s, it
must have been hard to get any sense of the history of the place, especially in
contrast to Carrickfergus, whose medieval castle and seventeenth-century stone
town walls still substantially survive.

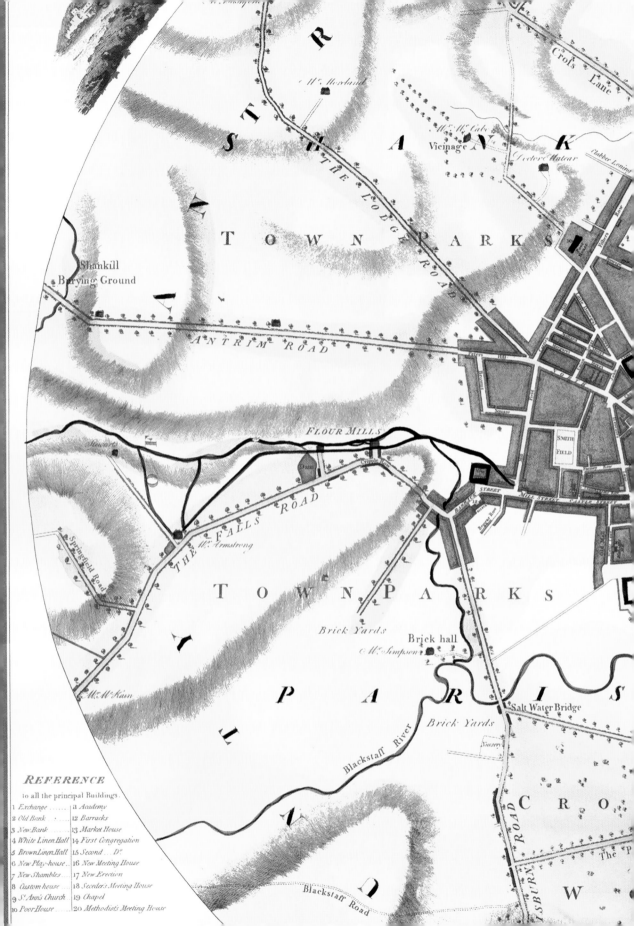

CRO^{fs} Lane

S T R A N K

Mrs Moreland

Mr Mc Cabe
Vicinage

Doctor Halear

Plabber Lonino

T O W N   P A R K S

Shankill
Burying Ground

SMITH
FIELD

ANTRIM ROAD

FLOUR MILLS

STEWART

THE FALLS ROAD

Mr Armstrong

Springfield Road

BARRACK STREET

MILL STREET

T O W N P A R K S

Brick Yards

Brick hall
Mr Simpson

Mr Mc Kain

P A R I S

Salt Water Bridge

Brick Yards

Nursery

Blackstaff River

L I S B U R N   R O A D

C R O

The P

W

Blackstaff Road

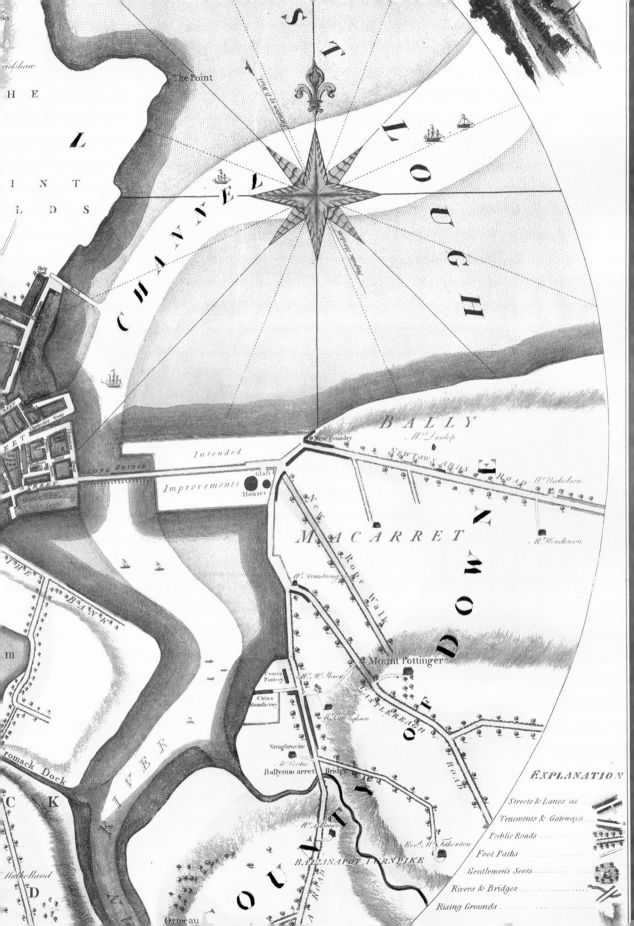

ST LOUGH

CHANNEL

The Point

L
INT
LDS

BALLY

New Foundry
McDunlop
NEWTOWN ARDS ROAD McNicholson

Intended

Improvements

Glass
Houses

MACARRET

McHenderson

Wm Armstrong

New Rope Walk

DOWN OF

LONG BRIDGE

STREET

Mount Pottinger

RIVER

BEANGR

Coates
Pottery

Wm McAlveen

LISNEREAGH Road

China
Manufactory

McCinCilgham

romack Dock

CK

m

Snugborough

McCoots
Ballymacarret Bridge

McBreen

Recd McJetherston

Mulholland

D

BALLINAPOL TURNPIKE

EXPLANATION

Streets & Lanes as
Tenements & Gateways
Public Roads
Foot Paths
Gentlemen's Seats
Rivers & Bridges
Rising Grounds

Ormeau

COUNTY

The Archaeology of Modern Belfast

In the nineteenth century, through its manufacturing and later its industrial, engineering and shipbuilding dynamism, Belfast became extremely affluent. The increased population required to sustain this economic power base meant that the town expanded dramatically, as did the building activity. Slowly the town moved away from its old historic core. The building of the White Linen Hall in the 1780s, where bleached linen could be marketed and sold, and the gradual development of south Belfast heralded this new prosperous age. The 1791 map of Belfast, drawn up by James Williamson, portrays the town just as industrial development was taking off. On it are marked buildings such as foundries, potteries, glasshouses, ropeworks, paper mills, breweries and brickworks. The old city was unrecognizable and this period ushered in what might be regarded as the fourth incarnation of Belfast. One of the buildings recorded on the 1791 map was rediscovered and excavated almost 200 years later. In 1993 Peter Francis carried out investigations at the site of the Downshire Pottery on the Ravenhill Road.[24] This pottery was one of the largest ever built in Ireland and it produced fine-quality, richly coloured Creamware vessels between 1787 and c.1806. Some of the pottery's walls are still standing.

From the end of the seventeenth century, as Belfast continued to expand, there were continued efforts to reclaim land. Archaeological evidence for this expansion has been found at several locations. In 2007 excavations were carried out at Custom House Square. The earliest evidence, dated to between 1685 and 1756, was deep-dumped deposits of sand and clay and a quayside wall of unbonded stones. This was followed by more dumping of material to reclaim land and the construction of the Salthouse Dock (1757–66), also composed of large unworked and unmortared stones. A last phase of construction took place between 1791 and 1846 with the creation of the Lime Kiln Dock and a quayside structure. These were backfilled in 1846 and later Queen's Square and Custom House Square were created. The well-known Belfast landmark the Albert Clock (more properly known as the Albert Memorial Clock Tower) was built nearby between 1865 and 1869. The structure leans slightly as a result of its being built on reclaimed land.

Excavations in 2005 and 2006 investigated some of Belfast's other docks. These included Donegall Quay, which runs from Ann Street to Corporation Street. It was built after the area was filled in when the course of the Lagan was altered in 1850, and was laid out over reclaimed land and the earlier Hanover, Merchant's and Tombs quays. Meanwhile other excavations carried out in advance of the construction of Victoria Square in 2004–05 uncovered a 70-metre-long stretch of May's Dock, built around 1815. The dock was built of large mortar-bonded, well-dressed stones on both the external and internal faces with a compact rubble core in between. Also uncovered was May's Bridge which allowed barges off-loading goods to approach the entrance to Church

A group of Creamware jugs made in the Downshire Pottery that operated on the Ravenhill Road from 1787–c.1806. Peter Francis excavated the remains of this important pottery in 1993 and some of its walls still survive.

Photograph © National Museums Northern Ireland. Collection Ulster Museum. MMCK12.

Lane. An earlier excavation on Oxford Street, in 2002, had already investigated the southern end of May's Dock. The docks were infilled when the River Lagan was deepened and widened to create the Victoria Channel, allowing ships to dock at Belfast quays rather than having to anchor offshore and unload their goods on to barges.

Two large-scale archaeological excavations in the last decade have uncovered evidence of Belfast's manufacturing and industrial history. The first took place in 2002 at the site of the Annadale brickworks that were in operation between 1888 and the 1920s.[25] The foundations of a Hoffman kiln, with a base diameter of 64 metres, were revealed along with ancillary buildings. The kiln was shown to have sequentially arranged chambers that enabled the continual firing of bricks with the surplus heat in the firing chamber used to heat each new chamber in turn. The brickworks was only one of a number in Belfast meeting the constant demand for building materials as Belfast continued to grow in size.

The second major excavation of an industrial site took place in 2005, and again between 2008–09, at the site of the old Sirocco Works at Short Strand, east Belfast.[26] When the factory was demolished archaeologists uncovered the foundations of two large glasshouses (kilns for firing glass bottles and other vessels). Glass bottles were being produced at both the John Smylie and Benjamin Edwards glasshouses on the site between 1776 and about 1830. Two glass kilns of different sizes are shown as being here on the 1791 map of Belfast produced by James Williamson.

Evidence of small-scale industry has also been revealed through archaeological investigations. In 1990 a rescue excavation in Winetavern Street in Smithfield uncovered clay pipe fragments and manufacturing debris from clay pipe kilns after they were discovered during road works.[27] No evidence of the kilns themselves was found but many different late nineteenth-century pipe bowls were recovered. Many of these pipe bowls were decorated in relief with floral designs or with Masonic symbols, suggesting that they may have been made to order for either the Masonic or Royal Black Institutions. Other bowls had stamped names such as 'Cavehill', 'Ulster Pipe Works' and 'Belfast', perhaps directed at the local market. Winetavern Street was once known as 'Pipe Lane' and renowned for its clay pipe makers. It seems likely that the pipes were manufactured by the Hamilton family (whose firm later became the Ulster Pipe Works).

Archaeology has also allowed an examination of the lives of the poorer Belfast people, whose former slum houses are now beneath the fashionable St Anne's Square in Cathedral Quarter.[28] An excavation took place here in 2006 in advance of the redevelopment of that part of Belfast. The investigation uncovered the foundations of red-brick terraces and cobbled streets dating to the nineteenth century. The stereotypically depressing picture of life in such slums, as recorded in an 1853 description of the area, was partially borne out by the large quantities of dumped alcohol bottles discovered during the excavation. However, two lovely artefacts that were also found restore the humanity of the people and provide a counter-balance to the jaundiced Victorian view of the poor. The first was an exquisite glazed clay pipe bowl, in the form of a fish, manufactured in France in the last quarter of the nineteenth century. The second was a dog collar with the words 'I AM JAMES PIPPARD DOG WHOS DOG ARE YOU'. The Belfast street directories record a baker, James Pippard, living on Talbot Street between 1819 and 1835 and the collar must have belonged to his dog. It is not very often that archaeologists can name the owner of a particular artefact that is found during an excavation they work on.

Conclusion

The variety of site types that still exist and the many wonderful artefacts that have been uncovered tell an exciting story about the peoples who have lived at Belfast over the last 9,000–10,000 years. However, the longevity and continuity of settlement in and around the city is one that, until recently, was usually neglected in the written accounts of the story of Belfast. Because the oldest visible buildings still standing in central Belfast are less than 250 years old, it is perhaps understandable that many Belfast citizens believed that their city was only a few hundred years old. With new archaeological publications about Belfast on the increase and the work currently being carried out, especially by Belfast City Council and the Northern Ireland Environment Agency, Built Heritage, to promote the city's heritage, the true story of the long and exciting history of settlement activity at Belfast is getting the publicity it deserves.

Most of the documentary evidence relating to the history of Belfast concerns the actions of the great and the good. From the material culture recovered from archaeological sites investigated in the city we are now able to get glimpses of the lives and lifestyles of the ordinary people not made visible in written accounts. Archaeological discoveries bring to life the predecessors of Belfast's current citizens in a very tangible way and help us appreciate our shared past.

There is still much to find out about the story of Belfast, especially concerning the Anglo-Norman and Clandeboye O'Neill settlements. We have yet to uncover the remains of any of the principal buildings from these periods, or those of Chichester's seventeenth-century town. However, given that excavations during the past thirty years have shown that there are still deep archaeological deposits surviving across the city centre, we can be fairly confident that there will be new and exciting discoveries in years to come.

The information recovered from archaeological excavations is a vital part of the resources that can be used to study the evolution and development of settlement at Belfast. Unless we uncover new cartographic or documentary sources, it is clear that most of the new information about the story of Belfast, certainly up to the seventeenth century, will come from archaeological discoveries and the analysis of material from previous excavations and find spots. For the later periods in Belfast's history, information uncovered from archaeological excavations can be used to complement and shed further light on such aspects as material culture, trade, the expansion of Belfast, its industrial history and the development of its harbour.

The Practice of Archaeology in Northern Ireland

Archaeological excavation in Northern Ireland is an integral part of the planning process. Both the archaeological profession and the practice of archaeology are regulated by the Northern Ireland Environment Service: Built Heritage. In legislative terms, the Historic Monuments and Archaeological Objects (NI) Order 1995 is one of the primary Acts used to protect the heritage of Northern Ireland, along with Article 42 of the Planning (NI) Order 1991, for historic buildings, and the Protection of Wrecks Act (1973) for maritime sites.

Prior to the mid-1990s, most archaeological excavations in Northern Ireland were carried out by one of the three main heritage institutions – the Northern Ireland Environment Agency, Queen's University and the Ulster Museum (now known as National Museums Northern Ireland). Since the mid-1990s, with the sharp rise in building development across Ireland, and the corresponding rise in the need for archaeological mitigation of many of these sites, most of the excavations in Northern Ireland are carried out by one of the several commercial, private-sector archaeological companies, overseen by the Northern Ireland Environment Agency: Built Heritage. The Centre for Archaeological Fieldwork, School of Geography, Archaeology and Palaeoecology in Queen's University undertakes the fieldwork requirements of the Northern Ireland Environment Agency: Built Heritage.

Further information

The Northern Ireland Environment Agency: Built Heritage (NIEA)

The Northern Ireland Environment Agency: Built Heritage is based at Waterman House, 5–33 Hill Street, Belfast, BT1 2LA; www.ni-environment. gov.uk/built-home.htm

The Northern Ireland Sites and Monuments Record (NISMR) holds information on over 15,000 archaeological and historic features. Information on each site can be accessed online through the Northern Ireland Sites and Monuments Record Database. The Northern Ireland Environment Agency: Built Heritage also holds the records of excavations carried out in Northern Ireland (called 'B' files), many of which contain as yet unpublished excavation reports. Other archives maintained by the Northern Ireland Environment Agency: Built Heritage are the Industrial Heritage Record which lists more than 16,000 features in Northern Ireland, the Defence Heritage Project, the Historic Buildings Database and the Northern Ireland Heritage Gardens Archive.

Belfast City Council

The Culture, Arts and Tourism unit of Belfast City Council promotes various aspects of Belfast heritage; www.belfastcity.gov.uk/culture/heritage.asp. The council seeks to contribute to the regeneration of the city through the positive use of tangible and intangible heritage, improving the quality of life and experience of all the people who live in, work in and visit Belfast.

National Museums Northern Ireland

The Ulster Museum is situated in Belfast's Botanic Gardens, right in the heart of the University Area of south Belfast (BT9 5AB): www.nmni.com/um

The museum contains many artefacts that were discovered at Belfast. Some of these are on display, including the Malone Hoard of Neolithic polished stone axes.

The Public Record Office of Northern Ireland

The Public Record Office of Northern Ireland (PRONI) is the official archive for Northern Ireland. It is based in Titanic Boulevard, Titanic Quarter, Belfast. It now operates as part of the Department of Culture, Arts and Leisure: www.proni.gov.uk

PRONI aims to identify and preserve records of historical, social and cultural importance and make them available for the information, education and enjoyment of the public. PRONI is the legal place of deposit for public records in Northern Ireland. In addition, it collects a wide range of archives from private sources. PRONI also advises on and promotes best practice in archive and records management to ensure that today's records will be available for future generations.

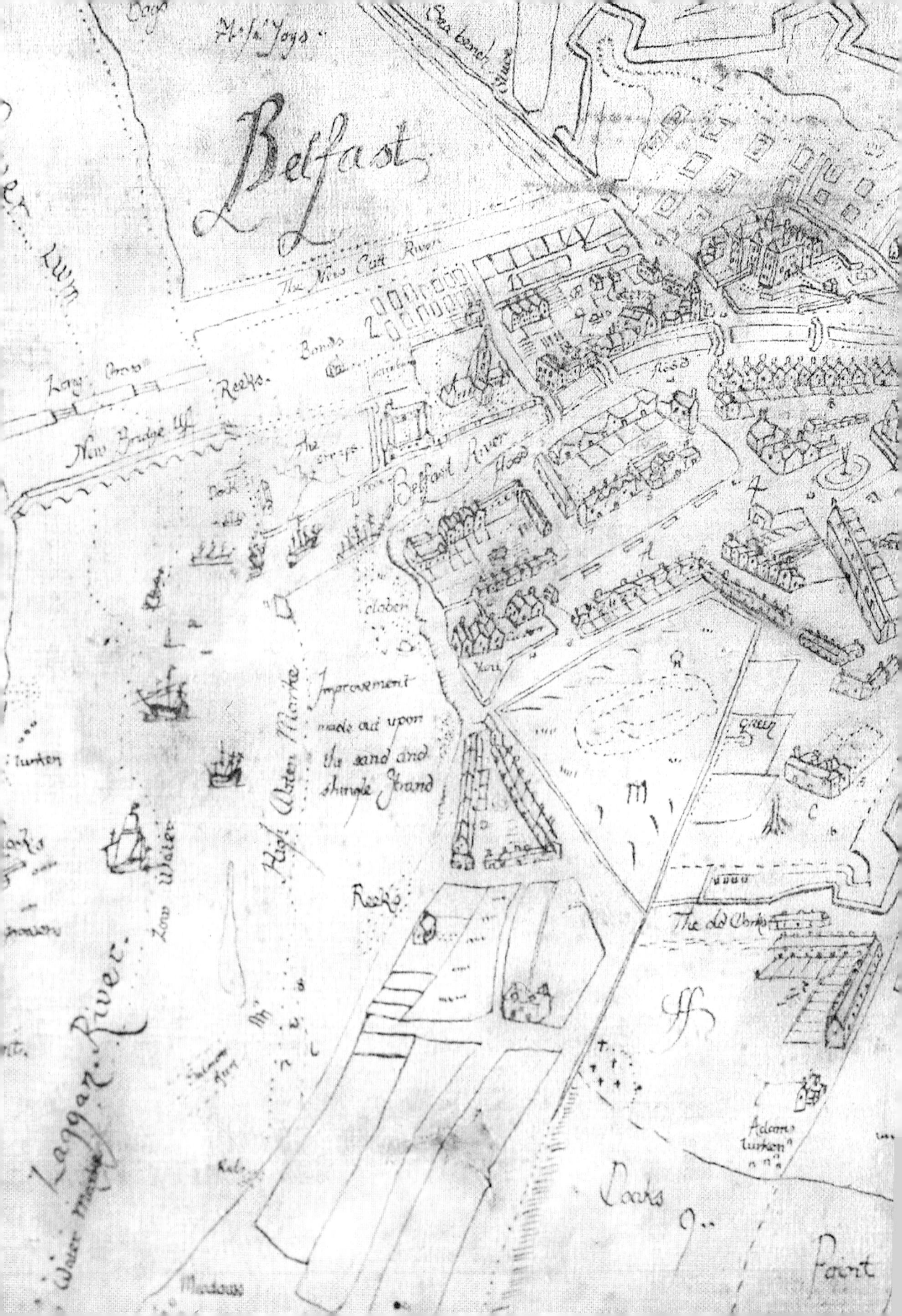

Belfast

The New Cutt River

Oogs

W.fa Yoys

Lang Corow

New Bridge W

Reeks

Bonds Cut

The Strips

Belfast River

Flood

Flood

Green

Dock

clober

High Water Marke

Improvement
made out upon
the sand and
shingle Strand

Reeks

Turken

Low Water

Lagger River

Water marke

Madows

The old Chrch

Adams
Turken

Poors

Point

3 The Medieval Settlement

Philip Macdonald

'Belfast, as a town, has no ancient history'

When George Benn chose this statement to begin his monumental *History of the Town of Belfast* (1877) he was reiterating an already long-established opinion.[1] This view was informed, at least in part, both by the paucity of available historical records of medieval date relating to Belfast and by the almost total absence within the town of any surviving buildings or monuments that pre-dated the seventeenth century. The nineteenth-century idea that Belfast had no medieval history of note has cast a long shadow over historical studies of the town. In terms of justifying an inadequate archaeological response to development within the city during the 1960s and 1980s it has almost threatened to become a self-fulfilling prophecy.[2] In addition to the lack of available evidence, the idea that the history of urban Belfast meaningfully begins only following the granting of the castle to Sir Arthur Chichester in 1603 is a consequence of the apparent break in permanent settlement during the later medieval period. Whether this break in settlement can be extended for any duration, beyond the disturbance caused by the wars and unrest of the later sixteenth century, is, however, a moot point. As described below, the use of certain units of land in seventeenth-century inquisitions suggests, at the very least, some continuity in boundaries and land divisions between the Anglo-Norman period and the early years of Chichester's town.[3] In addition to the paucity of evidence and the hiatus in late medieval settlement activity, the suggestion that Belfast had no early history has always had a political resonance. The lack of significance attributed to Belfast's medieval history by both nineteenth-century and later historians is arguably the product of the Elizabethan colonial myth, which portrayed Ulster as a depopulated wilderness ripe for plantation, fused with Victorian concepts of progress and modernity which sometimes saw even those individuals concerned to record the town's history advocating the removal of old buildings and even streets within the town.[4] This myopia towards Belfast's past has also been attributed to the influx of Scots settlers who migrated to the town during the seventeenth century and created a community that emphasized commerce, industry and the Presbyterian faith.[5]

In recent years, archaeology has begun to shed some light upon the early history of Belfast and historians have specifically begun to address the question of the town's 'lost' medieval history.[6] As a consequence, the early history of Belfast can be divided into four successive periods, which are as much delineated by variations in the quantity and quality of the available evidence as they are defined by historical events and changes in the character of the settlement. Belfast is first noted as a place during the Early Christian period. However, the earliest recorded evidence for a settlement dates to the thirteenth century when a castle and associated manor formed part of the Anglo-Norman earldom of Ulster. The later medieval history of Belfast is divisible into two parts: a period of Gaelic occupation reflected in a small number of annalistic references, and then, in the middle decades of the sixteenth century, a phase marked by an increased interest in Ulster on the part of the Tudor authorities, and by a concomitant rise in the number of available sources. In this chapter an attempt has been made to supplement the limited number of available historical references with archaeological, cartographic and place-name evidence. There are difficulties in both interpreting and integrating these diverse strands of evidence, however, and much of the story of medieval Belfast still remains, if not 'lost', then certainly obscure.

The Ford – The Early Christian Period

Bellum Fertsi eter Ultu agus Cruitne ubi cecidit Cathusach m. Lurggeni /
The battle of Fersat between the Ulaid and the Cruithin, in which Cathusach son
of Luirgéne fell[7]

This laconic notice dating to AD 668 was probably first recorded in the margins
of a, now lost, liturgical calendar in an Irish monastery shortly after the battle
itself. It survives to the present day only because it was incorporated into the
text now known as the *Annals of Ulster* – a chronicle of notable events, such
as battles, famines, plagues and the deaths of famous ecclesiastics and kings,
originally compiled in Fermanagh during the fifteenth century.[8] It represents
the earliest historical reference to the place that would subsequently become
Belfast.[9] The notice records a battle between the Dál Fiatach, expanding
northwards from their principal royal centre in Downpatrick, and the
incumbent Dál nAraide, whose king, Cathusach, was slain during the fighting.
In Ireland, the seventh century was a period of apparent cultural uniformity but
political fragmentation. At this time, Ulster was divided into a number of petty
kingdoms, each ruled by a military leader who was drawn from a ruling dynasty
and regarded as a sovereign king. Although kingdoms would have contained
a number of royal centres, these would have been essentially non-urban in

The ancient ford across
the Lagan as imagined by J.W.
Carey in one of his paintings
commissioned in 1903 for the
Ulster Hall. The figures are
modelled upon a well-known
drawing of Irish mercenaries
by the Nuremberg-based artist
Albrecht Dürer dating from
1521, providing an indication
of the period Carey intended
to depict.

Reproduced with the kind
permission of Belfast City Council.

character and the wealth that supported their elites would have been derived from a largely pastoral economy. The Dál Fiatach and the Dál nAraide were the two principal kingdoms within the over-kingdom of Ulaid, which extended across much of the modern counties of Down and Antrim.

The annalistic reference refers to the Dál Fiatach by the term Ulaid (meaning 'Ulstermen') and the Dál nAraide by the ethnic title Cruithin. Although the Cruithin periodically held the over-kingship of Ulaid and styled themselves the *fir-Ulaid* (meaning 'true Ulstermen'), the conservative compilers of the *Annals of Ulster* deliberately make an 'ethnic' distinction between the kingdoms because, in a strictly tribal sense, the name Ulaid referred specifically to the people who lived between Dundrum Bay and Belfast Lough and whose ruling dynasty was the Dál Fiatach. The name Cruithin is the Irish form for *Priteni* (meaning 'the Picts'). In Irish the Cruithin and the Picts of northern Britain were referred to by the same name; however, contemporary authors writing in Latin reserved the term *Picti* only for the latter group. This suggests that it is incorrect to view the Ulster Cruithin as meaningfully related to the Picts or distinct from other Irish peoples. In terms of language and other cultural practices they are typically Irish. For example, they followed the Irish system of regnal succession, rather than the system of matrilineal descent favoured by the Picts. Furthermore, their settlements, economic practices and material culture are archaeologically indistinguishable from those of other Irish kingdoms.[10]

The AD 668 annalistic reference indicates that the modern city's location, upon the lowest fording point of the River Lagan, was already considered significant enough by the seventh century AD to warrant a name – *Fearsat*, meaning sandbank or ford. This place-name survives to the present day. Although the earliest recorded form of the city's modern name, *Bel-feirste* (meaning 'approach or mouth of the sandbank or ford' and Anglicized from the sixteenth century as Belfast),[11] dates to 1476,[12] the earlier Anglo-Norman manor at Belfast was known as *Le Ford*, being named either independently after the site's defining feature or as a direct translation of the pre-existing Gaelic *Fearsat*. The long-term continuity in the place-name evidence reflects the strategic significance of Belfast's position upon the lowest crossing point of the Lagan, where the river is fordable at low tide. Just as today the river defines the boundary between counties Antrim and Down, this location has long been a fulcrum between neighbouring polities.[13] As the reference to the battle in 668 indicates, during the Early Christian period the ford was located upon the border between the kingdoms of the Dál Fiatach and Dál nAraide. Subsequently, it formed a crucial point on the route between Carrickfergus and the southern parts of the Anglo-Norman earldom of Ulster and, following the decline of the earldom in the fourteenth century, it came to be situated upon the border between the late medieval Gaelic lordship of Clandeboye and the Upper or 'Great' Ardes.

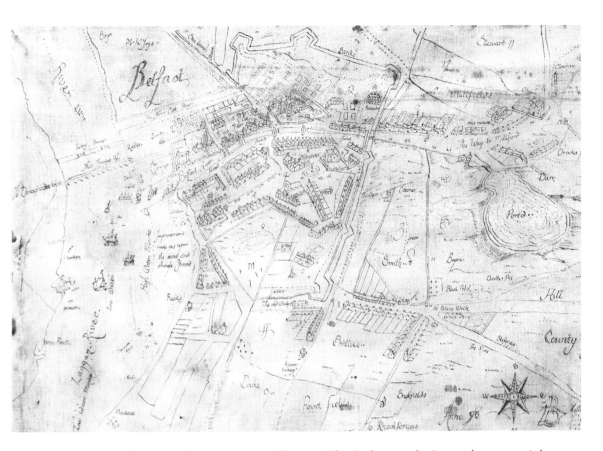

An eighteenth-century copy of a survey of Belfast dating to 1696, showing the position of the 'long cross' upstream from the Long Bridge.

Courtesy of the National Library of Ireland.

The strategic significance of the ford across the Lagan almost certainly pre-dates the development of any settlement at the site, possibly by a period of several centuries. Throughout the medieval period the ford, rather than any economic factor, formed the principal reason for the settlement's existence. Ironically, given its importance to the early history of Belfast, the precise position of the ford, formed by a sandbar deposited close to where the rivers Farset and Blackstaff (or, in Irish, Owenvarragh) entered the Lagan, is not known. The creation of a sandbar across the Lagan estuary was the result of a complex set of erosional and depositional interactions between the estuary's tidal regime and the silts transported into the estuary by the three rivers. During the medieval period the lower reaches of the Lagan would have formed a wide estuary whose western bank extended to the present-day junction of Ann Street and Victoria Street, while the Farset ran down the line of what is now High Street. The mouth of the Blackstaff probably formed a tidal inlet whose northern bank extended as far as the junction of Corn Market and Ann Street before turning eastwards to join the Lagan a short distance to the south of the Queen's Bridge.[14] Unfortunately, the early references to the ford fail to describe with any precision its location, while subsequent land reclamation, dredging of the Lagan, and the culverting and canalization of both the Farset and Blackstaff have made it difficult to assess exactly where a natural sandbar would have formed.

Although in essence it was a natural feature formed as a result of depositional processes, it is unlikely that the ford's position changed significantly during the medieval period. That the ford was used as a boundary in the grant of market rights made to Sir James Hamilton in 1605, and named as a place in a clause of his will in 1616, indicates that, in the early seventeenth century at least, it was considered a well-known, unambiguous and fixed feature in the landscape.[15] Cartographic analysis suggests that the ford was probably located between the outlets of the rivers Farset and Blackstaff, close to where the Queen's Bridge now crosses the Lagan. The Queen's Bridge was built in 1840 on more-or-less the line of the late seventeenth-century Long Bridge, which it replaced. During its construction an artificial, linear structure of stones was observed in the bed of the Lagan[16] and these stones probably represent an attempt to augment the ford formed by the sandbar. The recently discovered eighteenth-century copy of a 1696 survey of Belfast shows a causeway, labelled the 'long cross', immediately upstream from the Long Bridge, indicating that this location – which coincides with the stone structure observed in 1840 – was almost certainly the position of the ford during the medieval period.[17] This view is supported by a plan of Belfast harbour dating to 1785[18] which depicts the channel of the Lagan at low tide as being markedly wider in the vicinity of the Long Bridge than elsewhere in the lower reaches of

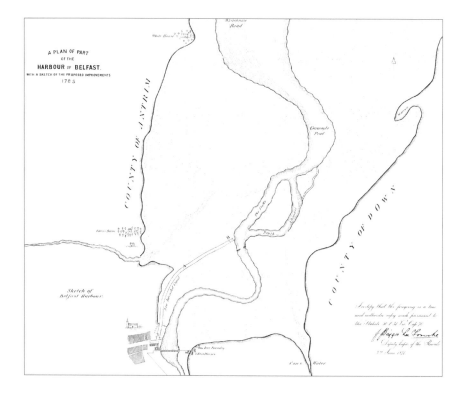

Detail taken from 'A Plan of part of the Harbour of Belfast', dated 1785 and reproduced in Benn's *History* of 1877. The image shows the channel of the Lagan as increasing markedly in width in the area around the Long Bridge. This implies a shallower depth, suggesting that the medieval ford was probably located at this point on the river.

Image kindly supplied by Blackstaff Press.

the river. Rivers that flow through sand tend to be wider and shallower than those that cut through silt and clay; this is because the comparatively coarser sand particles have less cohesion, resulting in greater instability and erosion of the channel's banks.[19] This suggests that in the immediate environs of the Long Bridge the Lagan's bed passed through a localized deposit of sand. Assuming that the area of a channel's cross-section remains fairly uniform across short lengths of a river, even if the deposits through which it flows vary, where the channel is wider it follows that it will also be shallower. Consequently, the considerably increased width of the channel at low tide represented on the 1785 plan in the area of the Long Bridge suggests that the medieval ford was located in this section of the river.[20]

The Anglo-Norman Castle and Settlement

Although place-name evidence indicates that following their victory in 668 the Dál Fiatach settled in various parts of the wider Belfast area,[21] the earliest reference to a settlement or castle located near to the ford dates to 1262 during the period of Anglo-Norman settlement in Ulster. In 1177 the Norman knight John de Courcy took advantage of dynastic rivalries within the Dál Fiatach to invade the kingdom. Following a decisive victory at Downpatrick, de Courcy spent the next five years or so establishing for himself an independent lordship in eastern Ulster.[22] De Courcy and the Anglo-Norman earls of Ulster who followed him tried, with limited success, to establish a European-type manorial system in their newly conquered lands. This marked a shift in the character of the local economy, reflecting an aspiration on the part of the earls to generate an income by exporting corn.[23] Although the relative importance of arable production to the local economy may already have increased in the centuries immediately preceding de Courcy's invasion, the establishment of manorial centres undoubtedly enabled the development of a denser settlement pattern than had existed in the preceding Early Christian period. Whether the creation of the earldom of Ulster resulted in a significant influx of new settlers into the region remains uncertain. It is likely, however, that most of the incumbent Irish population remained on the land, either as free tenants or as workers on the holdings of the settlers.[24]

The 1262 reference to a castle near the ford was contained in one of the pipe rolls held in the Public Record Office in Dublin until it was destroyed in the Four Courts fire of 1922.[25] The pipe rolls were long scrolls of parchment that contained the nominally annual compilations of audited accounts prepared by officials who received or spent money on behalf of the Crown. They were so named because they were stored as tight rolls resembling pipes and they represent an invaluable source for studying the activities of the Crown's authorities in Ireland.[26] A transcription of the relevant part of the document, which relates to the income and expenditure of Richard de Exeter, at that time an escheator in Ireland, was made during the nineteenth century.[27] In a section relating to various castles held by the Crown in Ulster, it is recorded that ten pounds was granted by Edward, who had been created Lord of Ireland by his father Henry III in 1254, to Richard de Exeter for the custody of the Castle of the Ford (*Casti de Vado*). This reference indicates that the castle existed by 1262 and that, at this date at least, it was a royal possession. Unless the castle had been built in the previous twenty years (and there are no extant sources that record what would have been a significant episode of expenditure by the Crown), it is reasonable to assume that the castle had previously been held by Hugh de Lacy. De Lacy had been the earl of Ulster and, following his death in 1242, the earldom and his possessions had reverted to the Crown. Significantly, the 1262 date indicates that the castle was not built after the acquisition of the earldom of Ulster by the powerful de Burgh family in 1264.

No physical trace of the Anglo-Norman castle survives and it is uncertain what form the fortification took. Most Anglo-Norman castles in Ulster were mottes – that is, substantial, usually circular, earthwork mounds that were surrounded by a ditch and whose flat summits would have accommodated various timber structures protected by a circumscribing wooden palisade. It is unlikely, however, that the Castle of the Ford would have been a motte. The underlying subsoil in Belfast is an estuarine clay known as 'sleech', a material both technically difficult to build into mounds and prone to subsidence.[28] Furthermore, because of their massive size, as a monument type mottes have a high survival rate. Consequently, it is surprising, had a motte been built in Belfast, that no trace or record of it remains.[29] Although the earls of Ulster apparently prohibited their barons from building masonry castles,[30] if the castle was indeed a possession of Hugh de Lacy prior to his death in 1242 then it is possible that it may have incorporated a stone-built structure. Even a small masonry castle, however, would have formed an important site in the earldom and the almost complete absence of historical references to *Le Ford* suggests that its castle was probably some form of earthwork and timber construction. It is possible that the Anglo-Norman castle was either a ringwork, that is, a circular or oval enclosure defined by a bank and ditch, or a more linear earthwork that cut off the low promontory formed between the Farset and Blackstaff rivers. Although requiring more men to defend than a motte, earthwork enclosures of this type would have been better suited to providing protected shelter for a large number of troops and horses while they waited for low tide in order to cross the ford.[31] Another possibility is that the fortified element of the Anglo-Norman settlement may have been a 'moated site' – that is, a rectangular enclosure comprising a central platform bounded by a bank and possibly water-filled ditch. The site's location adjacent to the Farset and Blackstaff, which could have been diverted as feeders for a moat, and in an area

The rectangular earthwork at Ekenhead photographed in 1928, prior to the construction of the Ekenhead Presbyterian church. The earthwork enclosure is probably an Anglo-Norman moated site.

© Crown copyright. Reproduced with the permission of the Controller of Her Majesty's Stationery Office.

where the water table lies close to the surface, would have been ideal for the creation of a wet ditch.[32] It is unlikely that most moated sites, conventionally considered to have functioned as protected farmsteads, would have been classified as castles during the Anglo-Norman period. However, it has been plausibly suggested that a small number did serve a military or strategic role.[33] Although moated sites are uncommon in Ulster, they are not unknown. The rectangular earthen enclosure at Ekenhead on the outskirts of north Belfast, which is associated with an early fourteenth-century coin hoard, is probably an example of the type.[34]

The precise position of the Anglo-Norman castle is also unknown. It has often been assumed to have been located in the immediate vicinity of Chichester's early seventeenth-century fortified mansion, which was recorded by the Plantation Commissioners in 1611 as being built over the remains of an earlier castle[35] – undoubtedly the Gaelic tower-house of the late medieval period (see below). That the tower-house had itself been built upon the site of the earlier Anglo-Norman castle, however, remains an unproven, though reasonable, suggestion.

Although the reference in the 1262 pipe roll does not mention a settlement or manorial estate associated with the *Casti de Vado*, it is unlikely that it would have existed in isolation in the landscape. That the castle formed a manorial centre that was transferred to the de Burgh family when they acquired the earldom of Ulster is confirmed by a record of a conveyancing document, known as a fine, recording the legal transfer of property from Richard de Burgh, the second earl of Ulster, to his son Edmund in 1293.[36] Notice of this late thirteenth-century document, which records the transfer of the *Manor de Vado* with its appurtenances, survives only in summary form in a calendar written in French and dating to the late fourteenth or early fifteenth century.[37] This calendar, reportedly contained within worm-eaten boards when it was donated to the British Museum in 1809, forms a catalogue of legal documents relating to the landed possessions of Edmund de Mortimer, the third earl of March, who had inherited the earldom of Ulster in the late fourteenth century.

The only other known reference to the Anglo-Norman settlement at Belfast records its decline. In 1333 William de Burgh, the fourth earl of Ulster, was murdered by his barons as a result of a local political dispute and divisions within the de Burgh lineage. The manor at Belfast (*Le Ford*) is detailed in the subsequent Inquisition Post Mortem[38] as formerly including a watermill and consisting of a 'ruined castle' and a 'borough town [now] totally burned and destroyed'.[39] The document notes that the destruction of the settlement was a consequence of 'de Logan's war'.[40] John de Logan was one of the earl's murderers[41] and the phrase 'de Logan's war' relates either to the dispute between de Burgh and his barons that led to the earl's murder, or, more probably, to the conflict that followed the murder between the rebel barons and John Darcy, the justiciar, in alliance with John de Mandeville and other loyal settlers.

The 1333 inquisition provides an insight into the character of the Anglo-Norman manor of *Le Ford*. Although as a result of the recent conflict the manor is recorded as being worthless, its former annual income, presumably assessed in 1326 following the death of William's father, Richard de Burgh, is quoted as being £28 15s 4d. This sum is comparable with the figures quoted in the document for other manorial estates in Ulster such as Greencastle and Dundrum, although significantly less than the income generated by the estates of Carrickfergus and Northborough.[42] It is likely that the manor would have had a larger income prior to the devastation caused to the earldom of Ulster following the Bruce invasion of 1315. The inquisition records that the demesne at the ford consisted of seven carucates. A single carucate is defined as the area a plough team of eight oxen could cultivate in a year (nominally equivalent to 120 acres). In practice, the size of a carucate could vary considerably and areas of other less productive land types, such as bog or wood, could also be appended to the cultivated land represented by a carucate.[43] Consequently, the figure of seven carucates indicates that the manorial estate of *Le Ford* was only approximately 840 acres (340 hectares) in size – it may have been significantly larger. Outlying possessions of the manor are recorded as including four carucates (approximately 480 acres / 195 hectares) at Castelconnaugh; two carucates (approximately 240 acres / 97 hectares) in Ymenaught (probably located in the area below Cave Hill and possibly administered from the probable moated site at Ekenhead noted above); six carucates (approximately

720 acres / 290 hectares) in an undisclosed location which Robert de Mandeville had held freely in fee of £4; and eight carucates (approximately 960 acres / 390 hectares) in Legolghtorp (probably part of the Lagan valley between Moria and Belfast), which David O'Coltaran, an Irishman, held in fee of £1 6s 8d and 24 days' work of reapers during August.[44]

Prior to its destruction the borough town of *Le Ford* is recorded as having an annual value of £1 in the 1333 inquisition.[45] This figure is small in comparison to the value attributed to other boroughs in the earldom and appears to be a nominal or conventional sum.[46] It is difficult to assess the size and status of the borough given the absence of any documentary evidence for either a market or the number of burgesses. However, the comparative wealth of the agricultural lands attached to the manor of *Le Ford* suggests that the settlement mostly contributed to the agricultural, and not mercantile, sector of the Anglo-Norman economy.[47] It is doubtful whether the Anglo-Norman borough ever formed a truly urban settlement that generated a significant income for the earls in terms of either the rents of properties with burgage tenure or fees derived from markets or fairs. Instead, the 'town' is more likely to have been a small nucleated settlement analogous to a village that consisted of several timber and clay buildings located close to the castle, chapel and mill. Such settlements have been classified as 'rural-boroughs', which were cynically established in order to tempt naive English settlers to Ireland with the promise of burgage tenure and its associated freedoms and opportunities.[48] That the manor was reliant upon Irish labour for hay-making suggests that the borough had failed to attract sufficient settlers to develop economically or become self-sustainable during intensive periods of the agricultural cycle.

In addition to the castle and the borough 'town', the other secular element of the manor would have been the watermill, which was recorded in the 1333 inquisition as having an annual profit, prior to its destruction, of 6s 8d.[49] Again, the precise location of the mill is not known, although it would have been built close to a watercourse, such as the Farset or Blackstaff, and would have been associated with a weir or dam, various feeder channels and a millpond. There is often long-term continuity in the siting of mills.[50] Hence it is possible that the millponds represented on Phillips's 1685 plans of the town,[51] which were located in the area between the Belfast Metropolitan College and Percy Street, may date back to the Anglo-Norman period.

The date at which the castle and manor of *Le Ford* were established is difficult to assess, although it is likely that securing the ford across the Lagan would have been an early strategic priority during the creation of the earldom of Ulster. The castle, it has already been suggested, was held by Hugh de Lacy prior to his death in 1242. However, the manorial estate of *Le Ford* and its castle are not recorded in either the itinerary or other papers relating to King John's incursion into Ulster to expel de Lacy in the summer of 1210.[52] It is not

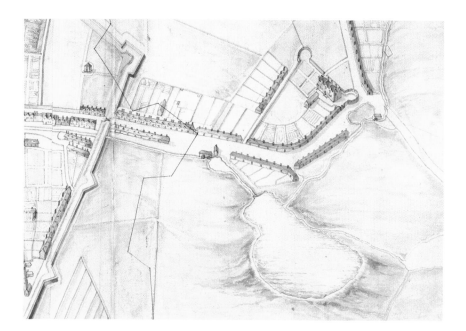

Detail of Thomas Phillips's 1685 map of Belfast (p. 78), showing a series of ponds created by damming the River Farset and used to power mills. The location, in the area between the sites of the modern College Square and Percy Street, was possibly the same as that used for the mill recorded in 1333.

© The British Library Board (Maps.K.Top.51,37).

unreasonable to assume that if the manor had been established prior to the early thirteenth century then it would have become a possession of King John's and therefore likely to have been mentioned in the Irish pipe rolls of 1211–12.[53] Although arguing on the basis of negative evidence is always problematic, these considerations suggest that the Anglo-Norman castle and its associated manor were established at some point during the second to fourth decades of the thirteenth century.

The devastation caused by both Robert the Bruce's Irish wars (1315–18) and the death of William de Burgh in 1333 marked the beginning of the decline of English power in this part of Ulster. The authority of the Anglo-Norman earls had always been dependent upon their warlike energy and diplomatic skills, qualities that William de Burgh's infant heir could not be expected to provide. The Crown authorities in Dublin proved incapable of filling the power vacuum, and there was no single pre-eminent Anglo-Norman family capable of taking control in Ulster.[54] Consequently, the earldom lost its fragile coherence and slowly declined as a political entity, although some isolated outposts of English settlement survived throughout the medieval period, most notably at Carrickfergus and in the Lower Ards and Lecale, where increasingly Gaelicized 'Old English' families such as the Savages maintained their pre-eminence. In the case of Belfast the Crown retained a nominal legal claim by descent from de Burgh's infant daughter, through the powerful Mortimer family, to Edward IV.[55] In reality, however, the ruined castle and its associated manor passed into the hands of the O'Neills of Clandeboye. Precisely when Anglo-Norman control of the Belfast area was lost is uncertain. It would be a mistake, however, to assume that the earldom rapidly declined to its fifteenth-century boundaries. As late as 1374 an Anglo-Irish lord controlled Camlin, a parish to the west of Belfast,[56] which suggests that a family of Anglo-Norman descent could have possessed the manor of *Le Ford* for at least one or two generations after the death of the last resident earl in 1333.

Later Medieval Belfast: the Gaelic Settlement

We know relatively little about the rise of the lordship of Clandeboye[57] and the long phase of Gaelic occupation of Belfast following the decline of the Anglo-Norman earldom of Ulster in the fourteenth century. This period is historically represented by only a handful of relatively late annalistic entries which indicate that the castle at Belfast was intermittently slighted and rebuilt over a single, thirty-six-year period during the late fifteenth and early sixteenth centuries. The first of these notices, dating to 1476, records that forces led by Hugh

A reconstruction of a typical tower-house of the fifteenth and sixteenth centuries (based upon Kilclief Castle, Co. Down). The vaulted ceiling of the structure's ground floor represents a common architectural feature of tower-houses, and helps to explain the reference in the report of the Plantation Commissioners in 1611 to the 'ruynes of the decayed Castle' being taken down almost to 'the valte of the Sellers' (p.104).

© Crown copyright. Reproduced with the permission of the Controller of Her Majesty's Stationery Office.

O'Neill successfully attacked and then demolished the castle of Bel-feirste.[58] Subsequent annalistic references record the taking of the castle of 'Bel-Fersdi' by Felim O'Neill and Robert Savage in 1486;[59] the taking and demolition of the castle in 1489 by Hugh Roe O'Donnell;[60] a hosting into eastern Ulster by the lord deputy, Gerald (Garret Mór) Fitzgerald, the eighth earl of Kildare, in 1503 during which the castle of Belfast was demolished;[61] and the taking of 'Beoil Fersde' in 1512 by an army led, once again, by the eighth earl of Kildare.[62] A sixth annalistic reference records another military incursion into Clandeboye in 1537 in which the son of Con O'Neill was taken prisoner at 'Bel Fersde'.[63] These annalistic sources are supplemented by a letter written by Gerald (Garret Óg) Fitzgerald, the ninth earl of Kildare, to Henry VIII in 1523 describing how, in retaliation for Hugh O'Neill rescuing the crew of a Scottish boat which he had been pursuing, 'I brake a castell of his, called Belfast, and burned 24 myle of his contre.'[64]

The castle of Bel-feirste slighted in 1476 would have been a markedly different structure to the Anglo-Norman castle that was described as a ruin in 1333. By the final quarter of the fifteenth century the castle would undoubtedly have been a tower-house, a defensible, stone-built structure of three or four storeys with a vaulted ground floor. Tower-houses began to be constructed in Ireland from the late fourteenth or early fifteenth century onwards, although at what date the example slighted in Belfast in 1476 was built is uncertain. The location of the tower-house can be identified with a reasonable degree of confidence. The 1611 report of the Plantation Commissioners records that the old castle had been taken down 'almost to the valte of the Sellers', that is the vaulted roof of the tower-house's first storey, and that the foundations of a 'bricke house 50 foote longe […] is to be adjoined to the sayd Castle by a Stayrcase of bricke'.[65] This 'bricke house' was the early seventeenth-century fortified mansion built by Sir Arthur Chichester in the area now occupied by British Home Stores on the junction of Castle Lane and Castle Arcade, and possibly represented on the extant maps of Belfast dating to the last quarter of the century.[66]

While there is no reason to question the veracity of the individual events that are recorded in the annals, they do present a partial, and therefore potentially misleading, view of the character of Belfast during the later medieval period. That all of the surviving references relate to military actions could give the impression that the site was not a place conducive to permanent settlement. Without denying that medieval Gaelic Ulster could, at least on occasion, be a violent place, it is the nature of annalistic entries to focus on recording sensational 'headline' events which, if accepted uncritically, could give the false impression of a highly dysfunctional and turbulent society. What is arguably of equal significance to the relatively short period during the late fifteenth and early sixteenth centuries in which the castle at Belfast is

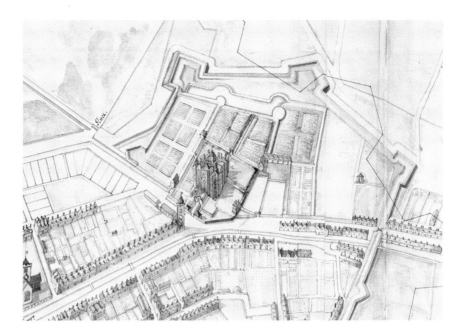

Detail of Thomas Phillips's map (p. 78), showing the Chichester family's mansion as it appeared in 1685. The relationship of this building to the house and adjoining castle described by the Plantation Commissioners in 1611 remains unclear. It may represent a wholly new building, as suggested by Raymond Gillespie (see p.126), or alternatively an extensive modification of the original fortified structure.

© The British Library Board (Maps.K.Top.51,37).

recorded as being repeatedly attacked and slighted is the total absence of any references to Belfast between the death of William de Burgh in 1333 and the slighting of the castle in 1476. Although this historical lacuna might represent a period when settlement at the site was largely abandoned, it could equally represent a period of relatively peaceful and near-continuous occupation. Certainly, it is unlikely that the late medieval castle would have existed in total isolation and, although they are not explicitly mentioned in the annalistic references, it is probable that it was associated with a small settlement, as well as the nearby chapel. Documents prepared during negotiations between the Crown authorities and Brian Mac Phelim O'Neill in 1568 concerning both the 'castle and manor of Belfast'[67] hint at the possibility that at least part of the Anglo-Norman manorial estate of *Le Ford* had survived intact throughout the Gaelic period. That the annals record that the castle was repeatedly slighted implies that it was also repeatedly repaired and re-occupied – a testament to the tenacity of occupation at the site. The status of any settlement associated with the castle and manor was not, however, apparently significant. The relative unimportance of Belfast at this date is reflected in two omissions. It was not noted as a reserved place in two, essentially nominal, grants of Clandeboye made in 1542 and 1543,[68] nor was it described in any detail in an extensive account of the progress through Ulster of the lord deputy, the earl of Sussex, in 1556.[69]

From the middle of the sixteenth century the castle at Belfast became of increasing interest to the English administration as Ulster became a focus for successive attempts at pacification, conquest and settlement by the Tudor authorities. Historically, the second half of the sixteenth century can be a difficult period to understand because the Tudor authorities had no settled, long-term policy, but alternated in an inconsistent manner between initiatives to anglicize the Gaelic lords and attempts to implement the first schemes of plantation. These changes in policy were as much informed by the cost implications for the Crown as they were by their likely outcomes. At this time, plantation itself was a broad concept, which ranged in scale from the establishment of military outposts, such as that at Newry under Nicholas Bagenal in the middle of the sixteenth century, to more radical attempts to replace one population with another, such as the colonial ventures attempted by Thomas Smith and Walter Devereux in the 1570s.[70]

As a consequence of this increased interest in Ulster on the part of the Tudor authorities, the number of historical documents referring to Belfast increases markedly after c.1550. Despite several short episodes of being garrisoned by English captains, often as an outpost associated with Carrickfergus Castle, the castle at Belfast generally remained either in a ruined state or in Gaelic hands for the remainder of the century as the Crown authorities intermittently pursued a policy of 'surrender and re-grant' and maintained an often uneasy relationship with the native Irish that periodically broke down into open conflict. 'Surrender and re-grant' is the name given by historians to a policy applied by the English administration in Ireland from c.1540 onwards by which Irish chiefs were encouraged to relinquish their traditional Gaelic titles and surrender their lands to the Crown on the understanding that they would receive them back as grants under English law. It was a not wholly unsuccessful attempt by the Crown authorities to pacify Ireland through a process of anglicization that involved redefining the relationship between the Crown and the Gaelic lords by bestowing English status and property titles upon them and involving them in both central and local government.[71]

The first recorded attempt by the Crown authorities to garrison Belfast Castle apparently occurred in 1551 when Sir James Croft, the lord deputy, reputedly took the castle from Hugh O'Neill of Clandeboye and repaired it as part of a campaign to address the threat posed by the Scots settled in eastern Ulster.[72] A document sent to the privy council implies that the English garrison established by Croft was maintained until at least the end of the year.[73] However, the site appears to have been given up by some point in the following year. A reference in the Annals of the Four Masters for 1552 records that a party of English troops were defeated by the son of Hugh O'Neill and obliged to cross the Lagan and erect a castle at Belfast.[74] The reference to the erection of a castle suggests that the existing castle had already been slighted. Presumably, the English troops either made sufficient repairs to the remains of the castle so that it could be temporarily occupied, or built a temporary defensive structure on the site. Later that year, Edward VI re-granted the castle to Hugh O'Neill 'in the same state as when he first possessed it'.[75] Given that Croft had overreached himself in his northern campaign,[76] the re-grant should probably be considered the best face-saving deal that the lord deputy could have made in the circumstances. In 1553 Lord Chancellor Cusacke recorded that 'Hugh [O'Neill] hath two castles, one called Bealefarst, an old castle standing upon a ford out from Arde to Clanneboy, which being well repaired, being now broken, would be a good defence betwixt the woods and Knockfergus'[77] indicating that, while O'Neill had indeed regained possession of the castle, it was still in a ruinous state the following year.

The rise in power across Ulster of Shane O'Neill in the 1560s prompted renewed interest by the Crown in the strategically positioned castle at Belfast. The castle had apparently passed back into the hands of the English administration by 1560 when the Crown authorities were able to assert that 'the Queen hath in quiet possession the Castles of Knockfergus and Belfast' which Shane O'Neill claimed.[78] A memorial of matters committed to Sir Francis Knollys in April 1566 indicates that the issue of 'fortifying Carrickfergus, Belfast, or some other straits or passages to be recovered from [Shane] O'Neill for his annoyance' was being considered,[79] although the ambiguous phrasing of the memorandum renders it unclear whether Belfast Castle remained in English hands or was held by Shane O'Neill at this date. A letter written in early November 1566 by Captain Thomas Browne at Carrickfergus states that large parties of Scots were able to use the ford at Belfast for raiding into north Down,[80] indicating that even if the English did maintain a garrison in Belfast at this date, their numbers were insufficient to control access to the ford. A brief of the state of Irish garrisons dated to 1567 confirms that an English garrison was present at Belfast.[81] Sir Henry Sidney, in his memoir of the time he spent in Ireland as lord deputy, boasted that after Shane O'Neill's death in 1567 he had planted 'the renowned soldier Captain Malbie with a company of horsemen in Belfast'.[82] Papers preserved in the National Archives[83] confirm that the captains based at Carrickfergus had indeed re-fortified and garrisoned Belfast, although the dispute over possession with the local Gaelic leadership, now in the person of Brian Mac Phelim O'Neill, was still ongoing.

Given the increasing political turmoil associated with both the tensions between the O'Neill lordships of Clandeboye and Tyrone and the increased focus of the Crown authorities upon Ulster, the economic status of the manorial estate associated with the castle at Belfast is uncertain. The manor was already recorded as being worthless in 1333. The Black Death of 1348–49 resulted in both a massive reduction in the Irish population and a concomitant reduction in the demand for agricultural produce. This would have had a direct impact on the viability of many of the surviving Anglo-Norman manorial estates, and prompted a long-term shift to an increasingly non-intensive pastoral farming regime based principally upon cattle.[84] Captain Malbie's report in February 1568 that he had 'set up two ploughs at Belfast'[85] suggests

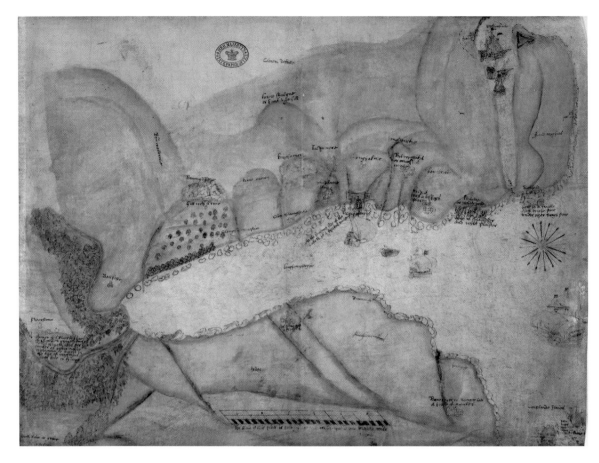

Map of Belfast Lough dating to c.1570 and attributed to Robert Lythe.

Reproduced with the kind permission of National Archives, Kew (ref. MPF/1/77).

that, despite these difficulties, at least part of the manorial estate associated with the newly re-fortified castle had survived intact. The use in seventeenth-century inquisitions relating to Belfast of units of land known as 'tuatha' or 'cinaments', whose origins are plausibly dated to the Anglo-Norman period, also suggests that land divisions defining the manorial estate associated with the castle survived throughout the later medieval period.[86] Despite this evidence for continuity, the degree to which the manorial estate remained a functional economic unit in the second half of the sixteenth century is debatable. That the nominally loyal Brian Mac Phelim O'Neill maintained his 'creaghts' [herds of cattle] around Belfast up until April 1568,[87] and that cattle being sent from Carrickfergus to Belfast had to be defended,[88] suggests that, although the Crown authorities maintained a garrison at Belfast, they did not meaningfully control much, if any, of the surrounding countryside. Furthermore, a detailed map of Belfast Lough, attributed to Robert Lythe and dating to c.1570,[89] depicts the castle of 'Bellfaste', but includes no representation of any houses or additional buildings associated with the castle. That settlements associated with castles elsewhere around the Lough were represented on the map, and two or three houses are depicted close to Belfast at 'Freerstone' (Friarstown or Friar's Bush), suggests that, at this date at least, the castle stood alone and that the associated manorial estate was not being significantly exploited.

Articles dating to 1568 indicate that the Crown authorities in Ireland were negotiating with Brian Mac Phelim O'Neill over the terms by which he could regain possession of the castle and manor of Belfast. These included building a bridge over the fording point, and providing hospitality and reimbursing Captain Malbie for the costs he had incurred in refurbishing the castle.[90] The negotiations must have been satisfactorily concluded because by 1571 O'Neill was apparently in joint possession of Belfast Castle with the English – he wrote to Elizabeth I in July of that year suggesting that the Crown maintain a small garrison in Belfast in conjunction with his own forces.[91] Unfortunately for O'Neill, the Crown's policy in Ulster had already shifted towards supporting the establishment of colonies in eastern Ulster in order to weaken the connections between Gaelic Ulster and Gaelic Scotland. By early 1572 O'Neill had become aware of an agreement made by the Crown with the English adventurer Sir Thomas Smith granting him significant holdings in Clandeboye and the Ards, including Belfast.[92] Outraged, O'Neill positioned himself against both Smith's colonists and the Crown's forces. In the conflict that followed it is not certain who held Belfast Castle. The privately financed adventure of Sir Thomas Smith proved to be a disaster and collapsed following the killing of Smith's son in 1573. Although seizing 'old castles' had been identified as a priority by Sir Thomas Smith,[93] it is doubtful whether his colonists ever managed to establish themselves at Belfast.

With his attempt to establish a colony in eastern Ulster failing, Thomas Smith agreed a deal with Walter Devereux, the earl of Essex, to give up a large part of the lands granted to him in the hope that Essex could bring the region under control. This arrangement was made with Elizabeth's approval and in July 1573 Essex received a grant of Clandeboye and other places. Essex quickly realized the strategic importance of Belfast in providing a base for his planned plantation of Brian Mac Phelim O'Neill's lands and proposed establishing a town at the site. In November 1573 he wrote to the privy council that

near unto Belfeaste is a place meet [suitable] for a corporate town, armed with all commodities, as a principal haven, wood and good ground, standing also upon a border, and a place of great importance for service, I think it convenient that a fortification be made there at the spring; the fortification for the circuit and a storehouse for victuals to be at her Majesty's charges, all other buildings at mine, and such as shall inhabit it; and for the doing hereof, I desire that Ligh, the engineer, or some other skilful in fortification, should be sent hither, who shall also build a Bridge upon the Laigan without her Majesty's charge.[94]

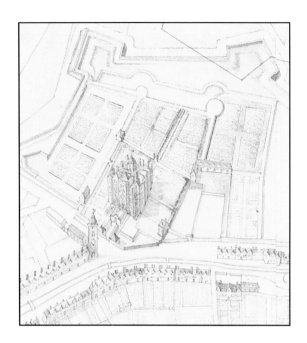
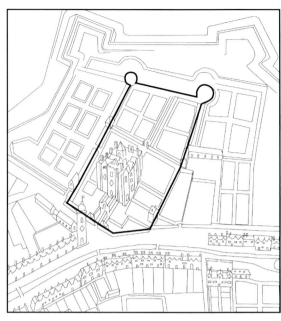

Although Essex never established a town 'near unto' Belfast, he did manage to re-establish a garrison at the castle, which was the site of a number of skirmishes during this period. An account of one of these engagements is valuable because it casts light on the character of the castle at this time. The skirmish took place in early October 1573 between a party of Essex's footmen and Scots from north Antrim. Essex records that his footmen were obliged 'to fight to the very ditch of the castle',[95] where presumably the Scots broke off their attack. In the sixteenth and seventeenth centuries, the word 'ditch' was commonly used in English to define a bank of earth, as well as an artificial hollow or cutting,[96] suggesting that the ditch described by Essex was probably a bawn, a fortified enclosure that was usually rectangular in shape and placed around a tower-house or plantation-period building. Essex's account continues that 400 of his men were 'left in the house of Belfast [...] which might have been defended with a small guard'.[97] That the castle could be held by a small garrison, while simultaneously being capable of accommodating several hundred men, is consistent with it being a tower-house augmented by a bawn. It is possible that the almost rectangular enclosure depicted surrounding Sir Arthur Chichester's seventeenth-century fortified mansion on one of Phillips's 1685 plans of Belfast represents the remains of this bawn.[98]

Hostilities extended into 1574 at which point an uneasy truce was established, suggesting that, although O'Neill had not been defeated, Essex had weakened him sufficiently to bring him to terms.[99] Negotiations between Essex and O'Neill, often apparently conducted at the now unknown site of the 'campe near Belfast', continued throughout most of the year.[100] The proposal to establish a town at Belfast was reiterated by O'Neill[101] and in July the privy

Detail of the Chichester mansion taken from Thomas Phillips's 1685 map of Belfast (left). The near-rectangular walled enclosure emphasized in the interpretive sketch of the map (right), although used to enclose the late seventeenth-century gardens, probably represents the remains of the bawn associated with the late medieval castle.

© Centre for Archaeological Fieldwork, Queen's University, Belfast.

council wrote to Essex suggesting that his troops should be 'induced to entrench and work there' and identifying the construction of fortifications, a brewhouse, storehouse and mill as priorities.[102] The privy council's instructions to Essex suggest that following the recent conflict these essential facilities for a long-term, self-sustainable settlement were not present at Belfast. The negotiations with O'Neill came to an abrupt end in November 1574 when Essex arrested O'Neill, his wife and brother, and massacred a large number of his people while they were being entertained at Belfast Castle. In a letter justifying his part in these events, Essex wrote that 'I gave order to lay hold of Brian in the Castle of Belfast where he lay [...] resistance was offered by his men lodged in the town and 125 of them were slain.'[103] His use of the word 'town' suggests the presence of, at the least, a temporary settlement of cabins or shelters that Brian Mac Phelim O'Neill's followers occupied. However, the contradictions and differences between the extant accounts of O'Neill's arrest and subsequent execution[104] suggest that this description might not accurately reflect the true character of the settlement at Belfast. Presumably, Essex either garrisoned or slighted the castle after the massacre took place. Essex wrote to the privy council in 1575 reiterating his wish to establish a town at Belfast[105] – an aspiration that was shared by other members of the Tudor administration close to Elizabeth.[106] By this time, however, his enterprise was failing and the available documentary evidence indicates that Essex never began construction of a new settlement at Belfast.

The End of Medieval Belfast and the Establishment of the Modern Town

In the years immediately following the execution of Brian Mac Phelim O'Neill, Belfast is not featured in many of the extant historical sources. A document dating to 1585 indicates that a garrison at the castle was maintained by the Crown authorities[107] and by the 1590s the castle was held either directly in English hands or garrisoned by Irish forces that were, at least nominally, loyal to the Crown.[108] As the rebellion of Hugh O'Neill, the earl of Tyrone, developed into the conflict subsequently known as the Nine Years' War (1594–1603), the strategic importance of the castle to the Crown authorities was reflected in the proposal to increase the size of the garrison at Belfast to 500 men.[109] Whether the defences of the castle were improved is unrecorded, but the lozenge-shaped earthwork known as Fortwilliam in the grounds of the City of Belfast School of Music in north Belfast[110] is of a form typical of the artillery forts of the late Elizabethan period and could date to the Nine Years' War.[111] Its position on a bluff overlooking the old shore road joining Belfast and Carrickfergus apparently reflects a concern to protect this vital route of communication and supply between the two English garrisons. It must be noted, however, that the

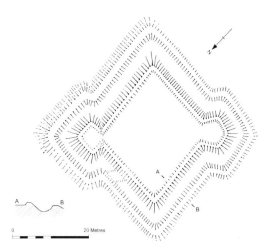

Plan of the earthen artillery fort at Fortwilliam in north Belfast.

© Crown copyright. Reproduced with the permission of the Controller of Her Majesty's Stationery Office.

form of the fort is not atypical of those built later in the seventeenth century and the site could post-date the Nine Years' War by several decades.

As an event, the Nine Years' War is important to the development of Belfast for two reasons. First, the war brought to Ireland an English soldier called Arthur Chichester who would subsequently become landlord and developer of the seventeenth-century town and founder of the Donegall dynasty. Secondly, the conclusion of the war in 1603, and the subsequent fleeing into exile of much of the Gaelic nobility of Ulster in 1607, provided the relatively stable conditions to enable the fledgling town of Belfast to develop as an economic centre.

Despite its strategic position, relatively little fighting occurred at Belfast during the Nine Years' War. However, one sequence of incidents is recorded, which accurately reflects the vicious character of the conflict. In June 1597 Shane Mac Brian O'Neill exploited a dispute among the captains at Carrickfergus and took Belfast Castle. As the eldest son of Brian Mac Phelim O'Neill, he apparently took the opportunity to avenge his father, as it is recorded that 'all the Inglishe men in the ward were hanged, and their throats cut, and their bowels cut oute of ther bellyes'.[112] It was also claimed that the castle was retaken the next day by a Captain Thornton, although if this was the case then the English evidently could not hold on to it, because Sir John Chichester subsequently found it in rebel hands when he assumed the stewardship of Carrickfergus Castle. Given its strategic position, Sir John identified regaining the castle as a priority and on 11 July, following an amphibious landing, he swiftly overcame the Irish occupants. Presumably as reprisal for the massacre of the English members of the garrison, he put all those he found in the castle to the sword.[113] That he lost none of his own men in the attack suggests that the surprised occupants offered no resistance and may well have surrendered. Although the English managed to hold the castle at Belfast for the remainder of the Nine Years' War, they did not succeed in controlling the land that surrounded it until the early 1600s. Until this point the eastern part of Ulster was largely in rebel hands and Belfast was an isolated outpost of Carrickfergus, which was itself an isolated stronghold precariously supplied by sea. Despite some significant initial successes, Sir John Chichester's career as governor of Carrickfergus Castle was short-lived and came to an abrupt end in November 1597 during an ill-advised and unprovoked charge against Sir James Macdonnell and a party of Antrim Scots.

Sir Arthur Chichester arrived in Ireland in 1599. Chichester was a complex man who played an important and controversial role in Irish history. As well as his significance to the history of Belfast, he played a pivotal role during the Nine Years' War, the Flight of the Earls and the subsequent plantation of Ulster. An Englishman from a family with puritanical sympathies, his unapologetic implementation of a scorched-earth policy during the Nine Years' War and near-zealous pursuit of religious conformity during his early years as lord deputy have earned him a reputation among some historians as being more malevolent than Cromwell.[114] He was a capable administrator who was prepared to push the boundaries of his position as lord deputy against the interests and express wishes of the Crown. Although he always retained a capacity for ruthlessness, by the end of his long term as viceroy there had been a marked change in his conduct that reflected the development of a more pragmatic, and concomitantly conciliatory, attitude in terms of policy.[115] For example, while vigorously championing the claims of the servitor class during the plantation of Ulster, he did not advocate the wholesale removal of the Gaelic Irish from the land they already occupied. The complexity and contradictions of Sir Arthur Chichester are exemplified in the Chichester Memorial in St Nicholas' church, Carrickfergus. This masterpiece of Jacobean sculpture and propaganda represents Chichester as a devoted family man kneeling in a pious manner facing his wife and surrounded by representations of his dead son and brother. It also depicts him wearing armour and includes panels of martial regalia, reflecting his pride in a successful military career.[116]

Following his arrival in Ireland, Sir Arthur Chichester rapidly distinguished himself as one of Essex's senior officers and was promptly appointed to the governorship of Carrickfergus – the post formerly held by his brother, John, and a role that Essex's successor as viceroy, Charles Blount, Lord Mountjoy, re-appointed him to in 1600.[117] As governor, Chichester demonstrated an exceptional military ability that was matched only by his ruthlessness in executing Mountjoy's scorched-earth policy. During the course of the conflict, Chichester's competence had impressed the Crown authorities in Dublin and London, and both the patronage of Mountjoy and his influential contributions to formulating a post-war policy in Ireland marked him out for advancement after the war was concluded. He was offered the lord deputyship in 1604,

A monument in St Nicholas' church, Carrickfergus, depicting Sir Arthur Chichester and his wife, Lettice, and between them the small body of his son, Arthur, described in the inscription as 'the only hope of his house, who lived not full two months after his birth'. The figure below is Sir Arthur's brother, Sir John, killed in an encounter with the Macdonnells of Antrim in 1597.

© Crown copyright. Reproduced with the permission of the Controller of Her Majesty's Stationery Office.

a post he accepted the following year and retained until 1616.[118] Following the Nine Years' War, however, Chichester was apparently more concerned to address his difficult financial situation by establishing several sources of income. He claimed that Belfast Castle was 'for the most part fallen to the ground'[119] and offered to rebuild it in exchange for a grant of the castle and the surrounding property.[120] While lobbying Robert Cecil over this grant in July 1603, Chichester demonstrated his skill in political negotiation by claiming that his future bride was of such an age that she was unlikely to bear him any children and that, as he would have no heir, he would leave his estate to Cecil's son.[121] Whether this gambit had any effect on Lord Cecil is unknown, but in the following month Chichester received a king's letter for the governorship of Carrickfergus and the castle of Belfast, together with its lands. Although a patent was issued in November 1603[122] this was subsequently surrendered as a new grant was issued to Chichester in 1604.[123] As described in the following chapter, Chichester quickly set about establishing a town at Belfast. The granting of charters for a market in 1605 and a fair in 1608 reflect the rapid initial development of the town which, as part of a scheme to ensure that the new parliament in Dublin had a Protestant majority, became a corporate borough in 1613. Chichester's wife did in fact give birth to a son in 1606.[124] However, the child died in infancy, and Chichester was succeeded as sole owner of Belfast by his brother, Edward, in 1625.

The Church

The earliest reference to the church in Belfast is contained within the Papal Taxation of 1306. This records the *Ecclesia Alba* (the White Church) and three dependent chapels, one of which is known as the *Capella de Vado* (the Chapel of the Ford).[125] The *Ecclesia Alba* was the parish church for the area which included the Anglo-Norman manor of *Le Ford* and was almost certainly located at the site of the old graveyard at Shankill approximately two kilometres to the west of the city centre. There is no extant historical evidence to indicate that the 'White Church' was a pre-Norman foundation. However, three decorative gilt copper-alloy mounts of either late eighth- or ninth-century date, all likely to have been fitted to the same crozier, have been recovered from the old graveyard at Shankill, suggesting that it was indeed an early ecclesiastical centre.[126] Excavation in the graveyard in 1959 also uncovered evidence of Early Christian period activity.[127] The organization of the Church in Ireland during this period is a complicated and not fully understood issue. It is probable that territorial episcopal dioceses existed in tandem with monastic confederations, and that there was a diverse range of ecclesiastical sites.[128] Both episcopal and some monastic churches would have served the needs of the local lay community and where early, undocumented sites can be identified by their physical remains it is frequently not possible to ascertain their status with any confidence on the basis of archaeological evidence alone. It is uncertain what status the site at Shankill had prior to the twelfth-century reform of the Irish Church that led to the creation of parishes within a territorially based diocesan structure; however, the crozier mounts suggest that it may have been an episcopal church associated with a monastic site.[129] While also suggestive of an Early Christian date, the bullaun stone associated with the Shankill graveyard, and now removed to St Matthew's parish church, does not refine our appreciation of either the dating or early status of the church.[130] The name 'White Church' was often attributed to early stone-built churches because of the whitewash that was used on their walls. Ulster was a region in which mortared stone churches remained in the minority until at least AD 1200.[131] Therefore any earlier church present at the site, contemporary with the crozier fragments, was likely to have been built from organic materials such as turf, wattle and timber. The earliest definite use of the place-name 'Shenkyll' occurs in an inquisition of c.1552 in which the church is included among the possessions of the Benedictine Cathedral Priory of St Patrick in Downpatrick.[132] The church was described as ruinous in the Calendar of Patent Rolls for 1604[133] and no record or trace of the medieval church building survives.

That the church building was a ruin by the early seventeenth century indicates that the *Ecclesia Alba* had lost its status as parish church by this date. Given that the name composition Shankill (*sean chill*, meaning 'old church') presupposes the establishment of a later church, it is likely that this loss of parochial status occurred before the middle of the sixteenth century. Although it is not directly historically attested, it is reasonable to infer that the parochial status of the *Ecclesia Alba* was transferred to its former dependent chapel, the *Capella de Vado*. This inference is suggested by the multiple occurrences in early seventeenth-century historical sources of variants of the hybrid name *Ecclesia Alba de Vado*, which combine the medieval names for the parish church and its

The decorative crozier mounts recovered from the old graveyard at Shankill. The mounts variously consist of a drop (top), tubular knop (middle) and ferrule (bottom). The line drawing shows how they may have been originally fitted.
Photograph © National Museum of Ireland.

The bullaun stone associated with the old graveyard at Shankill and now located nearby in the grounds of St Matthew's parish church.
© Philip Macdonald.

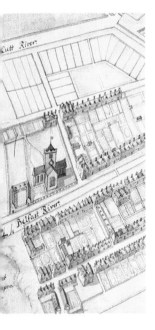

Detail of Thomas Phillips's map of 1685 (p. 78) showing the seventeenth-century parish church built upon the site of the medieval *Capella de Vado.*

© The British Library Board (Maps.K.Top.51,37).

dependent chapel.[134] That the medieval parish church at Shankill was a ruin by 1604, and that there is no evidence to suggest that it was subsequently rebuilt, suggests that the conflated name refers to the site of the former *Capella de Vado*. Presumably the place-names were amalgamated when the former dependent chapel became the parish church. What caused this transfer in parochial status, and whether it occurred before or as a result of the medieval church at Shankill becoming a ruin, is unknown. The medieval references do not specify the precise location of the Chapel of the Ford. However, a 1622 survey of the diocese of Down and Connor described the church (*Ecclesia de Albo-Vaddo*) as having been built 'from the ground and repayred',[135] indicating that Belfast's seventeenth-century church was located upon the site of its late medieval predecessor. This seventeenth-century church, which was pulled down in 1774, was located on the southern side of High Street in the position now occupied by St George's church.[136] This confirms that the hybrid name referred to the former Chapel of the Ford as during the medieval period this position would have been located immediately adjacent to the ford at the eastern end of the narrow and low promontory located between the Farset and Blackstaff.[137]

Previously it has been assumed that the *Capella de Vado* was established as a place for travellers to pray either prior to or after crossing the ford. However, it is also possible that it was founded as an integral part of the Anglo-Norman manor of *Le Ford*. There is no historical or material evidence to indicate that the chapel had a pre-Norman foundation. Although it was not unusual for early churches to be located both on routeways and adjacent to river crossings,[138] such positions were also chosen for Norman churches.[139] Consequently, the chapel's location is not indicative of the date of its foundation. That the church was rebuilt from the ground up in 1622 suggests that little of the fabric of the medieval chapel survived, but it is possible that elements of the ground plan of the medieval church were preserved in the new building depicted on Phillips's 1685 maps of Belfast.[140] No ruins of the seventeenth-century church are represented within the graveyard that surrounded the church on Williamson's 1791 map of Belfast.[141] This suggests that the demolition in 1774 was total and that no fabric from the earlier churches could have survived to be incorporated into that of St George's church when it was built between 1811 and 1816.

In addition to the *Capella de Vado*, two other dependent chapels of the medieval church of Shankill are noted in the Papal Taxation of 1306 – the *Capella de Henr* (Chapel of Henrystown) and the *Capella de Weston* (Chapel of Weston). Both of these chapels were apparently located in the northern outskirts of the modern city. The Henrystown chapel was probably located somewhere in Ballyhenry, which is now within the parish of Carnmoney,[142] while Weston was almost certainly located somewhere in Ballyvaston, now in the northernmost part of the parish of Shankill.[143] The Ballyvaston chapel is also recorded in the *Terrier*, a compilation of the ecclesiastical possessions of the dioceses of Down and Connor, dated on internal evidence to c.1615, but containing much detail derived from at least one lost pre-Reformation document that is speculatively dated to c.1500.[144] The reference to the Ballyvaston chapel in the *Terrier* indicates that it survived into the late medieval period. Five other dependent chapels are also recorded in the *Terrier*, as well as in several other early seventeenth-century inquisitions and visitations[145] – the *Capella de Crookmock*, the *Capella de Kilpatrick*, the *Capella de Killemna*, the *Capella de Clochmestale* and the *Capella de Tullerusk*.[146] The location of the *Capella de Crookmock* is uncertain. There is some confusion between the names *Cromac* and *Cranoge* in the various extant seventeenth-century sources. However, the chapel has been tentatively identified as being located in the district of *Croach Moch*, which is recorded on Williamson's 1807 map of County Antrim as being to the south of Belfast.[147] The *Capella de Kilpatrick* is described as being 'above Moses Hill's house at Stronmillis' and was probably located at the site of Friar's Bush graveyard beside the Ulster Museum.[148] No structure or monuments of medieval date survive within this graveyard, although the curvilinear mound located in a near-central position may represent the collapsed and denuded remains of an early ecclesiastical enclosure. The c.1570 map of Belfast Lough attributed to Robert Lythe represents a small cluster of houses associated with the townland of 'Freerstone' (Friarstown or Friar's Bush), but does not depict a chapel or church.[149] The name Friarstown does not necessarily indicate the presence of a church; it may simply signify a townland that had been donated to a friary established elsewhere.[150] The *Capella de Killemna* has been tentatively identified as being located at Kilwee, Dunmurry,[151] while the *Capella de Clochmestale* has long been confidently placed within the townland of Greencastle.[152] The *Capella de Tullerusk* was listed as a separate parish church within the Papal Taxation of 1306 and is readily identifiable with the ruined foundations of a simple rectangular church within the graveyard at Tullyrusk, near Dundrod.[153]

Friar's Bush graveyard in Stranmillis. The mound visible in the background may represent the collapsed and denuded remains of an early ecclesiastical enclosure.

© Crown copyright. Reproduced with the permission of the Controller of Her Majesty's Stationery Office.

The graveyard at Tullyrusk, near Dundrod, which was formerly the site of the *Capella de Tullerusk*. The site's rustic setting reflects the essentially rural character of the late medieval parish of Shankill.

© Philip Macdonald.

Given the relative paucity of sources and documents relating to both the secular and ecclesiastical history of medieval Belfast, archaeology has the potential to add greatly to our understanding of this first chapter in the city's story.[154] However, despite shedding a great deal of light on the conditions and development of the town from the seventeenth century onwards, the results of numerous excavations have yet to make a significant contribution to our appreciation of Belfast's medieval history.

Identifying the precise location of the Anglo-Norman and any later medieval settlement in Belfast remains an unfulfilled ambition of archaeologists. Conventionally it has been assumed that the medieval settlement was located in the area between the castle and the Chapel of the Ford, although it is far from certain that this locality would have been favoured for early settlement. During the medieval period this area, which roughly coincides with that part of the present-day town centre sandwiched between High Street and Ann Street, would have formed a narrow and low-lying strip of land between the rivers Farset and Blackstaff and would have been prone to flooding. In recent years a number of excavations have been conducted in this area, but to date the amount of evidence for medieval activity that has been recovered remains slight.[155] Near to the site of the later medieval castle, excavations on the site of the former Brands and Norman building in Castle Lane uncovered several ephemeral deposits of medieval date, including a pit and part of a sizeable ditch that were associated with sherds of medieval pottery.[156] Away from the immediate environs of the castle, however, excavation has produced little material of medieval date. A trench dug immediately adjacent to the High Street frontage within the Woolworth's and Burton building uncovered part of a curvilinear gully. This gully was inundated with estuarine clay that contained several sherds of local Medieval Coarse Pottery, but may represent nothing more significant than a short-lived drainage ditch.[157] The only other possible medieval feature that has been uncovered during excavations in the area between the Farset and Blackstaff was part of an east–west aligned waterfront. This feature consisted of a clay bank retained by a post-and-wattle breakwater and was located in the area beneath the former Kitchen bar, which was excavated in advance of the Victoria Square retail development.[158] A single sherd of glazed pottery, possibly of thirteenth- or fourteenth-century date, was recovered from within the clay used to create the bank. This has prompted the suggestion that the feature might represent a medieval waterfront or wharf located close to the mouth of the Blackstaff. That the bank was constructed from redeposited clay, however, means that the use of a single potsherd to date the feature is problematic and the waterfront could just as plausibly date to the seventeenth or early eighteenth centuries. Medieval

artefacts recovered by chance from the area are also few. However, a lead-alloy ring brooch of late twelfth- or thirteenth-century date and a gold signet ring of possible medieval date were discovered during works to renew parts of the Farset culvert between 1854 and 1860.[159]

The failure to find significant evidence of medieval activity is not apparently a result of the construction of nineteenth-century or later buildings removing evidence for earlier settlement. Presumably as a consequence of this low-lying area's tendency to flood, few of the buildings in High Street have deep cellars, and excavations of post-medieval sequences in the area have demonstrated that successive phases of building have tended not to involve significant truncation of earlier deposits. Therefore, if they were present, it is likely that archaeological deposits and features of medieval date would have survived beneath the foundations of the nineteenth- and twentieth-century buildings that have been excavated in central Belfast. Even if archaeological horizons associated with Anglo-Norman or later medieval settlement had been destroyed by subsequent building activity, it would be reasonable to expect significant quantities of medieval artefacts, especially potsherds, to have survived, residually deposited in later contexts. Excavation has demonstrated that this is not the case. Although arguments based upon negative evidence are always unsatisfactory, this lack of evidence for medieval activity between the castle and the Chapel of the Ford suggests the possibility that the main focus of the Anglo-Norman and later medieval settlement was situated elsewhere.

Where any alternative focus of medieval settlement might be located is unclear, although it would presumably be in relatively close proximity to the site of the castle and therefore somewhere within the immediate vicinity of the modern city centre. Numerous excavations have been carried out in the Cathedral Quarter area of the city, to the north of High Street, where cartographic evidence indicates the seventeenth-century town was located.[160] These excavations, however, have failed to recover any convincing evidence of medieval activity.[161] Topographically, a more likely focus for medieval settlement is the area of slightly higher ground to the west of the site of

Sherds of local Medieval Coarse Pottery recovered from excavations within the former Woolworth's and Burton building in High Street.
© Centre for Archaeological Fieldwork, Queen's University, Belfast.

Lead-alloy ring brooch of late twelfth- or thirteenth-century date recovered in the nineteenth century during the renewal of the Farset culvert in High Street.
Photograph © National Museums Northern Ireland. Collection Ulster Museum. BELUM.A32.1990.

'Blitz Square' (the corner of Bridge Street and High Street) following the air raid of May 1941. The photograph shows that few of the nineteenth-century buildings in the centre of Belfast have basements or cellars. This suggests that, if they were present, archaeological horizons of medieval date would survive relatively intact. The failure during the course of several excavations to find any significant evidence of medieval activity within this area, set between the known sites of the castle and the *Capella de Vado* (Chapel of the Ford), suggests that the main focus of medieval settlement was situated elsewhere within the immediate vicinity of the modern city centre.

Photograph © National Museums Northern Ireland. Collection Ulster Museum. BELUM.Y7003.

the castle in the Millfield area of the city centre. To date, only a couple of excavations have been conducted in this part of Belfast, but the work that has been carried out has also failed to uncover any definitive evidence of medieval deposits or artefacts.[162] The unresolved question of the location of the medieval settlement, coupled with the demonstrably high level of archaeological preservation within central Belfast, reflects the importance of continuing to conduct archaeological excavations in advance of development within the whole of the city centre. It is to be hoped that future excavations will not only provide evidence to indicate where the medieval settlement was located, but also challenge and complement the historical sequence outlined here.

Making Belfast, 1600–1750

Raymond Gillespie

In 1600 the site of Belfast was not a prime candidate for the construction of a significant settlement. Its importance derived mainly from the fact that it was the lowest fordable point of the River Lagan. On an isthmus of land where the rivers Blackstaff and Farset entered the Lagan stood a small medieval chapel, attached to the parish church at Shankill, and a tower-house. What else was on the site is a matter of speculation although attempts by the earl of Essex to fortify the place in the late sixteenth century had probably created some sort of settlement that may have endured. The area was frequently flooded and was underlain by unstable estuarine clays that made the construction of substantial buildings almost impossible. Despite these problems, Belfast a century and a half later was a town of over 8,500 souls crammed into 1,779 houses, making it the largest town in the province of Ulster.[1] It dwarfed its nearest rival, and near contemporary in foundation, Derry, which in 1738 had only 217 houses within its walls.[2] Belfast in 1750 had all the features that one might associate with a moderately prosperous regional centre. The economic infrastructure of a port with quays, custom house and warehouses was well established and its more local trading functions were obvious in the marketplace, linen hall and market house. On the streets industrial activity could be smelt as well as seen in tanneries, brewing, salt manufacture, sugar boiling and rope making. As the merchant John Black put it in 1766, Belfast was a place of 'smoke, hurry, bustle and noise'.[3] The Assembly Rooms, built a few years later, marked it out as a regional centre of sociability and, although it met infrequently, the corporation demonstrated the independence of the town in the management of its own affairs, although that was constrained by the desires of the landlord, who had been granted the town as part of the attempt to introduce royal authority into Ulster after the end of the Nine Years' War in 1603.

This town of 1750 had not come about by accident; it was the result of a process of construction. It existed in brick and timber, and those had to be assembled to create the physical environment within which people lived.

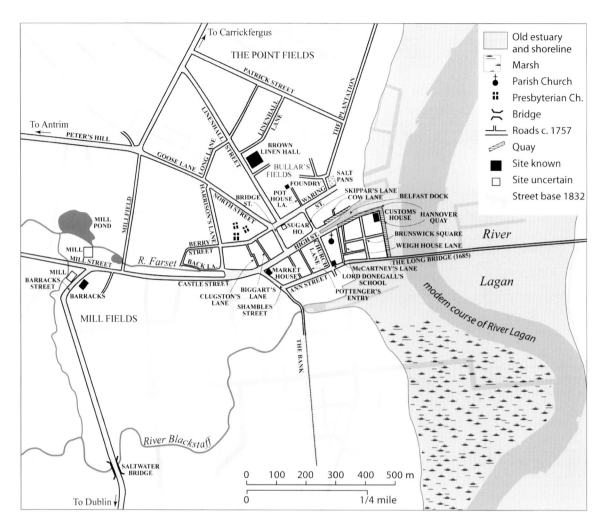

The following text labels appear on the map:

To Carrickfergus

THE POINT FIELDS

PATRICK STREET

THE PLANTATION

To Antrim

PETER'S HILL

GOOSE LANE

LINENHALL STREET

LINENHALL LANE

LONGLANE

HARRISON'S LANE

BROWN LINEN HALL

BULLAR'S FIELDS

SALT PANS

FOUNDRY

SKIPPAR'S LANE

COW LANE

BELFAST DOCK

POT HOUSE LA.

WARING ST.

BRIDGE ST.

NORTH STREET

SUGAR HO.

CUSTOMS HOUSE

HANNOVER QUAY

MILL POND

MILL FIELD

BERRY STREET

HIGH ST.

CHURCH LANE

BRUNSWICK SQUARE

WEIGH HOUSE LANE

River

MILL STREET

MILL

R. Farset

BACK LA.

THE LONG BRIDGE (1685)

Lagan

MILL BARRACKS STREET

CASTLE STREET

MARKET HOUSE

ANN STREET

McCARTNEY'S LANE

LORD DONEGALL'S SCHOOL

POTTENGER'S ENTRY

modern course of River Lagan

BARRACKS

BIGGART'S LANE

CLUGSTON'S LANE

SHAMBLES STREET

MILL FIELDS

THE BANK

River Blackstaff

SALTWATER BRIDGE

To Dublin

Legend:
Old estuary and shoreline
Marsh
Parish Church
Presbyterian Ch.
Bridge
Roads c. 1757
Quay
Site known
Site uncertain
Street base 1832

0   100   200   300   400   500 m

0   1/4 mile

However, Belfast was more than a physical space. It was also a centre of authority, a place that was able to generate and disseminate ideas and beliefs and that offered a social context not only for the exchange of goods but of political, religious and cultural values also. It provided a focal point for the creation of local societies for the exchange of information as well as a centre for sociability at which common ideas about what the town was and how it worked could be shared and shaped. This Belfast, the town of the mind, had to be made just as the physical fabric had to be built and the process was no less complex. This chapter concerns itself with the making of the many Belfasts that existed by 1750, not just in the physical landscape but also in the minds of those who occupied the town.

I

In 1772 the artist Jonathan Fisher sketched Belfast from the south. His view was of a town in a tranquil rural setting complete with cattle in the foreground.[4]

Belfast in 1757, based on the map of Belfast prepared for the Donegall estate in 1757 (p. 80).

Reproduced with permission from Raymond Gillespie.

This painting by the Dublin artist Jonathan Fisher (d.1809), dated 1772, shows Belfast from Cromac Wood to the south, with Cave Hill in the background.

Photograph © National Museums Northern Ireland. Collection Ulster Museum. BELUM.P236.1927.

The town itself was depicted as a compact settlement of packed buildings bounded on the south by the River Blackstaff as it entered the Lagan. What stood out were the spires and towers on the skyline, and the construction of those edifices was intended to mark these places out as important. On the east side of the town was the spire of the parish church, about to be swept away three years later by a new church on the newly laid out Donegall Street. In the west of the town was the tower of the market house. These were clearly the buildings that the shapers of the town laid great store by. By 1772 the parish church was a building of some antiquity. It had begun life as a chapel attached to the parish church at Shankill. By the early seventeenth century, however, that was in ruins so when in 1604 Sir Arthur Chichester was granted the site of Belfast and began to think about building a town, the old chapel was an obvious candidate for refurbishment as a more convenient parish church. Exactly when this was done is not clear but by 1622 it had been rebuilt in brick, as much of the early town was. The church provided a focus for many aspects of town life. Even later Belfast residents of a Presbyterian background saw merit in the church. Many Presbyterians were buried in its graveyard and their burials recorded in the parish register. In 1705 Isaac McCartney, although a Presbyterian, owned a seat in the gallery of the parish church and worried that it might be taken from him.[5] However, if they saw merit in the church, paying for its upkeep and for the maintenance of the clergy was more problematic. The collection of House Money for the payment of the clergy was always a potential flashpoint and in 1703 financial difficulties coincided with an unpopular incumbent to spark a revolt against the collection of this tax.[6]

The second building that the townspeople had chosen to mark out with a tower was the market house. This combination of corporation chamber, trading centre and meeting rooms was the second market house that the town had built. The first, whose location is not known but which was probably close to the marketplace in Bridge Street, was in place by 1639 but by 1663 it was deemed necessary to replace it, probably because of damage done by the military garrison in the 1650s. A prominent merchant, George Macartney, leased a new building at the corner of High Street and Corn Market, significantly adjacent to the landlord's house, and had it fitted out, presumably including the construction of the tower, as a market house and meeting place for the corporation. Until the construction of the new Exchange at the bottom of Donegall Street in 1769 the market house was the focus for the town and a tangible marker of its identity. Proclamations were read there and the bells located in the tower were rung for the funerals of important citizens. Auctions of land and goods were also held there in the early eighteenth century.

Fisher's view is, of course, a snapshot of the town at one moment in its life. By the time his engraving was made many buildings that were of importance to the town over the previous hundred years had disappeared. The most striking example was the earl of Donegall's castle. Sir Arthur Chichester had built a house for himself in the town by 1611, although he rarely resided there. His nephew and heir seems to have rebuilt that house in a much grander style, probably in the late 1620s. This was an impressive structure with some forty hearths as recorded in the hearth money roll of 1666. This castle dominated Belfast until it was destroyed by fire in 1708, leaving a large area of waste ground in the middle of the town that was not built on until the late eighteenth century.

For anyone acquainted with the origins of Belfast what Fisher's view does not show might seem surprising: the lack of provisions for defence. Other Ulster towns founded in the early seventeenth century, such as Derry and Coleraine, had walls and Chichester's other town, Carrickfergus, had its walls renewed and extended in the early seventeenth century. Belfast, like nearby Lisburn, had no such investment. The town was founded mainly as a trading centre and Chichester saw no need to invest substantial sums on walls for a centre that he had little interest in defending. Fortunately, throughout its first century and a half Belfast saw little military action. Only briefly, at the height of the insurrection of the 1640s, did fear prompt the inhabitants of the town to create a defensive line. In 1642 they began work on an earthen rampart which, on the evidence of later maps, was never finished. Even if it had been completed its construction was so amateurish that it would have provided little in the way of defence, since the sight lines for any guns defending the town were hopelessly confused.[7] Part of it was later incorporated into the boundary of Donegall's castle but the remainder was simply allowed to wear away, though parts could be seen in the nineteenth century since some fragments acted as property boundaries and hence were preserved.

While Fisher's view provides a profile of the town, it does not allow the reconstruction of the ligaments that held individual buildings together: the skein of streets. These streets might be seen as of two types. First, there were the older streets that followed the topography of the site, and secondly there

Sir Arthur Chichester.
Image supplied courtesy of Belfast Harbour Commissioners.

Sir Arthur Chichester

From the seventeenth century to the mid-nineteenth century the landlords of Belfast were the Chichester family, who in 1647 became earls of Donegall. The founder of the town, Sir Arthur Chichester, was granted the site of the castle and lands of Belfast in 1603. He was then 40 years old, having been born in Raleigh, Devon, in May 1563. In the 1590s he came to Ireland as a soldier in Queen Elizabeth's forces, having previously served in France and with Francis Drake in the New World. He was the architect of military policy in Ulster through the Nine Years' War (1594–1603), and especially of the scorched-earth policy that ended the war. In 1604 he succeeded Lord Mountjoy as lord deputy, holding the post until 1615. As such he presided over the Ulster plantation, although he would have preferred a settlement in which former soldiers played a greater part. After his recall in 1615 Chichester retired to Carrickfergus, although in 1622 he was sent on a diplomatic mission to the Palatinate and before his death, in 1625, he was spoken of as a potential lord treasurer of England. His own finances were chaotic. While he had large landholdings in south County Antrim and in County Donegal (worth about £6,000 a year in 1625), he was deeply in debt. Thus the development of Belfast was a speculative venture, intended to make money from rents and the profits of trade. In this it succeeded admirably, with a rental of about £400 in the 1630s, the highest amount of any of his properties. Most of this was achieved with little investment by the cash-strapped Chichester. The town had no defences and little harbour infrastructure, both of which he developed in his other town at Carrickfergus. Houses were built by tenants under the terms of their lease, rather than by the landlord. Chichester died childless in 1625. His lands passed to his brother, Edward, who probably moved the family residence from Carrickfergus to Belfast.

were those routeways that were created by planners to facilitate the workings of a rapidly growing town. Probably the oldest network of streets was that aimed at carrying those using the ford across the Lagan away from the marshland beside the river on to higher ground, along which they could continue their journey. What is now Ann Street probably continued north to Castle Street and hence to the 'sandy row' that led southwards. A spur off this led to what became North Street which bifurcated into the line of the Shankill Road, taking travellers past the medieval parish church and on to Antrim, and Queen Street, which followed the raised beach towards the medieval regional capital of Carrickfergus.

Overlain on this early network was a second type of street, one that was planned and formally laid out. The 1611 commissioners who reported on the progress of settlement in Ulster noted of Belfast that it was 'plotted out in good form', which implies planning.[8] The planned street can be identified as Broad Street (now Waring Street), which extended from the shoreline to what is now the junction of Rosemary Street and Lombard Street. This was a long and straight street, which was about the same size as the main axis of Carrickfergus though shorter than that of the contemporary foundation at Derry. The planning, insofar as it was done, was in the hands of the landlord of the town. Sir Arthur Chichester seems to have originated the idea of abandoning the old settlement on the south side of the River Farset and building anew on the north side. Before the middle of the eighteenth century, maps of Belfast show the Ann Street part of the town as a poorly developed area with only few houses, Waring Street and High Street being the main centres of housing. This east–west axis of High Street and Waring Street was, by the early eighteenth century, the most densely occupied part of the town. Of all the people attached to the Third Presbyterian church in Rosemary Street in the early eighteenth century about a third lived in this area. It was also one of the longest settled parts of the town and its building stock suffered badly in the early eighteenth-century recession in Belfast so that, when new leases were granted in the 1760s, those requiring rebuilding dominated in this area.[9] Chichester's initial enthusiasm for planning waned and the town was left to grow more haphazardly. High Street evolved as a trackway along the side of the River Farset that linked the quay, at the east end of the street, with the marketplace around Bridge Street. As a result it follows the course of the river and this is still apparent in the curved street today.

For most of the seventeenth and early eighteenth centuries the town grew around this framework of planned town and older topographically shaped streets. High Street extended up towards Castle Street and, by the late seventeenth century, Castle Street was being laid out in plots for house building. Waring Street expanded westwards by the addition of what became Rosemary Street and here the Presbyterians built their church in 1672 on previously unoccupied land. Eastwards, Waring Street extended on to the

Belfast in 1640.

Reproduced with permission from
Raymond Gillespie.

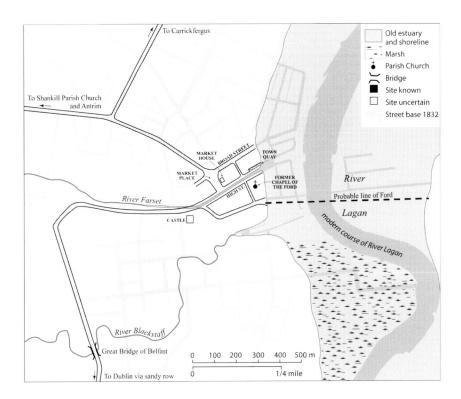

Belfast in 1640.

strand beside the river and there accommodated the noxious industries
of tanning and pottery making in the hope that smell and smoke would
be blown out to sea. The next major planning impetus was a speculative
development in the second decade of the eighteenth century by the
Presbyterian merchant Isaac McCartney. In 1711 McCartney acquired a lease of
unreclaimed land between the church and the River Lagan on which he laid
out the residential development of Brunswick Square, a new quay (Hanover
Quay) and a new custom house to deal with the expanding trade of the town.
This development can be clearly seen in Fisher's 1772 view as a rectangular
block of buildings at the east edge of the town, apparently at right angles to
the main orientation. By 1720 the work was well under way but it was never
completed and by the 1750s only the northern part of the square was finished.
Nevertheless, McCartney still cleared £400 a year from the development by
the end of the 1720s, much of which probably came from the quay and custom
house. Finally the Donegall family, after decades of neglect, once again began
to take an active part in urban development. Commencing around 1752 the
trustees of the fourth earl, in a fit of enthusiasm for urban improvement (and
rent increases), began a major overhaul of the property. In particular they
wanted to create a planned high-status quarter to the north of Waring Street.
The fourth earl did not live long enough to see his ambition realized, but the
development of the area continued as part of the far-reaching reform of the
town's fabric carried out by his nephew, the fifth earl. A new parish church, St

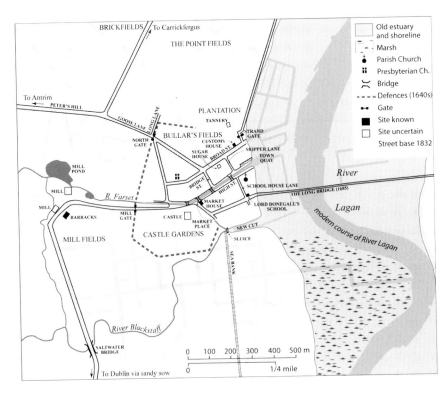

Belfast in 1685, based on Thomas Phillips's 1685 map of Belfast (p. 78).

Reproduced with permission from Raymond Gillespie.

Anne's, provided the focus, and at the start of the new straight street (initially called Linenhall Street but now renamed Donegall Street) a market house and assembly rooms created a civic space. The property around this area was set to developers who created a new network of streets with brick houses to a high specification as set out in leases.[10]

These Belfast streets were often unpleasant and sometimes dangerous places. Before the middle of the eighteenth century they were poorly lit at night and while the corporation ordered that lanterns be hung outside houses in winter 'when it is not moonshine' it is difficult to argue that candles had much impact.[11] By day the streets were rather better, being mainly broad to allow light and air to move freely, but the narrow alleyways connecting High Street with Ann Street that developed in the early eighteenth century, what came to be known as 'entries', had a narrower, gloomier appearance. This was a real problem since streets were often cluttered with timber and barrels, left there by shop owners and merchants, with the potential for fatal accidents.[12] Moreover, paving was irregular and before the 1760s, when clauses were introduced into leases by Lord Donegall requiring owners to pave the area in front of their houses, it was often non-existent. Before 1800 the houses on Belfast streets were not numbered, but then this was not necessary since the town was a small, face-to-face world in which most people knew each other. The recipient's name was sufficient address for letters sent within the town and in the 1730s letters from Dublin could easily be sent to 'Daniel Mussenden,

The author of this 1715 map, John Maclanachan, is a rather enigmatic figure who also mapped estates in Armagh, Londonderry and Tyrone between 1715 and 1724. His map of Belfast shows the town, not as it was, but with some significant developments. Isaac McCartney's development at the east end of High Street is shown as complete, although the map of 1757 (p. 80) makes clear that it was still unfinished even then. Again, the area around Smithfield is shown as built up although it was not yet developed in 1757. It is possible that the map was made as a preparation for the ending of the minority of the fourth earl in 1716. If so the concern for possible improvements suggests a greater engagement between the town and its landlord than has been generally accepted at this date. Another significant feature evident from the map is the development of the narrow lanes or 'entries' between the main streets, all named after merchants who were probably their developers.

Reproduced with the kind permission of the Public Record Office of Northern Ireland.

merchant, Belfast' and reach their destination. From London it was wise to add 'Ireland' to the address.[13] Most people knew where others in their social circle could be found without formal addresses. Publishers too saw little need to advertise where their wares could be obtained; most imprints mentioned only the printer's name and that the works were 'sold at his shop', assuming all knew where that was. Only recently established publishers, such as Wilson and Magee or Francis Joy in the 1730s, bothered to include an address. The streets of Belfast were both familiar and threatening places.

Added to these streets there were more specialized routeways that helped the townspeople navigate their way around the town. One obvious such feature was the quay and a second was the marketplace. The quay is visible on Fisher's view of the town as a forest of ships' masts at the east edge of the town. This new quay was part of Isaac McCartney's early eighteenth-century development but the older quay had lain at the north-east end of High Street, at the point where the River Farset entered the Lagan. This was connected to the main body of the town along Waring Street by Skipper Street and High Street. The quay was the point at which Belfast met the wider world. Smaller ships could tie up there directly while larger vessels had to anchor in the pool of Garmoyle and offload their cargoes on to light barges or gabbarts. The business of the quay was seasonal. Most shipping entering the port did so in spring and summer when sea conditions were best for travelling. In the mid-1680s no ships over 50 tons moved through the port of Belfast between September and March and

A

NARRATIVE

Of the Proceedings of seven General

SYNODS

Of the *Northern* Presbyterians in *Ireland*, with Relation to *their* DIFFERENCES in Judgment and Practice, from the Year 1720 to the Year 1726, in which they issu'd in a 𝔖𝔶𝔫𝔬𝔡𝔦𝔠𝔞𝔩 𝔅𝔯𝔢𝔞𝔠𝔥:

CONTAINING

The Occasion, Rise, true State, and Progress of the Differences; Expedients for Peace, offer'd by the Non-subscribers, and many other Original Papers; Synodical Debates, Overtures, and Decisions; the Conduct of the Parties, since the Breach; with General Observations upon the whole: And, an APPENDIX, in ANSWER to a late Pamphlet, Entituled, *A Seasonable Warning,* offer'd *by some Subscribing Ministers in the North, to their Congregations, &c.*

By the Ministers of the Presbytery of *ANTRIM,* in the North of *IRELAND.*

BELFAST:

Printed by JAMES BLOW, and are to be Sold at his Shop, *Anno Dom.* M. DCC. XXVII.

UNIVERSITY LIBRARY BELFAST

The intimacy of early eighteenth-century Belfast is clear from the printer's colophon on this 1727 work, *A Narrative of the Proceedings of Seven General Synods …*, printed in Belfast. It simply says that the work can be purchased at John Blow's shop, assuming that buyers would know that the shop was in Bridge Street.

Reproduced with kind permission from Queen's University, Belfast, Special Collections.

very large ships of over 100 tons, normally bound for the transatlantic trade, especially Virginia, tended to prefer the spring and autumn for their ventures. However, the quay did not grind to a halt during winter. There was a steady stream of smaller ships on shorter journeys from Glasgow or Irvine in Scotland and the ports of north-west England, as well as the coastal trade north to Ballycastle and south to Dublin.[14] All this inevitably gave a particular rhythm to Belfast's business life, speeding it up and slowing it down at particular points in the year. Indeed it may be no coincidence that marriages in the Third Belfast Presbyterian church for the 1740s were most frequently celebrated between October and April, the period when commercial life as measured by shipping movements was at its slowest, and the inhabitants of the town had time to engage in other activities.[15]

The goods offloaded at the quays were circulated through the marketplace. The earliest marketplace seems to have been on Bridge Street and by the late 1630s at least some of the stalls there had become permanent features, well on their way to becoming shops. However, after 1660 that site was abandoned. The building of a new market house opposite the castle determined where trade was conducted and a new marketplace was created in what is now Corn Market, although on a busy market day business regularly spilled out into most of the main streets of the town. As the old marketplace fell out of use, its triangular shape was filled in to create the line of Bridge Street, but the original shape is detectable in the pattern of the building plots in this area. In this marketplace the goods from the surrounding countryside were bought and sold by merchants. The influence of the Belfast merchants extended well into the Lagan valley, where they purchased butter for export, and also into County Down. The development of the Lagan valley and the expansion of Belfast in the late seventeenth century were closely connected processes. The completion around 1685 of the Long Bridge, which linked Belfast to County Down, certainly opened up the town's southern hinterland. One list of 200 debtors in a Belfast merchant's will of 1722 includes individuals located in Dublin, Cork, Liverpool and Fife, as well as evidence of more local trading at Comber, Broughshane, Doagh and Bangor.[16] Luxuries such as tobacco or sugar, sold in the marketplace, made their way through packmen into east Ulster and the middling sort looked to Belfast for things they could not obtain in rural areas. The late seventeenth-century rector of Dunaghy in County Antrim, Andrew Rowan, sold butter in Belfast and bought sugar, chairs and a clock there, as well as having one of his sons apprenticed to a merchant in the town.[17] Belfast by 1750 appeared to be a prosperous town. That prosperity was hard won, with periods of economic boom in the early and late seventeenth century being balanced by slumps in the middle of the century and at the beginning of the eighteenth century. By 1750 recovery was again under way. Through these vicissitudes the town had acquired not just a physical fabric but a complex economic infrastructure based on its own trading requirements.

II

In contrast to the solidity of its physical fabric, the population of Belfast in the eighteenth century was highly mobile and fluid. It was a town of migrants. In its earliest phase the town was a new creation and hence had to draw its people from elsewhere. The 1611 commissioners, surveying the progress of settlement in Ulster, observed that there were 'many families of English, Scotch and some Manksmen' already living in the town.[18] Migration continued in pulses after the initial settling of the town. In the late 1640s it was said that some 800 Scots who were in the town had come with their wives and children 'to plant themselves there'.[19] After the wars of the 1640s the town witnessed a new influx of settlers and many of Belfast's major merchant families dated their arrival there to the 1650s. By the early eighteenth century such large-scale migration from Scotland or northern England was a thing of the past. There were still trading contacts between Glasgow and Belfast and this undoubtedly promoted some movement and intermarriage between the inhabitants of both towns.[20] In the longer term, however, what was probably more significant in the growth of the population was not immigration but rather migration into the town from the surrounding countryside. The first Church of Ireland register from the 1740s and 1750s suggests that, while baptisms often outstripped burials, it was not by much.[21] The heavily polluted urban environment did not promote health and the threat of disease was an ever-present reality. The corporation complained in 1663 that the dumping of butchers' waste in the town gave rise to 'stink and evil and infectious smell (that if not timely prevented) will by all likelihood bring some ruinous and pestilent disease amongst the inhabitants' of the town.[22] Belfast, like most other substantial towns, stank. In the seventeenth century the corporation repeatedly demanded that streets be swept and that butchers refrain from dumping offal and blood in the streets and in the Farset, since such actions polluted the fragile water supply. All this had little success. As late as 1754 the Belfast merchant John Black was still urging the sovereign of the town to 'recommend the removal of all public nuisances as much as possible, slaughter houses etc. towards the shore and the frequent cleaning of streets from rubbish and dunghills before the doors' but it was not until the 1760s that clauses requiring this were introduced into leases.[23] To maintain population growth in this context the town was reliant on migration from the surrounding countryside. The evidence of the early eighteenth-century freemen's rolls, which sometimes mention the origins of freemen, suggest that they were drawn from all over the province of Ulster with occasional freemen being admitted from Drogheda.

This highly mobile population frightened many contemporaries. Mobile people carried disease and their lack of local roots meant that they were difficult to control. As early as 1620 the corporation decreed that no one in the town was to take subtenants or lodgers into their house without permission of the sovereign on pain of a fine, and these rules were repeated in the 1660s. Again in the 1680s further stringent rules were established to remove beggars from the town.[24] Yet many did take lodgers into their homes, thereby providing accommodation for those recently arrived in the town. When in 1726 the Third Belfast Presbyterian congregation conducted a census of those living within its area of influence, they grouped individuals together in what appear to be households. Many are simply listings of husband and wife (with the same surname) and children but in some cases there are what appear to be lodgers in the house. The Hanna household on the south side of High Street, for instance, comprised a husband and wife who were communicants, two children who were not communicants by virtue of their age, and two women, Elizabeth McClure and Isobel Irvine, who were not communicants and were probably lodgers in the house. Again the Medlton household in George's Lane had husband, wife and four children with two other men, both communicants, who were presumably lodgers. Such households were common in eighteenth-century Belfast, reflecting the substantial immigrant body within the population, some linked to churches while others were more loosely connected to mainstream society.[25]

Migrants adapted to Belfast life slowly. Some married and settled there or brought their families with them. The tailor Thomas Lightfoot probably came to Belfast shortly before he was admitted to freedom in 1650. He almost certainly brought his family with him, since by the end of the 1650s he had taken his son-in-law on as an apprentice and he, in turn, became free in 1666. Lightfoot rose in the world. He was a member of the grand jury of the town in 1667 and was one of the senior tailors in 1673.[26] Others were more reluctant to sever their connections with their place of origin. The 1643 will of the apparently well-established Belfast merchant Robert Nevin included legacies to a large number of his friends from Ayr, his home town, and he appointed two men from the same town as his executors, suggesting that connections were still strong.[27] The equally well-established merchant George Macartney showed a reluctance to cut his Scottish connections. In his will of 1691 he instructed that lands in Kirkudbright should pass to his son who was not to sell them, they 'having belonged for many generations last past to my ancestors of my name'.[28] Loose ties with the town and the high mobility associated with mercantile capital meant that the merchant elite could be very unstable, as men who made money in Belfast sought advancement elsewhere. In some cases they looked to other ports for trading advantages and a number of members of Belfast merchant families were part of a migration from Ulster to Carlingford in the early eighteenth century.[29] When the merchant John Black compiled a history of his family in the early eighteenth century he recorded that his sons had married in such diverse places as Edinburgh, Bordeaux and the Isle of Man as well as at home in Belfast, while two other sons were in Dublin and Bordeaux.[30] Others looked for land outside the town. Thomas Knox, for instance, resigned as burgess of Belfast in 1697 to move to his newly acquired estate at Dungannon and Edward Brice acquired a substantial estate at Kilroot in 1718. Others saw opportunities further afield. Hugh Eccles was born in Belfast and became a burgess there in 1688. Within a decade he had acquired an estate in Wicklow and was high sheriff of the county and MP for Carysfort in 1698, and a freeman of Dublin the following year. Another merchant, John Anderson, held land in Kildare and property in Dublin at his death in 1706.[31] On the other hand, residence in the town for more than one generation brought closer connections. In 1690 Thomas Theaker, who was Chichester's agent in the town in the 1640s, expressed the wish in his will that he should be buried 'in Belfast church among my ancestors and children', and later, in the 1750s, a Belfast merchant wandering in the graveyard attached to the parish church in High Street spoke of 'taking a walk among our ancestors' tombs and inscriptions'.[32]

Robert Leathes

In the late seventeenth century a second generation of Belfast settlers emerged: men who had spent so much of their lives there that they thought of the place as home and worked actively for the development of the town rather than seeing themselves as passing merchants. The Leathes family is a good example of this trend. Originally from Cumberland, William Leathes was a merchant who had become a burgess of Belfast in 1642 and was sovereign in 1645–46, 1657–58 and 1659–60. In 1657 his son, Robert, became a freeman and in 1669 followed his father and brother as a burgess. In the 1640s he served, like his brother John, as a royalist officer (and is shown in armour in a contemporary sketch), but stayed in the town during the 1650s and accommodated himself to the new regime, becoming town clerk in 1657. He worked for Lord Donegall after the Restoration as comptroller and later as seneschal of the manor of Belfast and served as constable of Belfast Castle in 1708 and 1717. He rose to the pinnacle of town life in 1687 as sovereign but the following year Leathes was removed by the new charter instituted by the Catholic James II. As a member of the Church of Ireland Leathes supported William III and was one of those who greeted the king when he arrived in Belfast in 1690. He became part of the new order and was sovereign again in 1696–97 and 1714–15. He contributed

Robert Leathes, from a contemporary drawing reproduced in R.M. Young (ed.), *The Town Book of the Corporation of Belfast 1613–1816* (Belfast, 1892).

significantly to the economic life of the town and was partly responsible, with George Macartney, for the installation of a piped water supply in the late seventeenth century. He was also involved in establishing the early eighteenth-century pottery near Hill Street which was later managed by four Belfast merchants. It survived to the mid-1720s and was significant in establishing industrial activity in a town that was mainly a trading centre. Leathes died in 1723 leaving a daughter, Mildred.

In addition to those moving into the town seeking opportunities there was a significant group who were professional migrants. Clergy of all denominations, for instance, moved into the town from elsewhere. Clergy of the Church of Ireland parish of Shankill, which included Belfast, came from a wide geographical area. Among the six vicars who served the cure from 1660 to 1750 three were born in England, one in Armagh and one in Dublin. All had seen something of a wider world since they were educated in Trinity College, Dublin, but at least three stayed in Belfast until their deaths.[33] Presbyterian clergy had equally diverse backgrounds. Two of the first three ministers were from Scotland and the other from England. The Scottish tradition remained powerful in selecting minsters for Belfast and between 1660 and 1750 the three who served the congregation in the town who were not from Scotland were all educated there.[34] The officials of the Dublin administration also came from outside the town. The importance of Belfast as a port meant that a customs administration needed to be maintained there. In the 1680s, for instance, there was a customs establishment of about twenty men based in Belfast.[35] Such men were rarely local (although the two collectors in the early eighteenth century were from the Belfast family of Macartney). Many were in fact English, and to prevent collusion with local merchants all officials were regularly rotated within Ireland, so that the Belfast cadre usually had wide experience of customs work in places as diverse as Dublin, Cork and Galway.[36] Whatever their origins, moreover, these Belfast-based officials had to engage in a continuous correspondence with the Revenue Board in Dublin about the application of revenue law to local circumstances. Again the army, based in the barracks, were posted from elsewhere in Ireland. Two companies of foot had been stationed in Belfast since the late seventeenth century and there is evidence of a barracks in Castle Street since at least 1685. A new barracks was built in Barrack Street at the beginning of the eighteenth century and extensively repaired in 1739.[37] Soldiers may have settled in the town for long periods of time and often put down roots there. Some, for instance, married locally and had families. The number of children who were offspring of soldiers recorded as baptized in the first Church of Ireland parish register for the town from 1745 to 1761 averaged three a year but varied from ten in 1749 to eight in 1760 and one in 1752, 1758, 1759 and 1761.[38] At least three soldiers can be identified in the Presbyterian marriage registers from the 1740s as marrying local women.[39]

There were other, more mobile, populations, most of whom are difficult to detect in the surviving evidence because of their transient nature. In the early seventeenth century many hoping to settle in Ulster landed in Belfast. One list of travellers from Chester in 1632–33 named 44 individuals bound for Belfast, yet none of these people appear as residents of the town in the census lists for 1640.[40] Again, seamen moved through the port of Belfast on a very regular basis and stayed long enough to assemble new cargoes. Some sailors, in the navy as well as the merchant marine, became ill and died there and their wills reveal a network of land and relations at their homes in England.[41] Some examples might illustrate the importance of sailors in the transient population of Belfast. On 7 March 1683 the *James* of Belfast, a vessel of 30 tons under the command of her master, James Glascoe, arrived from Ostend carrying hops. How long she stayed in port is not known, but on 1 October she was back, this time carrying bales and chests from the Low Countries. Between this arrival and 13 November 1685 the *James* plied in and out of Belfast six times, arriving mainly from Dunkirk and Chester and carrying hops, flax, 'goods' and often ballast.[42] Again the *Gabriel* of Belfast, a larger ship of 50 tons, entered the port on six occasions between January 1683 and December 1686 from Bordeaux, Dunkirk, Norway, Ostend and Nantes, carrying wine, timber, brandy, hats and ballast as well a crew who entertained themselves in the town while the ship reloaded.[43] The voyages of the *Jane* of Belfast, under a Scots master, Hugh Bell, were less exotic. The *Jane* was a small ship of 20 tons that plied between Belfast and Liverpool, Scotland and Dublin carrying coal, wine and salt, docking in Belfast seven times between January 1683 and December 1685.[44] These ships might bring exotic goods but the contents of many holds were more familiar. More than half of the ships entering Belfast carried coal from Scotland and this undoubtedly served to ensure that residents of Belfast were well informed on Scottish affairs, while the sailors who crewed them, given the regularity of their visits, probably developed connections with Belfast.

One particularly volatile group in the population of Belfast was the poor. Poor men and women were often attracted to the town by the opportunities it offered, but were very vulnerable to the dangers that it might present. A case in point is provided by the ballad 'William Montgomery's last farewell', composed for its subject's execution in the town on 15 April 1738 and preserved in a Belfast-printed song book of 1769.[45] The 21 verses relate the story of Montgomery, a Presbyterian who had come to Belfast from County Londonderry aged 14 and eventually established himself as an alehouse keeper. Falling into debt, he became bankrupt but set up in business again. Driven by poverty he fell into bad company with smugglers who stayed at his inn while engaged in shipping horses and other stolen goods into Scotland. He

In the eighteenth century, when the citizens wanted to acknowledge contributions to the town, they presented individuals with pieces of silver. In 1761 they presented silver cups to the officers who had defended the town when the French pirate Thurot attacked Carrickfergus. In January 1756 the weavers of the town presented the former sovereign, Stewart Banks, with a silver bowl worth £20 made in Dublin, 'in grateful acknowledgement of his extraordinary care of the markets and vigilant and impartial administration'. According to the *Belfast News Letter* the ceremony had 'a very genteel appearance with drums beating and colours flying'. Banks, then aged 30, had been sovereign of the town, and hence clerk of the market, in that year but had resigned early to go to England 'on his own private affairs' and the bowl was presented on his return. The weavers' appreciation was probably linked to the operation of the new linen hall, built in 1754 on Donegall Street, but it may also be connected with the poor harvests of that year that had begun to affect the poor in Belfast. Banks had endeavoured to maintain order in the town and to provide some relief. Conditions degenerated the following year, leading to riots. He was also presented with a sword by the Belfast Volunteer company in 1757 on the occasion of his election as sovereign for 1757–58.

Photograph © National Museums Northern Ireland. Collection Ulster Museum. MMCK6.

was caught in their company and hanged for being implicated in their crime, which he denied.[46] The ballad is cast in the form of a moral tale of an innocent brought up in the fear of God who found that when he dealt lawfully 'the Lord so blest my store', a sentiment often echoed in Belfast wills of the early eighteenth century. Perhaps inevitably, he was corrupted by the avarice of town life and the last verses of the ballad protest the innocence of his wife and offer a confession of his sins, asking for God's mercy:

> Now come, sweet Lord, I humbly pray,
> and wash me in thy blood;
> Then shall my tongue eternally
> thy praises sing aloud.

The literary model for this ballad was the gallows speech or confession which found increasing popularity with printers in the early eighteenth century. Such moral tales of what might happen to the naive and poor in the town circulated in a number of ways, as is suggested by the gallows speech of James Dunbar of Carrickfergus who, in his final words, thanked God for 'those learned gentlemen, the clergy of the presbytery of the town of Belfast etc, who was pleased to remember me in their public service, joined with their congregations on Sunday last'.[47] It seems highly probable that such remembrances were accompanied by an exposition of the sort of moral lessons that the ballad of Montgomery contained.

The plight of those on the edge of society is perhaps shown most clearly in the harvest crisis of 1756–57. Poor harvests were exacerbated by speculation and hoarding in the grain markets of the town. Food riots erupted and some 200

Belfast men were armed to put down the riot. To formalize this situation the Belfast Association for Suppressing Riots was formed. Coercion was balanced by compassion and in addition to arresting of a number of ringleaders a poor relief scheme was set up to ameliorate the worst effects of food shortages. The numbers of poor relieved under the scheme rose from 496 in January 1757 to 635 by the end of May. The impact of the crisis on these marginal people is clear from the percentage of 'poor' noted in the burials in the parish register, which climbed from 16 per cent of burials in 1756 to 36 per cent in 1757 before falling to a more normal 22 per cent in 1758. Among the burials noted as 'poor', men formed a greater proportion than they did subsequently, suggesting that it was not widows or poor women who were most affected but men surviving at the edge of society by relying on casual work or begging. With food shortages they slipped into the ranks of the destitute and were sufficiently weakened to become vulnerable both to hunger and to diseases that, in other circumstances, they might well have survived.[48]

One of the most important ways of dealing with the urban poor was the institution of schemes for their relief. Dealing with the poor was perceived as essentially a religious as well as a civic duty. In common with many other places the inhabitants of Belfast regarded their worldly wealth as the result, not only of their own endeavours, but of the outworking of God's providence that had placed them in their position in the social order. David Crawford, a 'gentleman' of Belfast, opened his 1734 will by referring to 'that worldly estate wherewith it hath pleased God to enrich me' and the wealthy merchant George Macartney acknowledged his success as 'it hath pleased Almighty God in his great goodness to lend unto and bestow upon me a considerable clear personal wealth'. Such attitudes were not the sole prerogative of the elite. Michael Biggar, a Belfast smith, began his will in 1718 by referring to 'such worldly estate wherewith it hath pleased God to bless me in this life', and the inn holder John Biggar in 1721 acknowledged the 'worldly substance' which 'it has pleased the Lord to bless me with'.[49] Material wealth thus brought the responsibility and the religious duty of sharing one's resources with the less fortunate, and this concern, coupled with the civic desire to maintain social order, meant that many made provision for the poor of the town. When the sovereign William Leathes died in office in 1660 he was praised as a just and upright man who was 'a support to the needy fatherless and widows'.[50] Such provision was often made in wills. At the pinnacle of the social order, Lord Donegall left £200 to the poor of the parish of Belfast in 1674 and others followed suit. In 1680 a board was erected, probably in the parish church, listing a number of donors who had left such bequests.[51]

Personal provision was a random activity and some tried to institutionalize these arrangements, often to their own advantage. Most obviously, churches became involved in poor relief as organizers of charity and as vehicles for its distribution. Thus John Biggar bequeathed in his 1721 will 'to the poor of the parish church of Belfast the sum of 20 shillings ster[ling] to be paid to such of them as Rev Mr Fletcher shall think most fit', while the richer burgess Thomas Waring allocated £40 for the poor.[52] Again in 1725 the Presbyterian merchant John Eccles left £10 to 'the poor of Mr Kirkpatrick's congregation of Belfast […] to be distributed by the elders of each congregation'.[53] The absence of parochial records for early Belfast means that little can be said about the effectiveness or confessional bias of this sort of relief. However, some evidence for its working may be contained in the corporation records. There are a number of acknowledgements in the town book for money received from the churchwardens by the sovereign for the relief of the poor but nothing is said about its distribution. The origins of this 'poor money' lay in a bequest of £40 to the poor of the town by a former sovereign, Edward Holmes, in 1631. The corporation had little income of its own, since the town was not provided with lands to generate income by the Chichesters, and they seized the opportunity to manage the money left to the poor of the town in their own interest. The corporation apparently used the money as working capital, lending it at interest and using the income for the original intention of the bequest. The original sum was added to over time, as in 1691, when George Macartney left £40 for the use of 'poor old decayed inhabitants of the town of Belfast', the interest on which was to be distributed half yearly among them. The former Belfast burgess Thomas Knox, who had moved to Dungannon, left £20 to the poor of the town where he had prospered to be used as part of this fund.[54] While the scheme was never completely satisfactory, there being problems with the security of the capital, it survived into the eighteenth century and presumably relieved the parish of the need to levy a cess for the poor.[55] Again the town sometimes shouldered the burden of caring for orphans and finding them apprenticeships, a function usually carried out in other places by the parish.[56]

In the case of the Presbyterian church a little more evidence is available. In the early eighteenth century the First Presbyterian congregation maintained 12 poor boys in the school attached to the church.[57] Further evidence of the involvement of the Presbyterian church in charitable work is available in the form of an account book for 1733–39 for the Third Presbyterian congregation, which allows some insight into the workings of charity.[58] The congregation maintained a number of women, between thirty and forty, whose names appear in roughly alphabetical order in every poor account, paying them 6d a month in the same way that many Church of Ireland parishes maintained groups of poor on a regular basis. There were also ad hoc payments to individuals to meet immediate need, with sums ranging from 6d to 1s to 'a person in distress', 'a person in want' or 'a stranger'. In addition, schooling the child of a widow might be paid for and coffins were also provided for the burial of the poor. At times of crisis, church and community might cooperate to provide relief for the poor. In the aftermath of the demographic crisis of 1750–51, indicated by a surge of burials in the parish register, a group of men in the town established a lottery to raise money for the building of a poor house and a hospital as well as a new church. The scheme failed as a result of a bank fraud and was discontinued in 1753 but it did lay the foundations for the establishment of the Belfast Charitable Society, which was responsible for the erection of the Poor House in 1761.[59] Again during the bad winter of 1755 plays were staged in the town as benefits for the poor.[60]

Thus by the 1750s the structure of Belfast's population was complex, ranging from the Donegall family at the social apex of the town through the wealthy merchant middling sort to the poor at the base of the social order. That population was assembled mainly through waves of migration, which inevitably meant that there were always some urban dwellers whose contacts with the town were recent and poorly formed, while there were others who had lived there for some time. The problem that contemporaries faced was to weld these individuals into a society that had a shared sense of itself as belonging to Belfast and common ideas about what the town was and how it could be shaped. This was not a theoretical exercise but a matter of practical survival. Merchants, for example, relied on friendships and bonds of trust to allow them to transact business. The notebook kept by the Belfast merchant John Black in the 1730s and 1740s contains not only accounts and memoranda but also a list of his trading contacts and how they were known to him, presumably indicating how trustworthy they were. Thus Edmund Field was 'Capt Williston's friend', William Black was 'brother in law of Alex Hume' and Sam Killell was 'late mayor, J.D's schoolfellow'. On the other hand one did not, presumably, do business with the 'cooper who failed' in Plymouth or the man described as 'formerly a knavish trick[ster] for hardware'.[61] Again, those two dozen or more Belfast merchants who issued tokens for coinage in the 1650s and 1660s relied on their own social position to make these acceptable.[62]

The process that created a sense of society and built Belfast in the minds of its inhabitants was what the first landlord of the town, Arthur Chichester, described in another context as 'a commencement or continual suppeditacion [exchange] of benefits mutually received and done between men'.[63] Social interaction was therefore crucial to creating networks along which personal trade, sociability and reputation could flow and these, in turn, created a corporate image of the town that reinforced personal images of prosperity and well-being. Merchants were prepared to invest in Belfast, such as Robert Leathes' and George Macartney's establishment of a water supply in 1678, for practical as well as financial reasons, since a prosperous-looking town encouraged trade in the way that a rundown one did not.

The framework within which the town of Belfast could begin to articulate a corporate identity for itself was the legal structures for the government of

This portrait of Thomas Gregg and his family c.1765, attributed to Strickland Lowry, shows how migrants could establish large and very wealthy dynasties in Belfast. Thomas Gregg's father, John, had come to Belfast from Scotland and was sworn free in 1723. Thomas married Elizabeth, the daughter of the Belfast merchant Samuel Hyde. Of the three sons standing to his left, two, Thomas and Samuel, later went to England while the youngest, Cunningham, remained as a merchant in Belfast. The family's evident wealth, demonstrated in their clothing and in the books, musical instruments and toys for the children, was made in trade, mainly with North America, by Gregg and his partner Waddell Cunningham, and the painting of the ship on the wall is a reminder of that connection.

Courtesy of Eileen Black.

the town. These were not invisible, theoretical constructs but could be given a tangible and visible form. Most obviously there was the charter granted in 1613, primarily to allow the town to send representatives to parliament. The document was not impressive in appearance. It contained none of the illumination of initial letters or the decoration that the contemporary charters for larger towns such as Dublin or Derry had. Chichester was unwilling to pay for such fripperies, presumably seeing the charter as a working document rather than an item for display. The contents of the charter did not seem to offer much to the urban inhabitants since it located power firmly in the hands of the Chichester family. In line with charters granted to other towns at the same date it established a corporation comprising a sovereign and 12 burgesses. The charter allowed Chichester to nominate the first sovereign and burgesses and provided that replacement burgesses would be selected by the existing group. Since the burgesses held office for life, or until they left the town, a small group could dominate the town for long periods. In the late seventeenth and early eighteenth centuries the average term served by a burgess was almost twenty years although this could range from one year to the remarkable fifty-five years during which George Macartney occupied the position. A sovereign was to be elected annually from within the burgesses and this election was to be confirmed by the landlord of the town. Long-serving burgesses meant that many men had multiple periods as sovereign, seven in the case of one man and five in the case of another.[64] The reasons for such arrangements are clear: an attempt to control the results of parliamentary elections. According to the charter the electorate was composed of the sovereign and the burgesses but, probably as a result of the disturbances of the 1640s, the electorate was

Iacobus ... Anglie Scotie Francie et Hibernie Rex fidei Defensor &c ... **Omnibus** ...

widened to include the freemen. After 1715 the desire for control led to the original constitution being restored and freemen excluded.[65] Given the small size of the town and the lack of a substantial middling group of men, in 1613 Chichester could not find suitable burgesses from within the town. Of the original burgesses, two, Waterhouse Crimble and Thomas Hibbots, were taken from Chichester's other town of Carrickfergus; another two, Humphry Norton and Moses Hill, were tenants on his estate; two more, Fulke Conway and Cary Hart, had served as army captains under Chichester; and one, John Vesey (the first sovereign) was Chichester's agent in Belfast. Since burgesses could occupy their positions for long periods the process of creating a local elite was a slow one. The last of the original burgesses lived until 1658, when he was replaced by George Macartney.

Local politics in Belfast thus emerged slowly. In the 1640s the radical politics of the Scottish Covenanters, who seized Belfast in 1644, was made manifest in the 'commonality' becoming involved in decision making in the town to a much greater extent than hitherto. Equally, there were disputes about the sovereign's authority in the town that a later commentator ascribed to the fact that in 1646 the mayor, Thomas Hannington, held his courts in the town without mentioning the king's name. Whatever the reason, Hannington was abused in the streets 'with scandalous words' and was also beaten by one merchant.[66] The years after 1660 saw the emergence of a substantial mercantile community who were prepared to engage with the problems of running the town as well as seeking public position to underpin their upward social mobility, in the same way as some sought land to confirm their new status. The result, perhaps inevitably, was arguments over the terms of the charter. Ten proposals for reform were advanced by the corporation in 1671 but nothing was done.[67] At the same time the charter came to represent something of the independence of the town and most were reluctant to see it undermined. When the Catholic king James II recalled the charter and granted a new one in October 1688 there was resentment, despite the fact that the new charter broadened the confessional range and power base of the town, effectively breaking the power of the Donegalls. The early eighteenth-century loyalist vicar of Belfast, William Tisdall, could think of no worse a condemnation of the Jacobites of the 1680s than that they 'made interest to have the old charter of that town broken and a new one granted'.[68] The defeat of James was marked in Belfast by the town clerk who copied the charter of 1613 into the town book to demonstrate that the old order had returned.

These structures of town government were made visible on a regular basis. By 1639 the corporation had acquired some of the public trappings of office. A seal was bought and a town hall fitted out, probably with the royal arms in a prominent position, and a mace was obtained. A second surviving mace was acquired in the 1690s.[69] The maces were the visible signs of the corporate

Previous spread: The charter of Belfast, granted on 27 April 1613, established the town as a corporate body with powers to hold courts and to elect a sovereign and burgesses for the government of the town, though without compromising the control of the landlord. As such it provided a framework for the management of the town's affairs that was to endure for more than two centuries. While the charter gave the landlord the power to appoint the corporation, the relationship between the landlord and the townspeople was generally good, with the Chichester family protecting the town's interests and being less rigorous in their dealings with Presbyterians than the law required. For a document of such importance its appearance is rather unprepossessing. Other charters granted to towns about the same time are more elaborately decorated but in this case the landlord clearly decided that such an investment in an illuminated document was not worthwhile for what was little more than a village.

Reproduced with the kind permission of Belfast City Council. Photograph © Bryan Rutledge.

This picture of Stewart Banks, painted between 1760 and 1765 and attributed to Strickland Lowry, is the earliest surviving formal portrait of a sovereign of Belfast. He was the son of Thomas Banks, a servant of Lord Donegall, who appointed him burgess of Belfast and constable of the castle in December 1711 and re-appointed him to both positions in 1723. In May 1746 Stewart succeeded his father as a burgess of Belfast. The shortage of suitably qualified people to hold office in the town meant that he was sovereign in 1755, 1758, 1762, 1766 and 1771. He supported the Donegall interest in the town and was commander of the larger of the two Volunteer companies that appeared in 1760 when it was thought Belfast might be invaded by the French. He was also instrumental in maintaining law and order during the agrarian disturbances of the Hearts of Steel in 1770. However, he may have had liberal leanings in politics, since during the later agitation for free trade and political reform he was a prominent member of the Belfast Company of Volunteers and was said to be a 'very good attender' at Volunteer meetings in 1778. He accumulated significant property in the town, especially in Castle Street, Barrack Street and in Lettice Lane. Banks died in 1802 aged 77.

© National Museums Northern Ireland. Collection Ulster Museum. BELUM.U206.

status of the town and hence were displayed on significant occasions, being carried before the sovereign and burgesses. One such occasion may have been the procession to church. As early as 1615 the corporation ordered that the burgesses and commoners accompany the sovereign to church and home again. Since most sovereigns lived in Waring Street and the parish church was on the opposite side of the Farset this would have involved a procession through the marketplace that would certainly have attracted some attention. Within the church building itself, the mayor and the burgesses had their own pews which marked them off from the freemen of the town.[70]

The beginning of the eighteenth century, however, saw a more dramatic clash between the power of the Donegalls and the emerging mercantile community in the town. This was a period of acute conflict at national level

The town mace, made together with the seal in 1639, was the symbol of Belfast's corporate identity and would have been carried before the mayor when he was on official business. When they were made, the mace and the seal cost £26, of which Henry le Squire, the constable of the castle and sovereign in 1635, 1636 and 1639, offered to contribute £6, although at the time of his death in 1643 he had still not paid the entire sum. It is likely that the town had acquired a second mace by 1659 since an account of the funeral of the sovereign, William Leathes, refers to 'two maces of the corporation' being carried in the procession.

Reproduced with the kind permission of Belfast City Council. Photograph © Bryan Rutledge.

between Anglican and Presbyterian interests, and an Act of 1704 required all holders of offices of profit or trust under the Crown to take Communion in the established church, the so-called 'sacramental test'. In 1707 an electoral conflict in the town led Lady Donegall to invoke this measure in order to exclude Presbyterians from the corporation, replacing them with members of the Church of Ireland.[71] Given the small numbers of wealthy Anglicans in the town, the corporation was emasculated and did little in the early eighteenth century except to return MPs at the Donegall family's direction.

While the processes of government, if not its appearance, involved an elite few, there were other places where the majority of the inhabitants of Belfast could mingle and forge a common sense of belonging. The most important of these was the church. Belfast before 1750 was mainly a Protestant town. According to the poll tax of 1660 'Irish', probably meaning Catholics, made up about a third of the town's population, but by 1708 it was claimed that there were no more than seven Catholics in the town. By 1757 the number had grown to 550, but this was a modest 6.5 per cent of Belfast's population. The Church of Ireland community was relatively small. In 1754 Archdeacon Pococke estimated it at 60 families, 'most of them of the lower rank'. This, to judge from the baptisms in the parish register, was probably an underestimate.[72] But Belfast in the late seventeenth and early eighteenth centuries was predominantly a Presbyterian town. By 1750 there were three Presbyterian congregations, all on the Rosemary Street site. According to a list of 'catechisable persons' produced by the Third Presbyterian congregation in 1726, there were some 1,313 individuals, not including children, in that congregation alone.[73] Presbyterianism emerged slowly in Belfast. In the early seventeenth century there was no sign of Presbyterian organization in the town and a congregation was established only in the later seventeenth century. In effect it was introduced by the Scottish army who occupied the town in 1644 and insisted that the

Solemn League and Covenant was taken by the inhabitants. The incident was an isolated one and throughout the 1650s Presbyterianism failed to make any headway in the town. It was the 1670s before a stable meeting was established there. While the Donegall family were well disposed to godly Presbyterianism, and indeed had Presbyterian chaplains in the late seventeenth century, it was politic to move slowly to avoid conflict.[74] In the 1670s, for instance, Lady Donegall objected to the removal of one Presbyterian minister from Belfast, leading to a resulting flurry of meetings between the Antrim meeting and Lord Donegall to resolve the situation.[75]

Attending church was not simply a religious event. It involved being identified with a particular social group with its own network of contacts and rights. The vicar of Belfast, William Tisdall, alleged in 1712 that Presbyterians would take only their own adherents as apprentices. This should not be overstressed, and religious differences did not prevent merchants cooperating when there was a profit to be made.[76] The young James Traill of Killileagh in County Down, a pupil in the Presbyterian school in Belfast at the beginning of the eighteenth century, boarding in the minister's house, described how he always attended church on Sunday 'either in the one church [Church of Ireland] or the other [Presbyterian] which were pretty much alike for me for I never enquired into the causes of their different sentiments with respect to the worship of God'.[77] However, most people in the town tended to associate themselves with the Church of Ireland or the Presbyterian churches, the latter attracting the majority.

Religion touched the inhabitants of Belfast at a range of points in the life cycle. This much is clear in the rites that the churches provided to mark the main stages of life. The most basic social unit of early modern Belfast was the family: an institution created by marriage that was solemnized in a church. It is difficult to measure the impact of this fully since the Church of Ireland registers appear to under-record marriage dramatically and the Presbyterian marriage records are available for only short runs. However, one way of discovering the strength of family connections may be in measuring illegitimacy rates. Presbyterian baptismal registers record no illegitimacies over this period but this was probably as much a matter of social discipline in refusing to baptize such children as an indication of extra-marital fertility. However, in the survey of the congregation of Third Belfast Presbyterian church in the 1730s all families had a father and mother listed. In the Church of Ireland registers for the 1740s the number of illegitimacies was small, never rising above four per annum with an average of two a year, though at least some of these were the product of stable, if irregular, unions.[78] Marriage, it seems, was the basis of social order for most.

At the other end of life, death again brought people into contact with churches. Preambles to wills are rather formulaic and the small number that survive for Belfast residents make it dangerous to attempt generalizations.

However, there are enough, with enough variety among them, to suggest that common ideas about the religious meaning of life and death were being put into their own words by testators. Most expressed the 'uncertainty of things temporal' and committed their souls to God 'nothing doubting but resurrection' while a few expressed contrition for their sins and begged forgiveness.[79] In the meantime their bodies were committed to the parish graveyard. Since, in law, all residents of the town were members of the established church, regardless of their own confessional preference, they had the right to be buried in the parochial graveyard and their burial was entered in the Church of Ireland register. As a result the Presbyterians did not keep burial registers. It was not until 1797 that an alternative graveyard became available with the opening of the New Burial Ground at the Poor House. Belfast had two parochial graveyards, one at the medieval church at Shankill and one attached to the church in the town. Whether the interments in each place were divided socially or by confessional allegiance is not clear.

Between these poles of birth and death the Belfast churches provided places for their members to worship and meet each other. Most obviously those events were at the regular services of worship offered by each denomination. Lack of evidence means that little can be said about the Church of Ireland experience of religion but the records kept by the three Presbyterian churches allow some reconstruction of that aspect of social life. Third Belfast, for instance, according to a note in the preaching register, offered services on Sunday morning and evening, a Thursday lecture and occasionally a sermon on Saturday.[80] Not all were equal at such events. Pews in the church were owned by those who occupied them and came in three sizes, presumably reflecting the standing of the occupants.[81] The poor had limited accommodation, although one Belfast merchant, James Anderson, in his 1706 will, left £20 towards the planned construction of the new meeting house to provide for 'the poorer sort' in the church.[82] More dramatic fare than these preaching services was available in the form of the Communion service. In the conservative Presbyterian congregation of Third Belfast in the early eighteenth century this happened twice a year, usually in February and August. This urban Communion service was a congregational event, unlike in the rural world where many local congregations joined to ensure that the celebration of the sacrament was on a grand scale. Admission was not straightforward and a Communion token, distributed by Elders, was required before one could be admitted to the sacrament.

A list of 'young communicants' for Third Belfast suggests that 15 was the youngest that one might normally be admitted (although there were a few younger communicants). Most new communicants were in their early twenties and it may be that marriage and forming a household prompted them into taking this step. Equally there were some in their late twenties and early thirties (and exceptionally one man of 49). This may suggest either that a number of people were indifferent to the Communion service or, and more likely, that the sacrament was not simply another rite but one that was entered cautiously, especially given the need to be a worthy communicant and not incur divine displeasure by making light of the ritual. Individuals may have pondered the need for the sacrament for some years before action was taken.[83] Lists of 'catechisable persons' from 1726, which were probably drawn up by Elders to ensure that communicants knew their catechism before they were issued with their token, indicate that probably only half of the members of Third Belfast congregation were communicants, again probably reflecting the gravity surrounding participation in the sacrament.[84] The account book of that congregation indicates that the Communion service lasted for three days beginning with a fast day on Saturday, the Communion service on a Sunday and a day of thanksgiving on Monday, although by the 1730s the thanksgiving seems to have been abandoned.[85] Several sermons were preached on each of the days both by visiting ministers and by the congregation's own minister. One Belfast merchant, Daniel Mussenden, kept notes during these sermons in 1704, presumably so that he could refresh his memory afterwards.[86] For some, this experience was a dramatic and spiritually charged one. The Belfast merchant James Rainey expressed a sense of union with God and a renewal of the Covenant after his Communion in the town in 1704.[87] Others, however, might be more akin to those whom the Revd Thomas Orr reproved at the 1704 Belfast Communion, telling them that 'you have been spectators here all this time' with little engagement in the emotion of the event.[88] Such religious events provided a focus for women, who are usually invisible in the records of the early modern town, except in wills and occasional property deeds. According to a list of communicants drawn up by the Third Belfast congregation in 1726, more than twice as many women as men were communicants in this church, pointing to the importance of churches and their worshipping life for urban women.[89]

Jennett Macartney

Women appear infrequently in early modern Belfast records and the glimpses of them are usually fleeting and poorly focused. Even in death the early eighteenth-century funeral register of the First Belfast Presbyterian church recorded women as 'wife of …' rather than by their own name. This was an easy way of locating women socially, measuring them by their husband's economic and social achievements rather than by their own. Men were the public face of the household and it is often only when that household changed that women appear in the records most clearly as widows. Jennett Macartney was one such woman. She was the wife of

'Brown' George Macartney, a Presbyterian merchant and shipowner of Belfast. When he died in 1722 he presumably made provision for his widow in his will as was normal with Belfast merchants. This included providing her with somewhere to live, furniture and plate for her house and enough to buy food and clothes, and possibly to speculate with. In all this Jennett was fortunate. Those with a less well-off background sometimes fell into poverty and, if lucky, were maintained by a church charity. By 1724, however, she was too infirm to live alone and moved to the house of her third son, the merchant John Macartney. In November 1724 an agreement was drawn up allowing Jennett to move into John's house. The document, formally registered in the Irish Registry of Deeds, allows us a brief insight into Jennett's lifestyle.[1] She was to have her own bedroom and bring her own furniture, which could be sold after her death, but the silver and gold plate that she had inherited from her husband would revert to John. Her son would supply her with 'sufficient meat, drink and washing, fire and candle light, tea coffee and sugar' for her lifetime. He would also pay any debts already incurred by her at the time of the agreement. John was to provide her with an income of £40 a year, paid quarterly, to be spent as she saw fit. In return Jennett surrendered to John all the property she had inherited from her husband two years earlier, as well as a field near Belfast that she had bought herself. Jennett clearly had a privileged and secure widowhood and when John died in 1729 his will stipulated that the agreement be continued and charged on his estate. Jennett died the following year and was buried in October 1730.

1   Registry of Deeds, Dublin, 44/16/27343.

Religion went further than simply providing people with a place to meet on Sunday and a way of shaping families through its rites of baptism, marriage and burial. The church also moulded ideas through the provision of schools in which the standards of behaviour expected of a resident of the town could be inculcated and contacts made among pupils that might well be of benefit in the future. Some certainly valued education highly. Hugh Rainey of Magherafelt, brother of the Belfast merchant William Rainey, related in his will how God had blessed him and in return he proposed to 'devote a considerable part of my sustenance to some pious uses', by which he meant the establishment of a school.[90] Before the middle of the eighteenth century Belfast had a small number of formal schools. A parish school certainly existed in the 1640s and 1650s and a charity school operated in the town in the 1720s under the auspices of the Church of Ireland.[91] In addition there were probably a number of informal, local schools that taught basic literacy skills necessary to live in the world of trade, but these have left little trace in the surviving evidence. Glasgow merchants exported large quantities of 'small books' to the town, possibly for the purpose of teaching reading.[92]

Undoubtedly the most prestigious of the formal schools was the earl of Donegall's school, established by 1666 and associated both topographically and in ethos with the Church of Ireland.[93] It educated the sons of the well-off for entry to university. In the late eighteenth century many of them went to the University of Glasgow, though in the early part of the century this was less common. The matriculation registers of Glasgow do not record the origins of students before 1728, but between that date and 1750 only nine students with fathers in Belfast are recorded as matriculating.[94] More common was Trinity College, Dublin, and from the matriculation registers of the university there is some evidence of how it worked.[95] Numbers from the Donegall school who attended Trinity were relatively small, probably not more than twenty in the years from 1666 to 1750, although the later Trinity registers are defective in recording students' early education. In the main this reflects the small Church of Ireland mercantile and gentry community in Belfast. Others from the town who matriculated into Trinity were educated elsewhere, at grammar schools in Lisburn, Dundalk, Armagh and, in one case, Eton. However, the Belfast school also pulled in students born elsewhere who subsequently went on to Trinity, including natives of Dublin, Bangor, Carrickfergus, Coleraine, Lifford, Sligo, Drogheda, Portaferry, as well as of various places in Antrim and Down. One student was born in Whitehaven in Cumbria, reflecting the trading ties between Belfast and north-western England. While nothing has survived to reveal the curriculum it seems that this school is identical with the Latin school which is mentioned in the early eighteenth century, which would imply the concentration on the classics that a university education would presuppose.[96]

By the 1690s the Presbyterians had also established a school attached to their church. It was attended by James Traill of Killileagh who described some of his experiences there in his autobiography.[97] According to Traill there were a great number of 'students of divinity' in the school and it was presumably used mainly as a preparation for university education in Scotland and ordination in the Irish Presbyterian church. Traill certainly described much 'going and coming from Scotland' in the school. However, it is clear that it was not rigidly confessional. Traill himself went to Trinity College, Dublin, and four students named on the Trinity matriculation list of the early eighteenth century were taught in Belfast by a Mr Collingwood, whom Traill named as the master in the Presbyterian school. However, given the number of 'students of divinity', the theological cast of the school must have been clear. This dominance of divinity in the curriculum meant that some subjects were clearly left to an individual student's own devices. Traill, for instance, attended a French master in Belfast for one hour a day, presumably to improve his language skills.

Religion was also a powerful force in shaping the intellectual life of early modern Belfast. Questions of belief, ecclesiastical organization and the related issue of loyalty to the monarch were rarely far from the minds of those who thought about the wider context of their lives. In particular they encountered a range of views in the books that were a common feature of the town from the later seventeenth century. The evidence of the customs returns from the 1690s, before the introduction of a printer to Belfast, suggests that the town received the largest quantity of books of any Ulster port and that the bulk of those came from Scotland.[98] The Scottish port books provide a little detail of what these were. In 1681 one Glasgow ship bound for Belfast had four gross of catechisms and another had Bibles. In 1685 ships destined for Belfast included one with 'one box and one cask of psalm books' and ten Bibles, and others had cargoes of Bibles, catechisms and the occasional copy of the Confession of Faith that continued to be shipped into Belfast in the 1690s.[99] The introduction of printing did nothing to diminish the supply of religious works and indeed the establishment of a printer in Belfast in the early 1690s may well have been a Presbyterian initiative.[100] Certainly his first effort was in printing the Solemn League and Covenant, which was in such demand that the printer ran them off on a regular basis.[101] For the first twenty-five years of its existence the press produced almost nothing but religious works and before 1750 very little that was not religious.[102] Such books provoked debate and at the beginning of the eighteenth century a number of Presbyterian ministers established the Belfast Society at which they could read and debate the books they bought, each buying a different one and lending it to the others.[103]

Such reflection and discussion perhaps inevitably led to controversy and, given the fissile nature of Presbyterianism, to splits within the local community. The initial controversy was over the issue of subscription to the Westminster Confession, which some refused on the basis of freedom of conscience while others had theological difficulties with the doctrine of the Trinity. In 1720 Samuel Haliday refused to subscribe to the Confession on his installation to First Belfast.[104] Haliday was quickly joined by the minister of Second Belfast, James Kirkpatrick, while a body of the congregation seceded and formed the Third Belfast congregation in protest. Matters did not end there and as late as 1743 the Presbyterian philosopher Francis Hutcheson could write to Kirkpatrick 'I am extremely concerned for your division in Belfast.'[105]

Closely linked to the question of religious belief was that of political loyalty, particularly that of the Presbyterians, which was placed under increasing strain by the demands for conformity from the Dublin administration in the early eighteenth century. Books, subversive and otherwise, circulated in Belfast defending the respective rights of each group. Covenanting works such as the *Hind Let Loose* were imported into the town in the 1690s.[106] One copy of the works of the republican John Milton, owned by Lord Donegall, was circulating

Much of the printing in early eighteenth-century Belfast was of religious works. However, where religion touched on politics, as in *A Historical Essay upon the Loyalty of Presbyterians in Great Britain and Ireland* (1713), one ventured into dangerous territory, even when the sentiments being expressed were, as in this case, moderate. The work was a reply to an attack on the Presbyterians by the vicar of Belfast, William Tisdall. The title page here does not identify either an author or a printer for fear of repercussions. The author was James Kirkpatrick, minister of Second Belfast Presbyterian congregation, and the printer was James Blow whose shop was in Bridge Street. Kirkpatrick was a significant figure in the intellectual life of the town. Not only was he interested in theology and political thought, he was also a medical doctor who was engaged with science. In the 1730s he owned a microscope and wrote a tract, also published in Belfast, on the then current debate about the treatment of kidney stones.

Reproduced with kind permission from Queen's University, Belfast, Special Collections.

AN
HISTORICAL ESSAY
Upon the
LOYALTY
Of
PRESBYTERIANS

In *Great-Britain* and *Ireland* from the Reformation to this Present Year 1713.

WHEREIN

Their steady Adherence to the *Protestant Interest*, our happy *Civil Constitution*, the *Succession* of *Protestant Princes*, the just *Prerogatives* of the *CROWN*, and the *Liberties* of the *People* is demonstrated from Public *Records*, the best Approv'd *Histories*, the Confession of their *Adversaries*, and divers Valuable *Original Papers* well attested, and never before Published. And an *ANSWER* given to the Calumnies of their Accusers, and particularly to two late Pamphlets *viz.* 1. *A Sample of true Blue Presbyterian Loyalty* &c. 2. *The Conduct of the Dissenters in* Ireland &c.

In Three Parts.

With a *PREFATORY ADDRESS* to all her Majesty's Protestant Subjects, of all Persuasions, in *Great-Britain* and *Ireland*, against the *Pretender*, on behalf of the *PROTESTANT* Religion, the *QUEEN*, the House of *HANOVER*, and our *LIBERTIES*.

Printed in the Year MDCCXIII.

in Belfast in 1712 as he lent it to both the Church of Ireland incumbent and one local Presbyterian minister, John McBride. More dramatically, one woman, the wife of a Presbyterian Elder, was seen in the marketplace in 1713 with 'a whole apronful' of one subversive work 'in order, as it must be presumed, to place them in the proper hands'.[107] The Belfast press also produced its defence of the loyalty of Presbyterians to the Crown, and in 1713 the Revd James Kirkpatrick's defence of the Presbyterian position, *An historical Essay upon the Loyalty of Presbyterians in Great Britain and Ireland*, was printed in Belfast although the printer deemed it wise not to identify himself on the title page. The Presbyterian minister John Abernethy was more practical in his demonstrations of loyalty, preaching a sermon on the accession of George I that was subsequently printed in Belfast.

If religion was one important centre of sociability then business was another, as was the entertainment provided on the streets and in various venues. The Plantation Commissioners noted the presence of an inn in the town as early as 1611. At the beginning of the eighteenth century the funeral register of the First Presbyterian church in the town mentioned three inns: the Adam and Eve, the Sign of the Sun and the Eagle and Child.[108] Others can be identified by the 1730s including the George, the Highlandman on the quay and the King's Head in Church Lane where 'good entertainment and lodgings' were offered. The Highlandman could not only provide the facilities of an inn but also sold tobacco and home-distilled spirits.[109] Such conviviality was likely to get out of hand. In 1616 the corporation attempted to control who should sell alcohol in the town and to prohibit such sales at the time of Sunday worship.[110] Controls had limited effect and there were complaints about rowdy drinking and gaming in inns. In 1665 the corporation responded by trying to prevent such activities after 9 p.m., probably with little success.[111] Entertainment existed at home also. In 1682 one Glasgow merchant imported into Belfast 12 dozen 'storie books' and another ship seized in 1682 had a gross of printed ballads for public or private performance.[112]

By the middle of the eighteenth century urban entertainment was becoming increasingly institutionalized. The rise of the theatre, for instance, provided a venue where individuals met and was as much a place for social mixing as it was for the display of wealth. In addition the plays staged contributed to the stock of common images and allusions that contemporaries could understand. Belfast probably had a theatre by 1730 and also had visits from a Dublin company through the 1740s. It seems highly likely that this theatre had a pit and a gallery, which suggests a wide social range of patrons, and a playbill of the early 1750s insisted that gentlemen were not allowed behind the curtain and servants and children were not to be admitted without paying. By the end of the 1750s the Belfast stage was presenting a range of plays, some of which had not yet made it to Dublin.[113] The theatre vied with the market house as a source

The arrival of the theatre in Belfast in the early eighteenth century marked a greater awareness of the importance of public sociability and increased the interest in and demand for plays produced by local printers. The number of play texts issued from the Belfast press grew significantly from the middle of the eighteenth century, even if the plays themselves were not staged in Belfast. Molière's *The Mock Doctor*, printed by James Magee of Belfast in 1762, followed successful printings of the text in London in 1732 and Dublin in 1752.

Reproduced with kind permission from Queen's University, Belfast, Special Collections.

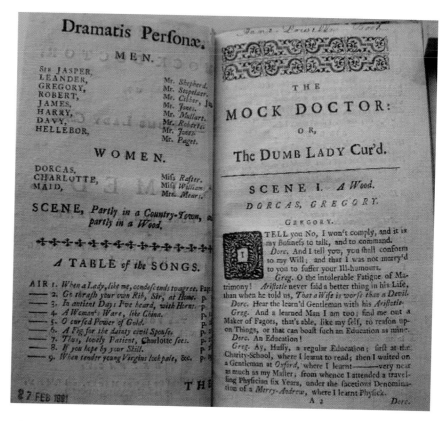

of entertainment. Polite society gathered in the market house for an annual ball in the early eighteenth century to mark the king's birthday and for celebrations of military victories. The birth of an heir to the earl of Donegall in 1739 was marked by feasting and drinking. Dancing was a frequent enough pastime in the town to support a dancing master by 1739.[114] In 1750 a party of professional musicians gave concerts in the market house and other concerts were advertised through the 1750s.[115] By the 1730s such balls were regular occurrences and one description of the town in 1738 noted that 'there is an Assembly kept there once a fortnight where you shall see a fine appearance of ladies and gentlemen, so trade don't always spoil politeness'.[116] This comment is of particular significance since it highlights the transition the town had made from being a place of trade to a centre of sociability and leisure where wealth was not just made but on display, reflecting a clear assurance of the central place of the town in its regional context. For those who doubted its regional importance the publication of the *Belfast News Letter*, probably from 1737, one of only three Irish provincial newspapers established before 1760 that lasted more than a year, demonstrated the importance of the town as a centre that gathered and disseminated news, forming local opinion in the process.

Like entertainment, business contacts showed a tendency to grow around institutions in the eighteenth century. In the seventeenth century the marketplace was one of the main sites to make connections. Apprenticeships bound master and servant, often introducing the apprentice to trading networks that would be useful later. At least one Belfast merchant remembered his apprentice in his will, leaving him £10.[117] Apprenticeship certainly provided one stabilizing influence in the town. Apprenticeship indentures were to be registered with the town clerk and were used to limit the excesses of youthful behaviour by prohibiting apprentices from attending unlawful games, or frequenting common alehouses, taverns or bawdy houses.[118] Apprenticeships tried to promote economic stability as well as fixing young men within a clear social network, but despite these restrictions there were clearly some who moved between trades to make most advantage of their skills. John Potts, for instance, became free of the town as a bookseller in 1731. By 1738 he was selling millstones in Bridge Street but later in that year he was selling books from the shop. The following year he set himself up as a woollen draper and when he died in 1760 he was described as a merchant.[119] By the late seventeenth century there is some evidence for the emergence of a guild system in Belfast at a time when it was already becoming obsolete in other towns. By 1674 the tailors in the town had bonded together to defend their rights. How extensive this system was is unclear but it certainly developed into the eighteenth century. By 1722 there was a well-organized trade guild structure in Belfast. In that year funeral cloaks were hired by the Presbyterian church to men who described themselves as 'captains' of the bakers, shoemakers and tailors.[120]

III

Belfast had a clear sense of itself by the middle of the eighteenth century. Its stock of buildings and streets had evolved through the previous 150 years to create its physical character. Perhaps more importantly the idea of Belfast itself had taken firm root. The disjointed group of immigrants who were the early town had developed into a self-aware society composed of networks of individuals. What had emerged by 1750 was a well-defined social order that was built gradually by integrating waves of migrants through a series of social institutions such as church or corporation. Moreover that social order had a sense of its civic duty to deal with the poor and maintain law and order. The powerful middle class of merchants who contended with the Chichester family for political power at the beginning of the eighteenth century, and who displayed their wealth at the Assemblies in the market house, contrasts strongly with Sir Arthur Chichester's inability to find enough local men of substance to be named as burgesses in the first charter. In the first half of the eighteenth century that middling group of people would find a role for itself in the town outside the formal structures of government. Their exclusion on religious grounds, together with the absence of the landlord of the town in England

The family portrait of the Belfast merchant Thomas Bateson in 1762, attributed to Strickland Lowry, demonstrates the extent to which the rising Belfast middle class were absorbing the new fashionable ways of their world. Two Bateson brothers had come to Ulster from Yorkshire and Thomas established himself at Belfast as a merchant. By 1760 he had acquired an estate outside the town at Orangefield. To the left, his daughters, with a harpsichord and sheet music, demonstrate their mastery of the social graces, while on the right three sons gather around a globe, reflecting the international trade from which their father has derived his wealth. All are dressed in the most recent fashion and the panelling on the wall behind them suggests their wealth. Two pictures on the wall of scenes near Belfast link them clearly with the town.

Photograph © National Museums Northern Ireland. Collection Ulster Museum. BELUM.U1664.

after the death of the third earl of Donegall in 1706 left only a minor to succeed him, and the burning of the castle in 1708, resulted in an absence of leadership in the town. In this context the Belfast merchants turned their attention from civic politics, from which they had been excluded, to civic improvement through a tradition of voluntary action. From the middle of the eighteenth century new associations and societies began to emerge in Belfast, including a musical society founded in 1768.[121] By the 1740s the Freemasons were also established in Belfast with two lodges and their numbers grew throughout the late eighteenth century.[122] The establishment of the Belfast Charitable Society in 1774 provided a structure not only for the maintenance of the poor but also for the provision of a burial ground (functions normally reserved for the parish church) and a water supply for the town.[123] Perhaps inevitably this voluntarism translated itself into politics with radical and loyalist clubs being founded in the town in the 1780s and 1790s.[124] All this was testimony to the success of the making of Belfast by those who not only built the town but shaped the minds of the people who lived there.

5 Improving Town, 1750–1820

S.J. Connolly

The London of the North of Ireland

The Belfast of the 1750s had come a long way from its humble origins as one of the lesser centres of the Ulster plantation. 'There are many merchants and traders of substance there', a visiting judge wrote in 1759, 'and it seems to me to be the London of the north of Ireland.'[1] By later standards, however, the town remained small and physically unimpressive. In the grid of streets clustered around the mouth of the River Farset – Waring Street, High Street and the connecting Broad Street – the houses were mainly slated brick structures of two storeys or more. Even here, however, there were humbler dwellings, like the 'row of low cottages, thatched with straw' that stood in Waring Street as late as 1800.[2] The two public buildings of significance, the late seventeenth-century town hall and market house and the parish church, were in poor repair. The whole town, moreover, was still contained within the line of the defensive earthen ramparts erected in 1642. There was even the wall and arch of a second gate, known as the Mill gate, in the south-west corner of the former perimeter. Sections of the ramparts themselves still stood, planted in places with decorative trees, testifying to the lack of pressure on space within their boundaries. The grounds of the Chichester family's castle, which had been destroyed by fire in 1708, were likewise still vacant, providing an attractive complex of field and woodland stretching down to the River Blackstaff.[3]

Against this background, the 1760s can be seen as beginning a new phase in the development of Belfast. In the three decades that followed, an extensive programme of urban improvement pushed the town well beyond its historic boundaries and gave it both a new appearance and a much-extended range of urban amenities. It was a development inspired by a new and highly active proprietor, but also underwritten by significant economic developments, including the beginnings of large-scale industrial production, and energetically supported by an increasingly sophisticated and self-confident body of inhabitants. Behind it there clearly lay the same ideal of cultivated urban living that was transforming the face of other provincial towns, in both Ireland and Great Britain, during the same period. It was during these last decades of the eighteenth century that the street pattern of the modern city centre came into being, along with some of its most significant older buildings. Four of those buildings in particular illustrate the transformation of the late eighteenth-century town.

Commerce and Sociability: The Exchange and Assembly Rooms

The earliest of these buildings is also, today, the least recognizable, thanks to extensive refurbishment in 1845 and again in 1895, when it was the headquarters of the Northern Bank. It began life as a market house erected in 1769 by the fifth earl of Donegall (later the first marquess), at the junction of Waring Street, North Street and Donegall Street. It was an unassuming structure: a simple one-storey rectangle in brick, with arcades along two sides giving access to the interior. Seven years later, however, Donegall commissioned a leading London architect to add a second storey, to be used as assembly rooms. The exterior remained fairly plain, but inside the new premises were elaborately decorated, with mahogany fittings, decorative plasterwork and a splendid vaulted ceiling. In this form it became for over half a century the town's most important social venue, and a hub of its corporate life.

Donegall's gift of this building to Belfast was just part of a much wider project. Succeeding to the title in 1757, and coming of age in 1761, the earl had entered upon a seriously dilapidated inheritance. The legal settlements imposed on his mentally incapacitated predecessor, along with a web of lawsuits and intrigues as relatives and others competed to gain control of the estate, had between them created a long period of virtual paralysis, in which

The Exchange (1769) and Assembly Rooms (1776), despite the modest external appearance of the building, confirmed Belfast's emergence as an important centre of polite sociability.

Reproduced with the kind permission of the Linen Hall Library.

The growing popularity of the personal portrait was one indication of the rising self-esteem of the Belfast elite of the late eighteenth and nineteenth centuries. For this they employed visiting artists such as the English-based Strickland Lowry, or later, local practitioners such as Richard Hooke. However, the fifth earl of Donegall, the highly active but absentee proprietor of the town, turned instead to the leading English portraitist Thomas Gainsborough for this painting, completed around 1780.

Photograph © National Museums Northern Ireland. Collection Ulster Museum. BELUM.U35.

there was no authority empowered to grant long leases of the kind that would be required by tenants proposing to make any substantial investment in building. By 1752 the town was reported to be in danger of losing its trade, as its physical fabric continued to deteriorate. An Act of Parliament in the same year at last empowered the fourth earl's trustees to let ground for periods of up to 99 years. This lifting of restrictions allowed the managers of the estate to begin granting new leases. By the 1760s, however, their efforts were overtaken by the much more ambitious plans of the new proprietor. The fifth earl was, like his uncle, an absentee, who spent his time at the large estate he bought at Fisherwick Park in Staffordshire, or in the London mansion he later acquired. But he nevertheless took a close interest in his town of Belfast, working constructively with leading local interests to promote mutually beneficial improvements, but also making free use of his authority as lord of the soil to dictate the overall pattern of change.[4]

The main instrument for this proprietorially led programme of urban development was a general issue, commencing in 1767, of new leases for the land on which the town stood. The leases were for long periods, the duration of three named lives, with a minimum of 99 years. But many carried with them a requirement that the tenant should build or rebuild, and contained detailed specifications as to the size and quality of the new houses. Buildings were to be of brick, with slated roofs and sash windows. Houses in Waring Street and High Street were to be a uniform 25 feet in height; those in Bridge Street (the modern Ann Street), reflecting its lower status, were to be 18 feet.

Donegall's efforts were not confined to the existing centre. His leasing policy also initiated a significant extension of the overall street pattern. A map drawn up for the estate in 1757 (p.80) illustrates the extent to which the shape of Belfast was still at that point dominated by its seventeenth-century past. The centre of the town was Waring Street, the site of the original plantation settlement. High Street, immediately to the south, had largely completed its transition from a dock along both sides of the River Farset, although its last third remained a waterfront, where masted vessels tied up in front of the houses and shops. Bridge Street was a shorter thoroughfare carrying traffic from the Long Bridge. North Street and Hercules Lane linked the two ends of this central area to what had been one of the gates in the earthen ramparts. There was further development beyond the line of the ramparts, along the road that led west past the former Mill gate, and along the main highway to Carrickfergus. But the buildings that lined these roads, the cartographer noted, were 'low thatched cabins of a mean appearance', representing the characteristic penumbra of poor housing that surrounded an early modern town.

By the time the fifth earl came of age plans already existed to expand the town beyond its long-standing limits. The map of 1757 shows the beginnings of a new development north of the built-up area, anchored by the location halfway along its projected length of a new Brown Linen Hall, completed in 1754 and giving the new thoroughfare its name. In the fifth earl's more ambitious development this Linenhall Street was renamed Donegall Street, extending to the line of the Carrickfergus road, with additional brick terraces growing up along side streets to right and left. The market house and assembly rooms were located at the bottom of this new development, on the corner with Waring Street. Further along Donegall erected an imposing new parish church, St Anne's. It stood on the site of the Brown Linen Hall, built only nineteen years earlier but now demolished and replaced by a new building on the other side of the street.

The Exchange and Assembly Rooms of 1769–76 were thus just one part of a wider redevelopment. Yet the building has a more particular significance. From the late seventeenth century provincial towns in Great Britain and Ireland developed a new social role, as increasing prosperity allowed both the urban middle classes and the country gentry to indulge in a widening range of leisure and cultural pursuits. Consumer demand supported the appearance of concert halls and assembly rooms, inns and coffee houses, walks and gardens. Town centres too became more attractive, as streets were paved, lit and cleared of refuse; in some cases roads were widened, and squares and public gardens laid out.[5] In the case of Belfast the early signs of this 'urban Renaissance' were already visible in the first half of the eighteenth century. With the construction of the Assembly Rooms, however, polite sociability was able to move from the crumbling market house to a new and more impressive venue. Meanwhile other social amenities became available. In the 1750s, for example, the ladies and gentlemen of the town had taken their summer evening walks along the Long Bridge. By 1791, on the other hand, Belfast had its own 'Mall', a bank of raised ground running across the waterlogged plain to the south of the town centre.[6] The wider urban environment was also being transformed, as the requirements of Donegall's building leases gave the streets of the town centre a new scale and regularity. Of particular importance in this respect was the relocation of the regular market from High Street to Smithfield Square on the western edge of the town, where a new purpose-built venue was completed in 1788. Citizens and visitors alike could now enjoy the inns and coffee houses of the town centre, free from the sights, sounds, smells and effluent associated with the sale of meat, fish and agricultural produce.

Alongside wider social amenities, new cultural facilities appeared. Belfast already had, in the *Belfast News Letter*, the longest-established newspaper outside Dublin. A circulating library established in the early 1770s was able by 1780 to offer subscribers a choice of more than 1,000 volumes. A Belfast Reading Society established in 1788 renamed itself in 1792 as the Belfast Society for Promoting Knowledge, and ten years later moved into premises in the Linen Hall, from which it took its modern name, the Linen Hall Library. The

St Anne's church on Donegall Street, completed in 1776, with its spectacular tower, could possibly be seen as Donegall's reminder to his mainly Presbyterian urban tenants of where the real power lay.

Courtesy of the National Library of Ireland.

Belfast Academy, opened in 1786, provided a grammar school education for the children of both the urban middle classes and the gentry of rural Ulster. A theatre opened at the Mill gate in 1768, followed by short-lived ventures in Rosemary Lane and Ann Street, and then by a more long-lived playhouse, opened in Arthur Street in 1793. The local taste catered for was not necessarily sophisticated. Shakespeare was the most popular single author. However, two-thirds of the plays performed were comedies, with comic operas becoming more popular over time. There was also clearly a taste for spectacle. In 1770, for example, audiences attending *The Rival Queens* were promised 'the grand triumphal entry of Alexander into Babylon with all the Grecian trophies, ensigns, banners, urns, vases and the triumphal car drawn by two captive kings'. Another performance in the same year had a more local flavour, with a panorama depicting the recent attack on Carrickfergus by the French privateer Thurot, as well as views of Belfast itself and of Joy's paper mill, whose location on the Blackstaff and impressive waterwheel made it one of the sights of the town. There was also 'an exact representation of a Patagonian man and woman brought [...] by the *Dolphin* man-of-war in her voyage round the world'.[7]

The polite society of late eighteenth-century Belfast, then, would probably have struck a visitor from London or Dublin as fairly provincial. Indeed even a resident of the town, the high-minded merchant's wife Martha McTier, writing in 1784, commented scathingly on the society she found herself keeping: 'you may be for months in what is called our best company without hearing a book named, an opinion stated, or a sentiment introduced, which could give rise to a conversation interesting to anyone above a chambermaid'.[8] What was important about the new culture of theatres, balls and assemblies, however, was not so much its intellectual content as the social values that underpinned it. The army officer who commented in 1738 on the 'fine appearance of ladies and gentlemen' seen at Belfast's fortnightly assemblies had felt able to add a condescending rider: 'so trade don't always spoil politeness'.[9] A few decades later, that conclusion would have come to seem superfluous and the assumptions behind it wrongheaded. By then authors such as the Scottish philosopher David Hume had begun to develop the argument that urban, commercial living should be seen, not as inferior to the pastoral world of the countryside, but as representing a more advanced stage of civilization. At the heart of this reversal of traditional attitudes lay a new emphasis on the virtues of politeness and sociability, permitting easy, mutually beneficial interaction between those who were neither relatives nor neighbours.[10] Whether Lord Donegall had ever read Hume is unclear. But in building an elegant social venue on top of a commercial exchange he showed himself to be fully in tune with one of the central values of the British Enlightenment.

Philanthropy and Association: The Poor House

At the other end of Donegall Street from the Assembly Rooms stands the second significant building of the period after 1750: equally tasteful in design, more fortunate in its later architectural history, and wholly different in its origins. This was the Poor House, opened in 1774. The committee responsible for its erection had obtained plans from leading architects both in Ireland and further afield. But the actual design appears to have been the work of an amateur, the paper manufacturer and joint proprietor of the *Belfast News Letter* Robert Joy, working in close cooperation with a talented master builder. The result, a two-storey building in red brick, with single-storey wings on either side, topped by a distinctive stone spire, was a low-key exercise in symmetry and simplicity. Its graceful lines belie its utilitarian purpose, testifying instead to a powerful fusion of philanthropy and civic pride. John Wesley, visiting in 1778, reported that the building 'stands on an eminence, fronting the main street, and having a beautiful prospect on every side over the whole country'. The apartments of the inmates, equally, 'are airy, sweet and clean, equal to anything of the kind I have seen in England'.[11]

The new building stood on land granted by Donegall, in response to a petition from the subscribers, in 1769. But that was the extent of his involvement in the project. Work towards the erection of a poor house

John Nixon's depiction of the Charitable Society's Poor House, dating from 1785–90, captures its original rural setting, at the head of what became Donegall Street.

Photograph © National Museums Northern Ireland. Collection Ulster Museum. BELUM.P1.1983.

had in fact begun long before, in 1752, when a group of leading citizens
had launched the first in a series of lotteries to raise funds. In 1774 one of
the town's MPs procured a clause in an Act then going through the Irish
parliament to authorize the establishment of the Belfast Charitable Society as
a legal corporation, managed by a committee elected by those who paid the
subscription of one guinea a year. The house provided accommodation for
people unable through age or illness to support themselves by work, and also,
from 1776, for orphaned or destitute children. Its upkeep was initially financed
through subscriptions, along with the income derived from the 'poor money'
held by the corporation.[12] From 1795 the committee sought to secure a regular
income by taking over the town's water supply. The next two decades saw the
Society spend thousands of pounds on wooden and later iron pipes, while
struggling to find new springs from which to meet a continually expanding
demand. An Act of 1817 empowered the Society to appoint nine Spring Water
Commissioners to take direct charge of the water supply, while receiving a fixed
income of £500 (later rising to £750) a year as a return on its investment.[13]

The establishment of the Belfast Charitable Society was a response, not just
to the distress of the poor, but to the threat posed to the social order by the
beggars and vagrants attracted to a growing town. Its aim, set out in founding
resolutions adopted in September 1774, was 'to provide for the real helpless
objects of distress among the begging poor of the town and parish, punish and
banish vagrant sturdy beggars, and consequently compel those that are able to
apply to useful industry'. Accommodation was for those incapable of providing
for themselves, with 'preference given to decent housekeepers, inhabitants of
the town, reduced through misfortune'.[14] Able-bodied beggars, on the other
hand, were to be seized and confined in a 'black hole'. Both elderly and child
inmates, moreover, were expected to contribute to their support by spinning,
weaving, picking oakum or whatever other work they were capable of. In all
these respects the philanthropy of the Society was of the strict, moralistic
variety characteristic of the age. But its contribution to the relief of human
misery was nevertheless substantial. By 1781 the house accommodated 80 adults
and 47 children; forty years later the number had risen to 149 children and 175
adults. The Society also provided some outdoor relief to the poor in their own
homes, as well as medical treatment both to outpatients and in the Poor House
infirmary.

In the decades that followed the Poor House was joined by a succession
of further philanthropic ventures. A meeting in 1792 led to the creation of a
public dispensary, initially based in the Poor House but from 1797 operating
in its own premises as a fever hospital. A Society for the Relief of Lying-in
Women, providing medical aid to those in labour, came into existence in 1793.
A new drive against beggars led to the creation in 1809 of a House of Industry,
which despite its punitive-sounding title was active not just in confining able-

bodied mendicants but in providing support to poor householders, in the form of food, straw bedding and raw materials for productive labour. All of these ventures had to struggle to survive. The Poor House itself went through a critical period in the early 1800s, when outdoor relief had to be suspended and the admission of children confined to the deserted; for a time the committee even revived the custom of issuing badges authorizing the deserving poor to beg in the streets. At the Fever Hospital in March 1801, a season of disease and food shortages, 'the patients are crowded and the attendants all ill, yet crowds and families rejected every day'. The Lying-in Hospital, in 1804, was suffering from a fall in subscriptions, with receipts of only £84 to meet costs of over £120.[15] Nevertheless this history of sustained effort to deal with the formidable social problems created by urban growth testifies to a strong sense of collective social responsibility on the part of Belfast's leading and middle-ranking citizens.

In another respect too the early history of the Poor House and the Charitable Society marks out Belfast's place as a centre of the emerging urban culture of the late eighteenth century. If one distinctive institution of that period was the Assembly Rooms and similar venues catering for the new cult of politeness, another was the wide range of voluntary societies, some devoted to religious or philanthropic purposes, others to cultural and intellectual pursuits or to simple sociability, that came into existence in towns and cities. At a time when neither central nor local government had yet begun to respond to the acute new social needs created by urban growth and the beginnings of industrialization, voluntary associations of this kind played a crucial role in mitigating some of the worst problems. But they also had a political importance. Decades in advance of even the most modest electoral reform, they offered a model of what has been described as subscriber democracy: associations where membership was open to all who could afford to pay the subscription required, where rights and obligations were set out in clearly defined rules and procedures, and where all enjoyed equal voting rights.[16] It was another respect in which Belfast, in common with other provincial towns, was becoming not just a larger urban centre, but a different kind of urban society.

Trade and Manufactures: The White Linen Hall

The third signature building of late eighteenth-century Belfast disappeared over a century ago, but its impact on the urban landscape remains as marked as if it still stood. The White Linen Hall, erected in 1785 on what had once been the gardens of the Chichester family's castle, became the focus for a decisive westward shift in the location of the town centre. The removal of the town's market to Smithfield made it possible to redevelop the former market square as the Parade, later renamed Castle Place, a broad street of newly built houses which the building leases required to be 28 feet in height, three feet more than

High Street itself. That development in turn led to the creation of a wholly new thoroughfare linking the Parade to the newly constructed White Linen Hall. Indeed the new street was initially (and confusingly, given the original name of Donegall Street) called Linen Hall Street, but later became Donegall Place. The three-storey terraces arranged on either side of a broad street became the preferred residence of the town's wealthiest citizens. A visiting English lawyer noted approvingly that the houses were built 'of good red brick on a modern London plan' and that one, belonging to the cloth merchant William Sinclair, was 'equal to many in Grosvenor Square'.[17] Piecemeal building over the next three decades extended this fashionable quarter to the four sides of the square, now Donegall Square, formed by the Linen Hall. The hall itself was a rather plain two-storeyed stone building with a central courtyard. However, the erection of railings created an attractive walkway round the exterior, the favoured promenade of fashionable Belfast until the outward spread of the shops and offices of the commercial centre gradually undermined its exclusive character.

The significance of the White Linen Hall was not confined to its influence on the evolving streetscape. It also marked Belfast's rise to undisputed pre-eminence as Ulster's leading centre of trade and manufacture. Already by the middle of the eighteenth century Belfast was Ireland's third busiest port, and probably its sixth largest town.[18] Its prosperity, like that of other Ulster towns, was based partly on linen. The first stages of production, the spinning of flax fibre into yarn and the weaving of yarn into cloth, took place in households across a wide range of northern counties. The 'brown' linen they produced was then bought up by bleachers and drapers to be finished, and the resulting 'white' linen sent to the ports for export. Initially much of the linen produced in Ulster was carried by road to Dublin, where a well-established group of dealers continued to dominate the export trade, and where there was a hall for the sale of white linens. In 1782, however, heavy-handed attempts at regulation in the name of quality control led Ulster dealers to take charge of their own affairs. At this point two east coast ports, Belfast and Newry, opened white linen halls in a bid to capture the new Ulster-centred trade. Newry, with an improved harbour and a canal linking it to Lough Neagh, was a significant challenger. But Belfast had a head start. Its existing linen exports were about twice those of Newry, and it had been the first Ulster port to open up a direct trade in linen with the American colonies. Hence it was the Belfast hall that flourished in the years after 1800, while its Newry competitor faded.[19]

The expansion of Belfast that commenced in the 1760s did not depend solely on the redirection of linen manufacture. The second half of the eighteenth century was also a period of rising agricultural prosperity, as Irish merchants and farmers responded to the growth of new markets across the Atlantic, in the colonies of North America and the British and French

The inner courtyard of the White Linen Hall as it was in the early twentieth century, with Robinson and Cleaver's department store in the background.
Courtesy of the National Library of Ireland.

An external view of the Linen Hall, showing the gravel walk that made it the location of a fashionable promenade.
Courtesy of the National Library of Ireland.

THE LINEN HALL, BELFAST. 1255. W.L.

LINEN HALL, BELFAST. 1251. W.L.

plantations in the Caribbean. Arthur Young, visiting Belfast in 1775, reported a huge trade in beef and pork, salted and barrelled for the long voyage west. Some of the cattle slaughtered in the town had come from as far away as Meath and Sligo. The main source, however, was the rich farming lands of east Ulster, for which Belfast, at the head of the natural corridor formed by the Lagan valley, and linked by the Long Bridge to County Down, was ideally placed to become the main outlet. A further important export was people, as a steady stream of emigrants chose the risks and opportunities of a new life in Pennsylvania, West Virginia or the Carolinas. The main imports, as elsewhere in Ireland, were wine and spirits, along with tea, sugar and tobacco. But in Ulster flaxseed, required because the flax grown to produce the finer linens had to be harvested before it produced seed, gave vessels engaged in the transatlantic trade an additional return cargo.[20]

Belfast's growing importance as a port inspired one of the major civil engineering projects of the period, the Lagan Navigation. The first phase, completed between 1756 and 1763, was a programme of works involving the construction of locks and the digging of new cuts across the river's winding course, to make the Lagan navigable as far as Lisburn. The project then stalled for want of funds, but from 1782, under the patronage of Donegall and other substantial proprietors, work resumed on a canal running west from Lisburn, now alongside but separate from the river. By 1793 a commercial waterway extended all the way to the shores of Lough Neagh. Its completion was further evidence of the enterprise and ambition of Belfast's merchant class, as well as of their ability to work fruitfully with the town's proprietor. The commercial benefits, however, were limited. Traffic moved slowly, hampered by the numerous locks and by inadequate depth, since linen bleachers refused to allow the water they used to drive their machinery to be diverted from the Lagan. The canal survived, carrying coal and timber into the interior and wheat and flour to the inhabitants of Belfast. But the greater part of the goods exported through the town continued to be carried along the good-quality roads that ran through the favourable topography of the Lagan valley.[21]

The other major economic engine of Belfast's rapid growth in the late eighteenth and early nineteenth centuries was the appearance alongside linen of a second textile, cotton. New techniques developed in England in the 1770s made possible the mass production of cotton thread with machinery powered by water or steam. The rapid extension of this technological breakthrough to Belfast depended on a combination of entrepreneurial alertness and sharp practice. A notice published after the death of one of the pioneers of the industry, Nicholas Grimshaw, himself a Lancashire man who had settled in Belfast in 1776, referred to an unnamed 'skilful mechanic' who 'at personal risk and considerable expense' had travelled to England and acquired details of 'the most improved British machinery'.[22] In 1778 Grimshaw, along with Thomas

McCabe and Robert Joy, persuaded the management of the Poor House to set some of the children housed there to work on machinery they provided. Within a few years Grimshaw and a partnership of McCabe and Joy had each established their own spinning mills, at Whitehouse just north of the town and in Rosemary Street, respectively. Other entrepreneurs quickly followed. By 1788 one, Nathaniel Wilson, employed 3,000 individuals in different phases of the spinning, weaving and finishing of cotton. Cotton mills also appeared in Cork, Dublin and elsewhere in the 1780s and 1790s. Belfast, however, had the advantage of expertise in handling finer textiles built up over decades of linen spinning and weaving. This is the most likely reason why by 1800 more than half of all factory spinning of cotton in Ireland was concentrated there and in the surrounding district.[23]

The mechanization of cotton spinning was a turning point in the growth of Belfast. The new factories, like their counterparts in England and Scotland, employed mainly women and children. But the adult men who wove the yarn produced into cotton cloth on handlooms, previously dispersed through the countryside, also flocked to the town to be close to the source of their raw material. By 1800, according to one contemporary estimate, there were 13,500 persons employed in cotton mills within a ten-mile radius of Belfast, as well as roughly the same number employed as weavers or in other work related to cotton manufacture.[24] Meanwhile the volume of goods passing through the town also continued to expand. North American farmers had by this time taken over the role of supplying the West Indies plantations with food. But the growing number of hungry mouths packed into the expanding cities of industrializing Britain provided an alternative source of demand. The prolonged war with France further increased the traffic of the port. In 1800 a single Belfast firm, Cavan and Heron, engaged in provisioning the navy, claimed to employ over 400 coopers, butchers, cutters, salters and packers.[25] There was also the heavy demand for labour arising from the rebuilding and expansion of the town itself.

The multiplication of opportunities for employment drew in migrants from the surrounding countryside. The population rose from an estimated 8,500 in 1757 to 18,000 by 1791 and 37,000 by 1821. This influx, just as much as Donegall's prestige projects, began to change the physical shape of the town. From the 1780s developers leasing plots of land to the west of the town, beyond the new high-status precincts of Donegall Place, began to lay out a denser network of streets, with houses designed for occupation by weavers and other artisans. Meanwhile the district of Ballymacarrett, on the other side of the Long Bridge, became home to a foundry, ropeworks, and glass and vitriol works, as well as to a colony of handloom weavers. Contemporary estimates suggest that the population of this industrial suburb rose from 1,208 in 1791 to 2,250 by 1811 and to between three and four thousand by 1822. Donegall, anxious to forestall rival developers, purchased the district in 1787, although it remained outside the municipal boundaries until 1852.[26]

Religion and Enlightenment: First Presbyterian Church, Rosemary Street

The fourth emblematic building dating from the transformation of Belfast in the second half of the eighteenth century is the First Presbyterian church in Rosemary Street, completed in 1783. Georgian Belfast, reflecting the mainly Scottish character of the settlement that had taken place in Antrim and Down in the seventeenth and early eighteenth centuries, was a Presbyterian town. The original meeting house, constructed in 1672, had already been rebuilt in 1717. By the late eighteenth century it was one of three buildings that had grown up on the Rosemary Street site. Second Presbyterian had been erected in 1708 and was to be rebuilt in 1790, while Third Presbyterian had opened in 1722 and was to be extended in 1803. The *Belfast News Letter*, whose sympathies at this period would have been with the established church, complained in 1813 of the disruption caused by 'coaches, post chaises and jaunting cars' coming from different directions to converge on the three meeting houses on Sunday mornings.[27] Meanwhile, a fourth Congregation had opened in Donegall Street in 1791.

The rebuilding of the First Presbyterian meeting house was the work of Roger Mulholland, a striking example of the opportunities for advancement that the expanding town offered to the talented and ambitious. Born in west Ulster, he had begun his career as a carpenter. He had risen to prosperity as one of Donegall's leading partners in the reconstruction of the town centre, taking leases for large plots around Donegall Street on which he had built houses. He was later to design the House of Correction erected between 1803 and 1817 in the south-west corner of the town, and may also have been wholly or partly responsible for the White Linen Hall.[28] But the Rosemary Street meeting house is his masterpiece, built to a novel elliptical design, with the woodwork of the pews and gallery curving gracefully to match the line of the walls.

The sophisticated design was testimony, not just to the prosperity and self-confidence of the town's Presbyterian elite, but also to a particular religious culture. From early in the eighteenth century Ulster Presbyterianism had been divided between two wings, generally referred to as Old and New Light. Old Light Presbyterians upheld the traditional Calvinist doctrine of a fallen humanity some of whose members were predestined to be saved through the bestowal of God's arbitrary grace, while the rest were doomed to eternal damnation. In New Light Presbyterianism this bleak vision gave way a more optimistic belief in an orderly universe, the essentially virtuous nature of humanity, and the harmony of faith and reason. Religion, from this perspective, became a rational instrument for the betterment of humanity. It was a theological outlook that appealed above all to the affluent members of an emerging commercial society, and it was for these that the Rosemary Street church was built. The building remained true to essential Presbyterian values: there was no frivolous ornamentation to distract the congregation from the words of the minister. But its spare elegance nevertheless reflected the sophistication and self-confidence of a new urban elite.[29]

The condition of the Church of Ireland contrasted sharply with that of its dissenting rival. A visiting clergyman, Archdeacon Richard Pococke of Dublin, reported in 1752 that the parish church, on High Street, was 'a very mean fabric for such a considerable place'. It seemed to him to be adapted from 'an old tower or castle'. Lord Donegall's intervention, twenty years later, transformed the physical presence of the established church in the town. The ambitious architecture of St Anne's, with its tall, slender tower dominating the Belfast skyline and visible for miles around, may perhaps have been the Anglican earl's reminder to his Presbyterian tenants of where ultimate authority lay. Later, in 1816, a second place of worship, St George's, opened as a chapel of ease on the High Street site of the former parish church. But new building could not compensate for the numerical weakness, and social inferiority, of the established church. 'The congregation', Pococke noted, 'is but small, and most of them of the lower rank, for of 400 houses there are about sixty families that go to church.'[30] Over the next few decades Church of Ireland numbers were to rise substantially, as the expanding town sucked in population from a widening circle of Ulster counties. By 1834 there were estimated to be 16,000 members of the Church of Ireland in the parish, as compared to 23,000 Presbyterians. But these mainly working-class migrants did nothing to change the concentration of wealth and influence in Presbyterian hands.

The sharp rise in migration from a much-expanded hinterland had implications likewise for Belfast's Catholic population. A return in 1757 counted 556 Catholics in a total population of 8,549. By 1808–09 this had risen to 4,000 in a population of around 27,000. Already in the eighteenth century the Catholic population appears to have been concentrated in the western part of the town, around Hercules Street and Smithfield Market. Newer arrivals settled nearby in the maze of new streets, taking its name from the former cattle pound, that had grown up on one side of an old road that continued the line of High Street and Castle Place into the countryside beyond the ramparts. All these were areas of poor working-class housing. The town's Catholic middle class, by contrast, remained insignificant. A return compiled for the government in 1818 listed just seven Catholics of substance: three provision merchants, two woollen merchants, a rope maker and a painter and glazier, who between them controlled at most £70,000 of capital, out of a total for Belfast of between £1.7 and £2.2 million.[31] Belfast had acquired its first Catholic

Following spread: Interior of Roger Mulholland's First Presbyterian meeting house, Rosemary Street (1783), its elegant simplicity perfectly reconciling aesthetic refinement and Presbyterian religious sensibilities.

© Scenic Ireland.

place of worship, St Mary's, only in 1784. This was a modest building, discreetly located in a lane off Castle Street. Even then, however, almost half of the £170 required to build it had come from Protestant donors. A second church, St Patrick's, completed in 1815, was notably more assertive. Decorated with Gothic pinnacles and battlements, it fronted boldly on to Donegall Street, only a few hundred yards from St Anne's. Yet the parish priest, William Crolly, preaching at the consecration of the church, nevertheless noted gratefully that £1,300 of £4,100 contributed to the building fund had been donated by Protestants.[32]

The generous contributions of Protestants to the erection of Belfast's first two Catholic places of worship reflected the generally friendly tone of interdenominational relations in the late eighteenth and early nineteenth centuries. In addition to their financial contributions, leading Protestants, including Donegall, his son Lord Belfast, and the earls of Londonderry and Massareene, ceremonially assumed the role of collectors at the opening service in St Patrick's, taking in a further £450. When Crolly was promoted five years later to the bishopric of Down and Connor the sovereign, along with senior members of the Presbyterian and Church of Ireland clergy, attended the two farewell dinners in his honour. Already by this time, however, rising Catholic numbers had begun to undermine the easy sense of security on which the religious liberalism of Protestant Belfast depended. As early as 1802 Martha McTier, sister and widow of leading United Irishmen and herself a staunch radical, was to confess to some alarm at learning that the town's Catholics had staged a 'singing procession' in the street. 'I begin to fear these people, and think like the Jews they will regain their native land.'[33]

Realities of Urban Life

The last decades of the eighteenth century thus saw Belfast enter a new phase of growth and urban improvement. The *Belfast News Letter*, in 1804, wrote enthusiastically of the continuing progress it saw all around it: 'On every hand stately and elegant edifices are rising, some designed for family residence, others intended for manufactories, but all of them denoting the taste, the opulence and the public spirit which reigns in the capital of the north.'[34] This, however, was Lord Donegall's showpiece town seen from its main streets. Much of the new housing growing up on the outskirts of the town to accommodate the expanding labouring class was of very poor quality, with whole terraces built back to back, leaving no space for the backyard ash pits that would have provided the only possible form of sanitation, and no water supply. In the town centre too, later reports described a growing population living in rickety, makeshift structures crammed into the courts and alleyways between the main thoroughfares.[35] Even further up the social scale there were, as in every property boom, losers as well as winners. As early as 1787 Martha McTier, as the widow

Martha McTier (1742–1827), sister of the radical pamphleteer and poet William Drennan and wife of Samuel McTier, a prominent United Irishman, was herself a committed reformer who took for granted her right to take an equal part in political discussion. Samuel's death in 1795 left her in straitened financial circumstances, but she remained a sharp observer of the Belfast social scene, mixing in circles that included the Donegalls as well as the town's leading merchants.

Reproduced with kind permission from Queen's University, Belfast, Special Collections.

of a local businessman fallen on hard times, complained bitterly at the influx of 'rich upstarts' thanks to whose presence 'a small, genteel house in a tolerable situation is not to be got at any moderate rent'.[36]

It is also important not to allow either contemporary rhetoric or the Georgian elegance of a handful of surviving buildings to cast too rosy a glow. Improvement was a gradual and uneven process. Part of the appeal of one of those survivors, the Poor House, for example, is its situation at the head of the vista up Donegall Street. But it was not until 1823, almost half a century after its erection, that the owners were able to remove a group of poor cottages that obscured that view. Another major building project, the new White Linen Hall, fell victim almost immediately to the perennial Belfast problem of subsidence. In November 1787, only two years after its completion, a visitor noted that 'the gateway and many houses in a very handsome street building in front of it [i.e. Donegall Place] have sunk or given way considerably', and that the gate was being rebuilt.[37] There were also the inescapable limitations of early municipal administration. A letter to the *Belfast News Letter* in 1780 complained of the piles of dung swept up following Friday's markets but then left to decorate the main streets of the town during the whole of Sunday.[38] Late eighteenth-century Belfast was a town being shaped by new aspirations to elegance. But any visitor would also have found it noisy, smelly and still visibly under construction.

By the same token the image of polite sociability embodied in the Assembly Rooms, or in the proceedings of the different literary and scientific societies, cannot be taken wholly at face value. There was also a less refined side to the social life of late eighteenth- and early nineteenth-century Belfast. The diaries of Theobald Wolfe Tone and Thomas Russell, young radicals at large in the town in the early 1790s, contain vivid accounts of the culture of extravagant drinking they encountered. 'Very drunk', Russell recorded after one night out in April 1791. 'Fall in the gutter and spoil my coat, bend my sword etc.'[39] Two decades later habits had apparently changed little. When concerned citizens came together in 1812 to institute a voluntary watch that would keep order on the night-time streets, their main concern turned out to be with the consequences of alcohol-fuelled sociability. Their response to these intoxicated fellow citizens, moreover, was revealingly indulgent. They were taken in hand and escorted safely home. Even the obnoxious individual who declared that 'he would knock the face off Mr Farrel that was taking him to his said home' was released on giving security for his future good behaviour.[40]

The other great source of disorder on the streets was, inevitably in a growing town, prostitution. Martha McTier, in 1797, admitted that there had always been some 'abandoned females', but complained that the recent flooding of the town with troops in response to the threat of insurrection had increased their number so much that 'all ladies must give up going out at night except in chairs'.[41] In the decades that followed the military barracks in North Queen

Street continued to be the centre of the town's red light district. But prostitutes also congregated, to the dismay of the respectable citizenry, around the town's cultural centrepiece, the Exchange and Assembly Rooms, where they attracted 'a number of drunken and profligate men and boys'.[42]

Most of these women are anonymous figures, appearing in the record only as a threat to the peace of the respectable. One, however, comes briefly into view. Bridget Kelly was living in Britton's Alley, near the barracks, when she was murdered in the summer of 1820. The house was owned by a woman who kept girls newly arrived from the country, giving them food and lodgings while taking for herself everything they earned from customers. Bridget had risen above this level; she was apparently 'mistress of the house'. But that status brought little security. A witness at the trial of the man accused of her killing explained that the defendant was one of those who, 'when unfortunate girls made any money [...] came in to them for treats and pints, and if they did not share with them they were beaten'. Bridget was also beaten sometimes by her brothers 'because she was light in her character'. Both brothers, along with her mother, had been present in the house on the night she was killed, but all three, according to the evidence given in court, were too drunk to know what had happened. It was a short, sad life. But it was as much a part of the story of Belfast's expansion as that of Roger Mulholland, or any of those others for whom the growth of the town and its industries brought the chance of prosperity and social advancement.[43]

A Perfect Boston

Throughout the second half of the eighteenth century, as Belfast's population more than doubled from 8,500 to around 19,000, the institutions charged with regulating the urban environment remained those specified in the charter of 1613. The corporation, consisting of 12 burgesses, was a self-perpetuating body whose members held office for life, with vacancies by death or resignation being filled by co-option. In practice its members were nominees of the Donegall family. This was so notoriously the case that when the lord lieutenant of Ireland visited the town in 1799 to solicit support for the Act of Union, he decided against the usual procedure of seeking an address from the municipal body, 'for as the corporation of that great and opulent town is entirely in the hands of Lord Donegall, it is necessary in some manner to obtain a public mark of approbation from the inhabitants at large'. Accordingly he had to go to the trouble, aided behind the scenes by Donegall's father-in-law, of organizing a public dinner at which toasts could be drunk to the proposed constitutional change.[44]

It would be wrong to suggest that the corporation was wholly indifferent to the needs of the growing town. Between 1761 and 1766, for example, successive sovereigns sought to organize the lighting of the streets with oil lamps, although even here the scheme eventually initiated was set up partly through the parish vestry. There was also at least intermittent provision for a night watch drawn from among the inhabitants.[45] In October 1768 the sovereign of the day personally shot two pigs left at large in the streets in contravention of a bye-law. A more regular function of some importance was to regulate the price of bread by fixing the minimum weight of a standard loaf. In addition there were occasional reports of the sovereign making a formal progress through the town's markets, checking weights and measures and confiscating meat not fit for consumption.[46] It was also his duty, on request, to summon a general town meeting on subjects of pressing concern. In 1771, for example, one such gathering agreed to institute a public subscription for the relief of distress due to harvest failure; another, in 1791, considered proposals to regulate the town's coal trade.[47] These meetings, open to all respectable citizens, provided some limited measure of consultation and collective decision making. Otherwise, however, the corporation remained under no real pressure to account for its actions to anyone other than the absentee proprietor.

Against this background, leading citizens responded to new economic needs as they had already responded to the problem of poverty and vagrancy, by setting up their own alternative structures. In May 1783, inspired by a similar initiative launched in Dublin three months earlier, leading merchants established a Chamber of Commerce to further the business interests of the town and 'have a watchful attention to the proceedings of parliament'. These, however, were early days in the development of an associational culture. At the first annual general meeting, in 1784, attendance was so poor that the proceedings had to be adjourned. The Chamber ceased to meet between 1787 and 1791 and again from 1794. One early initiative, however, proved to be of long-term importance. In 1785 the Chamber petitioned parliament for improvements to the harbour, where large vessels still had to anchor three miles from the port, at the Pool of Garmoyle, and discharge their cargoes on to smaller boats. In response parliament passed an Act creating a corporation, the Ballast Board, to manage the affairs of the port. The new body implemented some limited improvements to the harbour, including a dry dock completed in 1795, and also brought order to its traffic by regulating cargoes and navigation. Once again, however, it was not until the early nineteenth century that major works began the long task of reshaping the mouth of the Lagan into a significant waterway.[48]

These attempts by the business community to provide for the better regulation of the town's affairs took place against the background, not just of commercial and industrial expansion, but of political upheaval. Agitation against Ireland's constitutional subordination to Great Britain and a parliament largely unresponsive to public opinion had developed during the 1760s. The revolt of the American colonies in 1776 provided both a further stimulus to discontent and the opportunity to act effectively. Volunteer corps, initially formed to protect the country from Spanish or French invasion, turned to politics, campaigning first for the removal of restrictions on Irish trade and on the legislative powers of parliament, and then, unsuccessfully, for a reform of the electoral system. In all of this Belfast played a prominent part. By 1779 there were three Volunteer companies in the town. In 1780 and again in 1781 Belfast hosted major provincial reviews, when corps from all over Ulster attended to march, fire their cannon, stage mock battles and engage in political debate. During the review of 1781, accordingly to one disapproving observer, 'Belfast was a perfect Boston'.[49] In 1783 leading figures in Belfast public life, such as Waddell Cunningham, president of the Chamber of Commerce, and Henry Joy, proprietor of the *Belfast News Letter*, were among the delegates from Belfast at the great Volunteer convention in Dublin to demand a radical reform of parliament.

Belfast's prominence in this and subsequent radical agitations is hardly surprising. Rapid commercial expansion had created a self-confident and assertive middle class, its members acutely aware of the contrast between their economic importance and their negligible political influence. A sophisticated urban economy also produced a literate and prosperous artisan class, the potential rank and file for effective street politics. Close trading links, and a past history of substantial emigration, encouraged both a sympathy with the American colonists in their conflict with what was seen as an oppressive British government, and an openness to new political ideas from the other side of the Atlantic. As Presbyterians, equally, the citizens had much to complain of. The sacramental test, which excluded non-members of the Church of Ireland from local and central government office or employment, had been repealed only in 1780, and there was still resentment at the privileges enjoyed by the established church, including its power to levy tithes on persons of all denominations. Hence it is no surprise that one of Belfast's delegates to the Volunteer convention was Sinclair Kelburn, a minister at the Rosemary Street Presbyterian church. Demands for parliamentary reform, finally, had a particular relevance, since Belfast was a corporation borough. The town's two MPs were elected by the 13 members of the corporation. In practice this meant that they were the personal nominees of the earl of Donegall.

It was at this point that the rising radicalism of Belfast came into conflict with the town's sole proprietor. Donegall's relations with the Volunteer movement were initially friendly. On a visit to Belfast in June 1783 he formally reviewed the local corps, assuring them that their soldierly appearance 'would have done honour to veterans' and expressing his approval of the removal of trade restrictions.[50] When a general election was announced later in the year, the citizens sought to build on this mood of harmony by proposing that Donegall should have the corporation return Waddell Cunningham as their choice of member, while returning whomever he pleased to the other seat. When

Donegall ignored this petition, Cunningham put himself forward as a candidate at Carrickfergus, also part of Donegall's estate but with a larger electorate. He won the election but a committee of the House of Commons declared his return invalid on grounds of bribery. Meanwhile one of the two MPs returned for Belfast on Donegall's orders was burnt in effigy by disgruntled citizens.[51]

Waddell Cunningham
Photograph © National Museums Northern Ireland. Collection Ulster Museum. BELUM.U23.

Waddell Cunningham

The career of Waddell Cunningham (1729–97) typifies many aspects of late eighteenth-century Belfast. He was, in the first place, a self-made man, the son of a former ship's captain and small farmer whose emergence as possibly the town's richest merchant testified to the opportunities that the expanding port and commercial centre offered to the bold and talented. His wealth, as with much of the prosperity of eighteenth-century Belfast, was based on the transatlantic trade. Dispatched to New York around 1750 to assist a relative, he set up in business on his own account and made huge profits trading with both sides during the Seven Years War (1756–63) between England and France. Back in Belfast from 1763, he involved himself in commerce, banking and manufacturing. He was first president of the town's Chamber of Commerce, as well as taking a prominent part in the affairs of the Belfast Academy, the Linen Hall Library and the Charitable Society. In politics, he was an officer in the first Belfast Volunteer corps and a delegate to the major reform conventions at Dungannon in 1782 and Dublin in 1783. He also led the radical challenge to the Donegall interest in Carrickfergus.

If Cunningham reflected the opportunities that Belfast offered to the energetic and talented, he also encapsulated the contradictions of its late eighteenth-century radicalism. He helped to raise funds for the opening of the town's first Catholic church in 1784. But he also appears in the diary of Wolfe Tone as one of the most outspoken defenders of the continued exclusion of Catholics from political life. He was an active philanthropist, yet his dealings in land in County Antrim aroused such strong popular hostility that in 1770 his house in Belfast came under attack from the tenant protest group known as the Hearts of Steel. He was a strong supporter of parliamentary reform, but in the last years of his life, as advanced radicals turned to revolutionary conspiracy, he enlisted in the forces of the counter-revolution as a captain in the Belfast yeomanry. Most striking of all, he was a passionate supporter of political liberty who welcomed the American and French revolutions, yet his commercial dealings on the other side of the Atlantic included the trade in slaves. By the time of his death he had his own sugar plantation, worked with slave labour, on the island of Dominica.

With the failure of the parliamentary reform campaign, dismissed by a parliament that had decided to call the Volunteers' bluff, Belfast radicalism went into temporary eclipse. In 1789 news of revolution in France inspired a revival. In 1791 and again in 1792 the reformed Volunteer corps enthusiastically celebrated the anniversary of the fall of the Bastille. The banners displayed on the second of these occasions were eloquent expressions of a cosmopolitan radicalism confident that history was on its side. There were flags representing America, 'the asylum of liberty', and France, and another promising support for Poland in its resistance to Russian tyranny. The largest portrait, drawn on a triumphal car, showed on one side the storming of the notorious Paris prison. On the other, acknowledging the incomplete triumph of 1782, was a representation of Hibernia with one hand and foot free but the other in shackles, along with the motto 'For a people to be free it is sufficient that they will it.' The parade ended at the White Linen Hall, where the Volunteers and citizens crowded into the central square to debate and approve a congratulatory address to the French National Assembly. A second address, to the people of Ireland, denounced the 'unjust and ruinous inequality' of the political system and the corruption that resulted. The evening concluded with a public dinner, where 104 leading radicals toasted French liberty, the sovereignty of the people and the rights of man.[52]

There was more to these proceedings than met the eye. The resolutions debated at the White Linen Hall in July 1792 had been prepared by a young Dublin barrister, Theobald Wolfe Tone. He had been brought to Belfast by a small committee of radicals that sought to work behind the scenes to nudge the broader Volunteer movement towards militancy. In December 1791 these radicals formed themselves into a new body, the Society of United Irishmen. Their stage management of events, as demonstrated at the White Linen Hall, was highly effective. But there were signs from an early stage that they were seeking to lead reformist opinion in Belfast further than it wanted to go. In particular the suggestion that any effective campaign to extract concessions from the British government would have to include Catholics, however convincing in pragmatic terms, was more than many could accept. The Volunteers in 1784 had been happy, not just to contribute to the building of Belfast's first Catholic church, but to show solidarity by parading to the opening ceremony and attending the inaugural mass. But the issue there had been the removal of the obsolete restrictions on Catholic religious practice and Catholic property ownership. Where the admission of Catholics to political rights was concerned, the assembly at the White Linen Hall eventually accepted resolutions to this effect, but only after several spokesmen, including leading figures in the town, had sought to persuade them that the time was not yet quite right. Earlier, in October 1791, Tone had been present at a private dinner where leading radicals such as Waddell Cunningham and the Presbyterian minister William Bruce, whom Tone denounced as 'an intolerant high priest', had argued the same case with much less circumspection: Catholics, they insisted, were still committed by their religion to the elimination of heresy, and still hankered after a reversal of the land confiscations of the seventeenth century, so that they simply could not be trusted with power. 'Broke up rather ill disposed towards each other', Tone recorded in his diary. 'More and more convinced of the absurdity of arguing over wine.'[53]

'For a people to be free it is sufficient that they will it.' Some individual United Irishmen may from the start have recognized that change on the scale they demanded would require something more. At the outset, however, the aim of the movement was to return to the tactics of 1778–85, by orchestrating a demonstration of overwhelming popular support that the government would be unable to ignore. As part of this strategy the movement, in 1792, launched a newspaper, the *Northern Star*. But times had changed since the triumphs of the first Volunteer movement. To a British government horrified by the fall of the French monarchy, and from early 1793 at war with the revolutionary regime, political dissent was now potential treason. By 1795 the United Irish movement had been suppressed and had reorganized as an underground movement seeking French support for an armed insurrection to bring about an independent Irish republic. Belfast and its hinterland thus entered a vicious cycle of violence and repression. United Irish cells drilled and swore in members, raided houses for arms, and on occasion assassinated opponents or suspected informers. Moderate reformers, forced to take sides, transferred their support to the established order. In 1797, after only bad weather had prevented a French landing in the south-west, the army initiated a brutal campaign to break the radical underground before it could rise in arms. Belfast became crowded with aggressive soldiers, many quartered on the inhabitants. In June troops ran amok, smashing up public houses used by radicals and wrecking the offices and printing equipment of the *Northern Star*. Prominent radicals were arrested and held without trial under emergency legislation. Newgate prison in Dublin was jocularly nicknamed the Belfast hotel, from the number of Ulstermen confined there.[54]

Belfast, under curfew and swarming with soldiers, played no part in the insurrection that erupted in the summer of 1798. Instead what remained of the United Irish movement raised their standard in the surrounding countryside, and were defeated in bloody encounters at Antrim and Ballynahinch. The town's citizens did, however, have to witness part of the grim aftermath. Henry Joy McCracken, a member of two of the town's leading commercial families, who had commanded the rebels at Antrim, was hanged in High Street. In recognition of his status his body was returned to his family intact, but the heads of five other United Irishmen executed in the town were left to rot on spikes above the market house. There were also frequent complaints, in

the years immediately following the revolt, of the thuggish behaviour of the military garrison that remained in control of the town. In 1800, for example, two officers horsewhipped a ship's captain who had failed to get to his feet when 'God Save the King' was played in the theatre.[55]

Under New Management

By the time the fires of 1798 had died down in the surrounding countryside, Belfast had a new proprietor. The first marquess of Donegall died in January 1799. His eldest son and successor, George August Chichester, had already built up enormous debts during a decade of extravagant living and uncontrolled gambling. He had also forfeited his father's favour, and part of his inheritance, by an unsuitable marriage. The new owner immediately embarked on a further round of spending until in 1802, crippled by a new mountain of debt, he and his wife retreated to Belfast, to escape their creditors and seek new sources of ready money.

Belfast, for the first time in a century, had a resident aristocratic proprietor. There was a brief idyllic period when the marquess and marchioness became the centre of the town's genteel social life, hosting dinners and attending balls,

Although Belfast itself, swamped by government troops, was untouched by the rebellion of 1798, there was serious fighting in the surrounding countryside. Thomas Robinson's painting of the defeat of the County Down rebels at Ballynahinch on 12 June displays uniformed loyalists, some of whom had apparently sat for the painter, in heroic poses alongside a cringing rebel. The painting was displayed in the Assembly Rooms in November 1798, then successfully raffled – a reminder that political sympathies in the town were more divided than is often assumed.

Reproduced with kind permission from the Bridgeman Art Library (Private Collection).

Anna, Marchioness of Donegal

Anna, marchioness of Donegall (1774?–1849) was the daughter of Sir Edward May, a lawyer and moneylender from a County Waterford family. Her marriage in 1795 to the 25-year-old heir to the Donegall estates appears to have been part of an agreement under which May secured young Chichester's release from debtors' prison. The transaction had immediate repercussions. The first marquess, outraged at his son's choice of bride, altered his will to leave any property not covered by legal settlements, including lands in County Donegal and property in Staffordshire and London, as well as the townland of Ballymacarrett, to his younger son Spencer Chichester. More than two decades later, in 1819, the circumstances of the couple's marriage returned to haunt them once again, this time with potentially disastrous results. Investigations arising out of the proposed marriage of their eldest son revealed that Anna had been under age at the time of the marriage. The May family (who do not in fact seem to have known the exact date of her birth) had taken the precaution of obtaining a special licence recording her father's agreement to the marriage, but since she was illegitimate this did not meet the requirement that minors should have the consent of a legal parent. Instead the marriage was invalid and the couple's children, illegitimate in their turn, became ineligible to inherit the Donegall estate, which would descend instead to the son of the recently deceased Spencer Chichester. They were saved only by a change in the marriage law, partly inspired by their circumstances, which was enacted in 1822.

Despite the inauspicious circumstances of their match, and their life-long financial embarrassments, the couple appear to have been well suited. Martha McTier, meeting Anna for the first time in 1798, was unimpressed. 'Lady Belfast would be pretty if she had been left to nature, but paint, fashion and a posturing mother […] has turned her eyes – shoulders – and all – into supplicants for notice, and bold beggars they are.' Eight years later her attitude had softened. The marchioness was now in her view a good mother, 'chastely proper as to men and their admiration', her only fault being 'a too great attachment to worthless parents'.[1]

1   Jean Agnew (ed.), *The Drennan–McTier Letters* (Dublin: Irish Manuscripts Commission, 1998–99), II, p. 420, III, pp. 548–49.

Anna, marchioness of Donegall.

Image supplied courtesy of Belfast Harbour Commissioners.

and charming all by their willingness to mingle. However, it was not to last. As early as June 1803 a debt collector from London attempted to seize the contents of the house they had taken in Linen Hall Street, only to be forestalled by Donegall's father-in-law, who had already secured a pre-emptive judgement on the basis of monies supposedly owed to himself. By the end of 1806 the house had been shut up and the entire contents auctioned for the benefit of creditors. The marquess and marchioness moved briefly to Scotland and the relative security of a different legal jurisdiction. On their return to Belfast the following year they set up home in a villa at Ormeau on the other side of the River Lagan, where the marquess continued to dodge creditors as best he could: one, in 1817, managed once again to have the contents of the house seized by the sheriff.[56]

If Donegall's financial problems quickly ended his role as the chief focus of the town's social life, they in no way diminished his hold on its municipal institutions. On the contrary his financial problems created a new need to exploit his control of the corporation. The chief beneficiaries were his wife's family, who had accompanied the couple to Belfast. Thus the post of sovereign passed back and forth between Donegall's father-in-law Sir Edward May, Sir Edward's sons Stephen and Edward junior, and Thomas Verner, who was married to another of May senior's daughters. In 1835 an official inquiry into municipal corporations was to discover that some £3,000 had disappeared from the funds entrusted to the corporation for the relief of the poor, most of it appropriated by Donegall and his relatives. Donegall also enjoyed the right to appoint to the Church of Ireland parish of Belfast, and when the long-serving vicar William Bristow died in 1809 his successor was Edward May junior, who had been ordained just a week earlier.

The Act of Union had reduced Belfast's representation to one seat in the United Kingdom parliament, but this too was in effect a family possession. The post-Union MPs for Belfast were Sir Edward May (1800–14) and Stephen May (1814–16), followed by Donegall's cousin, Arthur Chichester (1818–20, 1830–32), and Donegall's son, the earl of Belfast (1820–30). The only short break, in 1816–18, occurred when the marquess was duped into returning an outsider, John Michel, in the hope of winning favour in high places. On other occasions he shamelessly lobbied successive governments for favours for himself and his relatives in exchange for the votes of the MPs for Belfast and Carrickfergus and his own vote in the House of Lords. In 1816, for example, he demanded that Edward May senior be appointed to the vacant collectorship of customs in the town. His presumption earned him a dressing down from the young but already formidable Robert Peel, then chief secretary. Afterwards, Peel reported, Donegall sat in his outer office 'nearly crying' as he wrote a letter of apology. Even then, however, the lord lieutenant's view was that, having 'brought the Belfast savage to a proper sense of himself', they should give him what he asked for, in order to secure his parliamentary votes.[57]

Donegall's ruthless exploitation of his prerogatives was less contentious than it might have been because by this time the corporation that was the basis of his power had lost even its former limited administrative functions. An Improvement Act introduced by the last session of the Irish parliament in 1800 created a new body, a Police Board charged with cleaning, lighting, paving and improving the streets of the town, and empowered to levy local rates for these purposes. The origins of the Act are unclear. During the decades preceding the general municipal reform Acts of 1835 and 1840 many of the growing towns of both Ireland and Great Britain secured local legislation of this kind, bypassing rather than removing unsatisfactory existing bodies. The Belfast Act, however, was introduced by Sir Edward May, suggesting a possible move by the Donegall interest to pre-empt more far-reaching reforms. That would explain the limitations of the new board. A lower tier, the Police Committee, was elected by ratepaying householders. Its role, however, was to implement decisions made by the Police Commissioners, returned on a narrow property franchise and holding office for life. Moreover the sovereign and all 12 burgesses were *ex officio* members of the Commission, giving the old corporation a majority within its 25-strong membership. The result was to institutionalize a division between oligarchic and more broadly based interests, with the former having the final say. Nevertheless the town now had a system of local government accountable, however imperfectly, to public opinion.[58]

During the next two decades the Police Board began the task of creating a system of regulation suitable to the needs of an expanding industrial town. The amount raised in police tax rose at a steady rate, from £1,567 in 1802 to around £5,000 in the mid-1820s and to over £7,000 a decade later. A large part of this income was spent on the paving of streets, the provision of raised footpaths along their edges, and their regular cleaning. Other basic amenities included the first public 'necessaries', erected in the years 1820–24. Meanwhile the Board also sought to impose a new sort of order on the expanding urban space for which it was responsible. One of its first acts was to have name boards erected at street corners, and to have houses numbered. There were also regulations governing behaviour in the increasingly congested streets. Butchers were an obvious target, now strictly forbidden to slaughter animals or dress meat anywhere except in their shops or designated slaughterhouses. Drivers of carts had to display their name and licence number. A bye-law in 1808 ordered that they were to lead their vehicles through the streets 'at no quicker pace than a walk'; by 1814 this had apparently been modified to a speed limit of four miles per hour 'within the precincts of the lamps'.[59] Drivers also faced fines for failing to keep to the left. Private householders too had their responsibilities. Under bye-laws agreed in 1808 they were required, on pain of a fine, to ensure that the footpath in front of their dwellings had been swept before 9 a.m., and no person was to shake or dust carpets or mats in any street or lane between eight in the morning and ten at night.[60]

The most ambitious innovation of the early nineteenth century was the replacement of the whale oil lamps that had previously provided street lighting with gas lighting. The gasworks, erected by a private company under contract to the Police Board, stood on the Ormeau Road, still on the eastern fringes of the town centre. The *Belfast News Letter*, reporting the first lighting of the new lamps on 30 August 1823, wrote enthusiastically of the novel night-time townscape. In place of 'the gloomy twilight, or rather darkness visible, which formerly issued from our dull and sombrous globes', there was now a 'mild radiance', so that 'the very shadows were well defined [...] Living objects [...] were distinctly seen, even at remote distances [...] each man could recognise his neighbour.'[61] In practice, economy dictated that for several decades the new system was to perform at well below its potential, as the council refused to light lamps, or lit only alternate lamps, during the brighter evenings of summer or the full moon, and extinguished all lights as early as 6 a.m. on winter mornings. But the technical achievement, with an estimated 14 miles of piping conveying the gas to street lamps and some large premises throughout the town, and an initial capital investment of some £40,000, was nevertheless impressive.

The term 'Police Board', introduced by the Improvement Act, reflected a contemporary usage that covered such matters as paving, street cleaning and lighting. The Act had also authorized the provision of a night watch, but here progress was slow. Full-time police forces were still widely seen at this time as a dangerous extension of the power of the state, and they were also expensive. In 1816, however, the Police Commissioners took advantage of public concern over crime to push through an unpopular new rating system, in which individuals were assessed solely on the value of their property within the town, rather than their total wealth. Once the rating bill had become law, the Board, in September 1816, created a paid police force of 30 men, almost immediately increased to 40. The new force was initially a night watch, patrolling between the hours of 9 p.m. and 6 a.m., but from October 1817 it included two day constables. By 1834 there were to be 11 day police out of a total force of 80. Their duties extended, not just to the preservation of public order and the pursuit of criminals, but to the enforcement of the growing body of bye-laws and regulations governing the movement of traffic on the streets, the disposal of refuse, or the obstruction of pavements. They were expected to prevent illegal trading, enforce the licensing hours in public houses, shoot stray dogs and deal with other public nuisances.[62]

The Rights of an Injured Queen

The unchecked profiteering of the Donegall clique and the humdrum, if sometimes contentious, workings of the Police Board are indications of the transformation that took place in the public life of Belfast in the years that followed the crisis of 1798. The campaign to secure the Act of Union met with sustained resistance in Dublin and other parts of the south. In Belfast, by contrast, there was either approval or apathy. For over a decade thereafter

William Drennan (1754–1820), son of the minister at the Rosemary Street First Presbyterian church, was a leading figure in the early United Irish movement, but withdrew after a traumatic prosecution for seditious libel in 1794. A poet as well as a radical pamphleteer, he introduced the term 'emerald isle' as a synonym for Ireland. This portrait is attributed to Robert Home (1752–1834).

Photograph © National Museums Northern Ireland. Collection Ulster Museum. BELUM.P3.1986.

The memorial plaque to William Tennent (1760–1832) in Rosemary Street First Presbyterian church reflects the successful rehabilitation of a leading radical of the 1790s. Tennent, a merchant and banker both before and after his imprisonment as a United Irishman, was a brother of Dr Robert Tennent (see p. 193), and uncle of Robert James Tennent, Liberal MP for Belfast 1847–52.

Photograph © Bryan Rutledge.

would-be spies and informers continued to send accounts of allegedly treasonable gatherings of radicals, and vague stories of clandestine contacts with Napoleon's France.[63] The consensus among informed observers, however, was that the north-east no longer presented a revolutionary threat. Instead leading radical activists of the preceding decade quietly reintegrated themselves into the town's life. William Drennan, a founder of the Society of United Irishmen who had stood trial for sedition in 1794, moved back to Belfast when he retired from his Dublin medical practice in 1807, and took his place as a prominent figure in its literary and cultural affairs. When he died in 1820 the politically conservative *Belfast News Letter*, while disassociating itself from his political views, paid tribute to 'the accomplished scholar, the well-bred gentleman, and the conscientious patriot'.[64] Another prominent radical, William Tennent, released after almost four years' imprisonment, returned to Belfast, where he quickly resumed a varied mercantile career in banking, insurance and the wine and sugar trades. By the time of his death in 1832 he was one of the richest men in Belfast, commemorated by a plaque in Rosemary Street Presbyterian church.

This apparent closing over of the deep ideological divisions of the 1790s is less surprising than might appear at first sight. Acceptance of the Union with Great Britain must be seen in context. The great issue for many radicals in the north-east had been one of representation rather than of Irish national rights. They had in any case little cause to lament the disappearance of an Irish parliament that had refused every call for reform, passed penal laws against Catholics and dissenters alike, and sanctioned the repressive measures introduced during the 1790s. Enthusiasm for revolutionary politics, meanwhile, had been doused by the harsh experience of that same repression, and also by the terrifying speed with which popular insurrection in the predominantly Catholic southern counties of Ireland had degenerated into a murderous attack on Protestants. Meanwhile France, now ruled by an emperor rather than a national assembly, had become all too clearly a potential conqueror rather than a liberator. This background of a declining radical threat in turn made possible the quiet rehabilitation of men such as Drennan and Tennent. The still small size of the urban community, the tight network of family and personal connections, and possibly a memory of how many others had shared in the original enthusiasm for change out of which the revolutionary movement had been born all made it undesirable, once the danger had passed, to indulge in vendettas or recriminations.

Despite appearances, however, a commitment to radical political causes did not entirely fade away. Drennan, after his return, launched the *Belfast Monthly Magazine*, which from 1808 to 1814 provided a regular critical commentary on local and national affairs. Some of the leading figures behind the Belfast Academical Institution revealed their continuing political sympathies at a

St Patrick's Day dinner in 1816, drinking toasts to the American and French revolutions and to the prospect of a reform of parliament. The outraged government initially sought to cut off the Institution's funding, but retreated when Presbyterians as a body revolted against the threat of interference. Although post-Union Irish politics offered little outlet for radical energies, moreover, there was now more scope to pursue radical causes within the framework of the new United Kingdom. In 1809, for example, the discovery that Mary Anne Clarke, mistress of the duke of York, second son of George III and commander-in-chief of the army, had been taking money to use her influence in military promotions gave radicals, in Belfast as elsewhere, a golden opportunity to attack the royal family from a stance of unimpeachable loyalty. A town meeting, ignoring the opposition of Donegall and the sovereign, voted an address of thanks to Colonel Wardle, the MP who had exposed the scandal.[65]

Two incidents in particular illustrate the conflicts and animosities that existed beneath the apparently tranquil surface of post-Union Belfast politics. In 1813 Dr Robert Tennent, brother of the reformed United Irishman William, became involved in a public argument with the Revd Edward May over whether there should be an inquiry into the violence that had followed that year's Twelfth of July celebrations. When Tennent laid a hand on the other man's arm, May arrested him for assault. Almost immediately afterwards Tennent became involved in the case of an itinerant pedlar who accused May's brother-in-law, Thomas Verner, of having raped her as she passed near his house outside the town. Tennent's retaliation, if that is what it was, backfired spectacularly. Verner was acquitted, and Tennent's alleged part in sponsoring the prosecution was widely regarded as having been responsible for the harsh sentence of three months' imprisonment, with a fine of £50, that he subsequently received for his purely technical assault on May.[66]

The second incident was in 1820, when George IV sought to divorce his long-estranged wife, Caroline of Brunswick, who had returned from exile in Italy to claim her place beside him on the throne. Once again radicals throughout the United Kingdom seized on the opportunity to attack the king and ministry, this time by defending the rights of an injured queen. When the House of Lords, in November, voted to throw out the divorce bill, the queen's Belfast supporters organized a public celebration, calling on the inhabitants to illuminate their houses as a sign of support. The event began well, with windows lit throughout the greater part of the town. Over time, however, the atmosphere became increasingly rowdy, as crowds paraded the streets dragging flaming tar barrels and firing rockets, squibs and pistols. Among their targets were the house of Thomas Verner, who as sovereign had refused to sanction the illumination, and the conservative Nelson club, whose members were showered with stones as they sat at dinner. Yet supporters as well as opponents of the queen's cause later admitted that the crowd became blatantly

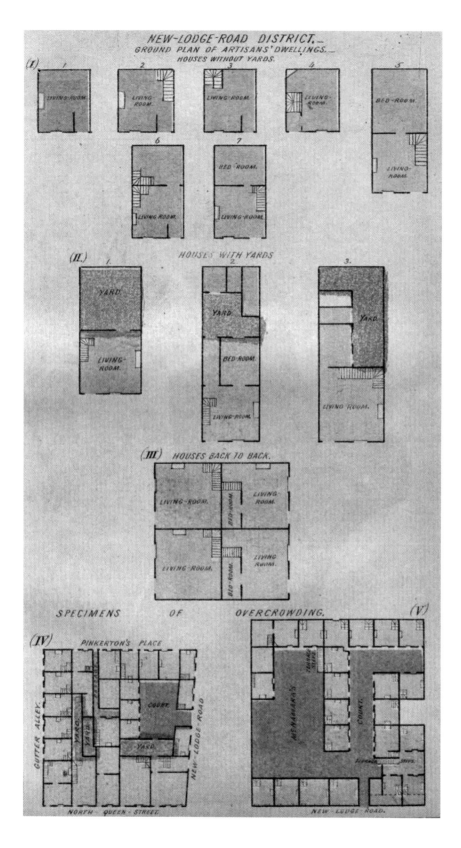

Plans of substandard working-class housing, from Andrew Malcolm's *The Sanitary State of Belfast* (1852). Back-to-back houses and overcrowding of the kind depicted blocked off light and air, while houses without yards could not have the ash pits which, in the absence of sewers, represented the only possible form of privy. Malcolm (1818–56), a doctor at the General Hospital, wrote a series of pioneering studies of the impact of industrialization on the working class of the town.

indiscriminate, smashing the windows of both illuminated and unlit houses, and in some cases allegedly demanding money in order to leave properties untouched.[67] In this sense the disturbances were evidence of what had and had not changed since the heady days of the 1790s. On the one hand there was still the potential, two decades after the defeat of the United Irishmen, to mobilize support for a radical cause, even if in the unlikely form of a German-born princess of dubious reputation. On the other hand the reform-minded middle classes, in a much-expanded town divided by industrialization along new lines of social class, could no longer be sure of controlling the forces they summoned on to the streets.

Belfast in 1820

In the twenty years after 1800 developments that had tentatively begun in the late eighteenth century continued and became more pronounced. The population, already more than twice what it had been in the 1750s, almost doubled again, from 19,000 in 1802 to 37,000 in 1821. The social geography of the town had also changed. Pococke, in 1752, had described a residential pattern characteristic of the pre-industrial town: the wealthiest inhabitants lived in the town centre, while behind and between the main streets were 'several lanes in which the inferior people live'.[68] In the 1820s the main streets of the town centre, High Street, Waring Street and Bridge Street, were still residential. Increasingly, however, their inhabitants were shopkeepers or tradesmen living over business premises. The urban elite, by contrast, had retreated from an increasingly crowded and commercialized centre to the new fashionable district focused on Donegall Place and Donegall Square. At the other end of the social scale too, residential segregation was becoming more clear cut. Large numbers of mainly poor householders continued to crowd into the lanes and entries of the old town. But there had also developed, to the north and west of the town centre, a wholly new type of working-class residential zone, as streets of terraced housing continued to multiply around the factories that had brought their inhabitants to Belfast.

There was likewise a further development of the town's associational culture. The Chamber of Commerce, which had had such a shaky start in the 1780s and 1790s, reconstituted itself in 1802 with 69 members. Its meetings were initially irregular, and there was a financial crisis in 1812–13, but by the 1820s the Chamber was an established part of Belfast's business life. In 1806, following the naval victory at Trafalgar, leading conservatives founded a Nelson club, which over the next two decades provided a regular round of dinners and balls. The club had its own premises in Donegall Place, where the presence of a head waiter and of 'a superior billiard table by one of the best London makers' suggests that its functions were as much social as political.[69]

The Commercial Buildings, opened in 1820, provided hotel accommodation, a newsroom and assembly rooms, replacing the more modest Exchange and Assembly Rooms as the hub of commercial and social life. Between 1921 and 1963 it became the offices of the *Northern Whig* newspaper. Detail from James O'Hagan's map of Belfast in 1848.

Photograph © National Museums Northern Ireland. Collection Ulster Museum. IA 1848.

MERCIAL BUILDINGS.

In 1820 the two-storey thatched cottages that had long anomalously stood opposite the Assembly Rooms on Waring Street were replaced by a set of Commercial Buildings. Funded by the issue of shares of £100 each, the new building provided accommodation for visitors, an extensive piazza for the use of merchants and traders, and a splendid newsroom offering accommodation for up to 100 readers, so that 'the lover of literature, the merchant, seaman, mechanic, stockholder and politician' could all be catered for.[70]

Other associations created in the years after 1800 further testified to an expanding field of cultural activity: a Literary Society in 1801, a Historic Society (1811), whose mission was to educate the town's young men through classes and debates, a Galvanic Society (1805), a Cosmographical Society (1811), and even a Society for Acquiring Knowledge (1806). Some of these were short lived. However, the Belfast Natural History and Philosophical Society (1821) was a permanent addition to the intellectual life of the town, particularly following the opening in 1831 of its celebrated museum in College Square. That location took its name from another important development: the establishment in 1814 of the Belfast Academical Institution, which until the creation thirty years later of the Queen's College provided the middle classes of the town with a third-level education in both the arts and the sciences. Meanwhile Belfast had acquired a second newspaper, the *Belfast Commercial Chronicle*, launched in 1805 and continuing until 1855. From 1824 it was to have a third, the *Northern Whig*, catering for moderate liberal opinion.

All of this progress, material and cultural, was made possible by economic growth, and in particular by the continued expansion of the partly mechanized cotton industry. One observer estimated in 1812 that there were some 22,000 individuals, who would have been mainly women, employed in cotton mills within a ten-mile radius of Belfast, as well as some 25,000 weavers and around 5,000 other workers.[71] Other rural migrants found work in the expanding port, or in the large building sector created by urban growth itself. Linen continued to be important to Belfast's economy. In 1810, in fact, it accounted for 80 per cent of Belfast's total exports, valued at £2.3 out of £2.9 million.[72] But the flax fibre from which linen yarn was produced was too brittle to be spun on the machinery used for cotton. Throughout the first quarter of the nineteenth century a variety of manufacturers, subsidized by the Irish Linen Board, experimented with machine spinning, but their products consistently proved to be more expensive than handspun yarn, and of poorer quality.[73] Hence linen continued to be spun and woven across a large area of the Ulster countryside, with Belfast serving as a depot rather than a centre of manufacturing.

By the end of the 1820s two further developments were to transform the town's prospects. The first was the decision of Lord Donegall, in 1822, to escape his continuing debts by a massive grant of leases in perpetuity covering virtually all of the land within and around Belfast. For a downpayment merchants, manufacturers and speculators acquired permanent possession of existing sites and future building land at a modest fixed rent, fuelling the building boom that over the next two decades was to transform the dimensions of the town.[74] The second was the introduction from around 1826 of a new process, wet spinning, in which a humid atmosphere made flax fibre more amenable to machine spinning. This in turn made possible a transfer of resources from cotton, where Irish manufacturers had to compete with giant, cost-effective enterprises in Scotland and England, to linen, where Ulster had an established supremacy, securing the future of large-scale factory-based industry. After a long apprenticeship as Lord Donegall's improving town, Belfast, no longer the private possession of an aristocratic proprietor, was on its way to becoming Ireland's Manchester.

WHITE STAR
ROYAL MAIL STEAMER
"OLYMPIC"

OLYMPIC

...PIC" AND "TITANIC" HARLAND & WOLFF'S BEL...

Workshop of the Empire, 1820–1914

Stephen A. Royle

In the nineteenth century, Ireland had the attractions of being reasonably exotic but at the same time reasonably accessible to travel writers from other parts of Europe who sought an outlet for their musings. The most famous of these is undoubtedly William Makepeace Thackeray, who wrote the *Irish Sketch Book* after his 1841 visit to Ireland in a straightforward ploy to make money. Belfast, with its 'docks and quays [...] busy with their craft and shipping, upon the beautiful borders of the Lough', shared in his wry observations, the most famous and perhaps now over-familiar of which being that the town 'looks hearty, thriving, and prosperous, as if it had money in its pockets and roast-beef for dinner'.[1] Rather than privilege Thackeray once more, this chapter uses as its spine the fresher, being less well known, observations of a visitor to the city from a later era, when the early phases of industrialization observed by Thackeray had matured. The French writer, Madame (Marie-Anne) de Bovet (1855–c.1935), who became Marchioness Deschamps de Bois Hébert, wrote novels, biographies and travel books, including two on Ireland, *Lettres d'Irlande*, in 1889, and *Three Months' Tour in Ireland*, in 1891.[2] All the headings below are quotations relating to Belfast from her second book on Ireland. The chapter considers Belfast over a period encompassing the reign of Queen Victoria, if extending a little in both directions beyond that monarch's long period in office. This reference to the British queen is deliberate, for in one of Madame de Bovet's most perceptive remarks, Belfast was cast as 'the least Irish of all Irish towns',[3] it being instead rather a good example of a British industrializing city, a workshop of the empire indeed. The political history of the period is well covered elsewhere; this chapter will focus mainly on the geography of Belfast, including its built form and structure.

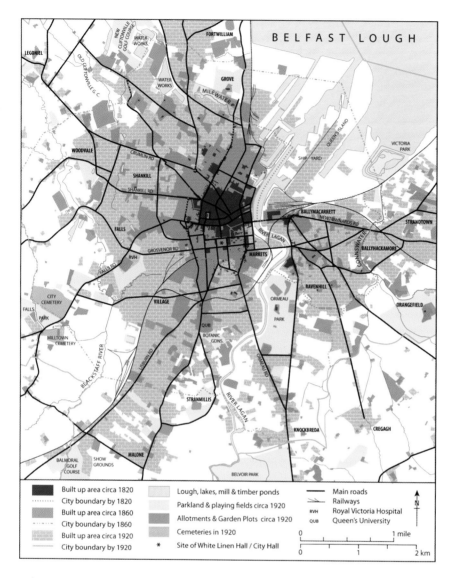

The growth of Belfast c.1820–c.1920. In 1820 Belfast was tightly clustered around its seventeenth-century core on the west bank of the River Lagan, with only pockets of development in Ballymacarrett in County Down on the opposite side of the river. Forty years later there had been considerable expansion – residential development to the south and industrial growth to the north and west. By 1920 the industrial city had reached its peak with the major areas of reclaimed land in Belfast Lough serving as sites for both shipbuilding and the harbour. East Belfast was now an integral part of the city with swathes of industrial workers' housing similar to that found in districts to the north and west. By this time the development of parks and open spaces had brought increased opportunities for leisure and recreation.

Map provided by Stephen Royle.

'The second town in Ireland is commercial, Protestant and wealthy, that is to say profoundly uninteresting'

That Belfast was uninteresting should, we hope, be countered by this entire book, although one rather imagines that Madame de Bovet's barb was directed at the perceived dourness of the 'Protestants' from her own French Catholic standpoint, rather than at the city itself. Her declaration might be challenged in its other aspects too. This is true even of the ascription to Belfast of the position of Ireland's second city. In 1841 Belfast had only 75,308 inhabitants compared to Dublin's 233,726. By the end of the nineteenth century, however, it actually exceeded Dublin in population, until boundary adjustments restored the latter's pre-eminence. Industrializing Belfast reached a population of 386,947 in 1911.

Another of de Bovet's claims was that Belfast was 'commercial'. This can be accepted only if 'commerce' be defined widely enough to incorporate manufacturing. At this period a strictly commercial European city would have been Hamburg, the German port sheltered some way along the Elbe, whose mighty Speicherstadt warehouse district took in and subsequently repackaged and redistributed goods from across the world; trade was its lifeblood. Belfast traded, too, but largely in Belfast-made manufactures, if constructed from imported raw materials; that was its commerce.

Was Belfast Protestant? Certainly in terms of the expression of political power it was. James Craig's declaration in 1934 that Northern Ireland was a Protestant parliament and a Protestant state needs be adjusted only for the name of the assembly and the scale of its reach to describe Belfast Corporation in the era leading up to partition. Were the people Protestant? Not entirely: Belfast's population was 31 per cent Catholic in 1834;[4] this reached 34 per cent in 1861, as Catholics from rural Ireland continued to move there in search of employment, before the proportion fell back to 24 per cent by 1901.[5] So Belfast was majority Protestant only. Indeed the city's narrative in the nineteenth century and beyond would have been very different without its substantial Catholic minority, for relations between Belfast's contesting groups formed a central theme of that story.

As to Belfast being wealthy, that, too, can be challenged, for while there was wealth in the city – some of its entrepreneurs lived very well, and the large and growing middle classes were comfortable – there was also real poverty. And the lack of wealth at the town's highest social stratum – the aristocratic family who entered the period under study here owning Belfast – explains a good deal of the way in which Belfast developed subsequently. This family was the Chichesters, granted the land of Belfast in 1603. Their title was Donegall, the fifth earl becoming the first marquess of Donegall in 1791. His eldest child had been born in 1769 – Chichester Quay being so named in commemoration of that event – and this infant went on to become one of the largest debtors in history. Even while still in his twenties Lord Belfast had accumulated debts of £30,000. Inheriting the Donegall title at his father's death in 1799, the new second marquess became something of a rarity, a significant Irish landlord who was not an absentee. Instead he moved to Belfast, living opposite the White Linen Hall before moving east of the river in 1807 to what is now Ormeau Park. Here he lived with his wife and their growing family; there were seven sons. Residence brought him and his family popularity in the town; the *Belfast News Letter*'s characterization of him as the 'best of landlords' in 1829 was not ironic.[6] But Donegall had moved to Belfast to distance himself from creditors in England, Although, as a peer, the marquess could not be arrested for debt, he was still in need of money since creditors did chase him to Belfast. In the 1820s he established a system of granting perpetual leases in Belfast in return for a cash payment called a fine. Those purchasing the leases were generally industrialists and entrepreneurs, who thus obtained ready access to land on which to build houses and develop their businesses, free from the sort of control that the first marquess had exercised over his urban tenants. The fines, amounting perhaps to £300,000, were supposed to clear Lord Donegall's debts; instead the marquess continued in his profligate ways, for example spending £86,000 building Ormeau House, a Tudor-style mansion in the grounds of his demesne.

Not all the family were wastrels. George Hamilton Chichester, who became the third marquess, had three children, a daughter and two sons. The elder boy died in infancy; the second, Frederick Richard Chichester, earl of Belfast, grandson of the second marquess, was a particular favourite in the town because of his good works. He supported the arts – being a writer and composer himself – and also practical worthy causes, such as William O'Hanlon's campaign for better sanitation. O'Hanlon wrote that the earl was 'noble by rank, but still more so by personal worth and accomplishments'.[7] The earl died in Naples in 1853 of scarlet fever at the age of 25, his brief life being celebrated by the statue that stood outside the Royal Belfast Academical Institution until replaced in 1876 by a statue of Henry Cooke.[8]

At the death of the second marquess in 1844 his debts, rather than having been reduced, had grown to around £400,000. Using the Encumbered Estates Court, which had been established more to deal with the impact of the Famine upon landed estates, the third marquess disposed of further property in Belfast and 30,000 acres (12,100 ha) in County Antrim.[9] Another way in which his family raised money was by the marriage of his only daughter, Harriet, to the eighth earl of Shaftesbury in 1857. The resulting restoration of the family fortunes might be seen in the building of the last Belfast Castle, the new family home from 1862 on the slopes of Cave Hill, erected to a Scottish Baronial style by Lanyon, Lynn and Lanyon.

The second marquess of Donegall's lasting impact upon what literally had been his town came from the use of Belfast as a vehicle for producing cash, which transferred the control of its development from the landlord family to the industrial and merchant classes. The substantial use such people were making of this opportunity was evident in the building boom that took the number of houses from just under 6,000 in 1821 to 11,751 by 1841. In 1853 the municipal boundaries were substantially increased, in order to accommodate what was described as Belfast's 'growing greatness'.[10]

'The busy harbour is a thing to rejoice the economist but is without interest for the artist'

Belfast's 'growing greatness' was, to a large extent, linked to its maritime location. As Madame de Bovet observed, its harbour was certainly busy and was in considerable need of extension and improvement by the early nineteenth century. The extension was in the requirement for more quayside; the improvement was in regard to easing access into Belfast itself from Belfast Lough. The River Lagan is a misfit stream, draining rather ineffectually a grand valley fashioned not by its own waters but by glacial action. The end of the ice age saw glacial deposition between the mountain barrier to the north-west, the edge of the Antrim plateau, and the smaller Castlereagh hills opposite, which further impedes drainage. As a result, the waterfront by Belfast and further into the lough itself is naturally shallow, characterized by banks of mud, the sloblands. This impeded the access of large or heavily laden ships into Belfast and they would have to wait in the Pool of Garmoyle for high tide or even discharge their cargoes into smaller vessels or lighters for the last few hundred metres of their journeys. In the 1810s a number of consulting engineers, including Sir John Rennie and Thomas Telford, drew up plans to improve access, but these were not carried out.[11] Instead, a scheme from the London engineer James Walker to dredge deepwater channels through the final two bends of the Lagan was adopted and a government grant of £30,000 was secured in 1832.[12] There was then delay as some interested parties, including the marquess of Donegall, objected. In 1839 the Corporation for Preserving and Improving the Port of Belfast, usually known as the Ballast Board, employed William Dargan, a railway and canal engineer from Carlow, to commence the first cut. The dredged material, the spoil, was dumped and formed Dargan's Island, later to be renamed Queen's Island, in which guise it became a site of considerable industrial significance. The Ballast Board's successor, the Belfast Harbour Commissioners, re-hired Dargan to construct the second cut in 1847, a project of considerable utility as a makework scheme during the Famine as well as being of value to the port of Belfast. The cut was completed in 1849 when the resultant deepwater Victoria Channel finally provided direct access into Belfast for the then largest ships. This helped Belfast to become the largest port in Ireland by 1852,[13] and the number of ships entering the port rose 30 per cent between 1860 and 1914, while their increased capacity saw annual tonnage grow from 800,000 to three million

Early shipbuilding on the Lagan, as depicted by J.W. Carey in his paintings for the Ulster Hall in 1903. The first shipyard, on the Antrim side of the river, was established in 1791 by a Scot, William Ritchie, who was later joined by his brother Hugh. By 1812 the brothers had built 40 ships. In 1820 they launched Belfast's first steamship. Set against this record of construction, Carey's depiction of handicraft production on a deserted beach is best understood as reflecting an imagined contrast with the massive industrial enterprise of his own day rather than as an accurate historical reconstruction.

Reproduced with the kind permission of Belfast City Council.

tons between those years.[14] This all required extension to the harbour; the town docks at High Street and the Lagan quays were replaced by new facilities such as Clarendon Dock (1851). The captain of the Royal Engineers who advised on Belfast's 1853 boundary extension noted that: 'The natural advantages of the town as a seaport have been fully developed by the spirit and enterprise of the Harbour Commissioners in the construction of quays and docks, and extensive improvements which enhance in an eminent degree the favourable position Belfast enjoys for commercial purposes.'[15] The developments continued apace: Spencer and Dufferin Docks (1872), Albert Quay, extended and rebuilt (1873), York Dock (1876), Alexandra Graving Dock (1885–89) and Thompson Graving Dock (1911). When there was no more space around the Victoria Channel, the Musgrave Channel was constructed from 1899–1903 between Queen's Island and the County Down shore to its south.

Port activity was only part of Belfast's story, for within the harbour area were also located major shipbuilding facilities. By 1820 there were a handful of shipbuilding concerns, mainly connected with the Ritchie family who had been constructing vessels on the Lagan since the late eighteenth century. These were wooden ships, but their designs might be innovative; thus in 1820 spectators lining the quaysides cheered off the first Belfast-built steamship, appropriately called *Belfast*, on its maiden voyage to Liverpool.[16] Its engines had come from the town's Lagan Foundry and in 1838 this foundry built the first local iron ship, *Countess of Caledon*, designed to tow lighters on Lough Neagh.[17] These small shipbuilding firms were located on the County Antrim bank of the Lagan but when in 1845 facilities there were removed in the harbour improvement scheme, an area was set aside for shipbuilding on Dargan's Island, although a little later a slip was reinserted on the County Antrim shore.[18] In 1847 the local newspaper reported that Lagan Foundry was building an iron steamer of 600 tons and, presciently, it predicted that this type of enterprise seemed likely to be both permanent and profitable and would employ many workers.[19] This prediction came true and it was expressed spatially on what had become Queen's Island following Queen Victoria's visit to Belfast in 1849. On the island there was a patent slip (an area of ground sloping into the water with a steam winch to drag vessels on to the land) which could be hired, and a small shipbuilding company, Thompson and Kirwan, moved next to it. In 1853 this assemblage was joined by another area let to Edward Hickson of the Eliza Foundry, which wished to extend its output by building iron ships. Hickson had use of the patent slip but also constructed his own facilities. The second manager he employed, from December 1854, was a young Yorkshireman, Edward Harland, who brought experience of working as an engineer and shipbuilder on the Tyne and the Clyde, having also been an apprentice to Robert Stephenson, the noted railway developer. Hickson's business ventures failed, he lost his foundry, and in 1858 he offered the shipyard to Harland.

Sir Edward Harland (1831–95), one of the makers of the nineteenth-century city. A Yorkshireman from Scarborough, Harland was an apprentice for Robert Stephenson, the railway engineer, on the Tyne before working in shipbuilding on the Clyde and back in Newcastle. In December 1854, aged just 23, he was appointed as manager of Edward Hickson's shipbuilding business on Queen's Island. Three years later he took on Gustav Wolff as his assistant. In 1858 Harland accepted Hickson's offer to buy the yard, forming Edward James Harland and Company, which became Harland and Wolff in 1861 when Wolff was made a partner. He served as a Harbour Commissioner, as mayor of Belfast in 1885 and 1886, and as Conservative MP for Belfast North from 1889 until his death. He was knighted in 1885.

Image supplied courtesy of Belfast Harbour Commissioners.

Harland had been seeking to establish his own business and, having failed to secure premises in Liverpool, accepted Hickson's invitation. He also bought up the original Queen's Island shipyard situated on the other side of the patent slip, giving his firm, Edward James Harland and Company, a parcel of 3.5 acres (1.4 ha) of land. By that time Harland was employing Gustav Wolff as his assistant. Wolff had useful contacts in the Liverpool maritime trade, in particular his uncle, Gustav Schwabe, and early orders for Harland's company came from the Bibby Line, of which Schwabe was a partner. In 1861 Harland and Wolff came into being when Wolff became Harland's partner.[20]

Only with hindsight can one regard as inevitable the success of this new company in the late Victorian era. A number of factors had to come together. Better facilities had to be established to enable the company to grow, such as the provision by the Harbour Commissioners of the tidal Abercorn Basin and the Hamilton Graving Dock in 1867, both on the Queen's Island side of the channel and thus adjacent to the Harland and Wolff site. Even this was not inevitable, for the investment was delayed for several years by poor economic circumstances following the Crimean War and the facilities might well have been built on the County Antrim shore. The Belfast region had no raw materials of any utility for shipbuilding, but Queen's Island did provide a sheltered site, which being reclaimed land was flat and easily worked. The era was also favourable, for despite economic slumps as in the 1870s there was a reasonable demand for shipping, especially passenger vessels (many for the White Star Line), given the mass migrations from Europe that characterized the late nineteenth and early twentieth centuries.

Another significant factor was the personal qualities of the first two partners: Harland, the engineer whose innovative design of long, slim ships – likened to coffins in their shape – proved to be efficient, and Wolff who brought financial acumen and good contacts. Later the yard's William Pirrie, a partner from 1874 and chairman after the death of Harland, became a significant figure in shipping circles, for example as Controller General of Merchant Shipping during the Great War. Pirrie worked tirelessly for the company for decades, and was rewarded by being appointed a viscount and becoming towards the end of his life a senator in the new Northern Ireland parliament. In 1878 Harland and Wolff had expanded by taking over another shipyard, McLaine's, and also by building new engine and boiler works. At this time the company was enabled to take in more land when the leisure facilities at the north-east end of Queen's Island were re-designated for industry – a replacement recreational site at Victoria Park at the mouth of the Connswater being provided eventually. Harland and Wolff was able to construct an additional four building berths on the former park site. Nearer the end of the century, when ships were increasing in size, major facilities such as the 800-foot (244-metre) Alexandra Graving Dock were built on Queen's Island, by then

"OLYMPIC" and "TITANIC". HARLAND & WOLFF'S. BELFAST   W.A.G. 2014

ALEXANDRA GRAVING DOCK

Olympic and *Titanic* side by side in the gantries of Harland and Wolff before *Olympic*'s launch in October 1910. *Titanic* underwent its sea trials on 2 April 1912 and embarked eight days later on the maiden voyage that was to end in its sinking on 15 April, following collision with an iceberg.

Photograph © National Museums Northern Ireland. Collection Ulster Folk & Transport Museum. HOYFM. WAG.2079.

much larger and no longer insular given continued land reclamation. The yard was further reorganized after a serious fire in 1896. This was just after Harland's death in 1895, his funeral in the city having been an affair of great pomp.[21] The Thompson Graving Dock was completed by 1911 and its 850-foot (259-metre) length was occupied first by the then largest ship ever built, *Olympic*, at 45,324 tons, followed a little later by *Titanic*, even larger at 46,328 tons. The infamous collision between this ship and an iceberg on its maiden voyage in 1912 led to the deaths of 1,517 passengers and crew, including Harland and Wolff's chief designer, Thomas Andrews. Harland and Wolff employed 2,400 workers in 1870 and 14,000 in 1914, mainly men, a counterpart to the female labour in the textile mills. Of 100,809 manufacturing workers in Belfast in 1905, 43.7 per cent were female, an unusually high proportion for a shipbuilding city.[22] This availability of work for all family members, together with Belfast's relatively good housing and cheap living costs, helps to explain how the shipyards could attract skilled workers to the city.

Of Belfast's other shipyards, the most important was Workman, Clark and Co., founded in 1879 by two former Harland and Wolff apprentices, Frank Workman and George Clark. This yard was on the County Antrim shore rather than Queen's Island and, despite being known in Belfast as the 'wee yard', it expanded to employ 14,000 workers by 1894. Twice, in 1902 and 1909, Workman, Clark launched a larger tonnage of shipping than any other shipyard in the world.[23]

'The manufacture of linen has ... attained large proportions ... in Protestant Ulster'

The opening of the Alexandra Graving Dock in 1889. The continuous development of the harbour was essential to Belfast's nineteenth-century growth.

Image provided by Mary Evans Picture Library. © Copyright 2001 British Photographers' Liaison Committee/Finers Stephens.

'The flax spinning business was introduced into Belfast and [...] began to take root. Then it flourished. And that year 1830 [is] the epoch which marks the time when the present extensive progress of Belfast may be regarded as having commenced.'[24] This comment by Thomas L'Estrange, written in the late nineteenth century, neatly summarizes the history of linen manufacturing in Belfast. Shipbuilding was of considerable significance, too, but – in its modern form of iron steamships at least – it came later, adding another economic sector to an industrial town already engaged in extensive textile manufacture. Captain Gilbert, in 1853, reported:

> The great staple of manufacture in Belfast and its vicinity is linen, and the spinning and weaving of linen yarn. From a recent trade report of this district I find that in the year 1829 there was only one mill, containing 15,000 spindles, in 1850 the number had increased to 326,000, and at the commencement of the present year they had reached 500,000 spindles, upwards of 100,000 having been added during 1852.[25]

The Brown Linen Hall in Donegall Street, built in 1773, held its market every Friday. By tradition its gates were still opened every Friday until the end of the nineteenth century, when the bulding had fallen into disuse and decline.

Photograph © National Museums Northern Ireland. Collection Ulster Museum. BELUM.Y2115.

Although Belfast had long traded linen produced in rural Ulster, with Brown Linen Halls being built in 1754 and 1773 and the larger White Linen Hall for the bleached linen trade in 1785, the original focus of its own textile manufacture was cotton. Indeed, George Benn noted in his history of Belfast of 1823 that 'there is very little linen cloth woven in this town or parish'; rather, cotton spinning, weaving, printing and bleaching were mentioned.[26] The transition to linen happened shortly after Benn's book appeared and the process was relatively swift. It depended, as so often in Belfast, upon both chance and the personal qualities and decision making of individuals. The principal actors here were brothers, Thomas and Andrew Mulholland. In 1824 it was reported that they were to move their cotton-spinning business from Wine Tavern Street to new premises in York Street.[27] This mill burnt down in 1828.[28] By that time the Mulhollands had already begun to experiment with flax spinning, having set up a mill for that purpose in Francis Street the previous year. The destruction of their York Street premises gave them the opportunity to rebuild their major enterprise for the manufacture of linen. Their partner, John Hind, investigated the latest techniques in Leeds and the Mulhollands had the necessary equipment manufactured in Belfast.[29] The new mill was, of course, steam-powered, unlike some earlier establishments in Belfast that had used water power. A contemporary passage based on an examination of the York Street mill exclaimed that:

> It is certain that the brain of man has given birth to a gigantic power [...] which is destined in all probability to become one day his master rather than his servant. This modern 'Frankenstein' though yet in his infancy beats all the exploits of

The construction in 1830 of the York Street mill, owned by the brothers Thomas and Andrew Mulholland, marked the beginnings of the flax-spinning industry that was to be one of the twin pillars of Belfast's prosperity throughout the nineteenth century. The number of spindles rose from an initial 8,000 to 25,000 by 1856, making the York Street mill the biggest factory of its type in the world. W.M. Thackeray visited in 1841 to find 'nearly five hundred girls employed in it. They work in huge long chambers lighted by numbers of windows, hot with steam, buzzing and humming with hundreds of thousands of whirling wheels, that all take their motion from a steam engine which lives apart in a hot cast-iron temple of its own, from which it communicates with the innumerable machines that the five hundred girls preside over. They have seemingly but to take away the work when done – the enormous monster in the cast iron room does it all. He cards the flax, and combs it, and spins it, and beats it, and twists it; the five hundred girls stand by to feed him, or take the material from him when he has had his will of it.'

'Barefoot worker, York Street mill', drawn by W.M. Thackeray (1842), from *The Irish Sketch Book* (1843).

fabulous giants into the shade. His progeny are already numerous and have divided themselves into three distinct classes or branches, but [are] all of the same nature and of similar Herculean might. One class have taken to the road and work their huge velocipedes with tremendous force and swiftness. Another have chosen water and impel by paddles a thousand vessels without the aid of oar or sail. But the third have located themselves in mills and factories where by the assistance of a few feeders, they whirl innumerable machines and myriads of spindles performing more work in an hour than half a million men would effect in a day.[30]

Other entrepreneurs followed the Mulhollands' example and produced linen powered by this Herculean steam, engendering a 'thinning out process' of cotton manufacture as it was to be described.[31] By October 1832 12 linen mills were at work;[32] by 1860 there were 32 linen mills in Belfast and only two spinning cotton.[33] The destination of Belfast's progress in its new venture was its nickname of 'Linenopolis', but the journey towards such a designation was not always smooth. In 1847 trade was depressed, as elsewhere in the United Kingdom, with short-time working and mill closures.[34] There was then expansion from 1850 and a positive boom during the American Civil War (1861–65) when supplies of raw cotton from the southern states of the USA were interrupted and linen made up some of the shortfall. Inevitably there was a post-war slump in linen when cotton supplies resumed after 1867.[35] This led to the establishment in 1873 of the Linen Merchants' Association, a trade body of 52 firms.[36] Competition from elsewhere in Europe was another problem. The demand for linen during the American Civil War had been met by manufacturers on the Continent, particularly in Eastern Europe, as well as those in Ulster, and the restoration of cotton led to excess capacity in the industry, especially spinning. Armstrong noted that the continental producers had easier access to supplies of flax than those in Belfast, and paid lower wages to a workforce that worked longer hours, so that they could undercut Belfast firms. Consequently there was an increase of yarn imported into the UK leading to a contraction of spinning in Belfast.[37] However, weavers in Ulster benefited from this cheaper yarn, while a high reputation for quality helped Ulster linen retain its place in international markets. The American consul reported in 1883:

There is reason to believe that in the manufacture of the finer linens no other country can successfully compete with those of Ireland. Germany already is a rival in the coarser manufactures, and it seems probable, with equal advantages in machinery and labour, that she will continue to increase her exports in linens of this quality. But it is doubtful that the climate will admit of the finer.[38]

In 1899 the president of the Linen Merchants' Association was still able to claim for linen the position of the 'staple industry in this province'.[39] In the new century, after a difficult time in the labour disputes of 1907, the

The Royal Ulster Works off the Dublin Road, home of the giant printing firm of Marcus Ward & Company. Marcus Ward began working as a paper manufacturer in Belfast at the turn of the nineteenth century, developing as a fine printer, bookbinder and stationer by 1833. During the 1840s the firm developed the expertise in colour lithography – the beginnings of the illustration process – that contributed to its fame as a publisher.

Reproduced with the kind permission of the Public Record Office of Northern Ireland.

Marcus Ward & Company, promotional leaflet. With the death in 1847 of the firm's eponymous head, the business passed into the hands of his three sons, Francis, John and William. Under their guidance the company developed further, becoming renowned for its illustrated books. By the 1880s, however, technology was leaving the firm behind; in the face of the evolution of photography its two main strengths, talented artists and chromolithography, were ceasing to be significant. The Royal Ulster Works was closed in 1899, when Marcus Ward & Co. went into liquidation.

Image © Roger Dixon.

industry was boosted by demand during the Great War. Thus the report of the Linen Merchants' Association for 1915 found that the year had been 'not unprofitable'.[40]

Indeed, then, 'the manufacture of linen […] attained large proportions' as Madame de Bovet observed. She concluded her remark with the words 'in Protestant Ulster', which might be challenged regarding this industry since linen, unlike shipbuilding, employed a large number of Catholics among its workforce, 70 per cent of which was female. William Topping, who spent a long career in Belfast textile manufacture from 1903, noted that the female millworkers, principally flax spinners, were predominantly Catholics, while about three-quarters of weavers were Protestants. Topping also remarked that they normally worked together harmoniously.[41]

Captain Gilbert presented a tabulated list of Belfast industries in 1853 (Table 2), indicating something of the range of different economic sectors then to be found. This certainly underestimates the number of factories in the town, given his exclusion of steam engines of less than five horsepower, but it does serve as a contemporary indication of the dominance of linen, for 31 of 78 mills and factories listed were employed in flax spinning. It also shows that steam by this time had become much more significant than water power. Gilbert's original analysis divided the industries into two spatial categories, inside and outside the boundary established in 1836 and, with the exception of cornmills, all the factories utilizing water power were located outside the boundary. The town factories had adopted a different architecture based around the steam engines at their heart. Another point to note from the table is the small scale of the shipbuilding industry at this time.

Table 2: Belfast Industries, 1853

How employed	Number of mills or factories	Steam (horsepower)	Water (horsepower)
Flax spinning	31	1873	180
Cotton spinning	3	172	40
Weaving	4	72	0
Foundries	9	120	0
Machine makers	3	20	0
Cornmills	6	115	90
Ironworks	1	275	0
Feltworks	3	28	0
Distillery	1	60	0
Sawmills	2	24	0

Railway	2	18	0
Bleachers and printers	3	136	171
Cement	1	26	0
Gas making	1	8	0
Shipyard	1	10	0
Alabaster works	1	10	0
Bark mills	1	5	0
Ropemakers	1	10	0
Printing and bookbinding	2	10	0
Brickmakers	2	12	0
Total	78	3004	481

Note: excludes small steam engines of less that 5 horsepower

Source: adapted from Francis Yarde Gilbert to Edward Granville, Earl of St Germans, Lord Lieutenant of Ireland, 11 February 1853, *Belfast Municipal Boundaries* (BPP 1852–53 (958) xciv.23).

Gallaher's tobacco and cigarette factory, York Street, the larger of the firm's two premises, completed in 1896. Thomas Gallaher had begun his business in Londonderry in 1857. His decision to transfer to Belfast in 1863 reflected the eclipse of Ulster's second urban centre by its larger rival.

Photograph © National Museums Northern Ireland. Collection Ulster Museum. BELUM.Y2839.

The total list of Belfast industries from 1840 to 1900 in the Royal Irish Academy's *Irish Historic Towns Atlas* fascicle shows 2,078 entries under 'Manufacturing' in 70 different categories.[42] Some of these industries, including engineering and chemical factories, were associated with textiles and shipbuilding. One example was Belfast Ropeworks, established in 1873 under Gustav Wolff, which made ropes for the shipyards. Its factory in east Belfast became the largest of its type in the world (the site is now the Connswater shopping centre). Other industrial sectors were independent of linen and shipyards and were significant in their own right, such as aerated water manufacture led by Cantrell and Cochrane, and the Sirocco Works of 1881, which specialized in heating and ventilation equipment. Belfast also produced whiskey and beer and contained important tobacco factories. A 1913 book noted that Gallaher's six-storey tobacco factory covered 4 acres (1.6 ha), employed 2,000 people and was one of the largest industrial concerns in the world.[43] There were several foundries, the largest of which, that of Victor Coates, was, like the ropeworks, located in east Belfast. The early industrial growth of that part of County Down had led its landowner, Baron Templemore, nephew of the second marquess of Donegall, to consider in 1853 an ambitious redevelopment project for Ballymacarrett. This would have seen the replacement of the streets and housing with a planned industrial suburb. However, the scheme proved too expensive to implement fully and it was abandoned, although the long, straight Templemore Avenue, the scale of which is out of character for east Belfast, was built under the plan.[44]

'Bare feet are rare, even in the lower orders'

Madame de Bovet's observation on the rarity of people walking the streets of Belfast unshod is a metaphor for the relative wealth of the city and its residents. Unlike some other parts of Ireland, she is suggesting, here is a place where people can afford shoes. However, one group in Belfast in the industrial era often did go barefoot. This was the linen workers, especially the women, and a focus on them under this heading enables a discussion of the social welfare issues raised by Belfast's industrialization. The bare feet of the flax spinners caused just one of the health problems to arise in their industry. As early as 1845 Friedrich Engels observed, if not specifically in relation to Belfast, that in 'flax-spinning mills, the air is filled with fibrous dust, which produces chest afflictions, especially among workers in the carding and combing-rooms […] Especially unwholesome is the wet spinning of linen yarn which is carried on by young girls and boys.'[45] Dr Andrew Malcolm brought such concerns into Belfast itself, the town specializing in this wet spinning of flax, which produced finer products. Malcolm worked at the General and Fever Hospital, for which he wrote a history,[46] and he was a campaigner for better sanitation and improved working conditions. At the Belfast meeting of the British Association in 1852 he spoke on sanitation but also mentioned industrial health problems, principally caused by poor ventilation.[47] He followed this up with a study of the morbidity of 2,078 female linen workers, which he presented at a later British Association meeting in Glasgow in 1855. He found that 73.2 per cent of these women did not complain about their health, 10.4 per cent were in tolerable heath but 'complained more or less constantly' and 16.2 per cent were 'decidedly delicate' and required medical attention. The early production stages of hackling and carding saw the most serious problems, given the flax and tow dust thrown into the air: 'the functions of the organs of respiration must be materially and injuriously interfered with'. In the spinning rooms, temperatures of about 32°C (90°F), together with the atmosphere being 'charged with vapour', would lead to perspiration. Further, the spinners would be sprayed by water thrown off the wet fibres. Such conditions Malcolm judged to be responsible for the 'marked preponderance of pulmonary infections' and he recommended better ventilation, artificial respirators for hacklers and carders, and special waterproof mill clothes for spinners, adding a note to mill owners about their responsibilities as employers towards their workers.[48]

Malcolm's message was not universally accepted, for another Belfast doctor, John Moore, claimed in 1867 that flax manufacture was healthy since the workers did not have to adopt constrained positions nor exert themselves unduly. The fibrous particles in the air he regarded as 'comparatively harmless'. Injuries in the hackling rooms did occur among young male workers, but 'boys will be boys' was his complacent response. Spinning itself, Moore accepted, did present problems from the heat and damp and here came the issue over the bare feet, for he was concerned about conditions caused by the women standing barefoot all day on wet floors.[49] Matters improved later as better equipment was developed and millworkers more often wore shoes, so Madame de Bovet's observation of 1890 about the lack of bare feet rings true. However, only in 1906 was it made compulsory in linen mills to extract dust from the atmosphere and to ensure that floors were drained.[50] William Topping's reflections on his working life in linen manufacture make some reference to poor conditions, but the threats to health posed by mill work do not appear to have been a serious concern. Indeed women employed in the first decades of the twentieth century, interviewed many years later, claimed to believe that the steam aided those with respiratory problems, while the moisture was good for the hair and complexion.[51] Instead the main focus of discontent was wages. For example, there was a strike by linen lappers in 1891, which saw members of the Linen Merchants' Association threaten to dismiss union members in their employment.[52]

'It is clean and the lamentable poverty seen in other parts of Ireland does not exist'

Observations regarding the cleanliness of Victorian Belfast depended on which parts of the settlement were being viewed, although in theory it should all have been clean. In an appendix to Francis Gilbert's 1853 report appeared a long letter from Belfast's Officer of Health, Samuel Browne. In this he detailed some of the Acts pertaining to cleanliness and sanitation in Belfast: the width of streets was regulated, householders could be compelled to clear drains, new housing had to be on properly drained sites, privies and cesspools could be inspected. Cellar dwellings were prohibited, as were earthen floors. Street cleansing and the removal of ashes were provided for. Hotels and taverns were regulated, as were common lodging houses. Whitewashing of places where contagious diseases had occurred could be and was ordered, as during the cholera epidemic of 1849. Some months before Browne's letter, Andrew Malcolm's paper at the 1852 British Association meeting in Belfast had focused on Belfast's sewers and drainage, mentioning also ventilation, water supplies, street cleaning, housing, schools, slaughterhouses and graveyards, all of which had impacts on sanitation and disease. He even suggested – with the aid of a drawing – improvements to sewerage systems. Despite this, Browne wrote that 'the great question of the proper drainage and sewerage of towns has not yet been sufficiently investigated so as to arrive at a conclusion as to what is really the best method'. He made a plea that this did not mean nothing should be done and one benefit of Belfast's proposed boundary extension would be to bring the outlying districts that were without planning regulations under the oversight of the Belfast authorities, for 'the parts of Belfast [...] without the limits of the borough must suffer from the lack of such sanitary control'.[53]

Although factually accurate, Browne's recitation of the sanitary rules and regulations cannot gainsay the different picture on the ground, where those regulations may not always have been put into operation. At the time Browne was writing, the Revd William O'Hanlon was perambulating the less salubrious parts of Belfast to research a series of newspaper articles subsequently published as a book, *Walks among the Poor of Belfast*. One passage, from a choice, exemplifies that in reality parts of Belfast, notwithstanding the regulations, were neither clean nor sanitary:

> Peel's Court with its twelve families in six houses, and shut in – narrow and close – between two nuisance yards, one for the front and another for the back, where we could not stand a moment without a sense of deadly sickness and loathing warning us to flee from the foul spot.[54]

W.A. Maguire has written of the problems caused by 'Belfast's unique addiction to the old dry closet system', partly explained by deficiencies in the

Slum housing, in Mitchell's Court, off Brown Square, c.1911. Although overall housing conditions improved significantly following the Improvement Acts of the late 1840s, some of the worst inner-city dwellings were cleared only in the early twentieth century.

Photograph © National Museums Northern Ireland. Collection Ulster Museum. BELUM.Y2475.

Floods in Donegall Square in 1902, when heavy rain revealed the inadequacy of recent drainage works.

Photograph © National Museums Northern Ireland. Collection Ulster Museum. BELUM.Y8537.

water supply that obstructed the adoption of the water closet.[55] The Belfast Water Act of 1840 transferred responsibility for supply from the Spring Water Commissioners appointed by the Charitable Society to a Water Board elected by ratepayers. The new Water Commissioners inherited sources of supply from a dam at Malone, which supplied a reservoir at Basin Lane from which pipes ran to public fountains. In addition, there were springs at Lisburn Road and Sandy Row. The Water Commissioners built a basin on the Antrim Road supplied by springs from Cave Hill, as well as a reservoir at Carr's Glen. Demand, of course, increased as Belfast grew. In 1855 a consultant water engineer, John Frederick Bateman, recommended a scheme utilizing the River Woodburn towards Carrickfergus in association with other sources,[56] but a decade elapsed before the civil engineer William Dargan built the new reservoirs at Woodburn, which were expanded in 1874. Later reservoirs were constructed at Stoneyford towards Lisburn, but there was an obvious need for a more radical solution to the continuing demands for water in the growing city. Lough Neagh was considered, as were a number of other sources, but in the end Belfast looked south to the Mourne Mountains where rights to a pure source of water at the helpful height of 2,500 feet (762 metres) were granted by the Belfast Water Act of 1893. A storage reservoir at Knockbracken was constructed, initially fed by river water from the Mournes, but to secure supplies the Silent Valley dam was built between 1923 and 1933.[57]

Only in 1887, when water supplies were becoming more reliable, was the Belfast Main Drainage Act passed, enabling the development of a sewerage system that carried untreated ordure across the mudflats to be dumped into Belfast Lough. Maguire captures the level of activity that took place below ground – and also above at this time, as streets were being paved – as a 'fury of paving and sewering'.[58] The scheme was not universally successful as the mudflats could be polluted as sewage leaked from the chute that carried the waste over them. A serious flood in 1902 covered central Belfast in a mixture of sewage and seawater. Following a viceregal commission of enquiry in 1906, the wooden chute was replaced by a concrete pipe, and new pumping stations aided the effective expulsion of sewage. From 1899, the corporation could require the replacement of cesspits and other dry closet arrangements by water closets, usually erected in the backyards of the houses, and this programme had been largely completed by the outbreak of the Great War.

'Belfast is the battleground of religions, a Protestant stronghold in the midst of Catholic and apostolic Erin and the zeal of both sides is quickened by contact'

There is no reason to correct Madame de Bovet's assertion here about Belfast being a battleground, for it has long been one of the major sites of conflict in

The Mater Infirmorum Hospital on the Crumlin Road, c.1900. The opening of the hospital in 1883 reflected both the increasing resources of the town's Catholic population and the steady drift towards separate development along denominational lines. The hospital was run by the Sisters of Mercy, a reminder of the central role of female religious orders in the spectacular growth of specifically Catholic institutions that took place everywhere in Ireland during the second half of the nineteenth century.

Courtesy of the National library of Ireland.

the seemingly unending struggles between Catholics and Protestants in this region. 'Sunday is no joke in Belfast', noted de Bovet,[59] for religion was taken seriously. Belfast citizens adhered to one of a range of Christian traditions. Protestants were dominated numerically by Anglicans (Church of Ireland) and Presbyterians, with the latter split into several different groups, as with the Wesleyan Methodists. Smaller Protestant groups were Covenanters, Congregationalists, Baptists, Unitarians and Moravians. There were various Iron and Mission Halls, the Evangelical Union, the Secession Church and some independent sects. There were Quakers and soldiers of the Salvation Army. By 1900 Belfast had over 200 non-Catholic places of worship, including a synagogue. By contrast, there were just 19 Roman Catholic churches. Catholicism has coherence, and so does not need a range of buildings for different sects. The small number of premises also reflected the poverty of many Catholics in Belfast at this time, which made it difficult to gather the funds necessary to erect new churches to relieve the pressure on accommodation, although there had been an expansion in the number of churches in the second half of the century and there were other significant Catholic institutions, such as the female religious orders and the Mater Infirmorum Hospital.[60]

The strife between Protestants and Catholics, de Bovet's 'battleground', is considered in Chapter 7 of this volume and specific events need not be covered here, although it might be noted that the council's police committee was 'well aware of the excitable character of our operative and labouring classes, and the difference in both political and religious views. If the slightest provocation be given on either side, a riot is sure to ensue.'[61] What is important to this chapter, with its focus on the geography of Belfast, is to note that these competing groups lived and moved largely in segregated spaces. 'The zeal of both sides is quickened by contact' was de Bovet's perceptive comment. Segregation lessened the possibilities of such unpleasant contact as well as offering members of the different religions the comfort of relaxing within their own group. On the other hand, segregation limited the opportunity for people to gain personal knowledge of those of other persuasions, allowing myths and demonization to be engendered. Thus, segregation might be seen as both cause and effect of sectarian strife. Catholic areas tended to be more highly segregated than Protestant, partly because of the class distinctions that saw Catholics working as domestic servants in Protestant households. The Catholic St Brigid's church on Derryvolgie Avenue in the city's exclusive Malone district was erected in 1893 to cater for the demand from domestic staff working in the large houses of what was then a mainly Protestant area. Nicknamed the 'Maids' Church' until recently, it now caters for a different type of clientele as affluent Catholic families have moved into Malone.

It was well known to Belfast people which religious group inhabited the different quarters of the town (indeed, this remains the case in the twenty-first century). For example, when the Twelfth of July procession of 1846 – held that year on 13 July as 12 July was a Sunday – was attacked by 'ruffians' from Smithfield and Hercules Street, the local newspaper did not need to explain that these were Catholic areas.[62] Another Catholic area was Pound Street (usually just called the Pound), while Sandy Row was synonymous with hard-line Protestants. Indeed, O'Hanlon had it as the home of the 'bludgeon-men' and he entered Sandy Row with trepidation: 'even though on a peaceful mission, I thought it just possible we might fare ill among men of blood'.[63]

There were strict social control policies to try to keep Belfast people in check regarding not just riots, but crime generally. This was the case especially at the start of the period when detection rates were low and law enforcement relied on exemplary terror to keep the citizenry under control. For example, in 1822 one John Agnew was subject to 100 lashes in public for abusing a child and another man had 70 lashes for stealing from Brown Street school.[64] Hangings, the ultimate public deterrent, generally took place at Carrickfergus, still the county town of Antrim. In 1816, however, the dramatic attack on the house of the cotton manufacturer Francis Johnson was seen as an outrage demanding special measures, and the two men sentenced to death were hanged on a temporary gallows in Castle Place. A Belfast woman, looking back to her childhood more than fifty years earlier, mistook the number of victims, but otherwise confirmed the vivid impression the event had left:

> I recollect well the procession in 1816 of the three unfortunate men to be hanged going down Donegall Street; three carriages with the creatures and then clergymen, the operator in an open cart covered with a white sheet. I fainted at [the] sight and my aunt took care I should not be at a window the next Friday when some of their accomplices were whipped up the street.[65]

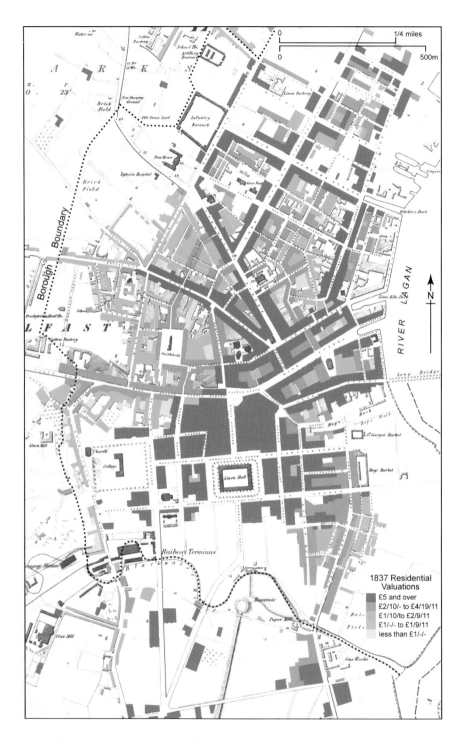

The Belfast Valuation of 1837 shows the town in transition, as the areas of highest value shift from the traditional centre around Waring Street and High Street to the new elite quarter around the White Linen Hall.

Map provided by Stephen Royle.

1837 Residential Valuations
- £5 and over
- £2/10/- to £4/19/11
- £1/10/to £2/9/11
- £1/-/- to £1/9/11
- less than £1/-/-

Following the transfer to Belfast of the assizes in 1850, two further hangings took place outside the newly constructed Crumlin Road gaol, in 1854 and 1863. By this time, however, opinion was moving against public executions, and from 1868 hangings took place behind prison walls. The change reflected the growth

The Belfast Valuation of 1860 shows the continued existence of pockets of poverty in the courts and alleys of the town centre, the huge tracts of low-value working-class housing spread to the west and north, and the increasingly density of high-value properties on the suburban periphery.

Map provided by Stephen Royle.

of more intensive policing. Already by 1864 the town police established in 1816 had expanded to comprise 160 officers and men. From the following year this local force was replaced by a detachment of the Irish constabulary, initially 450 strong. Social control was now maintained by surveillance and regulation rather than by the making of dreadful examples.[66]

Religious divisions and the associated trouble were, on occasion, joined by simple class strife. Especially noteworthy were incidents near the beginning and end of the period: the Corn Law riots of 1815,[67] and the labour disputes of 1907. These latter included the dock strike that united the Catholic and Protestant working classes, both groups being dismayed at low wages. In the end the strikers, led by James Larkin, were defeated on the quaysides and as John Gray has commented, 'opportunities for real social advance, albeit with attendant political risks, were lost'.[68] The Linen Merchants' Association noted that while they

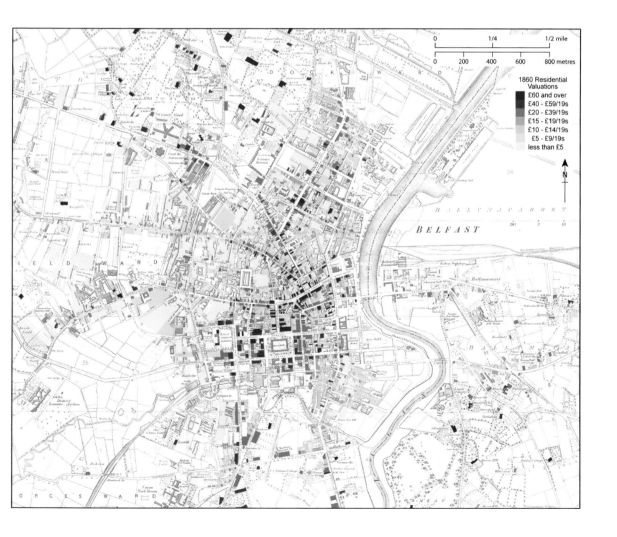

did not believe that employers as a whole had any desire to deal unfairly or oppressively by their workers [...] unfortunately during the past year the professional trouble-maker had been busy [...] the result has been [...] to make employers draw closer together, and to feel that what concerned one concerned all.[69]

'Outside the finer streets there is nothing but interminable ranges of brown brick buildings, mean and vulgar, afflicting the eye'

With this phrase Madame de Bovet identified the geography of social class within Belfast. The 'finer streets' of the wealthy contrasted with housing for the lower orders so vulgar as to afflict her eye, but that impaired organ of vision had remained perceptive enough to enable her to present a reasonable description of the residential patterns. More detail can now be added about this geography and how it changed during the years preceding her late-century visit.

The First Valuation of Belfast in 1837 took a record of each house in the town and assigned a value to the properties, which can be used as an indication of the wealth and social status of their residents.[70] 'Finer streets' at that time were those focused on the centre of the old town at the Four Corners (the intersection of Waring Street, Bridge Street, North Street and Rosemary Street), and also on High Street. This district was largely occupied by merchants and shopkeepers who lived on their premises. To the south, a newer area with high valuations was located near the White Linen Hall in Donegall Square. This residential district had begun to be built up from the 1790s and was almost complete by 1837. Professionals and business people such as industrialists and shipowners inhabited its tall Georgian terraces, described as 'large and handsome' by Mr and Mrs S.C. Hall who, like Thackeray and de Bovet, visited Belfast in their tour around Ireland in 1840.[71] There is evidence in statements in the valuation field books that some of the people in these southern 'finer streets' had moved from the Four Corners district when the introduction of shops and retail businesses, especially public houses, led to that area becoming less suitable for genteel families. Finally, some wealthy people resided on the edge of the town where there were a few country estates of high status, including Ormeau which belonged to the second marquess of Donegall.[72]

Regarding the less well-off, a government report in 1836 had found that 'the condition of the poor in Belfast is, in some respects, superior to that of other towns',[73] but still there were both pockets and entire districts characterized by poverty. The Halls identified the 'poorer and meaner' parts of the town as the northern districts and Ballymacarrett,[74] but the pattern revealed by the 1837 valuations was more complex. While Ballymacarrett was certainly poor, other working-class districts lay to the west as well as the north including Smithfield and Mill Street, largely Catholic areas of the inner west. Other low-value

Superior working-class housing from the late nineteenth century: McMaster Street, off the Newtownards Road in east Belfast, built between 1889 and 1899, consisted of parlour houses with running water and water closets connected to the newly completed sewer system.

Photograph © Stephen Royle.

Middle-class suburban affluence. Chichester Park off the Antrim Road, in north Belfast, c.1900.

Photograph © National Museums Northern Ireland. Collection Ulster Folk & Transport Museum. HOYFM. WAG.52.

property was located around mills and distilleries, or in the area surrounding Cromac Street in the south, near the gasworks and Long Bridge. These districts were usually associated with employment opportunities within Belfast's growing industrial sector and did not house the worst-off townspeople. They were more likely to be found in the areas of lowest valuation, pockets of extreme poverty tucked away in courts and alleys behind central high-status streets such as High Street and Donegall Street. O'Hanlon observed in 1853 that:

> When a representative of our most gracious Queen lately made an almost Royal progress through our principal streets and gazed at those proofs of opulence and prosperity which everywhere met his eye, how little could he [...] imagine the misery to be found in the immediate proximity to the brilliant and joyous scene.[75]

O'Hanlon's book, and also a report from another clergyman, Anthony McIntyre, from the same period, present a bleak depiction of an underclass living out lives of misery and degradation in the Belfast of the 1850s.[76]

By the time of the Second or Griffith's Valuation of 1860, the housing characteristic of the back streets and courts, for example from Great George's Street to Ship Street, now formed an ever more dilapidated, insanitary core. Elsewhere, as from Shankill Road to Grosvenor Road, lay what might be identified as the beginnings of the swathes of Victorian terraces that remained characteristic of Belfast until the clearance programmes of the 1970s and 1980s removed many of them. Belfast's housing stock quadrupled in the last three decades of the nineteenth century. Between 1867 and 1878 the corporation minute books record 796 new streets given approval to be built; 1880 alone saw 62 new streets approved with 1,826 buildings erected and a further 2,078 approved. Most of the housing was for industrial workers and was in the form of brick terraces with slate roofs. These 'brown [more often 'red'] brick buildings' were what Madame de Bovet saw as 'mean and vulgar'. But at least Belfast was spared the appalling housing of industrial towns such as Leeds and Nottingham, whose growth spurts had come earlier, so that they developed largely without planning constraints. In Belfast bye-laws of 1845, 1864, 1865, 1878 and 1889 had set minimum standards, the earliest, for example, imposing a ban on cellar dwellings and thatched roofs and requiring a yard and privy to be provided. Further, much of the clay for the bricks came from Belfast's own brickfields, enabling reasonable quality houses to be erected cheaply. Rather than back-to-backs, then, most Belfast workers occupied terraces that, if certainly small, at least usually had rear access, if only via an alley. Much of the housing was built by – or at least purchased by – speculators who let the houses out. 'Kitchen houses' would be available at 3s 6d per week; the roomier 'parlour houses' with a sitting room went for 5s. However, sub-letting was common and densities could be high, especially among the poorly paid textile workers.[77]

Towards the end of the century, the housing became more attractive, with polychromatic brick detailing seeking to draw tenants to take the houses. One street of this nature, McMaster Street off the Lower Newtownards Road, is now a conservation area, ensuring that this example of the 'interminable' Belfast terraces should remain.

Meanwhile the wealthy residents of the Four Corners or the Donegall Square area had over time moved to selected districts beyond the industrial area of the town. Suburbanization was in part a retreat from the growing clamour of city centre life; in part the growing demands of commerce for land and property in the centre helped to push residents out. In addition, the industrialization of Belfast was accompanied by a growing number of white-collar workers who also sought good-quality property. Many, whether those suburbanizing from the centre or newcomers setting up households, selected the Malone area of south Belfast. This occupies a gravel ridge, which helped to keep it free from flooding, and thus made it attractive to landowners and then to householders. The south became fashionable, the corporation minutes noting in 1863 that Malone was a preferred location for the wealthy and influential.[78] Botanic Gardens and Queen's College gave the area status and residential property of some pretension was erected, as in Upper and Lower Crescent and University Square. Malone developed into the archetypal leafy suburb, with relatively large houses, some detached with extensive gardens. Further north, Crumlin and Antrim Roads developed good-quality housing for the middle classes. Other people of middle rank took large terraced or semi-detached houses in outer east Belfast. The Lower Newtownards Road might have become associated with industrial workers, especially connected with the shipyard, but further up and off this road lived white-collar workers from the same companies. Those of greater wealth might even take small estates in east Belfast, such as Ormiston House, where Edward Harland and later William Pirrie lived in some luxury, Pirrie's improvements including the construction of a nine-hole golf course in the grounds.[79]

A local newspaper in 1869 both observed this process of suburbanization and explained how it could operate with reference to the need for those living in the suburbs to reach easily their employment in the centre:

> Of the many signs of rapid progress in Belfast the extension of omnibus accommodation is one of the most notable [...] We have excellent, well-appointed, and speedy omnibuses running hourly on nearly every leading road out of Belfast. There is one on the Malone Road to Windsor, one on the Lisburn Road, one on the Antrim Road to Fortwilliam, one on the County Down Road to Sydenham and Belmont and in a few days a new line will commence to Ormeau and Ballynafeigh. Almost without exception these are vehicles of the best class, keep time well, and are liberally supported by the public. The demand for house property a few years ago, for conversion into warehouses and offices, combined

A horse-drawn tram service began in 1872, but was replaced by electric vehicles in 1905.

Reproduced with the kind permission of the Public Record Office of Northern Ireland.

with the high taxation and dirty streets, has caused almost an emigration to the suburbs, and whole colonies of villas now stud the country round Belfast for a radius of three to four miles. The number of large dwelling-houses actually occupied as such in the town itself is greatly reduced and these new and prosperous lines of omnibuses are a great – indeed almost indispensable – accommodation to the business men of Belfast, who now, as a rule, reside outside the town proper.[80]

The omnibuses referred to were horse-drawn vehicles pulled along those dirty streets. Trams running on rails provided a smoother, quicker ride with less friction to overcome and thus reduced demand for horse power. Tram construction occurred on a large scale when the Belfast Street Tramways Company was founded under the Belfast Street Tramways Bill in 1872, despite the objection of the council, which wanted transport to be a municipal venture.[81] By 1885 the company operated six routes totalling 12 miles (19.3 km) and by the mid-1890s 11 million passengers were carried annually over 24 miles (38.6 km) of track. Under the 1899 Belfast Corporation Act the corporation built lines itself and the Belfast Corporation (Tramways) Act of 1904 allowed municipalization of the private company. The corporation immediately made plans to transfer from horse power to electricity, which took place 'without a hitch' with 174 new electric tramcars running for the first time on 5 December 1905.[82]

Railways also permitted commuters to travel from suburban stations. The Ulster Railway, running first just to Lisburn, opened in 1839, with its terminus in Great Victoria Street.[83] The Belfast and Co Down Railway, with its terminus east of the river, and the Belfast and Northern Counties Railway, with its terminus in York Road, both opened in 1848.

'Down to the hospitals and prison, everything is magnificent, everything is also new'

In 1832 the Irish Reform Act had deprived Belfast Corporation of its right to elect Members of Parliament, transferring this privilege to householders with property worth more than £10. Three years later, a parliamentary committee criticized Belfast Corporation for denying valid representation to the freemen of the town, noting also that no Roman Catholics had been members of the body. There was also censure for the way in which the corporation had worked, from its secrecy to its mismanagement of funds.[84] The Irish Municipal Corporations Bill of 1840 brought in reform throughout Ireland; for Belfast it saw Ballymacarrett added to the town and the municipal area divided into five wards, which were each to elect two aldermen and six councillors.[85] The Act marked the final stage in the decline of Donegall's influence over the town his ancestor had founded. The new corporation, under the control of a mayor, was elected in 1842 and was at first active and enthusiastic, passing three improvement Acts by 1847. The early reforms of 1845 regarding proper regulation of markets, widening of streets and regulation of housing standards were especially innovative. The activities of the reformed corporation received contemporary praise from Captain Gilbert in 1853:

> The powers [of the corporation …] appear to have been judiciously exercised for the improvement of the borough. This is particularly evident in the widened streets, and the architectural features of the buildings recently erected. The corporation […] have for the improvement of the borough, purchased and pulled down several streets and lanes in the old and decayed part of town and erected new and wide streets in their places.[86]

The new corporation was Conservative; no Liberal was elected until 1855, not least because of the chicanery of the Conservative town clerk, John Bates.[87] In the mid-1850s the Liberals got their revenge when a suit was filed in Dublin against Bates and 17 other Conservatives for having borrowed more than was allowed and using money raised to buy the gasworks for unauthorized purposes. Bates had to resign and died shortly afterwards while the accused councillors were held personally responsible for £273,000. The matter was finally settled under arbitration only in 1864, the decade-long dispute handicapping the corporation in the performance of its duties.

The settlement of the Chancery suit included the return without opposition of Liberal candidates to half the seats on the council, and the election in 1861 of Belfast's only Liberal mayor, Edward Coey. However, the party was too disunited and organizationally weak to capitalize on this temporary advantage, and throughout the rest of the century Belfast's local government was almost always dominated by Conservative interests. Its record was mixed.

THE TOWN HALL. BELFAST. 1261. W.L.

The Town Hall, opened in 1871. In his speech Mayor Philip Johnston articulated the ambition of the town: 'He did not know what the future of Belfast would be, but from present indications it was probable that a larger Town Hall – a real Town Hall – would be required.'

Reproduced with the kind permission of the Public Record Office of Northern Ireland.

The construction of the Town Hall in 1871, and the laying out in 1880–81 of Royal Avenue, testified to a continued enthusiasm for civic aggrandisement. However, the corporation was less effective in providing the infrastructure needed for the growing and industrializing settlement. The environment and the associated quality of life in Belfast suffered for years as a result, as exemplified in the story of water supply and sewerage provision. By the last thirty years of the century greater efforts had to be made to improve both infrastructure and the environment. The gasworks was municipalized in 1873 and output then increased 400 per cent by 1905. In the 1890s electricity supplies were installed. The telegraph was mentioned in 1863; telephone poles were being erected by 1888.

Another new feature of Belfast by the late nineteenth century was the growing number of parks and open spaces. Earlier in the century residents had resorted for recreation to the hills on the outskirts of the town, particularly to Cave Hill, a favourite resort on Easter Monday. A report in 1822 spoke of people there 'climbing, dancing, racing, tumbling, courting, egg-trundling, frisking [and] laughing'.[88] Occasional outdoor recreation of this sort was seen to be inadequate as the settlement developed. William O'Hanlon wrote that Belfast's 'miasm[a]-breathing population' needed to develop 'a taste for pure, open-air recreations'.[89] The health reformer Andrew Malcolm also identified a need for formal parks and open spaces in 1852, when he found Belfast to be 'sadly deficient in one of the most important requisites for the health and comfort of a town population – we mean public parks and pleasure grounds'.[90] In particular, he was concerned that the 'masses' were denied the use of free

Sir Charles Lanyon (1813–89), the premier architect of mid-Victorian Belfast, as portrayed by an unknown artist c.1845.

Reproduced with the kind permission of the Naughton Gallery, Queen's University, Belfast.

The Albert Memorial Clock by W.J. Barre was unveiled in May 1869 by Prince Arthur. The statue of the prince was by Samuel Ferres Lynn (1838–76), who later completed the contentious statue of Henry Cooke in College Square East (p. 37). The memorial, largely funded by the former mayor of Belfast John Lytle, began almost immediately to lean due to its unstable foundations. Belfast wits noted that it had the time, and also the inclination.

Courtesy of the National Library of Ireland.

Advertising hoardings surround the City Hall as it nears completion in 1905. Costing £360,000, as compared to an initial budget of £125,000, the new building replaced a town hall opened only thirty-five years earlier. In both these respects the new building aptly symbolized the headlong growth of the nineteenth-century city.

Photograph © National Museums Northern Ireland. Collection Ulster Museum. BELUM.Y8563.

open-air recreation. The one place within the town that partly fulfilled this need was Queen's Island, then an industrial site only at its south-west end, with the north-east devoted to recreation. There 'the People's Park' had its own Crystal Palace from 1851 until it burnt down in 1864. It was long realized that this land would one day be taken for industrial purposes and as early as 1854 a replacement was planned in Victoria Park. However, Harland and Wolff took the rest of Queen's Island in the late 1870s, while Victoria Park did not open until 1906.[91] Another early urban open space was the Botanic Gardens of 1828, but this was a private venture of the Belfast Botanical and Horticultural Society and access was restricted by membership subscription or entrance charge until the gardens were sold to the corporation for £10,500, re-opening as the Belfast Botanic Gardens Park on 1 January 1895.[92] After the passing of the Public Parks (Ireland) Act of 1869 the corporation negotiated with the marquess of Donegall to purchase his demesne at Ormeau. The cost was met by using 40 acres (16 ha) of the 175-acre (71-ha) site for residential development, on what became North and South Parade. The park itself was opened in 1871, with some parts of the demesne used for grazing; Ormeau Golf Club was founded on this parcel in 1892. Falls Park opened in 1876 on land originally planned to be part of the adjoining cemetery;[93] Woodville (later Woodvale) Park was announced by the council in 1887,[94] and opened in 1888. Alexandra Park had been opened the previous year. Dunville Park on the Grosvenor Road, an eponymous gift of Robert Dunville, the whiskey distiller, opened in 1892.[95]

That late-century Belfast appeared 'magnificent', as well as 'new' to Madame

St Ann's Cathedral, Belfast

St Anne's Cathedral, built between 1898 and 1904 on the site of the parish church erected by the first marquess of Donegall in 1776 (p. 165). In ecclesiastical geography, as in other respects, the massive growth of Belfast created serious anomalies. The city is in the diocese of Connor, whose historic cathedral is in Lisburn. By the end of the nineteenth century, however, it contained the largest concentration of Anglicans on the island of Ireland, and the erection of a cathedral, to be shared between Connor and the adjoining dioceses of Down and Dromore, was part of a wider programme of investment in clergy and places of worship. The cost of this investment, however, had to be supported by collections in the dioceses of southern Ireland, a reminder of the extent to which the massive wealth of turn-of-the-century Belfast was concentrated not just in Protestant, but specifically in Presbyterian, hands.

Courtesy of the National Library of Ireland.

de Bovet might be ascribed largely to the influence of local architects from the mid-century onwards. There were some good buildings earlier, such as the Royal Belfast Academical Institution by English architect John Soane, which opened in 1814, and the Commercial Buildings (Northern Whig House) on Waring Street, built in 1820 and described as being 'ornamental to the town'. This newspaper report mentioned that the Commercial Buildings included a newsroom, but it was rather more taken with the quality of the fine mahogany tables it contained and the fact that there would be a ballroom.[96]

The best-known of the later local architects was Charles Lanyon. He was actually from Eastbourne in southern England, but in his twenties had taken up a post in Dublin as a civil engineer with the Board of Works. He then became a county surveyor, first for County Kildare and then, from 1836, for County Antrim, where he worked on roads and railways, while also designing the new Queen's Bridge for Belfast in 1840. Lanyon remained as Antrim county surveyor until 1860, when he entered private practice in Belfast. He worked in a variety of styles, from the Gothic Revival of what is now called in tribute the Lanyon Building at Queen's University (1849) to the Italian Renaissance Custom House (1857). He designed the Crumlin Road gaol (1845) – hence de Bovet's comment that even the prison was magnificent – and the court house (1850) opposite. Sadly at the time of writing, the latter is in the later stages of dereliction and in urgent need of rescue. Lanyon also designed the Palm House in Botanic Gardens (1840), Assembly's College (Union Theological College) on Botanic Avenue (1853) and the Ulster Institute for the Deaf, Dumb and Blind on Lisburn Road (1845), sadly lost – although it had not been kept in good condition – to the uninspired Medical Biology Centre of Queen's University. Lanyon's range was wide, including churches: in Belfast there was Sinclair Seaman's Presbyterian church with its maritime theme (1856) and Falls Road Methodist church (1854), the latter lost to the Divis Flats in the 1960s.

On some projects Lanyon worked with his partner, William Henry Lynn, the latter normally being credited with leading on the Central Library in Royal Avenue (1884).[97] Lynn also designed the Old Library at Queen's (built in two stages, 1864–65 and 1911–13). Belfast Castle, with its Scottish baronial style, was designed in the 1860s by Lanyon's firm, Lanyon, Lynn and Lanyon, the second Lanyon being Charles's son, John. Now belonging to Belfast City Council, it is a popular venue for weddings. Charles Lanyon was knighted in 1868, by which time he had served as mayor of Belfast and was an MP. William Joseph Barre, from Newry, was a contemporary and rival of Lanyon. His most famous contribution to Belfast's Victorian townscape is the Albert Memorial Clock (completed 1869) on High Street, with its famous list. He also designed the Ulster Hall on Bedford Street (1862), acquired by the corporation in 1908 for civic musical entertainment.

Later, the new city of Belfast (a status awarded in 1888) was graced also by

Following spread: John Adams's panorama of Belfast provides a three-dimensional depiction of the main features of the Edwardian city. The port and the edge of the Queen's Island shipyard dominate the top right-hand corner, with the Custom House and the Harbour Office providing administrative services. High Street remains an important commercial thoroughfare, but the Albert Clock at its eastern end is no longer the centre of town. Instead Royal Avenue and York Street provide a broad artery running from the City Hall to the Northern Counties Railway terminus. Henry Cooke's statue stands prominently in Great Victoria Street. To the west working-class Belfast is represented by a landscape of factory chimneys and church steeples. The map shows the Town Hall as still located on Victoria Street, and includes but does not name the City Hall, suggesting that it was drawn around 1900, when the latter building was under construction.

Reproduced from plate 5 in Stephen A. Royle, *Irish Historic Towns Atlas, no. 17, Belfast, part II, 1840 to 1900* (Royal Irish Academy, Dublin, 2007).

high Victorian splendours such as the Grand Opera House by the English theatre architect Frank Matcham (1895).[98] Continuing the tradition of local architects was the Belfast firm of Young and McKenzie, founded in 1870 by Robert Young (a pupil of Lanyon) and Charles McKenzie. One of their notable commissions was for retailers Robinson and Cleaver who applied for permission to build a six-storey Italianate building on the corner of Donegall Place and Donegall Square in 1886. This was of such potential significance (as well as magnificence) that it merited a special meeting of the corporation to debate the proposal.[99] It opened in 1888. Young and McKenzie also designed another department store, Anderson and McAuley (1890) and the Presbyterian Assembly Buildings, Church House (1905). Their work is prominent in Donegall Square, once the site of high-status residences, but at the end of the century the favoured location for the financial sector. Two Young and McKenzie designs there are the Ocean Accident Insurance Buildings (1899–1902) and the Scottish Provident Institution (1899–1902), with its panels depicting images of Belfast's industries. Such office buildings themselves replaced residences and dwarfed the housing blocks that remained, the late Victorian and Edwardian city confidently breaking away from the Georgian town.

The same process can be seen in the centre of Donegall Square where another confident, even exuberant, building, the City Hall, was erected atop the site of the Georgian White Linen Hall. Belfast had been governed from the market house on High Street, but in 1866 the corporation had reserved £15,000 to build a town hall on the new Victoria Street,[100] and this opened in 1871. By the late 1880s a more impressive building was required for the new city of Belfast and in 1889 the corporation discussed a plan to demolish the White Linen Hall and reuse its site in Donegall Square for a city hall.[101] Four years later a budget of £120,000 was set up, which was expected to be met by rents from the municipal tram system.[102] Profit from the corporation-owned gasworks was another income stream. A competition for designs was launched in 1896,[103] being won by an English architect, Alfred Brumwell Thomas, whose Baroque Revival styled City Hall opened in 1906. The replacement of the White Linen Hall was paralleled by that of the Georgian parish church, St Anne's, also demolished in 1898 when the Romanesque cathedral was built around it. As a letter writer to the *Belfast Telegraph* stated, Belfast was becoming a city 'bare enough of monuments and relics of the past'.[104] Belfast, indeed, had become, at least regarding its public face, both 'magnificent' and 'new'.

'It is the least Irish of all Irish towns'

This final quote from Madame de Bovet might be challenged only regarding her use of 'town', for Belfast was by the time of her writing a city. That it was the least Irish of settlements on the island might be accepted. Belfast was ruled by a Conservative and Unionist council, membership of which tended to overlap with the group forming the city's leading businessmen and industrialists. It was an industrial powerhouse whose goods were largely for export, so that Belfast faced to the world, away from Ireland. Its people were largely Protestant and of British stock, although there was a substantial Catholic minority which had hardly been quiescent over their clearly inferior status, and the consequences of this unequal division were to blight the city in the new century. Matters would be worsened by political and social upheavals, including those associated with the losses in the First World War and the partition of Ireland. Industrial decline would add further pressures and destroy Belfast's Edwardian confidence; the twentieth century was not to be kind to Belfast.[105]

This chapter started with the views of visitors to Belfast; let us end with the prescient words of a Belfastman, Thomas Carnduff, born in working-class Little May Street in 1886. Of socialist leanings, Carnduff was a shipyard labourer who became a poet and dramatist, the 'shipyard playwright'.[106] He is perhaps best remembered for his first book of poetry, *Songs from the Shipyard* (1924). In this volume, his 'Men of Belfast' expressed the pride of residents at their mighty industrial city, but also pondered about its future. The first verse is triumphal:

> O city of sound and motion!
> O city of endless stir!
> From a dawn of a misty morning,
> To the fall of the evening air;
> From the night of moving shadows
> To the sound of the shipyard horn;
> We hail thee, Queen of the Northland,
> We who are Belfast born.

The last verse, by contrast, strikes a more sombre and rather prophetic note considering that the poem was published before the Depression and other evils that would be visited upon Belfast later in the twentieth century:

> With jealousy, cant and rancour,
> They would crush her world-wide fame;
> They would damp the flame of her furnace,
> To render her commerce lame;
> But her ships will traverse the ocean,
> Her sons will ply at their trade,
> Till the sheen of her glory will vanish,
> And the faith of her sons shall fade.[107]

AST. 8488. W.L.

7 Whose City? Belonging and Exclusion in the Nineteenth-Century Urban World

S.J. Connolly and Gillian McIntosh

The Victorian and Edwardian eras were the great age of the British city. It was a time when the worst of the social and environmental problems created by early industrialization were brought under control, but when the remorseless extension of central government supervision had not yet demoted urban management to the second tier of political life. The pride and self-confidence conferred by prosperity, social improvement and administrative autonomy found expression in distinctive buildings and institutions. Palatial town halls replaced the houses of the aristocracy as centres of social prestige and political power. Within their walls mayors and members of town councils, adorned with robes and chains, ceremonially acted out their role as representatives of the urban community, while also controlling an increasingly elaborate administrative system and steadily expanding municipal budgets. Museums, art galleries and concert halls, prominently situated in the wide streets and spacious squares created by inner-city improvement schemes, trumpeted the claim of the new urban centres to be the home of taste and culture as well as of enterprise and profit.

The extension of this same culture of civic pride is evident to anyone who walks through the centre of present-day Belfast. The Italianate elegance of the Custom House, the monumental buildings lining the wide passageway of Royal Avenue, the wedding cake grandeur of the City Hall all testify to the same determination to project an image of prosperity, order and civic harmony. Yet representation is not reality. The messages embedded in buildings and civic ceremony, however eloquent, cannot be taken at face value. Behind the impressive façade of the British Victorian city, and the rhetoric of a united urban community, lay deep divisions along newly defined lines of social class, equally deep if less contested inequalities based on gender, and in some cases local antagonisms based on religion or, by the beginning of the twentieth century, race. In Belfast there was in addition a deep political division that increasingly set it apart from the other great industrial cities of the United

Kingdom. It is thus necessary to balance an account of economic progress and civic grandeur with a recognition that this was a society of unequal rights and privileges – a city, in other words, that belonged to some more than to others.

Organized Labour and the Politics of Class

Belfast's first recorded experience of large-scale popular protest was in the summer of 1756. As food prices rose in the aftermath of a poor harvest, crowds took direct action, seizing grain from ships and warehouses. George Macartney, representing the town's merchants, bombarded Dublin Castle with alarmist reports. No magistrate, he claimed, would issue a warrant for fear of having his house torn down, and only the army could restore order. Yet in fact it is clear, from the details reported, that this was no mere outbreak of violence. The grievance being expressed was that local merchants were profiteering by exporting food to areas of high demand without first meeting local needs. The response of the crowd was not to plunder but to sell off the grain they seized at the price paid in normal years. It was a conservative form of protest, of a kind familiar in other urban centres of the period, based on the belief that the first duty of the agriculture in a region was to meet the wants of its inhabitants. Even the one act of violence reported, when a woman was put in a cart and taken to be ducked in the mill pond, had all the hallmarks of a ritual of popular justice.[1]

While the willingness of the crowd to take matters into its own hands might have alarmed men of property, moreover, the principle behind their actions, that the market economy should operate within a framework of social obligations, was for long widely accepted. As in other towns the sovereign and corporation continued throughout the eighteenth century to publish a regular assizes of bread, fixing the weight of a penny, fourpenny and sixpenny loaf in the light of current grain prices. The practice ended in 1800, although thereafter a public bakery, set up to produce bread at a fair commercial rate, continued to offer some check on profiteering by other producers.

The abolition of direct price control was part of a general move away from the paternalistic assumptions of a pre-industrial society, helping to set the scene for a new era of intensified social antagonism, developing into open class conflict. Already in the 1790s Belfast had experienced a new wave of popular action, this time taking the form of 'combinations' of workers organizing to protect wages and conditions of work. Those involved included traditional trades such as carpenters, stonemasons and shoemakers, as well as weavers in cotton and linen. The sudden surge of activity can be attributed to high food prices due to the long war with France. Rising popular political awareness may also have played a part, although if so those involved got no encouragement from the leaders of radical opinion in the town. Instead the United Irish newspaper the *Northern Star*, as progressive in embracing the new doctrines of the free market as it was in advocating far-reaching political reform, condemned the proliferation of associations among the town's tradesmen and called on the government and corporation to suppress them.

As the *Northern Star*'s reaction made clear, these early efforts at organized collective action met with massive hostility. Acts of the Irish parliament dating from 1729 and 1743 made all combinations of workmen illegal, while a new Act of 1803 extended to Ireland the recent codification of similar long-standing prohibitions in the British Combination Acts. Throughout the 1790s and early 1800s there were regular reports of would-be trade unionists being committed to prison. The consequence of thus outlawing peaceful forms of collective action such as the strike and picket was that early industrial action, in Belfast as elsewhere, frequently involved violence. In 1814 striking sawyers paraded a blackleg worker through the town, while in 1822 vitriol was thrown during a cotton spinners' strike. The most serious incident was in 1816 when cotton weavers attacked the home of the mill owner Francis Johnson, exchanging gunfire with those inside and forcing open the iron shutters protecting the building to introduce a bomb. Two of those involved were subsequently hanged, another transported for life and two more publicly flogged in High Street. Nor was the violence necessarily all one sided. In 1817 a cotton master, John McCann, was tried but acquitted for having shot the president of the weavers' society, with whom he had had a dispute.

The Combination Acts were repealed in 1825. However, workers downing tools could still be prosecuted for leaving their employment without giving notice, while anything resembling an oath or secret passwords left those involved in serious legal danger.[2] Employers, for their part, continued to regard the very existence of trade unions as a threat to the viability of their enterprises. A growing proportion of the workforce were by this time experiencing the transition to factory work, bringing with it longer working hours, the displacement of traditional skills through mechanization, and exposure to the competitive pressures created by technological innovation and improved transport. Workers in this category, however, had neither the resources nor the bargaining power to organize effectively in their own defence. Instead industrial action was for the most part carried on by skilled tradesmen, such as printers, shoemakers and bakers. By the 1830s some at least among these craft workers were moving beyond pure trade union activity towards political action. In 1834, for example, artisans marched in support of the Tolpuddle Martyrs, Dorset agricultural labourers transported for having formed a union. There were also branches during the 1830s of the cooperative movement, Robert Owen's visionary attempt to replace the brutality of early capitalism with a more equitable system of exchange based on the value of labour.[3]

By the second half of the nineteenth century industrial relations in Belfast had become more stable. Strikes still took place, but employers now accepted trade unions as legitimate negotiators, and even as useful partners in resolving disputes. When the Irish Trade Union Congress held their annual conference in Belfast in 1898 the lord mayor, Sir James Henderson, appeared in person to welcome them to the city and to proclaim the harmony of interests between business and worker:

> It was not at all necessary for him to say to them that Belfast was, he thought, an elysium for working men. In Belfast they had large steel and iron ship-building yards where fathers and sons could be employed. They had also what was termed their staple industry, the linen industry, where the wives and daughters found employment. If there was not sufficient employment in those places they had the largest rope manufacturing establishment in the world.[4]

This, however, was a comment addressed primarily to the craft unions who still dominated the Belfast labour movement. Skilled workers in Belfast were indeed well paid by United Kingdom standards, and they benefited from low-cost, good-quality housing and abundant employment for other family members. By contrast the wages of unskilled workers in the docks and carrying trades, as well as those of the legions of women employed in routine factory work, were lower than those paid in other industrial cities, reflecting the reserve army of underemployed that remained in Belfast's rural hinterland. When, over the next few years, what was known as the 'new unionism' began to mobilize these less fortunate unskilled workers, industrial relations once again developed a ruthless edge. During 1907 a dispute beginning on the docks escalated into something close to a general strike, with armed troops protecting strike breakers and two men shot dead in rioting in west Belfast.[5] Robert McElborough, who in the same year went to work for the city council, first as a tram conductor and later as a gas fitter, likewise recorded the long history of petty victimization he endured as an activist seeking to unionize low-paid municipal workers.[6]

The struggles for legitimacy, first of the craft unions, then of the 'new unionism' of the years before the First World War, paralleled those of workers in other industrial centres. Labour in Belfast, however, had also to deal with the additional handicap of a deepening political and religious division within the working population that it sought to organize. As early as 1835 a cotton manufacturer gave as a reason for the movement of capital from Glasgow to Belfast the absence of trade unions: 'there is so much political difference between the men that they cannot permanently cooperate together'.[7] After 1886, in a city now polarized along religious and political lines, the issue of Home Rule lay as an impassable barrier across every attempt to promote the politics of class. In the early 1890s the newly formed Belfast branch of the Independent Labour Party, seeking to hold meetings at the traditional speaker's corner provided by the Custom House steps, found itself under physical attack from Protestants outraged at the support of the British labour movement for Irish self-government.[8] Later, during the upsurge of militant Protestant violence in the summer of 1920, a full quarter of the supposedly 'disloyal' persons violently expelled from the shipyards and other places of work were in fact Protestants, targeted for their trade union activities or socialist politics.[9]

Sectarian and political divisions also blighted the electoral prospects of William Walker, the most able and charismatic spokesman for the Belfast labour movement. Standing for election in North Belfast in 1905, he was pushed by the Belfast Protestant Association into declaring his support for the Protestant constitution. He went on to lose the election by a margin of 474 votes, in a constituency estimated to contain 1,000 Catholic electors. A debate with James Connolly six years later, conducted in the pages of the Scottish labour journal *Forward*, summed up the predicament of the Belfast movement. Connolly, on the way to a personal fusion of nationalism and socialism into a single revolutionary commitment that was to bring him to his death in 1916, argued forcefully that a socialist Ireland could come into being only after the distraction of the national question had been settled by the achievement of self-government. Walker argued instead that the only way forward for labour was to abandon the irrelevant quest for Irish independence and instead combine with the stronger British labour movement to promote social justice within the United Kingdom. Each argument, taking its author's starting point as a given, made perfect sense; neither had any chance of being accepted by both working-class communities.[10]

Alongside the triumphal narrative of the rise to world prominence of Belfast's linen and shipbuilding industries, then, must be set the long struggle of workers in these and other sectors to challenge the structure of inequality and exploitation on which the success of these industries rested. At the same time it would be wrong to overstate the level of class conflict. Outbreaks of industrial militancy must be set beside evidence of the continuing importance of vertical ties of deference and respect. McElborough recalled the outlook of his father, a former soldier who in the 1880s and 1890s worked for the Belfast City Tramways.

> He never to my knowledge had a day off. I never heard him making any complaint. Mr Nance [the manager] was to him and the rest of the tram employees something far above them in the social scale. If he had asked them to go through hell they would have went if they knew the way.[11]

An oral history focused on men and women employed in linen mills and factories in the first three decades of the twentieth century, completed in the 1970s, likewise found that the proprietors of what were at that stage still generally family-owned firms were remembered as distant but benign superiors; any resentment of harsh working conditions was directed instead at foremen or factory managers.[12] Such sentiments could even cross sectarian and political lines of division. A report on the North Belfast bye-election of 1905 offered a different perspective on the defeat of William Walker, noting that his Conservative opponent Sir Daniel Dixon 'is a large employer of Nationalist labour', and that in the absence of a Nationalist candidate he would probably get the Catholic vote.[13] Employers themselves played their part in fostering ties of gratitude and respect, through the cheap but effective method of sponsoring parties, dances, excursions to the seaside or other minor treats.

A second influence working across the lines of class divisions was the continuing tradition of philanthropy. The late eighteenth and early nineteenth centuries saw a succession of charitable ventures: the Poor House, a Fever Hospital, the House of Industry. The introduction in 1838 of an Irish poor law, requiring property owners to pay rates, reduced the scope for private initiatives aimed at the straightforward relief of economic want. The House of Industry closed in 1841, while the Poor House narrowed its role to that of a refuge for the respectable elderly fallen on hard times. But other forms of philanthropic effort continued. At the beginning of 1845 the newly elected mayor, Andrew Mulholland, spoke of the need to improve the condition of the town's working classes, specifying public baths, parks, libraries and reading rooms. A public meeting the following month led to the establishment of a Society for the Amelioration of the Working Classes. Meanwhile specialist charitable bodies such as the Ulster Society for Promoting the Education of the Deaf and Dumb and Blind, established in 1831, went on with their work, and were joined by new ventures catering for specific disabilities, such as the Workshop for the Blind (1871) and the rather brutally named Cripples Institute (1878). The Belfast Female Mission, established in 1859, sent out paid women agents, drawn from the respectable and godly working classes, to provide spiritual and material support to poor families.[14] Men of wealth also made substantial private donations to public causes. The Quaker tea merchant Forster Green was estimated to have donated a total of £200,000 to charity, including £13,000 to the hospital, originally for the treatment of tuberculosis, that bears his name. On a smaller scale the distiller Robert Dunville in 1889 presented the city council with five acres at the junction of the Falls and Grosvenor roads for the construction of a public park, to which he also contributed £5,000.[15]

For those at the bottom of the social pyramid, education likewise came (if at all) through charity. Many of the town's Sunday Schools, in addition to religious instruction, taught literacy.[16] The Brown Street school, established in 1812 and catering for some 500 children, had separate schools for girls and boys. The first ragged school specifically for girls in Ireland was established in Frederick Street in 1847; originally a Lancastrian School established in 1811, it was supported by Mary Ann McCracken (1770–1866), social reformer, abolitionist and sister of United Irishman Henry Joy McCracken.[17] By 1852 the

Situated between the Falls Road and Grosvenor Road, Dunville Park was the gift of the distiller Robert G. Dunville. It was officially opened by the marquess of Dufferin and Ava on 10 August 1891– a date chosen, according to the *Belfast News Letter*, to link it with the visit of Queen Victoria to Belfast in 1849. In addition to its elaborate ornamental fountain, which was unveiled in 1892, the park provided sandpits for children, noted as a new phenomenon in the city.

Courtesy of the National Library of Ireland.

The public baths and wash house, located near Barrack Street, opened in 1847 but closed due to lack of funding in 1861.

Reproduced with the kind permission of Queen's University, Belfast.

Illustration taken from **The People's Magazine**

Belfast Street Directory noted that it was feeding, clothing and educating 'ninety poor girls, fitting them for domestic servants and other useful avocations'.[18] In 1851 the Society for St Vincent de Paul opened a school for boys and girls in Chapel Lane.[19] While Margaret Byers' educational campaigning was aimed primarily at the female children of the middle class, she was also active in her work for working-class women and working-class girls. In this – like many Belfast reformers of all convictions – she combined her advocacy of temperance with a drive for social reform

Philanthropic ventures of this kind inevitably operated within the limits set by the same bourgeois social and economic philosophy that had discontinued the assizes of bread and sought to outlaw any attempt by trade unions to curtail economic activity. In 1829, for example, a meeting to consider the case of distressed cotton weavers conceded that there was considerable hardship due to low wages. At the same time, leading citizens of impeccable humanitarian credentials, such as Dr Robert Tennent, flatly refused to consider a subscription in support of weavers' families, since this would be to subsidize low wages and so distort the local labour market.[20] The proceedings of the Society for the Amelioration of the Working Classes, equally, combined a genuine concern to improve the living standards of workers with an explicit desire to inculcate the approved virtues of industry, thrift and self-help. In September 1849, for example, its programme included a series of lectures on 'Political Economy'. The following month a leading barrister delivered a four-hour oration on the history of civilization from the Roman republic to the present, before concluding 'by strongly impressing upon all present the necessity of cultivating habits of self-dependence and self-respect'.[21] The Society's other main initiative, the opening of a public bath and wash houses, likewise reflected a characteristic middle-class priority. Even then, the venture was crippled by the assumption, shared with other cities, that such facilities, once provided, should become self-financing, and the baths and wash houses closed in 1861.[22]

If charity remained a prisoner of its social context, moreover, it was also apparently a virtue unevenly distributed within Belfast's social elite. The most detailed study of nineteenth-century philanthropy points out that it was the older branches of manufacture, such as the textile trades, whose proprietors appear on the committees of philanthropic societies. Leading figures in the shipbuilding and engineering sectors are by contrast largely absent.[23] The contrast may be somewhat misleading. Industrialists in these newer sectors of the city's economy came to prominence at a time when the provision of social welfare was becoming increasingly bureaucratized, so that cash donations became more important than personal participation. Thus William Pirrie of Harland and Wolff was, along with his wife, a tireless fundraiser for the Royal Victoria Hospital, and himself contributed £11,000 to the cost of a new building in 1904.[24] But there may also have been a difference in outlook, reflecting the presence in the textile sector of long-established families with historic ties to the town, as opposed to the new arrivals who predominated in engineering and shipbuilding. (Pirrie, it should be noted, was Belfast born, and the nephew of a doctor at the Royal Victoria.) Newcomers may also have been more inclined to take up residence in suburban villas well outside the city, further diminishing their sense of an urban community and their involvement in its problems.

Religion and Sectarian Conflict

The second line of division within Belfast, cutting across and for political purposes largely eclipsing that of class, was religion. In the 1780s and 1790s the town stood out as a centre of religious liberalism, symbolized by the famous occasion in 1784 when the first Volunteer Company provided a guard of honour at the opening of Belfast's first purpose-built place of Catholic worship. From the early nineteenth century, however, relations between Catholic and Protestant deteriorated rapidly. A violent incident on 12 July 1813, when Orangemen returning from their parade in Lisburn fired on a crowd who attacked them, killing two, may or may not have been Belfast's first sectarian riot. The location was Hercules Street, but the dead men were both Protestants, raising the possibility that it was radicals rather than Catholics who took to the streets to counter this demonstration of loyalist triumphalism.[25] However, further outbreaks of violence in 1822, 1824 and 1825, again associated with the Twelfth of July, were more clearly sectarian in character, and they established a pattern that was to continue throughout the nineteenth century and beyond.[26] Divisions were also reflected in a high level of residential segregation. By 1901 no less than 60 per cent of families lived in streets where at least 90 per cent of the householders shared the same religion.[27]

These deepening religious divisions were closely linked to the transformations brought about by the massive inward migration that caused the town's population to rise from 18,000 or so in 1791 to more than four times that number by 1841. The migrants were drawn from a countryside where feuding between Catholic and Protestant societies, Defenders and Peep of Day Boys, later Ribbonmen and Orangemen, had been well established from the 1780s. Rural custom, however, did not necessarily carry over directly to the new environment of the industrializing town, and indeed there seems to have been a time lag in this case. Residential segregation existed from the very start, with Catholics settling in the district known as the Pound. However, the tendency for new arrivals to cluster in ethnically defined neighbourhoods was a feature of urban growth everywhere. The attraction of the Pound may simply have been its proximity to St Mary's church, initially the only place of Catholic worship in the town, and to existing areas of Catholic settlement in Hercules Street and round Smithfield. Regular outbreaks of violence between the inhabitants of this district and their near neighbours in the Protestant Sandy Row seem to have come only after the residential pattern had already been well established.

Where inward migration was undoubtedly central to deepening hostilities was in the changes it brought to the town's religious demography. The Belfast in which the Volunteers had proclaimed their goodwill towards their Catholic fellow townsmen was one in which fewer than one in ten of the population fell into that category. Over the next few decades, however, inward migration from a much-expanded, and more religiously mixed, rural hinterland eroded that comfortable numerical superiority. Already by 1802 the growing visibility of the Catholic population was sufficient to alarm even a staunch radical like Martha McTier. In 1834 the first official religious census showed that one in three of the population was now Catholic. The next reliable count, in 1861, showed that their share of overall numbers had stabilized at this level (or perhaps risen somewhat, and dropped back as emigration rose during and after the crisis of the 1840s). By the end of the century it had fallen back to only one-quarter. That, however, is hindsight. Contemporaries in the crucial middle decades of the century knew only that Catholic numbers had risen sharply and might still be doing so. The disturbances of August and September 1857, arising out of Catholic objections to the activities of aggressively anti-Catholic street preachers, were fuelled partly by Protestant fears that to give way on this point would be to surrender ownership of the town to an increasingly assertive 'Romish mob'.[28]

Protestant fears were heightened by developments at national level. Even in the 1790s many Belfast Protestants, including some radical reformers, remained

R.C. CHAPEL, St MALACHI'S.

St Malachy's Catholic church, Belfast, completed in 1844, illustrates the growing visibility of the town's Catholic population. Where the first Catholic place of worship, St Mary's, built in 1784, had stood discreetly on a side street, St Patrick's (1815) was boldly situated on Donegall Street, not far from the Church of Ireland's St Anne's. St Malachy's, though erected to serve the overwhelmingly working-class Catholic population of the Markets area, was more flamboyant still, its design and scale suggesting ambitions to create a de facto cathedral. The cost, however, was beyond the resources of the diocese, resulting in a crippling long-term debt. Detail from James O'Hagan's map of Belfast in 1848.

Photograph © National Museums Northern Ireland. Collection Ulster Museum. IA 1848.

Table 3: Religious Denominations in Belfast, 1757–2001

	Church of Ireland	Presbyterian	Catholic	Other
1757			6%	
1808			16%	
1831	27%	39%	33%	1%
1861	25%	35%	34%	6%
1901	30%	34%	24%	12%
1951	30%	30%	26%	14%
2001	14%	16%	42%	28%

Source: 1757, 1808: contemporary estimates cited in Ian Budge and Cornelius O'Leary, *Belfast: Approach to Crisis* (London: Macmillan, 1973), p. 32; 1831: calculated retrospectively from census enumerator's lists for *First Report of the Commissioners of Public Instruction* (BPP 1835 (45) xxxiii), p. 216a; 1861–1951: W.E. Vaughan and A.J. Fitzpatrick, *Irish Historical Statistics: Population 1821–1971* (Dublin: Royal Irish Academy, 1978), pp. 58, 64, 70; 2001: census.

uneasy at the prospect of Catholics being admitted to full political rights. The debate was between those who argued that the removal of institutionalized discrimination would make religious divisions politically irrelevant, and those who insisted that if Catholics achieved political influence they would continue to pursue the interests of their denomination as a united, and now dangerously powerful, bloc. Subsequent events seemed to support the latter view. The insurrection of 1798 was an undoubted shock. The deterioration of what had begun as a secular republican movement into a brutal anti-Protestant crusade took place mainly in the south-east. But news of the Catholic terror in Wexford forced Belfast radicals, previously cocooned by their position in a predominantly Protestant north-east, to reconsider their position as part of a vulnerable minority within Ireland as a whole. Later, from the 1820s, Daniel O'Connell, supported by the Catholic clergy, organized the Catholic masses as an effective political force. His demand for repeal of the Act of Union united Belfast Conservatives and Liberals in determined opposition. The Act had been opposed by many Protestants at the time of its passage. But now, in a changed political environment, the great majority came to see its maintenance as their only protection against engulfment by an aggressive Catholicism. Fears were further heightened by the continuing presence of a current of revolutionary as well as constitutional nationalism. The Catholic bishop of Down and Connor reported to his Roman agent in 1854 that even liberal Protestants had become noticeably less friendly towards Catholics since the Young Ireland insurrection of 1848.[29]

The rise of the Home Rule movement from the 1870s completed the political polarization of the city. Up to this time the Liberal party had kept alive a measure of cross-denominational politics, even if the alliance between a leadership drawn from a small body of mainly affluent Presbyterians and a Catholic electorate that on polling day had no realistic alternative had become something of a marriage of convenience. In the general election of 1885, however, the Liberal party disappeared, leaving Belfast politics polarized between Protestant Unionism and Catholic Nationalism. The introduction in the following year of the first Home Rule Bill brought Belfast's most serious sectarian violence to date, with 32 recorded deaths during several weeks of fighting.

In considering the deepening of sectarian divisions, it is also necessary to take account of developments within the Churches themselves. By the middle of the nineteenth century, the growing influence of evangelicalism had given a new energy to the efforts of the clergy of different Protestant denominations. This was the case, for example, at Christ Church in Durham Street, built to serve the new working-class district growing up to the west of the town centre, where the vigorous preaching and committed pastoral work of the Revd Thomas Drew built up a substantial congregation for the Church of Ireland.[30]

An address to Charles Stewart Parnell, 'Leader of the Irish Race', presented during his visit to the city on 22 May 1891. Parnell's emergence as co-respondent in a divorce case the previous year had bitterly divided the Home Rule movement. Those who gave him their continued support, in the face of threats of excommunication from the Catholic clergy, were for the most part advanced nationalists. Indeed some of those involved in the Belfast address, like Robert Johnston, were members of the Fenian Brotherhood.

From the Collection of Queen's University Belfast.

But evangelicalism, with its insistence on intense personal conviction and its absolute division between false and true religion, also had the potential to exacerbate existing religious tensions, as was seen in Drew's own career as a religious controversialist. Meanwhile Irish Catholicism was undergoing its own transformation, resulting in a more vigorous pastoral regime, but also a more authoritarian and intransigent doctrinal and political stance. In Belfast the triumph of the new culture was confirmed by the replacement in 1865 of the scholarly but ineffective bishop, Cornelius Denvir, by the pugnacious Patrick Dorrian. Dorrian presided over a rapid expansion in the number of priests, churches and religious houses in Belfast, and robustly defended his Church's

The Presbyterian clergyman Hugh Hanna (1821–92), commonly known as 'Roaring Hugh', was a radical open-air street preacher, the founder of St Enoch's church at Carlisle Circus and also of several schools in the area. His inflammatory preaching was seen as contributing to outbreaks of sectarian violence in 1857 and again at the time of the first Home Rule Bill in 1885–86. The statue erected in Carlisle Circus in 1894 was blown off its plinth by the IRA in 1970. Though refurbished in the 1990s, it remains in storage.

Courtesy of the National Library of Ireland.

interests. But he was also critical of Catholics, such as the liberal-minded Bernard Hughes, who cultivated good relations with the town's Protestants and was dismissive of the Presbyterian Liberals to whom Catholics had traditionally looked for support.[31]

Sectarian divisions between Protestant and Catholic coincided with marked social and economic inequalities. An analysis of census data from 1901 shows that Catholics were significantly over-represented in unskilled and poorly paid occupations, while the average rateable valuation of Catholic houses was two-thirds that of Protestant dwellings.[32] The origins of these inequalities long pre-dated the growth of Belfast. A succession of confiscations during the seventeenth century had virtually wiped out the Catholic landed class, while pre-plantation Ulster had had no significant urban population to provide the nucleus of a Catholic middle class of the kind that survived in the three southern provinces. Catholic migrants to Belfast were thus for the most part unskilled rural labourers. (A similar historically based inequality continued within the town's Protestant population, where three centuries after the plantation the Presbyterian descendants of the more economically dynamic Scottish incomers still enjoyed an advantage over their Church of Ireland counterparts.) Within Belfast Catholic prospects for upward social mobility were limited by a system in which industrial workers were recruited informally by word of mouth or through family networks, and where apprenticeships went mainly to the sons and nephews of men already in the trade. There was also the likelihood of discrimination, intensifying as political divisions deepened during the nineteenth century. The major expulsions of Catholics from factories and other workplaces that took place in 1857 and during subsequent periods of heightened tension were purges of potential aggressors rather than a form of job protection. But they must still have acted to reinforce existing inequalities. In quieter times too the likelihood is that Catholic workers suffered either through direct hostility or through the desire of management to avoid problems with the existing, predominantly Protestant workforce in the more desirable occupations. Discrimination was undeniable in the case of municipal employment, where by 1912 only 9 out of 437 salaried officials were Catholic.[33]

In contrast to this growing unskilled or semi-skilled working class, the Catholic middle class remained small and economically weak. A few successful and wealthy businessmen emerged. Between the 1820s and the 1850s two Catholic entrepreneurs, Thomas Hamill and William Watson, took the lead in the development of the Pound as a residential district. Bernard Hughes (1808–78) became a household name in the city through his large and technologically advanced bread-baking enterprise. There were also some successful professional men. Dr Peter O'Connell, a senior surgeon at the Mater Hospital, was high sheriff of Belfast in 1907 and was knighted the following year for services to medicine. The majority of the Catholic middle class, however, comprised publicans and shopkeepers, or alternatively professionals such as lawyers and doctors providing mainly routine services to their own community.

Inherited inequality and present-day discrimination thus combined to condemn Belfast Catholics to an inferior economic position. Catholic disadvantage, however, did not necessarily equate with any general Protestant advantage. There was indeed a labour aristocracy, overwhelmingly Protestant, dominated by skilled workers in shipbuilding and engineering. But what a correlation of religious affiliation and housing quality (Table 4) reveals is above all the degree of overlap. Catholic families were significantly over-represented among the inhabitants of the poorest houses, and under-represented among those residing in the most desirable properties, such as substantial terraces or detached or semi-detached villas. Among Catholic and Protestant families alike, however, the largest single group, amounting to almost half the total in each case, were accommodated in the second lowest tier of housing. These would have been the standard terraces of 'kitchen' houses, comprising a downstairs kitchen with a door opening directly on to the street, a scullery behind, and stairs leading directly from the kitchen to two upstairs bedrooms. A detailed study of the Catholic Pound and the Protestant Sandy Row, two areas that featured repeatedly in sectarian clashes across the century, reveals an almost identical social profile in terms of housing and occupation.[34] Here at least violence in no way operated to protect Protestant privilege. Instead sectarian conflict largely served to pit two equally disadvantaged groups against one another, while also blighting any prospect of their improving their condition through joint political action in the cause of labour.

These religious divisions, periodically exploding into violence, quickly became part of the negative image Belfast presented to the outside world. Already by 1849 Queen Victoria had clearly been briefed on what to expect. 'The Protestants and Roman Catholics', she noted in her diary on the night before her visit, 'are nearly equally divided in Belfast, and religious hatred and

Table 4: Rateable Valuation of Houses by Religion of Head of Household, 1901

	Catholic	Protestant
Below £5	32%	13%
£5–£7.50	48%	45%
£7.51–£12	14%	26%
Above £12	6%	16%

Source: A.C. Hepburn, *A Past Apart: Studies in the History of Catholic Belfast 1850–1950* (Belfast: Ulster Historical Foundation, 1996), p. 62.

party feeling run very high.'[35] A London magazine, reviewing the official report on the riots of 1864, wrote severely of a town that was in most respects in tune with 'the most advanced notions of our time', yet that in matters of religion 'lives in the barbarism of the past'.[36] A few years later the lord lieutenant, Earl Spencer, reporting on yet another bout of violence, made clear how far he saw those responsible as lying beyond the boundaries of civilization:

> I confess that much as I dislike the idea of killing men in a crowd, I think it often would save great loss of property and life if at the outset after due warning an effective volley were fired. However it would be impossible to direct action of this sort from a distance, and few men have the moral courage to encounter the odium of giving the order, even in self-defence.

His correspondent, the Lord Privy Seal, was equally clear on the alien character of the behaviour on display, and the legitimacy of ruthless measures. 'What a set you have to rule over [...] I don't think that people in this country would grumble if less forbearance was shown to such wilful breakers of the law.'[37]

Comments of this kind are all the more striking because they were made at a time when Belfast's religious quarrels did not yet approach anything like the level of viciousness they were eventually to attain. Affrays between rival groups could be violent enough. In the run-up to the Twelfth of July in 1849, for example, two navvies were fatally injured after they had attacked a car driver who had decorated his vehicle with orange lilies.[38] For the most part, however, sectarian clashes led to broken heads and wrecked houses. The commissioners sent to investigate the riots of 1857 noted the ritualistic nature of what had taken place, as two communities that lived on reasonably good terms for the greater part of the year assumed a mutually antagonistic posture during the period on either side of the Twelfth of July celebrations. A relatively new feature, in 1857, was that both sides had equipped themselves with firearms. The use made of these, however, was primarily to exchange shots across the expanse of waste ground dividing the Pound from Sandy Row. Two children were wounded on separate occasions, in each case reportedly by a shot maliciously aimed directly at them. For the most part, however, the resident magistrate dismissed the shooting that took place as mere bravado, suggesting that those involved loaded with ball as well as powder only in the belief that it produced a louder noise.

The element of ritualized confrontation was also evident in an account of twenty Catholic mill girls dancing in a ring in a street joining the two districts:

> Hurrah for Mullan's corner
> And to hell with Sandy-row;
> And the Devil build Sandy-row up.[39]

Here there is a clear element of recreational violence, allowing people living in harsh conditions an opportunity to let off steam, of the kind that would have been found in working-class communities throughout the United Kingdom. Even the sectarian element, despite the patrician disdain of Earl Spencer and others, was in no way exclusive to Belfast. In English and Scottish cities the arrival from the early nineteenth century of large numbers of Irish Catholic migrants had also created the basis for serious antagonisms. In some cases, as in Liverpool and Glasgow, the resulting animosities continued into the twentieth century and beyond.

Where Belfast differed from other urban centres was in the lethal additional significance conferred on its sectarian quarrels by the wider context of a contested constitutional framework. Protestants in Glasgow or Liverpool might resent the Catholic intruders with whom they had to share their harsh and crowded urban environment, but they did not have to fear being ruled by them. In Belfast, on the other hand, it was precisely this prospect that over time gave local sectarian conflict a character wholly different to that seen elsewhere in the United Kingdom. The journalist Frankfort Moore, writing in 1914, recalled how it was the rising threat of Home Rule that had given the Orange institution, formerly regarded as 'an unmitigated nuisance', a new respectability in the eyes of middle-class Protestants.[40] The increasing level of violence likewise reflected political trends. The riots of 1864, coinciding with the rise of the Fenian movement, led to an unprecedented 12 deaths. In 1886, at the time of the first Home Rule Bill, prolonged disturbances caused 32 recorded deaths. In this case, however, clashes between Protestant and Catholic mobs were overshadowed by affrays between Protestants and the police. The Royal Irish Constabulary had in 1864 replaced the almost entirely Protestant Belfast town police, and inflammatory rumours now circulated that the Liberal government intended to use this predominantly Catholic force to impose Home Rule on Belfast.

The upward trend in sectarian violence during the second half of the nineteenth century, driven by the city's political polarization, is thus undeniable. But the conflict that erupted during 1920–22 must nevertheless be seen as representing a marked discontinuity. The background was a new and particularly destructive combination of circumstances. In the south the Crown was losing the war against militant Irish republicanism. Closer to home, the Government of Ireland Act had authorized the creation of a Northern Ireland state, whose success or failure would determine the foreseeable future for all of the inhabitants of Belfast. Meanwhile shipyard workers unemployed due to the post-war slump were outraged by claims that Catholics were still occupying jobs they had taken while loyal Protestants were serving in the First World War. Disturbances arising out of Orange celebrations on 12 July 1920 escalated into a round of unprecedented violence. By October 1922 498 persons had been killed, around 10,000 expelled from their places of work, and some 23,000

Nelson Street bedecked with
Orange arch and decorations,
July 1912.

Photograph © National Museums
Northern Ireland. Collection Ulster
Museum. BELUM.Y.W.10.21.205.

driven from their homes.[41] Killing also took on a new character. Reports of
snipers firing into 'enemy' streets superficially recall the riots of 1857. But this
time the shots were intended to kill. Random sniping, moreover, was backed up
by targeted assassinations. The aim on both sides was the same: to intimidate
their opponents into abandoning the struggle and accepting political
defeat. Andrew Magill, a former Dublin Castle official transferred to the new
Northern Ireland civil service, later provided a chillingly accurate summary of
the mentality involved. The subject was the murder in March 1922 of Owen
McMahon, a prosperous Catholic publican, and five members of his family, in
apparent reprisal for the shooting two days earlier of two Special Constables in
Belfast city centre. 'I would not like to say that it put a stop to the murderous
activities of the [nationalist] gunmen, for that would be too dreadful a thought,
but it undoubtedly made them pause as they realised that they were up against
a party just as sanguinary and evil-disposed as they were themselves.'[42]

Magill's condemnation was clear cut. But his comments nevertheless reflect
the inevitable ambivalence with which mainstream Protestant opinion, at a time
of crisis, regarded the violence of militant loyalism. The accuracy of his analysis,

meanwhile, was borne out by subsequent events. Although Catholics made up only a quarter of the city's population, they contributed three in every five of the casualties recorded. By the end of 1922 loyalist terror, combined with tough official security measures, had put an end to attempted resistance within Belfast to the new Northern Ireland government. Subsequent challenges were minor, the most serious being the 1942 murder of a policeman and a small number of other attacks during the Second World War. The renewed IRA campaign of 1956–61 focused on the border, leaving Belfast largely untouched. Belfast became the capital of an assertively British and Protestant Northern Ireland, its Catholic minority denied any role, even if they would have been willing to assume it, in the city's civic life. Discrimination in both public- and private-sector employment, and the social and economic inequalities for which they were partly responsible, continued or deepened. The development after 1945 of a welfare state improved overall living standards, but also created new areas of exclusion, particularly in the discriminatory allocation of housing.

Against this apparently static background, one episode made clear that the potential for violence had not disappeared. In October 1932, as the world economy slid into depression and the numbers out of work rose to crisis levels, street protests against the miserable relief offered by the town's Poor Law Guardians seemed for a time to promise a revival of the working-class unity across lines of sectarian division that had been briefly glimpsed in 1907. However, a succession of other incidents during 1933–35, including a murder in

The aftermath of riot, 1932. Cobblestones have been lifted for use as potentially lethal projectiles.

Photograph © Keystone-France / Gamma-Keystone / Getty Images.

1933 and riots following the celebration of the king's silver jubilee in May 1935, reflected a parallel build-up of sectarian tension. Matters reached a head in a week of violence following the celebration of the Twelfth of July in 1935. There were ten deaths, seven Protestants and three Catholics. Families were driven from 214 Catholic and 64 Protestant houses, and some hundreds of Catholic workers were expelled from factories and the shipyards. The destruction of lives, homes and livelihoods was on a smaller scale than in 1920–22. But the episode made clear that the calm so ruthlessly imposed during 1920–22 was not to be taken for granted.[43]

Three decades later the calm came more decisively to an end. In 1966 militant Protestants organized a revived Ulster Volunteer Force and carried out a series of sectarian attacks resulting in three deaths. Their actions were a response to what were by any standards some mildly conciliatory gestures by the Unionist prime minister, Terence O'Neill, towards Northern Ireland's Catholic minority. Two years later an initially peaceful campaign for civil rights faced repeated violent assaults from Protestant counter-demonstrators. On the Catholic side a revived IRA reacted to this Protestant violence and the subsequent appearance of Crown forces as peacekeepers by launching its own campaign of bombings and shootings. In time these were to become targeted attacks, designed to wear down British and Unionist resistance to a united Ireland by a 'long war' of attrition. In its early stages, however, the violence was indiscriminate, intended to bring about victory through the immediate collapse of the Northern Ireland state. Of 693 deaths between 1969 and 1972, 438 took place in Belfast and about half were the work of Republicans. The grotesque disparity, on both Catholic and Protestant sides, between grievance and response reflects the depth of the animosities and suspicion that had been allowed to build up within an outwardly stable but divided and unequal society.

Women

In 1795 Martha McTier wrote to her brother William Drennan about a public meeting she had attended on the subject of political reform, 'where indeed I was the only woman'.[44] Yet her presence, as a confident, opinionated individual of some standing in the community, was not all that surprising. In the traditional political system that obtained until 1832, attendance at many of the patchwork of local assemblies that managed urban affairs was regulated by custom and practice. The great reform acts of the first half of the nineteenth century brought consistency and greater rationality to the process of representation. But in giving the entitlement to participate in public life a strict legal definition, they also made it exclusively, rather than just predominantly, male.[45] Women regained their right to take part in the management of their community only a century later. When they did so, as it happened, Belfast led the way. Determined lobbying by the North of Ireland Women's Suffrage Society (NIWSS) ensured that the 1887 Act to create a new municipal franchise for the city conferred the vote on 'persons' rather than 'men'. This was eleven years before Irish women elsewhere gained the vote in local government elections. In 1896 the NIWSS became the Belfast branch of the Irish Women's Suffrage and Local Government Association. An early NIWSS member, Belfast MP William Johnston, otherwise noted mainly as a champion of popular Orangeism, introduced the Bill in 1896 permitting Irish women to vote and stand as candidates in the election of Poor Law Guardians. Largely motivated by a desire to bring Ireland into line with English and Scottish legislation, the Local Government (Ireland) Act 1898 admitted women as voters and candidates in district council elections.[46] In parliamentary elections, on the other hand, women, in Belfast as elsewhere, had to wait until 1918 to gain the right to vote; those between 21 and 29 had to wait until 1928.[47]

This long exclusion was all the more anomalous in the case of Belfast because in other respects this was, throughout the period concerned, a city dominated by women. In 1901 there were in fact 1,290 adult women for every 1,000 adult men, while just over a quarter of all households were headed by a woman. This marked numerical preponderance reflected the unusually wide range of employment opportunities available to women – or, to put it another way, the extent to which the city's economic fortunes depended on the contribution of female workers. At the beginning of the twentieth century women comprised 38 per cent of the labour force, as compared to 29 per cent in Ireland as a whole and 30 per cent in Great Britain. Only 20 per cent of these Belfast women workers, moreover, were employed as domestic servants, as compared to 40 per cent in Great Britain. Instead women formed the backbone of the city's linen industry, in both spinning and weaving sectors, and were also crucial to other manufacturing enterprises such as Gallaher's giant tobacco factory.[48]

In addition to this growing legion of factory workers, women also played a role in the small commercial enterprises that remained important within the expanding urban centre. Throughout the first part of the century, for instance, there was a female presence even within the male-dominated butchering trade of Hercules Street.[49] More typical were the women, such as Ann and Mary Allen, recorded in the directory for 1807 as running haberdashers' and milliners' shops clustered in and around Castle Street and High Street. Lower down the social scale, in the poorer district of Carrick Hill, a Mrs Graham and a Mrs Mulgrew worked as clothes dealers.[50] Others again earned a living through taking in lodgers – one reason for the high proportion of female heads of household. Some trades traditionally dominated by women, such as the straw bonnet manufacturers, declined and disappeared with the advent of mass production. But economic change also brought new opportunities. As the industrial economy matured, an expanding commercial, legal and

Isabella Tod (1836–96) was the best-known feminist of her generation, and also campaigned vigorously for female education and temperance. Her strong opposition to Home Rule cost her friends in the British suffrage movement, instinctively inclined to sympathize with the campaign for Irish self-determination. The portrait is by Marguerita Rosalie Rothwell (fl. 1881–89).

Photograph © National Museums Northern Ireland. Collection Ulster Museum. BELUM.U4493.

financial services sector created a growing number of office jobs, and the rapid rise from the 1880s of the typewriter, stereotyped from an early stage as a woman's instrument, helped to ensure that a proportion of these went to female workers. The appearance of large city-centre department stores created openings for shop assistants. The census of 1901 provides other, more exotic, examples: women such as 18-year-old Phoebe Quinn and 19-year-old Isabel Whisker were employed as telephone operators, while 25-year-old Sarah E. Whiteside and 17-year-old Gertrude Noble were recorded as photographers.[51]

Further new opportunities for women's employment arose through developments in education and public health. Already in the mid-nineteenth century women such as Margaret Byers, who established her first school in Belfast in 1859, ran small private schools in the town.[52] The census of 1911 recorded just over 1,300 female teachers. Training colleges for elementary teachers were under the control of the separate denominations, and supported by the state from 1883. In 1900 the Dominican order opened St Mary's Training College, on the Falls Road, to educate and train Catholic women as primary school teachers. (Protestant would-be teachers continued to attend training colleges outside the city until the establishment of Stranmillis College in 1922.) Where health is concerned, visiting the sick poor had long been a charitable duty accepted by middle- and upper-class women. A Ladies' Committee also took part in managing the Lying-in Hospital on the Antrim Road, opened in 1830, which offered care during childbirth to poor married women. The routine work of caring for patients in hospitals, by contrast, was generally in the hands of untrained pauper women. In 1871, however, the Belfast Nurses' Home and Training School was established to provide trained nurses both for Belfast

Margaret Byers (1832–1912), an educationalist and advocate for temperance, is most associated with the school she founded in Belfast in 1859, which was named Victoria College in honour of the Queen's jubilee in 1878. While this catered for the daughters of the rising middle classes in the town, Byers also established homes for the underprivileged children of Belfast. A founder of the Belfast Women's Temperance Association (1874) she was a campaigner for alcoholic and vulnerable women, particularly former prisoners through the Prison Gate Mission. She was a member of the first senate of Queen's University, Belfast, and the photograph shows her receiving an honorary doctorate of laws from Trinity College, Dublin, in 1905, in recognition of her services to education.

Copyright of Victoria College, Belfast.

Margaret Byers and her staff in the school at Lower Crescent.

Copyright of Victoria College, Belfast.

General Hospital and for service as private nurses. In the first year 27 nurses and probationers were accommodated in the home.[53] The Society for Providing Nurses for the Sick Poor, established in 1874, also trained and employed a small group of nurses to work alongside the 'ladies' in caring for poor people suffering from illness. In the Workhouse Infirmary change came with the appointment in 1884 of an energetic new superintendent and head nurse, Ellie Pirrie. Previously some 15 paid but untrained nurses had supervised the work of 65 pauper attendants. Pirrie, however, persuaded the Poor Law Guardians to introduce a formal training programme, admitting the first three probationers in 1887.[54] By 1899 the number of nurses employed in the Infirmary had risen to 78.[55] In the same year, the Sisters of Mercy opened St Philomene's Training School for nurses.[56] The census of 1911 recorded a total of 554 nurses in Belfast.

New employment opportunities were directly linked to improvements in women's education. Mid-nineteenth-century Belfast had a profusion of small 'ladies' seminaries', offering classes in music, drawing and other suitable accomplishments. The second half of the nineteenth century, however, saw the establishment of new schools: the Sisters of Mercy's Young Ladies' School at St Paul's convent (1857), Margaret Byers' Ladies' Collegiate College (1859), which later became Victoria College, Belfast Ladies' Institute (1867) and Methodist College Belfast, co-educational from 1868. By 1880 the town's directory claimed that there were more than 40 private day and boarding schools for young ladies. The Intermediate Education Act (1878), providing prize money to individual pupils and fees based on results to schools, was crucial to the opening up to girls of a secondary education leading to recognized qualifications. Byers, along with Isabella Tod, was prominent in the agitation required to ensure that the Act included girls' as well as boys' schools.[57] The Sisters of Mercy were also keen supporters of the Act, entering their students in intermediate exams, despite the objections of their bishop, Patrick Dorrian, who criticized what he saw as 'an attempt to subvert society to establish a blue stocking in every family by the introduction of a system of education which would not be in keeping with the positions of females'.[58] In the first year that exams were held, one Mercy student received a gold medal for the best results (for girls) in Ireland, while Byers' school became one of the top prize-winners in the 1880s and 1890s. In 1882, as a result of agitation from Byers and the Belfast Ladies Academy, Queen's College admitted women to its arts classes, three years before Queen's College Cork and six years before Queen's College Galway.[59] In practice, however, few women attended Queen's College, choosing instead to attend the collegiate departments of girls' schools. Between 1891 and 1900, for instance, there were 19 women graduates from Queen's College, compared to 95 from Victoria College.[60] Byers herself was given an honorary degree of doctor of laws by Trinity College, Dublin, in 1905, and was made a member of the first senate of Queen's University, Belfast.[61]

For a select number of Belfast women, widening educational opportunities opened up the possibility of entering the professions. Jean Bell was the first woman to be admitted to medical classes at Queen's in 1889.[62] By 1901 six women were listed as medical students in Belfast. Notable among them were the children of William Hastings, clerk of the Union, Eva, Ethel and Arnold. There was clearly also a religious dimension to becoming a doctor; Presbyterian Sarah Brown Keers, for instance, was a medical missionary, married to the Revd John Keers, while her brother David McMordie was also a medical student. In 1911 Marion Blaidforth Andrews and Elizabeth Bell Fisher were two of Belfast's only four female doctors. Meanwhile 20-year-old Florence Hobson, only sister of the Irish nationalist Bulmer Hobson, having trained in Belfast School of Art, appeared in the census in 1901 as the lone female architect in the city, apprenticed to Messrs James J. Philips.[63] She later joined the architectural staff of Belfast Corporation, assisting on projects such as the new electricity station on east Bridge Street and in 1910 the new abattoir. In 1911 she became the first female licentiate of the Royal Institute of British Architects.[64]

In addition to providing a range of new employment opportunities, the changing city centre offered women a greater freedom of movement. On its periphery millworkers, many still instantly recognizable by their shawls, continued to troop from narrow streets of terraced housing to nearby mills. But now there were also other women making their regular journeys to work in the city centre, the dress codes of employment behind desk or counter serving to blur previously obvious social distinctions. For the leisured middle-class woman, meanwhile, the giant new department stores, such as Robinson and Cleaver (1886–88) and Anderson and McAuley (1895–99), offered a wholly new type of public space: one where an unaccompanied female could saunter at her own pace, inspect what attracted her attention or linger to meet a friend without becoming the object either of suspicion or of unwelcome attention. There were also more basic conveniences. By providing a tea room, a restaurant and a 'ladies' parlour', the department store permitted middle-class women to extend their stay in the newly expanded centre beyond what the need for rest, refreshment and acceptable toilet facilities would otherwise have permitted.[65]

The breakdown of traditional boundaries and restrictions, not surprisingly, made many uneasy. A correspondent to the *Irish News*, in 1909, found it 'actually indecent' that men and women should be packed together into the crowded trams leaving Castle Junction for the suburbs between 5.30 and 7 each evening, to be thrown on top of one another at every jolt.[66] In this context many social reformers attempted to change, regulate and police the behaviour of women in public space. Girls and women newly arrived from the country, or living apart from the supervision of relatives, were perceived to be particularly at risk. Some employers provided accommodation for such employees. The 'Ulster Arcade', as early as 1858, provided accommodation for both its male and female assistants in premises fronting on to Callendar Street, near the arcade. The Bank Buildings, thirty years later, boasted of providing bedrooms, 'dispensing with the objectionable dormitory principle', for its employees.[67] In other cases religious and philanthropic bodies filled the gap. Between 1889 and 1898 Belfast's Sisters of Mercy ran a home 'providing temporary accommodation for girls in service and in retail employment who had come up from the country until they were able to find themselves suitable permanent accommodation'.[68] The census of 1911 reveals that the residents of the Girls' Friendly Society in Donegall Pass were mainly shop assistants and dressmakers.

Another area of concern to reformers was women's use of alcohol. Margaret Byers (who became the first president of the Irish Women's Temperance Union in 1894) and Isabella Tod organized the Belfast Women's Temperance Association (BWTA), which added Christian Women's Union to its title in 1883. When she moved to Belfast in the late 1850s Byers had quickly become a supporter of the town's Band of Hope children's temperance movement.[69] The aim of temperance work such as that of the BWTA was 'to rescue women of the working-class who had fallen into the temptation of drink'. By 1875 three BWTA temperance food houses had opened in Belfast, particularly aimed at women factory workers. The BWTA also ran the Prison Gate Mission for Women from 1877, in addition to a home for alcoholic women. In 1902 they also opened an Inebriates' Home for Women at Strandtown. In 1882 the BWTA opened a home for destitute girls, complementing the orphan societies run by the Presbyterian Church, Church of Ireland and Sisters of Mercy, but motivated to remove children from alcoholic parents. Ultimately this BWTA home moved to Lagan village and was named Shamrock Lodge, an industrial school accommodating over a hundred children by 1902.[70]

Closely related to alcohol, and forming the true heart of concern over women's behaviour, was the issue of prostitution. From 1860 members of the Belfast Midnight Mission toured the less savoury streets at night, seeking to persuade women to spend the night in their rescue house. More permanent accommodation was available in the Ulster Female Penitentiary, which dated its foundation to 1839 (although an institution of that name had been in existence as far back as 1816), and defined itself as catering for 'penitent victims of seduction'.[71] Its driving force was the Presbyterian clergyman John Edgar, and in 1892 the institution was renamed the Edgar Home in his honour. The Ulster Magdalene Asylum, established in 1849, was closely associated with the charismatic champion of the Church of Ireland's mission to the working classes, the Revd Thomas Drew. Both institutions, however, accepted women of all denominations. On census night in 1901 the 36 inmates in the Presbyterian Edgar Home comprised seven Catholics, 19 members of the Church of Ireland and 10 Presbyterians.[72] At this social level at least Belfast's notorious sectarian divisions seem to have lost their force. There was also a Catholic institution, opened in March 1860, run by the Sisters of Mercy.

The aim of these different institutions was to reclaim women who had strayed beyond the limits of conventional morality through discipline, religious practice and arduous manual labour, most commonly in laundry work. Not all of those subjected to this punitive routine were necessarily prostitutes. The Sisters of Mercy also took in teenage girls described as 'wayward' or in moral danger, or who had been disowned by their families.[73] In other cases too there is evidence that those confined included women who had been caught engaging in sexual activity, or who had become pregnant outside marriage, or even those simply considered to be keeping 'bad company' or otherwise behaving in a way that caused concern.[74] Yet the reformers must also be given credit for seeking to rescue women from what was indeed a nightmare world. Margaret Ann Rocks was habitually before Belfast's magistrates on charges of being drunk and disorderly, a life of alcoholism and homelessness which stretched back to the late 1860s; by the age of 27 she had spent a total of ten-and-a-half years in jail, which her short spells in the Edgar Home did not rescue her from.[75] In January 1874 Eliza Nichol was prosecuted for keeping a 'bawdy house' in Donegall Street, where Catherine Moore and Eliza Walker worked as prostitutes. The constable who arrested them observed perceptively to the magistrate that 'landlords got higher rents' for houses rented to prostitutes 'than to ordinary people'.[76] It was the start of a life of drink, prostitution and violence for Catherine Moore, who by 1881 had been before the magistrates 81 times, regularly convicted of being drunk and disorderly, involved in petty crime and the victim herself of assault.[77]

In less obvious ways also, social reformers sought not just to improve the living conditions of the city's expanding working class, but to impose appropriate models of female behaviour. Women were viewed as the anchor of family life, and there was a societal expectation that they were naturally responsible for its domestic economy, the care of children and the sick, and the morality of the family unit in a way that men were not. Child poverty and neglect was partly judged on the cleanliness of the child, its home and clothing, all regarded as largely female spheres of concern. Middle-class women activists, themselves liberated from a purely domestic sphere by philanthropic activity, thus imposed a domestic ideology on the lives of the very poorest, despite the fact that those lives could not fit such an idealized model.[78] The same emphasis on women's particular responsibility was evident at the level of state intervention. For instance, it was predominantly mothers who were the focus of the authorities' ire and punishment when children truanted from school or were caught begging. In Belfast, Charles McLorinan, JP, laid the blame for begging squarely on mothers, who he claimed stood outside public houses sending girls in under the pretext of selling matches.[79] With the beginning of

Following spread: The Edgar Home for the 'penitent victims of seduction'. As the historian W.A. Maguire has observed: 'whatever their religious denomination, fallen women did a lot of washing'.

Photograph © National Museums Northern Ireland. Collection Ulster Museum. BELUM.Y3013.

child protection policies and institutions at the end of the nineteenth century – the National Society for the Prevention of Cruelty to Children opened a branch in Belfast in January 1891 – it was again mothers, rather than fathers and husbands, who were mainly the targets of aid and instruction.[80]

In thus devoting themselves to attempts to alleviate the massive social problems of a growing industrial city, middle- and upper-class women did not wholly escape the confines of traditional gender roles. Although the work of the Belfast Female Mission was managed by a committee of 25 women meeting monthly, their report on the year's activities to the annual meeting of the society was read out by a clergyman, and other speakers at the meeting were exclusively male.[81] For others, however, philanthropic and voluntary work was an essential stage in their politicization. Involvement in organization and fundraising meant taking charge of staff, managing large budgets, writing reports and, in other organizations if not in the Belfast Female Mission, developing confidence and expertise in public speaking. It also brought middle- and upper-class women – regularly unchaperoned – into contact with sections of Belfast and its population with which they would not normally have engaged. Through charities, hospitals and schools they took part in appointments and in the formulation of policy. The ethos underlying the heavy involvement of women in philanthropy – the belief that they were by nature suited to the care of the sick and poor, as well as morally and spiritually superior to men – was also of use to those who, at the end of the nineteenth century, campaigned for the appointment of women as Poor Law Guardians.[82]

The close connection between women's social reform work and the development of female political activism is evident in the case of Fisherwick Presbyterian Working Women's Association, established in 1884 to inspire and instruct women of the church to engage in work for women both at home and abroad. Seven of its most active members, it has been pointed out, also served on the 13-strong committee of the North of Ireland Women's Suffrage Society,[83] founded by Isabella Tod in 1871, and counting among its members Margaret Byers, William Johnston MP, and the Revd E.L. Berkeley, moderator of the Irish Presbyterian Church. Following the success in 1887 of the campaign to grant the municipal suffrage to propertied women in Belfast, Tod helped to establish a women ratepayers association to promote 'temperance, sanitary reform and the observance of peace and order on the streets'. By 1895 the number of female voters in Belfast was not far short of the total number of voters in the exclusively male municipal electorate in Dublin.[84] Reformers saw education and the franchise as closely linked. Education would enable middle-class women to improve society, while the extension of the franchise would give women a means of bringing in legislation to protect women's rights, not least in the workplace.

Women activists in Belfast, despite their shared commitment to female rights, were not immune to the political polarization that marked the last decades of the nineteenth century. Margaret Byers, like Isabella Tod, actively opposed Home Rule for Ireland and was a member of the Irish Women's Liberal Unionist Association which Tod helped to set up in Belfast in 1888.[85] Tod's Unionism drove a wedge between her and the British feminists with whom she had up to this point cooperated fruitfully. Her conviction, however, was that subordination to an intolerant, Catholic-dominated Home Rule government would be fatal to the gains that she and others had achieved. 'I perceived that [it] would be the stoppage of the whole work of social reform for which we had laboured so hard. I saw a large portion of my life work shattered, and endangered.'[86] Other women, too, justified their opposition to Irish self-government primarily in terms of the threat to the social and economic progress they had striven for in recent decades.

Others among Belfast's politically active women took a radically different view. In 1896 Alice Milligan and Anna Johnston, who wrote under the pen name Ethna Carbery, founded an advanced nationalist newspaper, *Shan Van Vocht*. Milligan, inspired in part by the successful political activism of Irish women Unionists, also joined with Jennifer Armour in founding branches of the Irish Women's Association (IWA) in Belfast in 1894, holding meetings in the Rosemary Street lecture room, former meeting place of the United Irishmen.[87] In addition to its commitment to Irish nationalism, and its literary and cultural remit, the IWA sought to redefine the role of women in Irish society.[88] For example, the Quaker Mary Hobson (mother of the architect Florence Hobson) presented a paper dealing with the political and social work 'which women might attempt' in March 1895. Hobson argued for the extension of the sphere of women's civic activity and influence:

> It is the duty of every woman to take an interest in the country in which she lived, to know something of its history, past and present, and, if the conditions under which she and her sisters are placed are likely to lead to a fair development, she should be prepared with the experience she has gained through many years to extend her help and sympathy outside her own home. Who is better fitted to fill the position of guardian of the poor than such a woman as I have tried to describe?[89]

In the last decade of the century Home Rule had become the dominating political issue, dividing a Victorian Belfast already fractured along class, religious and gender lines.

Newcomers

Any discussion of identity or community, belonging and exclusion, must also take account of the extent to which Belfast, at the late nineteenth-century peak of its success, was a city of newcomers. The massive growth in population, from perhaps 20,000 in 1800 to 350,000 by 1901, could have taken place only through a massive process of migration. At the beginning of the twentieth century no fewer than three out of every five inhabitants, and almost four in every five heads of households, had been born outside the city. Even among the city's youngest inhabitants, around one-third of all children under nine had been born elsewhere.[90]

The importance of migration to the growth of Belfast was reflected in the make-up of the city's business elite. Of the managers of the two great shipyards, Edward Harland had been born in Yorkshire and Gustav Wolff in Hamburg, while George Clark was Scottish. Only Frank Workman was Belfast born. Many of the city's leading linen merchants, such as Sir David Taylor and Sir Robert Boag, both of whom served as mayors of the town, were likewise Scottish born. From further afield the opportunities held out by Belfast's linen industry also attracted Daniel Joseph Jaffé, who came from Hamburg with his family in 1852. His son, Otto, was to be Ireland's first Jewish lord mayor and high sheriff, and the first Irish Jew to be knighted.[91] Gustavus Heyn from Danzig, who moved to Belfast via Liverpool in 1826, became a commission merchant and agent. A street directory listing for 1861 identifies him as consul for Belgium, Prussia, the Hanseatic cities, Mecklenberg, Oldenberg, Spain, Turkey, Greece and the Kingdom of the Two Sicilies, providing some indication of the port's growing international reach. He also established an important local connection by marrying into the Pirrie family, Harland and Wolff's William Pirrie being Letitia Heyn's nephew. The Heyns themselves went on to create a successful shipping business (Headline), becoming significant figures on the city's Harbour Board and Chamber of Commerce.[92]

The arrival of figures such as Harland, Wolff and Jaffé testifies to the extent to which the developing mid-century town had become a magnet for ambitious and energetic businessmen. At the same time it is also clear how much its subsequent success depended on this fund of imported entrepreneurial talent. At a lower social level, but still of major importance, Belfast's success as a latecomer in the technologically sophisticated shipbuilding industry depended heavily on the imported skills of workers from the Mersey and the Clyde, attracted to Belfast by high wages, the availability of housing and the additional employment offered to family members by the city's linen mills and factories. Demand for a different set of specialized skills encouraged the establishment from the 1850s and 1860s of an Italian community, drawn mainly from the Lazio region and including gilders, carvers, sculptors and other craftsmen attracted to a town which in the 1850s and 1860s was creating impressive monumental buildings with elaborate decorated interiors.[93] Immigration from Italy continued into the early twentieth century, but the 1901 census revealed that later arrivals predominantly brought with them the skills of the ice-cream vendor rather than the artisan. From the 1880s eastern European Jews, ethnically distinctive in a way that middle-class German immigrants

Sir Otto Jaffé (1846–1929), whose father had come to Belfast from Hamburg in 1852, was a successful linen exporter who served as lord mayor in 1899–1900 and 1904–05. Despite his distinguished record of public service and philanthropy, he was accused of pro-German sympathies during the First World War and left Belfast for London, where he spent the rest of his long life.

Reproduced with the kind permission of Belfast City Council. Photograph © Bryan Rutledge.

such as the Jaffés had never been, also settled, working as traders, dealers and tailors. Other migrant streams commenced only in the twentieth century, as an overspill from movement to Great Britain. A small number of Indians settled in Belfast in the 1920s and 1930s, working mostly as door-to-door salesmen. Further arrivals from the 1960s, including a stronger professional and middle-class element, strengthened what became a thriving community. The 1960s also saw the arrival of immigrants from the New Territories. The first recorded Chinese restaurant, 'The Peacock', opened in Belfast in 1962, and it is mostly catering which has occupied the city's Chinese community since.

As in other cities, immigration left its mark on the social geography of nineteenth- and early twentieth-century Belfast. Eastern European Jewish migrants clustered in the area round the Antrim Road. While the town's first synagogue, opened in 1871, was located in Great Victoria Street, its successor, in 1904, was in Annesley Street off Carlisle Circus. Meanwhile Little Patrick Street, in the docks area sandwiched between St Patrick's and St Joseph's churches, became known as Little Italy. Little Italy was in turn part of a larger docklands area, known as Sailortown, lying between Great George Street and Whitla Street, where the coming and going of seamen, along with the presence of Italian and other migrants, created a greater degree of cultural variety than was found in other parts of the city. At a very different social and cultural level the town's middle-class Scottish population cultivated their own expression of ethnic distinctiveness. The Benevolent Society of St Andrew, established in 1867, hosted regular dinners while also organizing philanthropic assistance for their less fortunate countrymen and their children. In the 1890s the city also boasted a Burns club, a Scottish Association and three curling societies, as well as a Highland Games.[94] Over time this determined maintenance of an identity, combined with the strength of Presbyterianism in Belfast and its hinterland, were to mean that Belfast's political Britishness was to be identified with ethnic Scottishness, even though in 1911 Belfast's 12,451 Scottish-born residents were in fact outnumbered by its 15,446 English-born.

Table 5: Birthplaces of the Population of Belfast, 1901

Belfast	39%
Antrim and Down	38%
Other Ulster counties	12.5%
Other Irish provinces	3%
Great Britain	6.5%
Other	1%

Source: A.C. Hepburn, *Catholic Belfast and Nationalist Ireland in the Era of Joe Devlin 1871–1934* (Oxford: Oxford University Press, 2008), pp. 9–10.

Belfast, then, had its ethnic minorities, both real and self-defined. At the same time, in a city of newcomers, the proportion who had travelled any significant distance was small. In 1911 just 1,990 residents of the city, 0.8 per cent, had been born outside the United Kingdom, the two largest groups being the 867 who had been born in America and the 424 born in Russia. Just over 7 per cent of the city's population, 27,897, had been born in Great Britain. The number coming from more distant parts of Ireland was also small: 3 per cent from the three southern provinces, and 13 per cent from the seven counties beyond Belfast's immediate hinterland. By contrast 38 per cent of all inhabitants, more than half the non-Belfast born, had come no further than from the counties of Antrim and Down.

Late Victorian and Edwardian Belfast would thus have had nothing like the mix of accents and backgrounds to be found in the immigrant quarters of a contemporary American city. Its newcomers, with a few exceptions, took up residence, not in neighbourhoods defined by ethnicity, but rather, as in the Pound and Sandy Row, in areas demarcated by religious affiliation. The

In the first decade of the twentieth century York Street was a busy, multi-ethnic area of Belfast. Its great landmarks were the York Street mill, Gallaher's tobacco factory and the Belfast and Northern Counties Railway terminus. A noisy, bustling thoroughfare, nearly every corner of the densely populated area was marked by a public house. This photograph shows the railway station (centre right). The junction, being passed by the tram, gives an insight into the diversity of the area in 1911. Frank Puleo, an Italian Catholic, and his second wife Hessie, a Presbyterian from County Antrim, ran a refreshment room and confectioners with Frank's son, Francis, at the corner of Ship Street. Married for less than a year, they were supplementing

YORK ST.BELFAST.330.W.L.

their income with the rent from three lodgers. Frank's neighbours on the opposite side of the street were the Barrs, Charles and Essa Jane, Presbyterians from County Tyrone, who ran the Elephant Tea House. On the other corner of Brougham Street was the public house, run by George A. Bennett, a Scot, who lived in a terraced house in Rosemount Gardens, off the Antrim Road, with his wife Eva and their four children.

Courtesy of the National Library of Ireland.

dominant cultural influence on the city, meanwhile, was that of the immediate rural hinterland, whose inhabitants had long been famous for their dour manner and lack of ceremony. The farmers and weavers of County Antrim, one visitor noted in 1839, believed that they had no superiors, 'and that courtesy is but another term for servility'.[95] It was a description that would remain instantly recognizable to visitors to the town to which so many of this same population were to move. In 1921 the journalist Frankfort Moore, brought up in Belfast but returning after a long absence, found himself temporarily disoriented by the changes that had taken place in the urban landscape. The sensation lasted only until his first conversation with a local.

> The car pulled up.
>
> 'Five shillings', said the driver.
>
> Then I knew it was really Belfast I had come to. The car was one that I might have jolted on 40 years before, and the driver was looking me straight in the face.
>
> 'Ay, five shillings – that's what I'm telling ye.'
>
> Yes, there was no change in the tone. I was in Belfast.[96]

8 An Age of Conservative Modernity, 1914–1968

Sean O'Connell

Between 1914 and 1968, sweeping cultural and economic changes transformed the tapestry of Belfast life. Suburban development and the re-planning of inner-city districts changed the city's social geography radically. The local economy also underwent transition, as once booming industries went into long-term decline. This caused hardship for many families, particularly during the 1930s. The Second World War, and the years thereafter, brought greater affluence to the city, even though pockets of inequality and poverty hung on stubbornly. In each of these respects, Belfast's story bears comparison to that of numerous industrial cities in Britain. Where it differed was in the continued significance of ethno-sectarian conflict and identity, which remained important in many aspects of everyday life.

The analysis that follows is distinct from that offered in earlier chapters, because it is possible for the first time to explore the period through the voices of ordinary men and women. Testimony gleaned from autobiographies and oral histories can enrich our understanding of the cultural, social and economic life of twentieth-century Belfast.[1] This chapter also examines a number of individual streets and communities, to provide insights into how the tides of historical change affected the city. The chapter begins by exploring housing and community in the city, probing, in turn, inner-city working-class communities, the development of suburbia and the impact of public housing estates. The focus then shifts to the topic of work, through discussions of work and welfare, and the social composition of the labour force. The final sections of the chapter explore the broad area of consumption, via discussions of spending and leisure.

Working-Class Life in Inner-City Belfast

Belfast was home to many districts that exhibited the features of the 'traditional working-class community' which became the object of sociological investigation in the 1950s. How did that cultural framework operate in a city beset with sectarian tensions? Autobiographical accounts and oral histories of working-class Belfast frequently offer positive accounts of neighbourhood life, even though community often had to be chiselled out of adversity. John Young Simms's account of growing up on Shankill Road, in the 1930s, is one example:

> But there was humour in the streets [...] And it was this humour, plus the friendliness and tenaciousness, that made for survival. Who on Saturday night, when out walking amongst the bustle and the talk of the Shankill Road, could believe that life for many in the throng was perpetual grind [...] Hoots of laughter would often rise above the din, for Saturday night on the road was a relaxed and happy occasion. But in times of trouble, or when a death was dutifully recorded in the daily papers by a bereaved family, or when the horror of an impending eviction for non-payment of rent to some unknown landlord was near to crushing the spirit of a struggling family, then tears would be understood and absent friends would join with neighbours and help to dry those tears by door to door collections.

Cynical readers may dismiss this as rose-tinted reminiscence, but Simms provided the example of how a neighbourhood collection saved his own family from eviction for non-payment of rent. The motivations of those involved in this generosity are unclear, although it is possible that there was a degree of reciprocity stemming from the significant role Simms's father undertook in the community: 'One thing my da was good at was putting a letter together, and he was much in demand when it came to communicating with officialdom. People would come from near and far to have letters written or to get advice on dole matters, or to trace dates of birth when seeking a pension.'[2]

According to May Blood, moments of crisis united Catholic and Protestant neighbours. She recalled women, in the Donegall Road district, engaging in reciprocal arrangements around childcare or financial crises.[3] The traumatic events of the Second World War also feature in accounts of mutual support crossing the religious divide. During the Belfast Blitz, New Lodge Catholic Terry O'Neill took refuge in a stranger's house: 'The people's house we were in were Protestant and my only reason for stating this is to illustrate the way old sectarian and political divisions were set aside as folks tried to comfort one another during that fearful night [...] God if it only had stayed that way!'[4] In his view, this nascent community unity was broken after the war by political interlopers:

> In 1945 they came round our district – the Protestants – waving red flags saying 'Vote Labour'. And they put a guy called Downey in. Well, the next election came four years later [...] The same people were out with the Union Jacks, shouting 'Vote Cole. Keep the Fenian bastard out!' They wrote on the walls 'Downey's a Fenian – vote Cole.' Of course the Catholics started writing 'Don't vote Cole he's as black as your hole!' What happened is a man called Paisley come in and

Public houses were frequently targeted during sectarian violence, as in this scene photographed in 1935. Widespread Catholic ownership of bars in Protestant districts made them an easy target, while civil unrest provided an opportunity to loot alcohol.

Photograph © R. Lock / Hulton Archive / Getty Images.

offered to be Cole's election agent and he went round and spoke to the people and reawakened old sectarian fears and sectarian hatreds and the people naturally voted for Cole.[5]

Others offer alternative, less politicized interpretations of community relationships. Helen, an east Belfast Protestant, recalled working in the Ulster Spinning Company in the 1930s: 'on St Patrick's Day we all wore shamrocks and there was always a bit of a wee party and they called it drowning your shamrock'. She had equally positive memories of the Twelfth, in the years after the Second World War:

> When we lived on the Cregagh Road, my friend lived on the Ormeau Road, and she used to bring folding chairs, one for me and one for Joe – my husband – and we sat at Shaftesbury Square to watch the Orangemen. She was a Roman Catholic, and we were Protestants, and they went out to see the Orangemen and like it was just a day out. Times have changed terrible.

Kathy, an Ardoyne Catholic, also remembered going to watch the Twelfth:

> Him and I – on the Twelfth Day – would have went out and looked at the Orangemen. Took the two childer with us, down to Agnes Street and watched the Orangemen coming up and then went down to the chip shop and took the childer in with us and that was a great Twelfth Day. There was no fighting in them days, like, when the bands were coming home at night. The kids thought that was great. I don't know how many more [Catholics] went, but I went.[6]

While these accounts remind us of the danger of assuming that a total religious apartheid existed, analysis of residential segregation is sobering. In the period under consideration, Catholics made up around one-quarter of Belfast's population. In 1901 almost 60 per cent of Belfast's population resided in streets that were either more than 90 per cent Protestant or 90 per cent Catholic. By the late 1960s the figure was 67 per cent.[7] This segregation both reinforced cultural and political divides between Catholics and Protestants and made religion 'a considerably more potent force for social segregation than was social class'.[8] Even in the few working-class districts that were 'mixed', micro-level segregation was significant. Dock Ward, home to large numbers of carters, dockers, labourers and millworkers, had a Catholic population of just under 40 per cent in 1911 and 45 per cent in 1937. Analysis of one of its thoroughfares, Vere Street, provides rich insights into a number of aspects of Belfast life during this period. Catholic families occupied only three addresses between numbers 1 and 34 in the street. Patrick Quinn, a spirit grocer, lived at Number 1. Catholics predominated in this trade, as Protestant involvement had been reduced by a vociferous temperance campaign. In 1911 640 Belfast publicans were Catholic, while only 137 were Protestant.[9] At Number 3 was Susan Grant, a Catholic linen weaver, and her two children. Sharing this address was Elizabeth Hill, another Catholic widow, with her children. There was then a long gap to the next Catholic residence, which was at number 29. Number 35 was home to a Belfast rarity, a 'mixed marriage'. It was the only one on the street and it was perhaps no coincidence that this household marked a transition point between Protestant and Catholic predominance. Of the 41 households between numbers 36 and 77, 31 were Catholic.[10]

Residential patterns such as this ensured that Vere Street, and others with similar demographic profiles, featured prominently in the sectarian violence that scarred the years 1920–22 and 1935. Newspapers reported the violence and provided insights into the motives of those involved. They also offered glimpses into other aspects of community life. In July 1921 Matilda Ferran told a court that her Vere Street home was attacked by a group of up to 50 men shouting 'We will rid the Fenians and rebels out of the street', during what police acknowledged was a long passage of conflict in the street.[11] The following month a Catholic man was shot dead and another man was wounded. There were also arson attacks on several houses.[12] In September Sarah Dunlop and Jane Carol were wounded and Eva Blair and Maggie Ardis were killed by gunmen. John Corr, a Catholic labourer, was charged in connection with the fatalities.[13] Despite the fact that this neighbourhood, and many others like it, was experiencing extraordinary times, what a later generation would call 'ordinary decent crime' continued. When a suspected burglar failed to appear at Belfast Custody Court in November, his wife explained that he could not attend because shooting was continuing in

Vere Street. She had to 'creep through the holes in the walls in order to get to the court'.[14]

This sense of a community besieging itself re-emerged in the testimony of Mrs Rafferty who, in 2002, recalled events in Grove Street, adjacent to Vere Street, eight decades earlier:

> The very first day there was a man shot outside our door – a man called Ned Burns. He was leaving his wife up at his mother's – she lived facing us. And he come over and he said to my mam 'I'll put on your shutters.' And he put on the shutters – and he was shot. That man lay in my house from five o'clock that day to nine that night, for they couldn't carry the corpse up to his mother's house […] I seen him dying on our floor. We had to stay off [work] for them couple of days, until it all ceased and I remember we had to dig the holes in the walls in the kitchens. We had holes in the walls – that was a coalhole and this was a cupboard and you had to dig into the woman's coalhole. Everybody had the right to a coalhole, for to let the people walk out. You see, there was Protestants at the back of us. Earle Street – they were all Protestants there and we had to dig out holes in the kitchen […] They used to come from Tiger's Bay to Spamount Street. That's as far as ever they got. Because the next street was our street [Catholic] and the next street was Grove Street and then Brougham Street and then Sussex Street. And there were Protestants at the bottom of the street and that's why we had the big holes in the walls. We had them for years.[15]

Grove Street and Vere Street featured again when, in the fevered atmosphere that surrounded the celebration of George V's silver jubilee in 1935, violence erupted once more. On 9 May two hand grenades were thrown into Vere Street and there was sporadic gunfire. An orgy of shootings, looting and arson led to numerous arrests and the press coverage again provided insights into more mundane aspects of community life. One case hinted at inter-communal flirtation. On 2 June Grove Street's Robert Lenaghan admitted shooting and wounding 15-year-old Annie Quinn, who was on her way to chapel. Eighteen-year-old Brigid Corr identified Lenaghan as the gunman. She claimed to know him from the Henryville Dance Club, 'which she used to frequent'.[16] Dance halls were one of the few social spaces in the city where there was a good deal of mixing across the sectarian divide, as this case illustrates. Etiquette dictated that no young woman could refuse an invitation to dance, ensuring a degree of inter-denominational mixing under the ballroom lights.

The precise dynamics of Lenaghan's transformation from dance hall charmer to violent assailant remain unexplained. However, historian Tony Hepburn identified a number of factors explaining the involvement of individuals in the 1935 violence. He concluded that the desire to avenge an earlier attack was a common motive. Others, driven by the shortage of housing, took the opportunity to seize a home. A court was told that the battle cry

'Whoever throws out the furniture will get the house' was issued, in July 1935, by Henry Cahoon, a 26-year-old unemployed Protestant father of two. For others, being at the centre – or the fringes – of violent disorder provided macabre entertainment. Schoolboy Sam McCaughtry 'was there in the crowd' and recalled being 'excited to hear that a Fenian was being burned out' of a Tiger's Bay house. His excitement dimmed when he discovered 'that it was my poor uncle Thomas, a dock labourer, who used to give the children his pennies when he came home, full of beer, singing, up the street'. For the majority of those involved in violence, however, the primary driving force was 'fear or a perceived threat'.[17]

Religious affiliation was not, of course, the only marker of difference. Belfast was home to small Italian and Jewish communities. The former settled initially in 'Little Italy', around Little Patrick Street. Many skilled Italians assisted in the construction of new Catholic churches, while others were involved in the 40-plus Italian ice cream and fish and chip shops that were operating by 1914. The Jewish community, which was 1,500 strong in 1951, was centred on the upper Antrim Road. Overall, immigration was insignificant. Between 1926 and 1971 the proportion of Belfast residents born outside Britain or Ireland did not rise above 1 per cent.[18]

Various forms of economic and cultural hierarchy created more commonplace forms of distinction between families. During the 1930s Sam McCaughtry's family moved from a house in Cosgrove Street, in Tiger's Bay, to Hillman Street, off the New Lodge Road. He recalled that the 'distance involved in the move wasn't any more than a couple of hundred yards or so, in a straight line, but in terms of progress on the social scale it was a vertical take-off of a good half mile'. The new home had 'a parlour, and […] front and back attics. And as if that wasn't heady enough, the back attic had been converted into a bathroom.' The parlour offered a room in which guests could be entertained. It was off-limits for normal family activities, which took place in the back of the house and 'respectably' away from the public gaze, unlike the prized best furniture in the parlour. Status and respectability came at a cost and the McCaughtrys' weekly rent climbed from 4s 6d to 8s. This increased outlay was made possible when several of the McCaughtry children entered employment and began contributing to family finances. McCaughtry associated the physical move with a degree of social mobility also: 'My mother joined the Mothers' Union soon after […] She used to come back from the meetings and tell us about the addresses that the bishop's wife and the rector's wife had given.'[19]

Mrs McCaughtry's outings to the Mothers' Union were a sign of increasing respectable status, at a time when notions of the 'rough' and 'respectable' were central aspects of identity formation. John Boyd grew up in Chatsworth Street, off Templemore Avenue, in a 'parlour house with a kitchen and scullery at the back, a back yard with a water closet and two bedrooms'. The 'respectable' nature of his home was symbolized by 'the musty parlour, which was seldom used except on Sundays'. The bookish Boyd, and his father, regretted their proximity to the less respectable Lord Street. Boyd got 'little peace to do my homework' because these neighbours were always 'gossiping, shouting and laughing' and the 'corner boys' played 'noisy games of marbles' or got 'drunk on a Friday or Saturday night'. Boyd's father labelled them 'good for nothing' and instructed his son not to go near them.[20] Respectability was linked strongly with religious observation and the donning of Sunday best outfits. May Blood recalled that each year 'my sisters and I got new coats and hats, while my brothers each got a new suit. This shopping excursion usually took place at Easter, and you wore the new outfit through to the following Easter.'[21]

Middle-Class Suburbia

While the Blood, Boyd and McCaughtry families kept up appearances in their working-class neighbourhoods, middle-class families pursued new suburban lifestyles. Interwar suburban development centred on the middle classes, exacerbating the physical buffer zones between them and inner-city communities. Housing styles and standards articulated economic disparities. Suburban homes built between the wars often followed the vogue for the 'Tudorbethan' style common in England, with features such as half-timbered gables. These houses were much smaller than the villa houses associated with Victorian suburbs and were built for middle-class salary earners. Semi-detached suburban homes brought new forms of living, which involved embracing labour-saving devices that replaced live-in servants. Middle-class housewives were encouraged to turn to new magazines, such as *Good Housekeeping*, for advice on managing their homes.

While sectarian mayhem took place in Vere Street, a few minutes' walk away leafy Somerton Road was witnessing the arrival of new suburbanites to a series of semi-detached houses, completed in 1922. Running parallel to the upper Antrim Road, Somerton Road was part of a neighbourhood that was home to some of Belfast's finest Victorian villas. The area hosted an affluent population that included the families of businessmen and lawyers, and that was now being augmented by salaried workers and their families. In 1951 Protestants made up four in five of the area's residents.[22] Many among the area's Catholic minority worked for the more affluent families that still employed servants. An advertisement in the *Irish Times* in 1948 sought a 'general servant' for 116 Somerton Road, which was – the prospective employee was told – 'near Catholic church'.[23] The placing of the vacancy in a Dublin-based newspaper indicated that female employment opportunities in Belfast were extensive enough to allow local women to avoid low-paid and low-status domestic service. Any young woman taking the post at Number 116 would have been invited to the local Catholic Girls' Club. This was set up in 1933 to provide 'girls resident as domestic servants in the vicinity' with 'safe surroundings and legitimate recreation'. Its meeting times – Wednesday and Sunday afternoons – indicate the limited leisure time these domestic servants received. As the 'members of the local branch of the Legion of Mary were asked to take charge', the servants taking part did not escape middle-class supervision in their free time, with the authority of a Protestant mistress being replaced by that of a middle-class co-religionist.[24]

The local parish was St Therese's, which opened in 1937, and was one of several churches built in the suburbs to minister to female domestic servants and 'the emerging Catholic professional and business class'.[25] Its presence, and that of the Catholic bishop of Down and Connor on Somerton Road, signifies that residential segregation by religion did not operate in the same way among the middle classes as is it did among the working classes. Instead, divisions were 'more effectively measured by membership of ethnic associations, schooling and kinship links'.[26] Thus, Somerton Road was one of the 'good residential areas that used to be exclusively Protestant' where, a journalist noted in 1958, 'well-to-do Catholics have been moving'. The article was part of a series on the 'Northern Catholic' by the writer Desmond Fennell, for the *Irish Times*. Fennell claimed that to purchase a home in such an area, a Catholic family engaged a Protestant solicitor and only revealed their faith 'when it is too late for anything but Protestant dismay'. While this suggested sectarianism with a bourgeois slant, Fennell also quoted a middle-class Catholic living in a 'mixed' area who had told him there was 'hardly a flag put out now on the Twelfth'. It was claimed that 'Catholic and Protestant children built bonfires' together and that 'if the Catholic children didn't go to see the bonfires, their share of the hand-out of lemonade and cakes was delivered to them in their homes'.[27]

Thus, the average suburbanite was unlikely to encounter naked sectarianism and was more likely to meet his or her maker as the result of a car accident than through inter-communal violence. In 1929 Somerton Road resident Helen Newel, the widow of a tailor, was killed by a car at a local tram stop. Six years later, her neighbour, businessman Alan Carswell, was seriously injured when his car collided with a bus carrying Linfield supporters.[28] The car symbolized mid-twentieth-century suburban living. As well as increasing road casualty figures, the arrival of middle-class motoring gave rise to another modern scourge, the car thief. The term 'joyrider' was used first in Belfast when 24-year-old mechanic Anthony Bradin stood accused of the larceny of his former employer's car. Bradin had been spotted, at Christmas 1912, driving up the Newtownards Road with a woman and two men. He maintained that he did not intend to steal the car and the judge remarked that 'probably the prisoner was taking what was called on the other side of the channel a "joy ride"'. He was

The interwar years witnessed the rise of mass motoring, with car ownership extending into the middle classes. In this photograph, from 1918, Mr Pyper proudly poses with his car.

Photograph © National Museums Northern Ireland. Collection Ulster Museum. BELUM.Y2692.

found not guilty, because there was no intent to deprive the car's owner of his property permanently.[29]

It took the introduction in 1930 of a new offence (taking a vehicle without the owner's consent) to empower the courts to deal with this phenomenon. By the mid-1930s, when there were 27,000 private vehicles registered in Northern Ireland, one in every hundred was stolen each year for 'joy rides'. Offenders came from a range of social backgrounds. In 1930 16-year-old message boy Arthur Peacham, from inner-city Lindsay Street, was sent to borstal for three years for a number of car thefts. Prior to his arrest, up to two cars a night were being stolen in the city. He returned to car crime on his release and, despite several subsequent prison sentences, was involved in all the activities that late twentieth-century Belfast came to associate with the joyrider. Peacham was the quarry in a number of high-speed chases, was fired on by the RUC, and was injured in his final, 70 mile-per-hour police pursuit in 1938. Ironically, he later became a Dublin taxi driver. While Peacham journeyed from the inner city to the suburbs to steal cars, other offenders were themselves from well-heeled families. In 1933 18-year-old Alfred Mandale Fisher, a stockbroker's stepson from Myrtlefield Park, was one of a group of teenagers arrested for the theft of a series of high-performance sports cars, including a Riley and an MG. Unlike Peacham, Fisher avoided prison initially, due to his family background and expensive legal team. He did receive a month's imprisonment when he re-offended later in the year. Thereafter, his family despatched him to South Africa. He returned to serve – and die – in the RAF during the Second World War.[30]

The car's attraction to young car thieves reflected its increasingly important role as a signifier of status in a middle-class hierarchy that was highly stratified and based on rich cultural codes. Observers, occupying very different positions on the social scale, offered contrasting perspectives on the Belfast bourgeois lifestyle. Caroline Blackwood, who preferred London's bohemia to life in the aristocratic Ulster circles in which she was raised, was scathing of Belfast's suburbia:

> And day after day – post-war, just as they had pre-war – in the wealthy suburbs of Belfast the wives of industrialists went on reading the Bible, drinking their sherry and eating scones [...] In those days all those houses were meant to contain that most curious of rooms known as the 'parlour'. The parlour was always musty and unused [...] with plaster Peter Scott geese, which were nailed so they appeared to be flying past the photograph of the Royal Family in a freedom arc up the side of the wall. Sometimes one had the feeling that these status-symbol geese themselves secretly knew that their flight was an illusion and they were just as static as their owners, that they would never fly out of the stifling, expensive interiors.[31]

In his short story 'The Land of High Hedges', Sam McCaughtry narrates the tale of a working-class boy delivering messages to houses with names such as 'Penmawr and Oakdene', and with 'long drive ways, high hedges, and extensive well-kept gardens'. These were the homes of 'school principals, senior civil servants, bank managers, and area heads of insurance companies' and their 'self-assured and cool' wives. On reaching adulthood, and after fighting the Nazis and becoming 'a diligent, semi-skilled worker', he learns that 'houses in the land of high hedges that he loved rarely went up for sale and when they did, the price was hopelessly out of his reach'. Instead, he borrows the money to buy a 'cramped semi-detached house' built to 'minimum specifications', and proudly christens it 'Shangri La', with a name-plate purchased from Smithfield Market, 'where they were selling in their thousand'. He decorates it every two years and when his daughter brings her fiancé home he is 'quietly pleased that she had not had to bring her young man to the kitchen house in the old street'.[32]

While this tale encapsulates the warmth that many felt towards suburban living, academics have not always responded so positively. One architectural historian argues that the special features that had set some Edwardian villas apart 'from the normal red brick monotony of the city' were adopted later 'on a more widespread scale, but at a debased level'. For example, houses were constructed with 'a minimal amount of half-timbering in their gables' in a 'dilution and commercialisation of earlier Edwardian Arts and Crafts ideals' that 'brought its own monotony to the suburban housing scene'.[33] Even worse, for some commentators, was the onset of suburban sprawl, which saw villages lose their original character as residential development took place along the city's major arterial routes. Glengormley provides an example of this process. Its development as a suburb originated with the arrival of the electric tram in 1913. Its population rose from 500 to 2,200 between 1911 and 1951, at which point it was said to 'exhibit all the worst attributes of piecemeal suburban development', being made up of a 'haphazard conglomeration of detached and semi-detached houses and bungalows' created by speculative building.[34] In 1901 it had a public house, a smithy and a police station. Half a century later it had a number of shops, two doctor's surgeries, a post office, a primary school, several churches, branches of the British Legion and the Women's Institute, a social club and a Ratepayers' Association. These were signs of a new community taking shape, but the fact that a large number of Glengormley's residents chose to worship in their former areas indicates that community often functioned differently in suburbia.[35] Glengormley's growth was symptomatic of population dispersal. In 1951 Belfast had 443,671 citizens, with around 100,000 living in the 'urban area' outside the city boundary. Twenty years later the city's population had dropped to 362,082 and the suburbs had boomed. The number living in Andersonstown, Dunmurry, Lisburn, Newtownabbey, Castlereagh and Holywood was over 240,000.[36]

Rehousing the Working Classes

Vast new public housing schemes were partly responsible for these population shifts. They also promoted an alternative form of suburban development. No local authority housing was built in Belfast until 1917, but the political environment after the First World War appeared to offer the prospect of a more dynamic approach. The Westminster government promised 'homes fit for heroes', and the proportional representation system by which the city council was elected in January 1920 radically altered the political landscape. Of the 60 seats contested, Labour candidates, who rode the tide of socialist sentiment created during a bout of industrial conflict in 1919, won 12 and claimed a new political influence. However, the Unionist government established after Partition swiftly passed legislation ending the PR system.[37] This ensured the return of Unionist hegemony to the council in 1923. One result was an unwillingness to follow the example of those cities that built corporation houses to be rented for moderate sums. A combination of Unionist philosophical antipathy to state intervention, the stagnation of the local economy and a financial scandal ensured that Belfast's house-building programme got off to a lamentable start. In 1926 a report on the Housing Committee's activities found that inferior materials were being used in construction, and that contracts had not been put out to tender. The city solicitor and members of the Committee had financial interests in sites that were selected on the basis of 'profit to the vendor and not suitability for working-class housing'. Thereafter, housing schemes proceeded limply. Only 2,187 corporation houses were available by 1930, compared to the 28,450 houses constructed by the private sector in Belfast during the interwar decades.[38]

The best-known private estate built in this period was Glenard in north Belfast. In summer 1935 it consisted of 1,477 houses of 'superior working class type', in various stages of completion. The developer's intention was to create 'a 100 per cent Protestant colony'. However, when violence erupted in July, the estate's proximity to the nationalist Ardoyne transformed it into a safe haven for Catholics forced from their homes elsewhere in the city. Around 200 Catholic families began squatting on the estate, many in uncompleted houses. In a typically pragmatic Belfast solution to the problems fomented by sectarianism, the estate's developer accepted most of them as tenants, while the Catholic Church bought the 48 homes squatted by persons deemed unacceptable. The developer's decision followed the Church's offer to guarantee the safety of Protestants already living in Glenard, in the wake of threats that they had received.[39] This guarantee did not prevent Protestant drift out of the estate and a large part of it eventually became known as 'new Ardoyne'. In the years after 1935 further Catholic families moved in. Kathy's family was one of these and she recalled their move from the Markets: 'my mummy went and she got a house up in Glenard. It's Ardoyne now, it was Glenard then. There was a bathroom in it and it was great and there was a wee fire and wee boiler at the back. You got hot water and it was great, that was

A Second World War air raid shelter. Many shelters were constructed only after the attacks of April and May 1941 had produced widespread destruction and loss of life.

Photograph © William Vandivert / Time & Life Pictures / Getty Images.

Surviving against the odds. This photograph was taken in North Derby Street, off York Road, two days after the air raids on Easter Tuesday, 15 April 1941. The poignant note on the back of the photograph reads: 'The tears were still falling when this was taken at the loss of all our homes.' It is signed Grannie Kernaghan. Mrs Kernaghan's husband, an Air Raid Precaution warden, stands behind her in his overalls.

Reproduced with the kind permission of the Public Record Office of Northern Ireland.

luxury then.'[40] The Glenard affair was an early indication of how the sectarian cultural politics of the inner city could transfer to the new suburban housing estates.

Belfast's housing problems were exacerbated by the Luftwaffe's savage bombardment of the city in 1941. In a few short weeks, during April and May, there was a series of shattering air raids. The first, on 7 and 8 April, killed 13 people. It targeted the docks and the shipyard but also destroyed numerous homes and other buildings in adjacent neighbourhoods. This rocked a city that had long assumed it was beyond the range of German bombers. Rancour and recrimination followed, amid bitterness at the authorities' failure to prepare adequate air raid shelters and other precautions. More traumatic still was the Easter Tuesday raid of 15 and 16 April that took the lives of 900 Belfast citizens. On the night of 4 and 5 May German bombers returned, this time dropping incendiary devices that were designed to create a maelstrom of flames in industrial and commercial areas. Finally, on the following evening, a further raid led to 14 more deaths.[41]

The Impact of the Blitz

Personal testimony best indicates the impact the Blitz had on individuals, both on the nights of terror themselves and in later years. Terry O'Neill spent the night of 15 April 1941 at home in the New Lodge. He remembered that, having previously gone through a series of mock air raid drills, 'we started being a little contemptuous of them and making fun of the "oul ejits" doing their A.R.P. drill'. As a result, the first air raid

> took us a bit by surprise. When the sirens went off we just sat back to wait as usual for the all clear and the lights to come back on. Instead there was the boom boom of anti-aircraft guns being fired from Victoria Barracks […] and the blasting sound of bombs not far enough away for comfort […] I can truthfully say that I have never had another frightening experience to match that night. The thunder of the bombs and the anti-aircraft guns combined with the drone of the bombers never ceased until the following morning. The most frightening of all was the 'whistling bombs', so called because they had holes specially designed in their fin-tails that produced a high-pitched screeching noise like an approaching train whistle as they came down seemingly just over our heads. So the object of the raid was, not just to destroy strategic targets like the shipyards, aircraft factory and docks etc, but to terrorise and destroy the morale of the civilian population.[1]

Florence was a young married woman, living in Ainsworth Pass, when the bombers struck. Her account reveals the painful, long-term impact of the Blitz. It changed Florence's life irreparably:

> Well that just wrecked everything. I was the oldest of ten – and the youngest was only two weeks old and I was left to rear her because of the night the Blitz happened in Ainsworth Pass. I lived on one side and my mother lived on the other side; and she lived in number thirteen and that was the house was hit. They were all in it when the house was hit and my mother was killed. I had a brother killed; my husband was killed. I had twin brothers and they both had fractured skulls and the wee one, well, I reared her she had shrapnel. And all I got was a finger cut to the bone with shrapnel, you know, that's all I got. There was a sister seventeen – and we thought she was going to lose her leg. We thought she was going to lose her hand too, it was so badly mangled. And because my father died soon after, and because of that Blitz, I was left with twin boys of ten-year old, a girl of seventeen and that wee one to rear and I was only twenty-six years of age. I'd been married five years, just, and I had no family, which was a good thing, you know, because they say God works in mysterious ways. It just was to be, you know.[2]

1   Terry O'Neill, 'Raining Bombs', *Belfast Magazine*, 14, p. 13.
2   Interview with Florence (born 1915), 12 February 2003.

German bombing destroyed 3,200 houses in Belfast, aggravating what was already a serious problem of poor conditions and overcrowding. It was calculated that of the city's 114,995 houses, 18,440 lacked basic amenities and/or required serious repair work.[42] Writing in 1960, an academic described one badly affected district:

> the highest densities in the city are to be found in some of the small streets which are sandwiched between mills and warehouses in the grid-patterned streets on either side of York Street; the generous width of the main streets in this area belies the squalor of the streets behind them; most of the comparatively few bigger houses which had been built here are now grossly overcrowded, and the whole area constitutes a slum. These high densities extend northwards into an area of small nineteenth-century byelaw houses, some extending along the side of the docks.[43]

Joan, who married in the late 1950s, faced a long struggle to find decent housing for her husband and four children. She lived in a dilapidated two-bedroom millworker's cottage. The house, in Legoniel, was also home to her father-in-law. It lacked an indoor toilet and electricity and – as the row of terraces behind it had been knocked down – 'when it rained, believe it or believe it not, it rained in the inside of the house. The water ran down the inside of the house.' Joan, a Protestant who converted to her husband's Catholic faith at the time of their marriage, felt that her inability to secure a corporation house was due to discrimination, particularly as some of her sisters and brothers 'were getting offered houses and flats and they weren't even married'.[44] Joan was not alone, as many families struggled to acquire corporation housing. In 1956 the corporation was instructed to deliver a programme of slum clearance, but it built only 470 houses per annum between 1945 and 1972. This tardy housing programme did have one positive outcome in that fewer high-rise flats were built than in comparable cities.[45] Belfast did experience schemes such as Unity Flats (at Carrick Hill) and the Weetabix Flats (on the Shankill Road), which were demolished after short lifespans. More successful were the city's first high-rise flats, built on the Cregagh estate in 1961.[46] In that year Belfast's housing density levels were lower only than those of Liverpool and Glasgow. Furthermore, a good deal of the housing that was built was 'not built to the generally recognized standards of the day'. The limited success of post-war public housing schemes is revealed by the fact that almost 30,000 houses were still deemed unfit in 1974.[47]

It has been stated that where possible the corporation 'mixed tenants of both religious groups'.[48] Ballymurphy is often cited as an example of this attempt at social engineering and there was some inter-communal engagement on the estate. For example, in March 1969 work began to clear a site for a community centre. Funds had been raised by a tenants' association, set up in

1962 and chaired by Mrs Frances McMullan, a Presbyterian. Digging the first sod, the High Sheriff of Belfast felt the centre could 'blaze a trail that would do away with the necessity for marches and counter-marches, demonstrations and counter-demonstrations'. However, by that point only 1 per cent of Ballymurphy residents were Protestant.[49] Even by the late 1950s it had been identified 'whether by accident or design' as 'a sort of clearing house for Catholic Belfast'.[50] Families making the move from traditional working-class areas to new public housing estates demonstrated what one geographer called 'a tendency to sector movement'. Those who associated themselves with either the Shankill or the Falls, for example, made 'axial movements along these roads' to new homes.[51] What this dry academic language did not reveal was the extent to which rehousing and population movement aroused controversy. Potential electoral change in corporation wards was the most obvious debating point, but there were often others. In the late 1950s plans for the redevelopment of Carrick Hill created some interesting alliances. It was proposed that the overcrowded and poor-quality housing in Upper Library Street, Millfield and Carrick Hill be replaced by an estate consisting of four blocks of multi-storey flats, maisonettes and terraced houses that would rehouse most, but not all, of the area's residents. A number of Unionist councillors and aldermen united with the Eire Labour Party in Dock Ward, the Independent Labour Group of Falls and Smithfield, and a local residents' campaign group to oppose the plans. Ranged against them were the majority of councillors and the Belfast Trades Council.

Those Unionists campaigning against the plan were 'not unconnected to the coal trade' and did not object to redevelopment per se. They wanted the new homes to be in the form of terraced housing with fireplaces, 'something the people have always been used to'. There were charges and counter-charges about gerrymandering. The Unionists accused the Independent Labour Group of being motivated by concerns to protect the Central Belfast seat it held at Stormont. The Unionists were suspected of planning to shift Catholic voters out of Carrick Hill, as part of a wider programme of electoral musical chairs devised in the aftermath of their defeats at the hands of the Northern Ireland Labour Party. The residents' main objection was that they did not wish to live in the 15-storey-high flats that were included in the plans. They also feared that community bonds would be shattered by redevelopment.[52] In subsequent years, a number of adjacent communities experienced this process of dispersal and destruction. Ron Weiner's *The Rape and Plunder of the Shankill* reflected local resentment about the way in which that community was redeveloped, while the Sailortown Local History Project's website laments the loss of a colourful dockside neighbourhood. Former residents of both these communities felt they were subjected to 'piecemeal dismemberment', as their homes made way for the Belfast Urban Motorway and the Westlink during the 1970s.[53] The

Domestic idyll? One of the better examples of public housing built in Belfast after the Second World War.

Photograph © National Museums Northern Ireland. Collection Ulster Museum. BELUM.Y3973.

Carrick Hill scheme eventually produced Unity Flats. Their name, as well as their design, was a triumph for the planners' misplaced ambitions.

The poor quality of Unity Flats indicated that Carrick Hill residents were right to be distrustful of the rehousing plans. Unity Flats were, like many of the corporation's estates, 'laid out solely with an eye to accommodating as many people as possible', with densely packed homes that were far from spacious.[54] A combination of poor accommodation and repeated rent rises led to the formation of the Amalgamated Tenants Committee in 1961, to represent families on over 50 'Catholic, Protestant and "mixed" estates'. Their campaign won some sympathy. The *Belfast Telegraph* cited Ballymurphy as an example of 'houses rushed up' to accommodate families 'who had been bombed out in the war'. With nowhere 'for the young people to amuse themselves or the older ones to meet socially', there was 'boredom and vandalism' at one end of the age spectrum and 'frustration and loneliness' at the other.[55] Despite the unattractive characteristics of some estates, housing demand exceeded supply and while Belfast Corporation's housing allocation was not as controversial as that of other authorities in the North, there were allegations of unfairness. In 1961, for example, one councillor stated that only 1,860 of 11,000 corporation houses were home to Catholic tenants.[56]

The Northern Ireland Housing Trust (NIHT) was also active in the city, building 21,000 houses between 1944 and 1968.[57] Its homes were more spacious and of a higher standard than corporation housing. However, rents of around 14s per week meant that less affluent workers could not afford these homes.[58] This ruled out many Catholic families due to factors associated with income,

The controversial Unity Flats development.

Reproduced with the kind permission of Pacemaker Press International Ltd.

as well as family size. However, the historian Marianne Elliott, who spent her childhood on the White City estate, observed that the NIHT allocated affordable housing without discrimination: 'In our corner of the estate there were three Catholic families and five Protestant.' In her view, 'sectarianism impinged rarely enough to be truly memorable', although children 'knew the codes of behaviour and said nothing to upset in mixed company'. She recalls friendships between children that dwindled in teenage years, as new bonds were formed with 'classmates of the same religion'. As Elliott grew older, she noted that her family's difference was signified by choice of newspaper, doctor and holiday destination (the south of Ireland). Those holidays were taken in July, when the estate 'took on a new character' and was 'festooned with Union Jacks'.[59]

Although the NIHT's stated policy was to seek low-income tenants who could afford its rents, 8.6 per cent of its renters in 1957 were in professional or commercial occupations (such as civil servants or clerks). Similar surveys in Liverpool and Sheffield found no public housing tenants in these categories. This illustrated the strong pent-up demand for housing, further emphasized by the fact that 54 per cent of tenants had previously been living with relatives.[60] The clamour for homes was such that some individuals tried unusual methods to secure one. In 1953 an inquiry investigated allegations that a Belfast woman had been taking payments of up to £36 to use her 'influence' with officials at City Hall to secure houses. One of her methods was to direct her 'clients', both Catholics and Protestants, to doctors who assisted with false declarations about tuberculosis.[61] The presence of tuberculosis in a family, along with the loss of a home in the Blitz or a record of war service, ensured that individuals gained maximum points in the housing allocation system. Before the war, Belfast had the highest TB-related death rates in Britain or Ireland.[62]

Once a home was secured, experience of life on the new estate depended on a number of factors. These included the quality of the housing and amenities on the estate, its proximity to the tenant's former neighbourhood and family, and whether or not they had moved willingly or felt pushed out by a slum clearance programme. Estates varied markedly. In 1960 Ballymurphy had 700 homes built around a small central square that featured a few shops and accommodated a doctor and dentist. There was no playground or primary school and a report noted that its amenities 'are very poor for an estate of this size'. In contrast, Flush Park estate had access to the existing amenities of Rosetta.[63] There were also contrasting experiences on NIHT estates. The Dundonald estate had no shops, while at Suffolk there were waits of up to three hours for the bus. Better facilities were available at Castlereagh (a large hall, shops, two churches and a school) and at Andersonstown (a small hall, shops and churches and a primary school). The Finaghy estate benefited from pre-existing facilities in this suburb, such as its cinema.[64]

A survey of housewives on NIHT estates, in 1953, indicated that only 15 per cent were in any way dissatisfied. The most common concern was the cost of 'keeping up'. Of those surveyed, 44 per cent admitted having hire purchase agreements to pay for the furniture and consumer goods with which they augmented their new homes.[65] The researchers found mixed evidence when they assessed whether or not social relations on the estates were as strong as in the tenants' former communities. Asked whether they provided help to neighbours, 69 per cent replied yes. Of these, a third reported helping with 'messages', and 20 per cent with child minding, while 7 per cent admitted to assisting in terms of the more delicate matter of 'lending or borrowing'. However, one-quarter reported that they had no contacts with neighbours.[66] The researchers divided respondents into four groups, 'the superior', 'the respectable', 'the ordinary' and 'the rough', and speculated that those in the first and last categories were more likely to remain aloof. They felt this was most probable if they lived 'in a street where their standards are noticeably different from their neighbours'. Large numbers also retained strong bonds with their former neighbourhoods, with 59 per cent of the women questioned visiting relatives in their old communities at least once a week. Meanwhile, the NIHT prohibition of public houses on its estates prevented the development of particular forms of communal activity and indicated the form of respectability that it expected of tenants.[67]

There were differences also in household size on various estates. In 1960 the Flush Park average figure was 4.3, at New Barnsley it was 5.0, and in Ballymurphy it was 7.5. This factor clearly brought the greatest economic challenges to families on the latter estate. It might have been offset by the fact that the average weekly wage of male householders in Ballymurphy was £12 14s, compared to the £10 18s recorded for the men of New Barnsley. However, only

50 per cent of the Ballymurphy householders were in employment, while only one New Barnsley male (of 32 surveyed) was out of work. It is not surprising that Ballymurphy had the greatest number of tenants in arrears.[68] The Catholic Church's moral teaching on sexuality and birth control was clearly a factor in this. For example, Catholics marrying in 1936 went on to have an average of 4.5 children, compared to 2.69 in Protestant marriages.[69] However, inequalities in the city's labour market also left many families in economic difficulty and these issues are addressed next.

Work and Welfare

Myriad factors created a patchwork of workplace conditions across Belfast. The city was home to large-scale textile, shipbuilding, engineering, rope-making and aeronautical industries, as well as significant transport and commercial sectors. It also fulfilled major educational and administrative functions. Its workers thus experienced a wide range of employment opportunities and conditions. There were also markedly differing experiences between those in the professional, commercial, skilled, semi-skilled and unskilled categories. Entrance to each of those categories was often heavily dependent on an individual's gender and religious denomination.

Economic historians have employed the concept of an inner and outer Britain to describe the different economic experiences of the UK's regions during the interwar years. Inner Britain, which included the English south-east and midlands, benefited from the development of new consumer-based industries, such as motor manufacturing. Much of northern England, Wales and Scotland struggled economically as their traditional industries stagnated. Belfast's economy fell into the latter category. Moreover, despite the fillip it received during the two world wars, it lagged behind the rest of the UK for the whole period between 1914 and 1968.

The First World War presented the city's employers and workers with a series of challenges and opportunities. New types of demand boosted industries that had been in recession in 1914. The textile industry struggled to cope with order books swollen by the need to supply military and hospital equipment. The numbers of textile workers who were tempted to move to more remunerative war work complicated the task. As military conscription was not imposed in Ireland, women workers had fewer new openings than were available in Britain. Nevertheless, the engineering company James Mackie & Sons poached many female workers to assist in the production of 75 million tonnes of munitions. Opportunity knocked, also, for Dr Margaret Purce, who became the Royal Victoria Hospital's first female house surgeon. Meanwhile, Harland and Wolff's contribution to the war effort drew on traditional and new strengths: it produced 200,000 tonnes of merchant shipping in 1918

A sad departure? A family
pictured as they were about to
emigrate in 1929. Persistently
high unemployment produced
a steady stream of migrants
through Belfast docks for
much of the twentieth
century.

Photograph © National Museums
Northern Ireland. Collection Ulster
Museum. BELUM.Y2362.

and developed an aircraft works to produce heavy bombers.[70] Following the
war, there was a short economic boom until 1920. At that stage, the 29,000
employed in the shipyards was up 45 per cent on the 1914 figure. Demand for
shipping, to replace that lost to German U-boats, had continued. Linen also
thrived briefly, spurred on by consumer demand for its traditional products.

Thereafter, the interwar years were turbulent ones for Belfast's staple
industries. The city's workers experienced an increase in their real incomes of
between 10 and 15 per cent in these years, but this was significantly lower than
the UK average increase of 25 per cent. By 1937 the average income in Northern
Ireland was only two-thirds of the UK figure.[71] A major factor in this statistic
was the incidence of unemployment. Belfast's population increased by 61,000
to 444,000 between 1901 and 1937, at a time when its spluttering economy was
not creating employment opportunities. Between 1923 and 1930 the number
of unemployed insured workers hovered just below 20 per cent, before rising
to 27 per cent between 1931 and 1939.[72] Over 50,000 Belfast workers were
unemployed in 1932, providing the bleak context for the Outdoor Relief
Protest. The Belfast Board of Guardians had to provide support for the 14,500

unemployed who did not qualify for state unemployment benefits. The Guardians' response was to offer grants that the Presbyterian Church described as 'inadequate to provide the barest necessities of life'. On 3 October 60,000 protesters converged on the Custom House to voice their anger. When a protest march was banned, one week later, rioting erupted throughout the city. The resulting backlash forced the Guardians to increase payment levels.[73] This was, however, a rare success for working-class collective action. More often it was to their churches that the poor turned for welfare support. For example, the North Belfast Mission provided ultra-violet treatment to undernourished children who had developed rickets.[74]

While the Great Depression weakened Belfast's staple industrial sectors, other factors also contributed. Demand for linen declined due to quicker turnaround in fashions, making durability less significant in the buyer's mind.[75] Harland and Wolff met changes in demand by diversification, constructing diesel trains and steelwork to meet the boom in cinema construction. However, Workman, Clark did not survive the Great Depression, closing in 1935. Other Belfast stalwarts came through the period relatively unscathed. Gallaher's was the largest independent tobacco manufacturer in the world, employing over 3,000 workers. Many of these were women, toiling at its huge York Street factory. Its products were marketed as a symbol of modernity and sophistication, often to the growing bands of female smokers. The company also claimed a modern approach to working conditions. It hosted Ireland's only workplace welfare centre, looking after the health of 'girls' who worked in its 'great family circle'.[76] Meanwhile, Belfast's new status as a centre of political power created opportunities in administrative roles. Employment in the service sector grew from around 80,000 to 100,000 in the interwar years. A further positive development was the arrival of aircraft manufacturers Short Brothers in 1937. The company employed 6,000 by 1939.[77] This development was part of an economic upturn ushered in by the anticipation of war. The local economy grew with 'unprecedented rapidity' between 1938 and 1947, and some ground was made up on the rest of the UK. Whereas income per head had been only 55 per cent of the UK average in 1938, by 1945 it was 70 per cent.[78] Many hard-pressed families appreciated the rise in wages at the time. Fifteen-year-old Bob earned 29s working in a laundry alongside his mother before the war. He then obtained a job at Mackies, producing armour-piercing shells:

> I remember when I come home from Mackies and I got my first pay I never forget; it was three pound fifteen shillings. And do you know, I think I run down the Springfield Road and down the Falls Road and down Broadway and into the house; I don't think I stopped. I gave it to my mum: do you know what she said to me? 'Take that back Bob! Take that back, they've given you a man's wages!' She couldn't believe it. I think it was more than she was getting, you know? And she

Howzat! The Shankill Mission provided these delighted young boys with a rare excursion to the seaside where they indulged in a little beach cricket.

Reproduced with the kind permission of the Public Record Office of Northern Ireland.

says: '£3 15s?' I says: 'Aye, but mum that's twelve hours a night, sixty hours a week.' 'Oh yes', she says, 'isn't that great money?'[79]

By 1944 80,000 were employed in shipbuilding and engineering. Linen struggled, however, due to a shortage of raw materials, and over a third of its workforce was unemployed in 1941. As a result, many female linen operatives found alternative work. The number of women in engineering was just 250 in 1939, but had soared to 12,000 by 1943.[80] Unemployment was not eradicated during the war, but the lowest dole queues for a generation gave Belfast workers a degree of workplace power. Shipyard and engineering workers gained a reputation for flexing their muscles in industrial action.[81]

In the immediate post-war years, linen and shipbuilding both benefited from relatively favourable economic waters. Linen prospered until 1952, but its employment levels then slumped from 31,000 to 8,000 by 1972. Shipbuilding's post-war employment peak was 20,000 (in 1960), but in 1968 the number was only 8,000. However, employment was generated in new industries, such as precision engineering, food processing and toy manufacturing. Employers such as British Tabulating Machine Company (later incorporated into ICL) and the German electronics firm Grundig located production on greenfield sites at Castlereagh, Dunmurry and elsewhere.[82] The service sector also continued to grow. Meanwhile, the extension of the welfare state increased numbers in the health services, public administration and teaching. In 1901 there had been one teacher for every 58 children; by 1961 the ratio was 1 to 34. Professional services also expanded.[83]

The experience of work was rosier during the 1950s and 1960s than it had been before the war. Wage levels, compared to the UK average, were higher than they had been in the 1930s, partly because trade unions negotiated equal rates of pay for equivalent jobs. Yet hourly manual earnings in Northern Ireland in 1960 were only 82 per cent of the UK average. In other respects, too, the people of Belfast were not having it quite so good (to paraphrase Prime Minister Macmillan) as those elsewhere in the UK. Unemployment in Northern Ireland stood at 6.1 per cent, compared to the UK figure of 1.5 per cent.[84] Even on the NIHT estates surveyed in 1953, where male unemployment stood at 4 per cent, living standards were lower than in Britain. Whereas Seebohm Rowntree's famous study *Poverty and the Welfare State* suggested that only 5 per cent of households were living below his minimum needs standard, on Belfast's relatively privileged NIHT estates the figure was 12 per cent.[85]

The impact of poverty was cushioned, in these years, by the safety net provided by the welfare state. The working classes welcomed the social reforms of the 1940s, due to the advances they offered in terms of economics and health. Many Unionist politicians were resistant to increasing 'socialism', but their arguments lost ground for a number of reasons. The poor organization of Belfast's civil defences, which had left it so vulnerable during the Blitz, shifted the public mood in favour of greater state planning and intervention. In creating refugees, the Blitz also increased the visibility of the city's poor, shocking many observers. One senior Presbyterian declared that 'I have been working nineteen years in Belfast and I never saw the like of them before. If something is not done now to remedy this rank inequality there will be a revolution after the war.'[86] In this fevered atmosphere, two reports on the health services, both issued in 1941, provided further stark evidence of the need for reform. An inquiry undertaken by the former deputy Chief Medical Officer at the Ministry of Health in London found that Belfast's medical services 'fell far short of what might reasonably be expected in a city of its size and importance'.[87] A further damning report, on the malpractices of Belfast Corporation's Tuberculosis Committee, led to the council's suspension and a much wider investigation of corruption in City Hall.

Tuberculosis was gradually brought under control; by 1954 its incidence stood at the same levels experienced in England and Wales. This was in no small part due to the formation of the Northern Ireland Tuberculosis Authority in 1946 and to the mass radiography unit opened in Belfast in 1945.[88] Wartime campaigns for tuberculosis patients to receive allowances at the rates granted in Britain were also successful, creating popular demand for similar initiatives in other welfare schemes. Advances by the Northern Ireland Labour Party, in the 1948 election, convinced Unionists to overcome their ideological principles and to plant Westminster's welfare innovations in local soil.[89] The comprehensive medical service that ensued had numerous benefits. One assessment suggests that free false teeth and spectacles made the biggest difference, as they had been beyond the means of almost everyone 'with the exception of the very wealthy'. More measurable was the notable fall in death rates. In 1946 the figures for the whole of Northern Ireland were 12.5 per 1,000 population compared with 12 for England and Wales. By 1962 the respective figures were 10.6 and 11.9. It is impossible to separate the role of the NHS from other factors, such as improved housing or diet, but it clearly had an impact.[90]

The welfare state was influential in other ways. Ethel, who was born in a Welsh mining village, met her husband during the war and settled with him in east Belfast, raising seven children. Ethel's husband withheld a significant proportion of his wages for his leisure pursuits, giving her a level of housekeeping money of which she said 'sometimes I suppose it was adequate, sometimes it wasn't'. The introduction of family allowance payments was a boon to her and she remembered that it 'always went towards the rent'.[91] The disbursement of this benefit directly to mothers provided valuable income for many hard-pressed women. Other individuals benefited from educational maintenance grants, enabling them to go on to higher education instead of being forced to find work and contribute to family income. In the ten years following the implementation of the Education Act of 1947, undergraduate numbers at Queen's University climbed by 50 per cent and the proportion of Catholics rose to 20 per cent.[92] Increasing opportunities such as this led, in the opinion of one historian, to a 'softening of many Catholics' attitudes towards continued inclusion in the United Kingdom'.[93] At the same time a long-running squabble between the Catholic hierarchy and Unionist ministers about the governance and funding of the Mater Hospital marred the NHS's impact on community relations in Belfast.

The Social Composition of the Workforce

While the rising number of Catholics at Queen's was evidence that education in post-war Belfast was becoming more meritocratic, there was a lot of ground to make up in the city's labour market. Family connections and cultural networks were a common route into employment. Jimmy Penton, a Protestant, got work at the shipyards because 'it was tradition; my father put my name down'. Only later did he 'realise fully the extent of Masonic influence' that lay behind recruitment.[94] Factors such as this led to Catholic fatalism about employment practices. This sentiment surfaced in a darkly comic tale related to the journalist and writer Desmond Fennell in 1958: '[a] story is current among Catholics of a man who went to be tested for a post as a B.B.C. announcer. When he met his friends in the local afterwards he declared with an uncontrollable stutter: "They wouldn't take me because I am Catholic."'[95] The power of this story lay in the fact that it was open to multiple readings. At one level, it could be interpreted as evidence of unjustified bitterness about anti-Catholic employment practices. An alternative allegorical reading was that the job-seeker's stutter represented his community's limited political voice and that his Catholicism, not his speech, was his impediment.

Tony Hepburn has probed the history of Belfast's labour market. He noted that because skilled employment was relatively scarce, it became an area in which narrowly defined sectarian interests were central. Protestants dominated the city's skilled worker elite, in which Catholic representation was minimal. For example, in 1911 only 10 per cent of those employed in engineering were Catholics. This contrasted with their over-representation in dock labouring, where 46 per cent were Catholic. However, the fact that Protestants made up three-quarters of the city's workers meant that they also outnumbered Catholics in the majority of unskilled and semi-skilled jobs. Thus, in Hepburn's striking phrase, 'to say that the Protestant community had nearly all the plums is a long way from saying that nearly all the Protestant community had plums'.[96] In a similar vein, Sam McCaughtry was fully aware of the Catholic critique of nepotistic and sectarian employment practices, but argued that not all Protestants were favoured:

When I was a youngster in Tiger's Bay we had poverty equalling the worst of
that suffered by Catholics; we had no uncles, fathers, brothers in regular jobs to
speak for us, no Freemasons, and, what a surprise, we were gamblers and heavy
drinkers [...] Our homes weren't little palaces, like those of the Protestants on
the Newtownards Road, stable families who lived stable lives. They knew that
they could plan out their lives from Friday to Friday, while our men waited their
turn for a day's work at the docks, or ploughed the ocean shovelling coal into
furnaces, or sat at coke fires taking sulphur into their lungs as nightwatchmen
on outdoor relief work, and they were the ones who got work at all. The Catholic
men who spent half the day with their backsides against the bookie's wall along
North Queen Street wouldn't have had to look far to see us doing the same.[97]

Being Protestant was also not necessarily a defence from the demeaning
comments of those empowered to dole out financial assistance. The Unionist
Dehra Parker told one Shankill Road man, appearing before a panel assessing
his right to benefits during the 1930s: 'Let's hope you bring no more [children]
into the world.'[98]

Hepburn's statistical analysis does demonstrate, however, that the already
limited Catholic presence in trades such as engineering, shipbuilding and
printing declined between 1910 and 1951. Notoriously, the high unemployment
of the 1930s produced nakedly sectarian calls from Unionist politicians for
Protestant workers to receive preferential treatment. In the improved economic
conditions after 1945 the economic effects of occupational segregation were
'somewhat mitigated', as Catholics made some advances in the building sector
and as wage rates for semi-skilled and unskilled manual workers improved.[99]

Catholics had a more 'substantial representation' in the white-collar sector
of the labour market. They were over-represented among shopkeepers and
in the licensed trade. In fact, publicans constituted a third of the Catholic
middle class.[100] Catholics also dominated among Belfast's street bookmakers,
leading the *Irish Times* to comment that 'it is Catholics who control the double
key to the irrational and unpredictable – the realm where money lies. All the
bookmakers and nearly all the publicans are Catholics.'[101] There was also a
sizeable representation within the public sector, particularly in teaching and
the health service. The employment of large numbers in Catholic schools and
in Belfast's Mater Hospital effectively represented a mini-state within a state.
Increased numbers of Catholic graduates also found positions in a variety of
managerial and professional categories.[102]

Belfast also demonstrated particularly marked gender dynamics in the
workplace. The 'ideal family' consisted of a male breadwinner, whose earnings
were sufficient to enable his wife to operate exclusively as household manager.
While this was possible for skilled workers in shipbuilding or engineering,
it featured much less in other families. Females made up 38 per cent of the
labour force in the city in 1901 and 36 per cent in 1951.[103] They included a

significant number of married women, who worked sporadically. The presence of large numbers of married women in the linen workforce was driven by the availability of work for them in that sector and the modest male wages in many local industries. High male unemployment in the interwar years also encouraged many married women back into employment. Thus, in Belfast's textile communities the populist view that a married woman's place was in the home was subordinated to economic considerations. A wife's wage was often what kept the working-class family afloat during periods of depression.[104] High participation rates by married women in the textile sector were also fuelled by their exclusion from newer areas of female employment. There was a ban on married women working in the public sector until 1975.[105] The marriage bar also operated in clerical jobs. Harriet, who was born into a middle-class family in 1913, worked her way up the pecking order at the Ulster Spinning Company and was earning £8 per week when she married in 1940. At that point, she had to 'retire from working' and the family lived off her husband's much lower wage.[106]

Occupational factors also created different levels of female/male population balances in various parts of the city. A female predominance in the Shankill and

Belfast's linen industry employed many women workers: one of them enjoyed being placed in the spotlight by BBC radio in 1949.

Published with permission from BBC Northern Ireland Archives.

Falls emerged from employment opportunities for women in local mills. In the east of the city, where shipbuilding and engineering were concentrated, greater demand for male workers produced a smaller female majority.[107] The decline of the textile industry affected women workers, but job losses were offset by gains in the service sector. These involved increased numbers of retailing and catering jobs, and others in education and health care as the welfare state developed. Kathy, who was born in 1920, had an employment trajectory that illustrates some of these changes. Her schooldays were curtailed, as was the case for many others in interwar Belfast, and she put family before her own aspirations:

> My father died in the thirties and there were seven girls and a boy. My mother couldn't get no help and she had to go out to work and she had to leave me with all the seven children. So, I didn't go to school and I was twelve going on thirteen and she did the best she could. There were days I was able to get to school and days I wasn't. And I had to do the washing, I had to learn to cook, I had to look after my sisters while my mother went out to get the money. Whenever I was the age for work, my mother sent me into the spinning room. And I hated the weaving, but I knew I had to stay in the weaving because there was no money coming in. So, when I got married, I went down the town and got myself in till the shop; no education nor nothing and I went in till the shop. I always had big ideas [laughs] and I did not want to be a weaver.

Drudgery and glamour: a group of women hard at work at the Devonshire Laundry, during the 1930s, are watched over by the photos of their favourite Hollywood movie stars.

Photograph © National Museums Northern Ireland. Collection Ulster Museum. BELUM.Y3817.

Kathy worked for several years in Anderson and McAuley. Later in life, after raising her children, she heard that 'they were looking for auxiliary nurses in the Mater Maternity and I went down and I got a job as an auxiliary nurse'.[108]

Kathy's testimony reveals commonly held distinctions about work in the spinning room, the department store and the hospital. Similar distinctions operated in male employment, but here the apprenticeship system formed a powerful barrier to upward mobility. A fortunate minority gained access to a skilled trade and then hoped that the economic waters of their chosen industry remained calm. Lily's father qualified as an electrician during his service with the Royal Navy, which he joined as a boy. On his return to Belfast in 1919 he worked as a foreman at Harland and Wolff. He saved avidly, helped by a navy pension as well as his wage. In 1938 the family owned their own terraced house in east Belfast, making them one of a select group of working-class owner-occupiers. Lily's father also lived a particularly 'respectable' lifestyle. He drank only in moderation, often choosing the anonymity of a city centre pub rather than one close to home.[109] His wage brought him a level of economic independence and status that many other Belfast men did not have.

Among dockworkers a complex system of work delegation operated. Catholics worked on the deep-sea wharfs and were members of James Larkin's Irish Transport and Workers Union, while Protestants toiled on the cross-channel wharfs where the Amalgamated Transport and General Workers Union (ATGWU) operated. There was also a hierarchy at work within the docks, as the example of the ATGWU demonstrates. During the Second World War it had established a first- and second-preference system among dockers, to limit the impact of unemployment on its members. First-preference men were given 'blue button' union badges and guaranteed work, while second-preference men, who had 'red buttons', worked only when all the blue-button men were employed. Blue buttons were rarely made available, and then only to sons or close relatives of existing first-preference men. In 1962 the 1,100 blue-button men and 250 red-button holders in the ATGWU became embroiled in a bitter fight over the system's inequalities.[110] The dispute was intensified because family members and neighbours were pitched against one another. Lower down the pecking order were the numerous casual dockers, known as 'Arabs', who scavenged for employment at the docks. The insecurity caused by these labour conditions formed the bedrock for a particularly rugged, often violent, masculine culture in the dock district. Tough men, who could hold their drink and take the bookmakers to the cleaners, were valued.[111] The extent to which male breadwinners took part in this form of masculine associational culture often had a critical impact on the family economy.

A Woman's Life in Twentieth-Century Belfast

Mrs Jane Rafferty was born in 1904 and christened Ann Jane McGrady. She was raised by her widowed mother, a millworker in Grove Street, off North Queen Street. Her life story is unremarkable in many respects but she was an example of the many resourceful, tough and humorous characters that emerged from the adversity of Belfast life. Like many others, Mrs Rafferty was a 'half-timer' during her childhood. From the age of 12 she spent 'a day at work and [then] a day at school', until leaving school at 14. Mrs Rafferty explained that her mother 'put me into Gallahers' because 'the mill money wasn't as good'. She earned 25s a week at Gallaher's. She jokingly recalled how people were shocked to learn that she was a stripper, although it was tobacco leaves that she removed, not her clothing. She enjoyed her work, although she remembered that in the run up to the Twelfth the 'good Protestant' people she worked with would 'kind of drop away from you. Union Jacks were flying all around the place' and the radio played 'party tunes'. Mrs Rafferty left work when she had the first of her eight children (she also had five miscarriages), but returned during the Second World War. Her husband, William Rafferty, was a carter and family finances were often tight. She received assistance from her mother, but occasionally surreptitiously pawned William's best suit. On one occasion, a funeral in the street almost revealed her secret. Mrs Rafferty remembered that her husband announced that he was going to pay his respects to the deceased: 'I says "Oh Jesus, Mary and Joseph!" I was sitting sweating, stuck to the stool. The suit was in the bloody pawn. And I looked at him and I said, "Oh the coffin's out now." The bloody coffin came out and saved me. "Dear God", I said, "never again will I take his suit to pawn – you never know what's going to happen"' [laughs]. The family were bombed out of their home in the Blitz and moved to Ardoyne. Despite the fact that Mrs Rafferty had seen a neighbour shot dead amid the carnage in Grove Street during the 1920s, she warmly recalled that community as her home: 'I was born and reared there and confirmed and married and all. I had five children down there.' Remarkably, sixty years after moving to Ardoyne she still felt like an 'import'.[1] Mrs Rafferty died in 2003.

1   Interview with Mrs Rafferty (born 1904), 10 October 2002.

Jane Rafferty, pictured with her husband William in the 1920s.

Reproduced with the kind permission of Dr Paddy McNally and the McNally family.

Spending

In the typical Belfast household, monetary management was the wife's task. This role was frequently demanding. It had to be approached with one eye on available finance, the other on watchful neighbours. Harriet was by no means in dire financial straits, but still felt these pressures:

During the war I went to Robb's and I got a remnant of gabardine and I made my husband's trousers and I made the boys' trousers – although I never served my time but I just was able to do it. Must do is a good master. I wouldn't want, when the boys grew up, anybody pointing at them [and saying] 'I remember them when they were running about with no arse in their trousers.'[112]

Others lived a more hand-to-mouth existence. Trips to the pawnbroker or local moneylender were common, particularly before 1939. The 100 pawnbrokers of 1930 were reduced to 40 by 1960, due to the impact of the welfare state, rising incomes and lower unemployment. The nature of pledges received by pawnshops provides insight into Belfast's various sub-cultures and the changing nature of working-class consumerism. At the end of each summer in the 1930s, the ice-cream sellers of Little Italy pledged their carts at McKeown's pawnbrokers. One Shankill Road pawnshop took up to 700 pledges on busy Mondays, with Orange sashes pawned regularly. By the 1970s only items such as 'transistor radios, record-players, tape-recorders and good watches' were accepted.[113] Moneylenders were also commonplace. Female street lenders typically provided loans to women for household bills, while male lenders operating at the docks, gasworks, pubs and other areas of male employment or leisure provided cash to pay for gambling or drink. These individuals usually came from the communities in which they practised their trade, which was often a sideline to other work. In some cases a moneylending career began when a gambling windfall or other cash acquisition brought neighbours to the recipient's door to request a loan. In March 1921 a bullet fired by a British soldier struck Sarah Bannon, of New Lodge Road, in the mouth.[114] She used the proceeds of her compensation claim to launch her family's lucrative moneylending enterprise. Mrs Rafferty, a former neighbour, remembered the circumstances:

At the time of the trouble she walked down the room to look down Vere Street and a shot come up, shot her in the lip and it took the whole roof of her mouth away. She got a claim – it was a big claim worth about £100. That was a big claim then and she would lend out money.

Prior to that point she was 'like ourselves, robbing Peter to pay Paul'.[115]

The various religious denominations were highly active in offering charitable provision that might circumvent the need to pawn or use a moneylender. Among the most committed were the Shankill Road Mission, the Methodist Belfast Central Mission and the Roman Catholic Ladies' Clothing Society.[116] The most effective intervention was the promotion of credit unions, run by local volunteers as equitable savings and loans institutions. Belfast's first was Clonard Credit Union, in 1962. Promoted by Redemptorist priests, it was built up by the Clonard Confraternity and other lay groups. A similar pattern occurred throughout Catholic Belfast in the following decade. Newington Credit Union, formed in 1968 in Holy Family parish, had 500 members within a year. What made credit unions so successful was that the common bond of church membership brought together a variety of social groups with different skills and requirements. Middle-class and more affluent working-class savers provided the cash for low-interest loans accessed by harder-pressed families. Credit unions were a vehicle through which an increasingly confident Catholic middle class demonstrated financial independence, at a time when their thoughts were turning towards seeking greater social and political status. Credit unions did not become a feature in Protestant areas until the 1980s, when Shaftsbury Credit Union, in Sandy Row, was among those that created a common bond based on Orange Order membership. This development model proved as successful as that which operated in the Catholic parishes of the 1960s.[117]

Credit unions were not the city's first thriving co-operatives. The Belfast Co-operative Society was formed in 1888 and became a city institution, particularly its York Street department store, which was opened in 1910. The store's 1930–32 revamp introduced the splendid Orpheus Ballroom. This modernization was a response to intensifying retail competition. In 1930, for example, Woolworth's and the tailor Montague Burton opened stores in a purpose-built Art Deco building on High Street.[118] By 1937 the Co-op had 49,526 members. The payment of a dividend to members four times a year – the famous Co-quarter – was eagerly anticipated and had an important function in family finances. However, the 'Co' was circumspect in its attitude towards consumer credit. It did offer it, but in 1937 it lamented that the 'habit of thrift had been relegated to the background in recent years'.[119] Growing use of consumer credit also attracted political comment. In 1930 Northern Ireland's prime minister Lord Craigavon lambasted 'easy terms' and advised 'Ulster people not to tie such loads around their necks'.[120] Consumers often chose to ignore such advice. Those seeking the signature goods of the consumer society often turned to stores such as Gilpins, on Sandy Row, which was one of the first to advertise credit facilities. In 1935 it encouraged buyers to 'enquire for our famous No-Deposit Out-of-Income Convenient Terms'.[121] Consumers' willingness to ignore the paternalism of politicians surfaced again after the Second World War, when the UK government attempted to control consumer demand by placing restrictions on hire purchase. In 1961 Crawley and Quinn of York Street faced a Grand Jury at Belfast City Commission for selling a refrigerator to a Mr and Mrs Adair without requesting the deposit required by law. In a victory for popular consumerism, the Grand Jury returned a 'no bill' verdict for the first time since 1925.[122]

Memories of childhood deprivation prompted many to embrace the affluent society, as Kathy explained:

An interwar shopping scene. Many Belfast districts had a thriving commercial sector. Sandy Row and the Shankill Road were among those that attracted consumers from across the city.

Photograph © William Vandivert / Time & Life Pictures / Getty Images.

I tried always, I was obsessed with the house, making the house nice because we never had much in our house, it was just a big scrubbed table and there were five of us in one bed [laughs]. So, I always was very obsessed with the house. All the luxuries that I didn't have I went out, earned it, and got them. When the television came out first, I got it. I brought all the children out of the street to see the Queen's Coronation.

Kathy also recalled other expenditure on items ranging from children's bikes to an extension to her terraced house. Women such as Kathy wanted to establish a better lifestyle for their families than the one they had had in childhood. Kathy met most of her aspirations for a more modern lifestyle, but she was thwarted in her desire to own a car by her husband's traditional views. He told her '"You're not going to take no driving lessons and go and kill somebody!" That's all, that's all I got out of him and I would have had a wee car today only for him.'[123]

SECRETARIES OF SPORTS CLUBS, CHURCH PARTIES, etc. . . . .
LEAVE YOUR ARRANGEMENTS IN OUR HANDS
(No Charges)
For DAY TRIPS (either Land or Sea) — For SUMMER HOLIDAYS — Write, 'Phone or Call.
Belfast Accommodation Booking Bureau
Excursion Organisers
30. HOWARD STREET, BELFAST   'PHONE: 25010

● 'PHONES:
BELFAST
21677 - 3 lines

Victor LIMITED.

YOUR PRESENT CAR TAKEN IN PART PAYMENT OF

ANY MAKE of NEW CAR

●

HIRE PURCHASE TERMS ARRANGED

SOLE DISTRIBUTORS in NORTHERN IRELAND For . . .

— SS — MG — OPEL and **CHRYSLER** Cars

● NEW CARS: DONEGALL HOUSE, DONEGALL SQ., W.
● USED CARS: 56, HOWARD STREET
● SERVICE: 17, QUEEN STREET

M. R. PERRY   Art Florist and Fruiterer

FRESHLY CUT FLOWERS. DAILY SUPPLIES OF SELECTED FRUIT. EARLY VEGETABLES.

WREATHS, BOUQUETS and SPRAYS ARTISTICALLY DESIGNED ON THE SHORTEST NOTICE.

CONVEY YOUR EXPRESSION WITH FLOWERS IN A TASTEFUL DESIGN BY PERRY.

'Phone Day and Night 66044.   **141, LISBURN ROAD**

2

RITZ CINEMA :: BELFAST
:: FEBRUARY ATTRACTIONS AT A GLANCE ::

MONDAY, FEBRUARY 7th.
NORTHERN IRELAND PREMIERE OF THE FILM THAT HAS CAPTURED THE WORLD!

VICTORIA THE GREAT

ANNA NEAGLE
has the honour to portray
Queen Victoria

ANTON WALBROOK
has the honour to portray
Prince Albert

FEBRUARY 21st, FOR SIX DAYS.
OUR FIRST GREAT STAGE AND SCREEN SHOW OF 1938!
ON THE STAGE
WELCOME RETURN PERSONAL APPEARANCE OF
NAT GONELLA & HIS GEORGIANS
ON THE SCREEN
THE LEAGUE OF FRIGHTENED MEN
with WALTER CONNOLLY — IRENE HERVEY — LIONEL STANDER
— Also —
WINGS OVER HONOLULU
with WENDY BARRIE — RAY MILLAND

FEBRUARY 28th, FOR SIX DAYS.
FRANCHOT TONE — MAUREEN O'SULLIVAN — VIRGINIA BRUCE
in
BETWEEN TWO WOMEN
— Also —
MICKEY ROONEY — ANNE NAGEL
in
YESTERDAY'S HERO

JOSEPH SEAL, our Brilliant Broadcasting Organist, will render a SPECIAL INTERLUDE at every performance.
3

This programme for the Ritz Cinema, from 1938, indicates that the luxury cinemas of the interwar years attracted increasing numbers of middle-class patrons.

Reproduced with the kind permission of the Public Record Office of Northern Ireland.

The Ritz Cinema: one of Belfast's interwar Art Deco 'dream palaces'.

Photograph © National Museums Northern Ireland. Collection Ulster Museum. BELUM.Y2221.

There was a similar mixture of tradition and modernity in the development of leisure. Cinema, in particular, achieved incredible popularity. In doing so, it promoted new ideals about consumerism, as audiences saw the cornucopia of consumer goods portrayed in American movies. In 1914 Belfast's 12 cinemas had a dowdy image, but in the interwar years national chains glamorized the 'picture palaces'. Filmgoing offered cheap, comfortable entertainment and was particularly popular among children, youths and adult women. By 1935 Belfast had 28,000 seats in 31 cinemas. The following year, the UK's biggest movie star, Gracie Fields, attended the opening of the Ritz, in Fisherwick Place. The Ritz was a cinema for the more affluent moviegoer or for a young man courting a young lady in style. Cinema retained its popularity until the rise of television in the 1950s. By the early 1970s the number of picture houses had contracted to seven, including the newly established Queen's Film Theatre, with its menu of independent movies.[124]

Most cinemagoers went once a week or more. Bob, who grew up in Sandy Row, recalled that

> we used to go to the Coliseum – that was on the corner – and the Sandro. My father used to bring me to the Sandro every week. Thursday night and that was in the dear seats, up at the back. Then we used to go to matinees, when we were kids. I remember *Flash Gordon*.

A few years later, yet another cinema provided the venue for the next stage in Bob's lifecycle, courtship: 'I met my wife when I was walking down Donegall Road and I was in uniform and with a mate and we just got talking. And then we made a date and I took her to the pictures – the Majestic, on the Lisburn Road.'

The apparently casual encounter that Bob described was part of a traditional mating ritual, variously called 'dolling' or the 'Sunday Parade'. In 1937 Sam McCaughtry was an eager participant.

> Almost as far as the eye could see the Antrim Road seemed to be black with sixteen-year-old fellas linking girls that they'd picked up on the Sunday Parade [...] Two dolls would come along letting on not to look right or left, but actually missing nothing. Before they would reach our length a couple of fellows like ourselves standing at the wall would call out something like: 'Does your Ma know you're out?' or else: 'Would you go for a loaf?' or maybe: 'Hey you – you've a quare leg for button boots.' The girls would slow up if they fancied the boys: then the boys would be over to them like greased lightning.

McCaughtry's use of the term 'dolls' indicates the Americanization of youth culture. He also indicated cinema's influence in this respect. A 'rage' for black shirts with pearly buttons 'started when George Raft wore one in a gangster picture: like magic they had appeared all along York Street and Tiger's Bay', where they were donned by 'sixteen year olds, with short haircuts and their hair smothered in brilliantine and parted in the middle'.[125]

Belfast's numerous dance halls were also courtship hotspots. Dances were often held at Catholic or Orange halls, but most venues saw a degree of religious mixing. The Plaza, owned by the Mecca chain, was the best known. It offered regular competitions, such as Miss Slim Ankles, Miss Shop Assistant, Miss Belfast and Miss Linen contests. In 1954 a journalist described the 'exciting feeling of sumptuousness' in 'the richly carpeted and elegantly furnished foyer' and the 'impeccable' Nat Allen and his orchestra. Other notable venues included the Maritime Club in College Square, and the Floral Hall which, from 1936, occupied a majestic position on Cave Hill. The ability to dance was an important factor in most successful courtships, and dance studios, such as those run by John Dossor, offered lessons for up to 450 eager learners at a time.[126] Revellers even had the opportunity to take part in lunchtime sessions. Florence, who worked in her father's shop on Peter's Hill in the 1930s, fondly recalled that there were 'all different places, you know, but I liked the Plaza. I used to go out of work at lunchtime. We didn't take our lunch and we went to the Plaza and had a wee dance and back into work again.'[127]

Some parents declared certain venues, or even all dance halls, out of bounds. The Plaza's association with Teddy Boys in the late 1950s and early 1960s led some to shun it for this reason. Harriet's leisure time was closely monitored by her middle-class parents: 'Mum was strict but it was for our own good. She didn't allow us to just go to any dances that there used to be then, unless it was a thing with the Masonic. That was the only one we were allowed to go, where dad and her were.' As a result, Harriet met her husband via their

Georgina Lauder, dressed as a fortune teller, pictured with James Daniels in Donegall Avenue. Fortune telling remained a popular form of entertainment, particularly among working-class women, well into the twentieth century.

Reproduced with the kind permission of the Lauder family.

The Floral Hall. This striking Art Deco building, dramatically located on the slopes of Cave Hill, was a mecca for dancers between the 1930s and 1960s.

© The Francis Frith Collection ®.

shared membership of a cycling club rather than through a penchant for the Rumba.[128] Norman, who was born in 1924 and raised on the Shankill Road, was prevented from dancing by his father. Like many parents, he feared the medical as well as moral consequences:

> You see going into a dance hall and coming out sweating – he thought – You see the plague of those days was TB – Oh it was a terrible plague! [...] Well my father didn't approve of it and it wasn't that he kept us down, but we didn't go against his wish. My sister didn't dance either.[129]

Many young people secretly attended the forbidden territory of the dance hall. Sam McCaughtry's future wife would go out with 'her dancing shoes wrapped up in brown paper under her arm [...] worrying about whether her dad would find out' that she had gone dancing rather than for the 'quiet stroll with her chum' that she had claimed.[130]

Parental attempts to restrict dancing reflected concerns about their children's moral well-being, particularly that of their daughters. Such concerns reached a peak during the Second World War, with the arrival of over 100,000 American GIs. For local women they had an erotic appeal, kindled by the Hollywood movies that made up 95 per cent of all films exhibited, and further fired by the GIs' ready supplies of chocolates, stockings, cigarettes and other rationed commodities. Women seen in their company were immediately suspected of licentiousness, producing a variety of initiatives. American service personnel were barred from particular areas. Amelia Street, notorious for prostitution, was one such zone. In September 1943 local women established 'voluntary street patrols in the hope of exercising a moral influence on members of their sex'. They were trained by the police and patrolled the city centre in pairs, in an attempt to thwart over-excited transatlantic special relationships. The American Red Cross employed local women to investigate the characters of women who became engaged to GIs. The allowances available to wives of US servicemen constituted, it was feared, 'a certain lure for a certain type of girl'. Around 1,800 women, from across Northern Ireland, married US servicemen during the war. This figure represented the most obvious sign of amorous relations between GIs and local women, but even flirtatious encounters caused tension between Americans and local men. This led to many incidents, such as one in May 1944 when three Belfast men assaulted a GI after spending the evening watching him romance a local woman in a pub booth.[131]

Despite the best efforts of the GIs, it appears that the Americans did not usher in a new sexual permissiveness in Belfast. Doris, from Roden Street, who was a 21-year-old when the Americans arrived, explained the outlook in her family:

> If you were single and expecting a baby you were shipped away across the water or somewhere, out of the road, until that baby was born and it was adopted [...]

Following spread: Bellevue: Belfast's pleasure gardens, home to the city's extremely scenic zoo, opened in 1934.

© The Francis Frith Collection ®.

Beatlemania reaches Belfast.
The Fab Four played the Ritz
Cinema in November 1963.

Courtesy of the National Library
of Ireland.

the mothers and fathers was very, very strict on you. My mother's sex instruction
for me was – 'if he kisses you too hard you'll have a baby' – and that was it and
that was stuck in my head. I really believed it, honestly that was it.

The churches continued to wield moral authority in matters of sexuality. This
influence was also reflected in Belfast's experience of the 'swinging sixties',
when it was not a particularly radical centre of cultural experimentation.
It was significant that the 14lb of hemp found at the docks in August 1961
was destined for Liverpool rather than the local drug market. Belfast's most
symbolic contribution to this hedonistic decade came in the person of George
Best, who achieved the label 'the fifth Beatle' only after leaving the Cregagh
estate for the nightclubs (and football pitches) of Manchester.[132]

Evangelicalism's continuing influence meant that Belfast literally did not
swing on Sundays: its children's playgrounds remained closed on the Sabbath.
In 1964 the corporation overturned the Education Committee's decision to
open them, even though an opinion poll suggested that a majority favoured
the original pronouncement. The Northern Ireland Tourist Board warned of
the dangers to the city's £12 million annual tourist trade from its reputation as
'a strict sabbatarian place'.[133] However, cultural shifts were taking place. Terri
Hooley's autobiography demonstrates this and also provides a perspective on
life within one family which, although idiosyncratically colourful, indicates the
extent to which outward signs of respectability often masked a more complex
family life:

Sunday was a big day in our house, Mum wouldn't even bake a cake on the Sabbath and my brother and I weren't allowed out to play. Church dominated everything. There was a service in the morning, then Sunday school and church again in the evening. We always went to church meetings, and every week we would go to the Grosvenor Hall, in town, to watch a religious film.

By 1968, when the RUC formed a drug squad (led by future journalist David Dunsieth) to deal with the city's growing cannabis 'problem', Hooley was a potential target. He had begun to experiment with drugs in slightly unconventional circumstances. As his mother was 'always concerned about my friends in case they got into trouble', she 'said we could smoke dope in her house so that the police wouldn't catch us'.[134] Hooley's embrace of 'free music, free drugs and free love' led him to set up an 'underground folk club' in a room in High Street in 1967. Charging women 1s 6d and men 2s for entrance, he claims 'we had some great nights there – a lot of sex and drugs'. Music played at the club included that of Jimi Hendrix, The Move, Pink Floyd and, ironically, The Temperance Seven. Hooley was not the only one experimenting musically in 1960s Belfast. Another east Belfast boy who was also the product of slightly unconventional parents, Van Morrison, produced his own influential music. However, Morrison and Hooley were in a minority. The majority of young people were still getting their musical kicks in more staid venues, such as the Strand Presbyterian Church Hall, where Hooley had been a teenage DJ, or in city centre dance halls that hosted the popular show bands of the 1960s.[135]

There was also a strong tint of conservatism surrounding gender and leisure. This was exhibited most obviously in the case of pubs. Norman explained that on the Shankill Road a 'barman wouldn't serve a woman'. Instead, many pubs offered 'a family compartment where a man could have took his wife in for a drink'. Norman did remember that:

> you could have bought whiskey by the pint and you would have seen women going to the pub with a shawl on them. And they carried a white enamel jug underneath the shawl – if they could afford it – and they bought some whiskey. But other than that, they weren't served. The barman wouldn't serve women at all. They had to get a man or somebody that'd get it for them.

Kathy explained that her experience of pubs was limited to one local bar:

> I only went with my husband. I went into The Wheatfield. They played the organ up the stairs in it. That's the only one I was ever in. When I was a young women, if you were seen going into the pub you were classed as a bad woman [laughter]. So I didn't go into pubs when I was a young woman.

Kathy was one of an increasing number of working-class wives who began to accompany their husbands to the pub after the Second World War. Previously it was more common for them to visit relatives to engage in 'colloquing' (gossiping), while their spouse spent Saturday nights in the pub.[136] In 1958 the *Irish Times* remarked that Belfast's numerous suburban golf clubs, such as Knock, Fortwilliam, Cliftonville, Balmoral and Belvoir Park, brought 'Catholics most effectively together with Protestants. The golf clubs have a camaraderie of their own.'[137] However, as in the pubs of the Shankill and the Falls, it was male fellowship that was cemented at the nineteenth hole.

Gambling was a further area of leisure that occupied men's free time. It also provided Belfast with an unaccustomed pole position in the race towards the permissive society. In 1957 the Stormont parliament legalized bookmakers' shops, pre-empting by three years similar legislation at Westminster. The Northern Irish initiative proceeded despite vocal opposition from Christian groups. The Council of Social Welfare of the Methodist Church in Ireland called the legislation a 'retrograde step' and betting a 'running sore'. The issue also caused a spat with the BBC. A torrent of complaints followed an Alan Whicker film about Belfast's legal gambling establishments that featured, in 1959, on the *Tonight* programme. The Northern Ireland Tourist Board felt it showed the 'most sordid part of Belfast'. Whicker's remaining five films on Northern Ireland were shelved amid the furore.[138] The tax revenue available from gambling lay behind Stormont's early action. It was a profitable enterprise, with three in every four people admitting to at least an occasional bet.[139] It produced one of Belfast's best-known businessmen, Leonard Steinberg, who built up the Stanley Leisure Group from its origins in 'a discreetly placed illicit betting shop' behind a Belfast milk bar.[140]

Others made smaller profits from illegal activities associated with gambling. From 1928 punters had been indulging their passions at Dunmore Stadium's greyhound racing track. It claimed to be 'unrivalled for accessibility, comfort, and charming situation'.[141] The venue's 500 car parking spaces indicated that it attracted affluent gamblers, not just the local working class. With money to be made, Belfast's hardmen took an interest. In the late 1940s Alexander 'Buck Alec' Robinson, from York Road, and Patrick 'Silver' McKee, from the Markets, fought for control of the Dunmore protection rackets that relieved bookmakers of a percentage of their takings. The younger man, McKee, triumphed, but was then challenged by the equally formidable James 'Stormy' Weatherall, from the Shankill. This produced violent gang fights that spilled over into the city's nightclubs.[142] These men were part of a Belfast criminal fraternity about which comparatively little is known, perhaps because the authorities of the time were not overly concerned about them. Lord Justice Porter declared, in 1953, that unlike London, Manchester, Liverpool, Glasgow and other big cities, Belfast was comparatively free of the professional type of criminal. 'Our criminals', he observed, 'are mostly bungling amateurs.'[143]

The Gunman turned Lion Tamer

Alexander Robinson (Buck Alec), captured by a *Belfast Telegraph* photographer.

Reproduced with the kind permission of the *Belfast Telegraph*.

Buck Alec (Alexander Robinson) was one of the most controversial and colourful figures in twentieth-century Belfast. His life, and its subsequent commemoration, is an example of how the city has come to terms with the uglier aspects of its history through a process of selective remembering. Robinson was born in 1902 and grew up in the tough York Street area. First arrested in 1913 (for larceny), he had a long list of convictions by 1921, at which point he joined the RUC's C1 Special Constabulary. In 1922 he won the RUC middleweight boxing championship. At this time, he was also a member of the notorious Ulster Protestant Association, which was responsible for numerous sectarian murders. Among the killings with which Robinson was linked was that of a Catholic woman who lived on his street. A police informer claimed Robinson's comment on her death was: 'I put another spy out of the way, I put three through her head.' After a brief period of internment, he was released and spent a period as a bootlegger in the USA, rubbing shoulders – he claimed – with Al Capone. On his return to Belfast, he again found himself before the courts for criminal activity and was involved in gambling and protection rackets, his fearsome reputation as a street fighter enabling him to enforce his authority. In later years he became best known for his succession of pet lions and his image became somewhat sanitized. At his funeral in 1995, the Revd Ian Paisley carried his coffin and described Robinson as 'a rare character, a typical Ulsterman'. Members of the nationalist community, such as dramatist Martin Lynch, were also among the mourners. Importantly for Lynch, Robinson had told his father that he regretted 'being used by the Unionist establishment' in the 1920s. Robinson's significance, according to Lynch, lay in his role as a 'legend' and 'hardman' in the masculine culture of the dockland community that the playwright had recreated on stage. After his death, Robinson was commemorated in murals (complete with lion) and in a Northern Ireland Tourist Board publication about celebrated residents of north Belfast, in which he appeared in the company of Mary McAleese, James Galway and Kenneth Branagh. This is a prime example of Belfast's repackaging of its violent past. Alexander Robinson, 'a gunman of the most notorious type' according to police files in 1922, was transformed into Buck Alec, 'one of Belfast's extraordinary characters'.

Buck Alec (and his lion) commemorated in a mural celebrating noted individuals from the York Street area.

Photograph © Sean O'Connell.

Lord Justice Porter was more exercised about juvenile crime. Belfast was not immune from the bouts of moral panic about youth that beset Britain in the 1960s. In 1964, for example, one press story claimed that a children's playground in Castlereagh was the battle zone for local Mods and Rockers.[144]

Soccer hooliganism also surfaced. Games between Linfield and staunch rivals Glentoran frequently resulted in violence. Trouble at a match in May 1967 led to the jailing of seven young men for one month. The next game between the teams, in September, saw ten arrests as fighting broke out in the stadium at half time and 'a penknife with both blades open was found in the Glentoran goalmouth'.[145] The rivalry of Belfast's 'big two' was long-standing, being based on geographical and occupational rivalry within the Belfast Protestant working classes, but it had been heightened by the demise of Belfast Celtic. The club withdrew from the Irish League in the aftermath of a stormy game at Christmas 1948. At the match's denouement, Linfield fans invaded the pitch and attacked Celtic's Jimmy Jones, knocking him unconscious and breaking his leg.[146]

On that occasion, sport was divisive, but it could create common bonds among individuals who were potential antagonists in other circumstances. Boxing is a case in point. Belfast's pugilistic culture was widely cherished. This was particularly true in working-class areas where the hardened self-image of shipyard workers, dockers and others created 'a physically tough and exclusively male occupational culture which cast a long shadow over popular recreation'. In this context, the ring work of flyweight world champion Rinty Monaghan was admired across the sectarian divide.[147] This was also true of Belfast's most famous sporting celebrity, the soccer star George Best.

Mass television ownership created a new medium that brought popular entertainers to extensive audiences, who followed the careers of a number of Belfast celebrities. The arrival of UTV, in 1959, meant that the BBC was not the sole outlet for this coverage. Ruby Murray, who at 19 was dubbed 'the North's first TV star', began her career in Richview Presbyterian church choir. She gained widespread recognition by appearing on the BBC's *Quite Contrary* programme, in 1954, and first topped the charts the following year with her song 'Softly, Softly'. Another remarkable vocalist was Van Morrison. His talents were honed playing with Irish show bands, before he formed the band Them. The Maritime Hotel in College Street was their base before the group, and then Morrison as a solo performer, went on to international acclaim. Belfast audiences basked in the reflected glory of viewing local heroes on *Top of the Pops*. Similarly, the weekly diet of English soccer served up on *Match of the Day* established the legendary status of George Best, who left the Cregagh estate in 1961 to seek fame with Manchester United. Best became a prototype for the modern-day celebrity, with his 'brand' being used to market products ranging from Cookstown sausages to the Great Universal Stores catalogue. Its George Best range offered 'colour, impact, slickness [...] all you need to look and feel great'.

While Best, Murray and Morrison achieved national and international fame, James Young's career catered for more local tastes. A talented actor, his comic abilities shone when playing Derek the window cleaner in the radio serial *The*

Belfast's most celebrated songstress, Ruby Murray (1935–96), photographed at the peak of her fame in 1956.
Copyright © PA Archive/Press Association Images.

Van Morrison, born George Ivan Morrison in Belfast in 1945, pictured in a publicity still in 1977, ten years after he had left Belfast for the United States and an international career.
Photograph © Michael Ochs Archives / Getty Images.

McCooeys, based on a Belfast working-class family of indeterminate religion, which had the highest listening figures in the BBC regions, with around 500,000 dedicated followers.[148] Thereafter he specialized in local, often topical, humour. During the controversy over the Sunday closure of parks in the 1960s, he quipped: 'If you had to bail out of a plane over Belfast on a Sunday, sure they wouldn't let you open your parachute.' While the modern medium of television made Young famous, his performances were suffused with traditional elements of music hall entertainment. As Young rose to prominence on local television, the equally telegenic Ian Paisley was offering viewers 'a form of evangelical vaudeville' that included 'humour and knockabout vilification of enemies'.[149] Television coverage of his theatrical street politics made him a phenomenon.

Conclusion

As this chapter has demonstrated, Belfast underwent a great deal of change between the First World War and the late 1960s. Like many other industrial cities, it struggled to cope with the economic forces that undermined several of its formerly thriving industries. Despite this sluggish economic performance, there were gains in the standard of living for the city's population, particularly after 1945. This was due to factors such as the emergence of the welfare state and the success of trade union negotiators, mainly in the public sector, in securing higher wages. In the same years many of Belfast's worst slums were removed and replaced by public housing estates that varied between the good and the bad via the indifferent. Their cumulative impact improved housing (and health) standards, although many lamented that redevelopment schemes diminished Belfast's character. However, the city's resilience remained visible in its responses to two very different forms of foreign assault. Belfast took the worst that the Luftwaffe could throw at it, and made a significant economic contribution to the defeat of Nazism. Its citizens also embraced mid-twentieth-century popular culture, with its heavy American influences. In this respect, Belfast resembled other cities that were taking on twentieth-century forms of modernity. Elsewhere, notably in the workings of its labour market and in the survival of long-standing religious antagonisms, the political and cultural life of the city remained anything but progressive. The years between 1914 and 1968 were, for Belfast, years of conservative modernity, marked by a dichotomy between new forms of work, consumption and recreation and a regressive cultural politics.

In memory of
the eight men who died
during the construction and launch
of Titanic

William Clarke

James Dobbin

John Kelly

Robert James Murphy

Samuel J Scott

Unknown

Unknown

Unknown

We raised a monument of fame
Upon these banks; and thus unfurled
An honoured scroll to Ulster's name,
nequalled yet around the world.

Reflections of a Shipyardman
Thomas Carnduff

9 Titanic Town: Living in a Landscape of Conflict

Dominic Bryan

The stopped clock of the Belfast Telegraph seems to indicate the time
Of the explosion – or was that last week's? Difficult to keep track:
Everything's a bit askew, like the twisted pickets of the security gate, the wreaths
That approximate the spot where I'm told the night patrol went through.
Ciaran Carson, 'Gate', from *Belfast Confetti*

The forces of conflict that have shaped Belfast since the late twentieth century have been, in many ways, shared with cities all over the world, particularly those of western industrial countries. The city struggles with modernity as global capital flows mean that the old manufacturing industries no longer thrive in the ageing Victorian urban landscape. Labour costs too much, so that the ships can be built and the textiles woven more cheaply in the Far East. The local businesses either disappear or become part of bigger multinational conglomerates. Working-class people start to move out of the central areas of the city due to the decline in work. The unique stores of the high street give way to international brands and in turn the out-of-town shopping centre competes with the high street. Road, rail and air networks struggle to provide the desired connectivity. Planners attempt to reinvent the city, while local councils re-brand it. The city that built the *Titanic* no longer builds ships but, in the strangest of twists, it sells itself as 'the *Titanic* town'.

1968 was a year of global political unrest. Protests took place as far apart as Yugoslavia, Poland, Spain, Brazil, Germany, Britain, France and Czechoslovakia. The Civil Rights movement in the United States had developed into the Black Power movement in the northern cities and there were numerous protests over the Vietnam War. In London one anti-Vietnam War demonstration in Grosvenor Square on 17 March erupted in serious violence. The Civil Rights protests in Northern Ireland, originating a year earlier, thus developed in a global context.[1] In many ways Belfast in 1968 was just another urban area of Europe struggling to come to terms with poorly performing industries and significant political change. Yet it had local

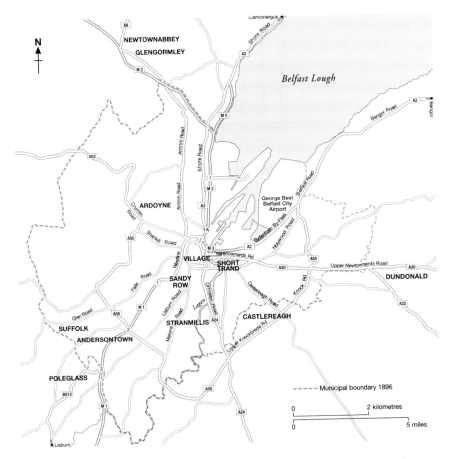

The rise of greater Belfast. The population within the municipal boundary laid down in 1896 peaked in 1951 (see Table 1, p. 17). Thereafter a combination of official housing policy and improved public and private transport led to a massive outward shift of population. Proposals to extend the boundary, in 1947 and again in 1964, were rejected. As a result much of the population of Belfast now lives beyond the city limits, in areas such as Poleglass to the west, Castlereagh to the east, and Newtownabbey and Glengormley to the north, as well as along the east shore of Belfast Lough. Meanwhile the towns of Bangor, Newtownards, Carrickfergus and Lisburn, as well as the more distant Antrim and Comber, have become for practical purposes part of a single metropolitan area.

Map by Stephen Ramsay Cartography.

dynamics that were to mean that civil unrest developed in more specific forms.

Unsettled by protests, Northern Ireland erupted into violence in the late 1960s, resulting in bouts of what could, in retrospect, be called ethnic cleansing. Parts of Belfast became no-go areas for the forces of the state. On 15 August 1969 British soldiers were introduced into west Belfast to restore order as Unionist and nationalist groups clashed at the boundaries of highly segregated districts. Catholic residents and businesses were burnt and threatened out of Protestant areas and some Protestants in Catholic areas suffered the same fate. The residential demarcation between Catholic and Protestant areas that had always been present became much more severe with violent policing of the boundaries. In working-class Catholic areas the Provisional IRA organized into an efficient non-state paramilitary organization in order to oppose the British presence in Ireland. The legitimacy of the state, particularly in the form of the police, the Royal Ulster Constabulary (RUC), withered in Catholic areas of the city. Loyalist paramilitary groups, the Ulster Volunteer Force (UVF) and the Ulster Defence Association (UDA), gained significant control of working-class Protestant areas, leading ironically to a further loss in legitimacy for the state that they claimed to support. Modern

Belfast became divided through the widespread use of organized political violence, involving state and non-state actors.

Any discussion of the changing identity of Belfast must begin with the concept of space. This involves more than just the geography of a city divided along sectarian lines. Space is not simply a dimension in the physical world. It is a cultural artefact, which imposes meanings on the people who inhabit it, at the same time that they give it meaning by the way in which they live there.[2] On the one hand there is a direct relationship between the spatial structure of the city and the nature of identity divisions within the city. Planners seek to design or modify the spaces of Belfast to provide more security, or to improve living facilities, or to boost the commercial viability of the city. On the other hand, meaning in everyday life is reproduced through the lived experiences in the landscape in which people reside and move. In the case of Belfast, the dominant experience of many parts of the city in the last three decades of the twentieth century was high levels of organized political violence. Sandy Row, the Shankill, the Falls, the New Lodge were not just residential areas in Belfast, they were stages for that violence. For some they were a safe refuge, while to others they were places of fear. The Europa Hotel was not simply a hotel but was reputed to be the most-bombed hotel in western Europe since the Second World War. The Rex bar in west Belfast, the Avenue bar in east Belfast, the Felons club on the Falls are more than just bars, as they carry with them important political meanings. The fatal bombs at McGurk's bar and the Abercorn restaurant mean these places no longer exist; but they reside in people's memories of the city. And beyond the everyday, the city is re-imagined by artists, writers, poets and singers in murals, poems, books and songs. The city is narrated through the poems of Ciaran Carson and the murals that cover many gable wall ends.

August 1969. A man has his bag searched by soldiers before being allowed to re-enter the sealed-off area at the mouth of Divis Street. Such security checks became a part of everyday life in Belfast after 1969.

Reproduced with the kind permission of the *Belfast Telegraph*.

4 June 1970. A lorry is piled high with furniture and personal belongings as families move out of the riot zone. Fear and intimidation had a lasting influence on the choices people made over where to live.

Reproduced with the kind permission of the *Belfast Telegraph*.

The distinctive nature of territorial division in Belfast at the start of the twenty-first century is dominated by class, ethnicity, gender and age. This is true of both the residential areas and the 'civic' centre of the city. A host of archives, recordings and memories reveal what it was to be a young unemployed man in west Belfast in 1969 compared to being a middle-aged mother living in the same place. Growing up in the middle-class Malone Road area and drawing a pension on the Newtownards Road in east Belfast offered very different social spaces within the same city. Belfast is both ranked by the same differentials of class and status that exist in other urban centres, and polarized by its more distinctive ethnic and religious conflicts.[3] And the nature of its spaces changed dramatically through the 1980s and 1990s. The forces of capitalism and ethno-national violence combined to make Belfast in the early twenty-first century almost unrecognizable from the city convulsed in 1969.

Belfast 1969

Belfast in 1969 was mostly industrial on the outside and mostly Unionist on the inside. Tall red chimney stacks emanating from mills and factories stood in contrast to the small chimney stacks of the two-up two-down working-class houses that accommodated much of the population of the city. In many areas the housing stock was poor, often lacking basic amenities.[4] Belfast in the 1960s shared much with its industrial counterparts in other parts of the United Kingdom. Like Glasgow, Liverpool and Bristol it had a civic pride built on modernity and Britishness. The ostentatious City Hall was surrounded by statues of the industrialists who built the city and stood next to the Cenotaph that recalled the sacrifice of so many of its citizens in the defence of Empire.[5] As the capital of Northern Ireland, Belfast had a status greater than those other British cities of shipbuilding and trade. The grand Parliament Buildings at Stormont in the east of the city stood testament to this. Yet unlike those comparator cities, Belfast was on the island of Ireland and its politics reflected the ethno-national politics of the island. Ulster Unionists controlled the Northern Ireland parliament and Ulster Unionists controlled Belfast City Council.

Industrial Belfast was going into decline. The last liner built by Harland and Wolff had been the *Canberra* in 1960. Like other shipbuilding centres across the UK the yard could no longer compete with low-cost producers in the developing world. From 1964 onwards Harland and Wolff made a loss and its workforce fell from 20,000 in 1960 to 9,000 in 1968.[6] Other manufacturing jobs in Belfast had sustained at a reasonable level up to the 1960s,[7] in part due to outside investment by multinational companies.[8] But between 1973 and 1979, while GDP in Northern Ireland grew due to heavy public expenditure, manufacturing industry showed a steep decline.[9] Industrial output in 1988 was

Children play near a patrolling soldier on Independent Street in west Belfast. Like so many others in Belfast this street disappeared after redevelopment.

Photograph © Keystone / Hulton Archive / Getty Images.

lower than that of 1973. Between 1973 and 1979 manufacturing jobs were lost at a rate of 3 per cent per year and from 1979 to 1982 at 8 per cent a year. By 1987 the labour force in manufacturing was around 100,000, less than two-thirds of that in 1973.[10] Northern Ireland, with Belfast at its heart, was rapidly becoming a post-industrial society. In 1986 the Belfast urban area had an unemployment rate of 20 per cent and in some areas of the city male unemployment was thought to be as high as 50 per cent.[11]

Unionism dominated the City Hall and the streets. The largest event of the year was the Twelfth of July parade, with thousands of Orangemen marching through the city centre. The Orangemen and their bands took routes from the various Protestant parts of Belfast, meeting at the city centre and heading south along the Lisburn Road towards 'the field' at Finaghy where a religious and political assembly was held.[12] In an early paper on the sectarian divide, Fred Boal describes the symbolic manifestation that accompanied the celebrations. He noted 'the pattern of street decorations in the area running west from the city centre, erected for the Orange (Protestant) July the Twelfth celebrations. The complete absence of decorations in the Falls Road area and their concentration in the Shankill Road area are notable features.'[13] By contrast the Irish Tricolour was never allowed into the centre of Belfast and was problematic even when flown in Catholic districts. The Flags and Emblems (Display) Act (NI) 1954 forbade the display of 'provocative emblems'. In 1964 the Revd Ian Paisley famously threatened to march up the Falls Road to remove a Tricolour from the office window of the Republican Party. This forced the RUC to remove the flag, provoking serious rioting in the Falls Road area.

John De Lorean (1925–2005) sitting in one of the sports cars that bear his name. De Lorean, a former executive with General Motors, received substantial government funding in a high-profile but short-lived attempt to revive manufacturing in the city. His factory in west Belfast opened in January 1981 but closed in December of the following year. However, the car, with its stainless steel body and distinctive gull-wing doors, achieved subsequent fame through its appearance in Robert Zemeckis's 1985 film *Back to the Future*.

Reproduced with the kind permission of the *Belfast Telegraph*.

From 1967 the Civil Rights movement offered a serious threat to this Unionist, Orange hegemony. Its main demand was for basic rights for all citizens, particularly focusing on issues of fair housing, jobs and votes, but it also called for 'guarantees for freedom of speech, assembly and association' and organized very public events.[14] The Civil Rights movement really had only one success in gaining access to the centre of the city, on 9 October 1968, when the People's Democracy marched from Queen's University before being stopped by the RUC and a counter-protest organized by Ian Paisley. They sat down in Linenhall Street.[15] Other than that the police effectively excluded the different elements of the Civil Rights movement from the city.

In May 1969 serious clashes took place between the RUC and Catholics in the area around the Edenderry Inn, also known as Kilpatrick's, a pub located at the junction of Crumlin Road and Hooker Street. The violence further undermined confidence in the police, and at the same time served as the genesis of one of the most significant boundaries in Belfast. The pub and even Hooker Street itself were soon gone as an interface was created. In July and August further clashes took place around the newly built Unity Flats, a predominantly Catholic area on Peter's Hill at the bottom of the predominantly Protestant Shankill Road. Riots on the Twelfth of July and again on 2 and 3 August centred on Orange parades. The events on 3 August, which became known as the Battle of the Shankill Road, were largely clashes between the RUC and Protestant groups and prefigured increasing tensions between the police and residents in working-class Protestant areas.[16]

The Twelfth of July parades, Bedford Street, 1969. Although parades like these were to be a source of recurrent conflict in the decades that followed, the influence of the Orange Order in working-class communities in Belfast declined during the 1970s and 1980s.

Reproduced with the kind permission of the *Belfast Telegraph*.

Corporation workmen guarded by troops remove the barricade at Herbert Street while engineers arrive to retrieve a bus, 19 August 1969. Disruption to public transport led to the development of a distinctive alternative transport network using London-style black taxis.

Reproduced with the kind permission of the *Belfast Telegraph*.

On the afternoon of 14 August the area around the lower part of the Falls Road exploded into rioting, house burning and gunfire. On 15 August, after successive nights of disturbances, the RUC decided to concentrate their resources on defending their police stations in west Belfast. They were thus absent from the streets as serious rioting developed in the Clonard area of the city. This small run of predominantly Catholic streets abuts the Protestant Shankill Road district. Rumours of a possible attack on the Clonard monastery building gripped Catholics in the area. In Protestant areas rumours persisted of gunmen in the monastery. With the police failing to act on information, anxiety and tension eventually broke in the area between Cupar Street and Bombay Street. Barricades were built by the afternoon of 15 August. Stones, petrol bombs and guns were used without any intervention from the RUC. Later in the afternoon a young Catholic man, a Republican, Gerald McAuley, was shot dead. Bombay Street burned and by the end of the evening the British army, having been deployed in Derry earlier, was deployed on the streets of Belfast.[17]

At the end of a day of violence, the *Belfast Telegraph* described the scene in Catholic west Belfast:

Every street running off the Falls Road is barricaded. Groups of people, many of them wearing crash helmets and carrying dustbin lid shields, were stopping traffic and diverting it away from the Falls Road area. At Howard Street a six-wheel lorry had been turned on its side and set on fire. Other streets in the area had been cordoned off with telegraph poles, lamp posts and paving stones.[18]

29 June 1970. An Irish Tricolour is waved from the top of an army lorry during the rioting at Crumlin Road/ Hooker Street, Belfast.

Reproduced with the kind permission of the *Belfast Telegraph*.

The key thing here is to look at the control of space. While the area in which fighting took place was limited, and most areas of Belfast were peaceful, this was not a small-scale civil disturbance. Instead it represented the start of an attempt by groups to control working-class residential space. It was that attempt that was to define Belfast in the years that followed. Civil Rights activists set up Radio Free Belfast while Radio Orange and the Voice of Ulster broadcast to Loyalist areas. In September the army erected barriers on roads between the Shankill and the Falls. These were the first of the physical 'interfaces', boundaries that would endure for decades to come.

The introduction of soldiers clearly marked the crossing of a Rubicon in terms of policing. The legitimacy of the RUC had certainly been problematic but the presence of British soldiers policing British citizens on the streets of a British city was redolent with symbolism. Within this highly contested space, meanwhile, paramilitary groups now began to organize. The perceived lack of defence of Catholic areas in the north led to a split in the IRA, with Provisional IRA becoming the dominant Republican force in Belfast. In Protestant areas, by 1971, the local vigilante defence associations and tartan gangs became the Ulster Defence Association. Some estimates have put its numbers by 1974 as high as 50,000.[19] In 1973 the UDA formed a more overtly paramilitary wing, the Ulster Freedom Fighters (UFF). The UVF, which had murdered three people and been declared illegal in 1966, remained active. Different streets of Belfast were patrolled by the RUC, the British army, UDA, UVF, Provisional IRA and Official IRA, as well as by numerous community groups and similar associations, all trying to establish forms of control.

August 1970. Across a rock-strewn street a frail chain brings a touch of sanity to a mad situation. The women, from Unity Flats, were stopping their own people from stoning police and troops. Many ordinary citizens did what they could to cope with the violence that was surrounding them.

Reproduced with the kind permission of the *Belfast Telegraph*.

Acts of violence gave new meaning to the streets. For example, on 1 March 1971 three Scottish soldiers, two of them brothers, were shot at point blank range in the Ligoniel area of Belfast. Two schoolchildren discovered the bodies. Between 9 and 11 August 1971 the army shot 11 men in the Ballymurphy area of Belfast. On 4 December 1971 the UVF planted a bomb in McGurk's bar in the New Lodge, killing 15 people. 'When the explosion came, little Marie McGurk and a young friend killed with her were playing cards in the flat above the bar.'[20] On 21 July 1972 the Provisional IRA exploded 22 bombs in Belfast in just eight minutes, killing nine and injuring 130. Among the dead was 14-year-old Stephen Parker, killed by a bomb on Cavehill Road as he sought to warn people. This became known as Bloody Friday.

A range of strategies were developed by the security forces in order to recover some sort of control, particularly over working-class residential areas. From 3 to 5 July 1970 the army imposed a curfew on the lower area of the Falls Road using 3,000 soldiers, 1,500 rounds of ammunition and 1,500 rounds of CS gas grenades, with four civilians killed, 57 wounded, 18 soldiers wounded and over 300 people arrested.[21] On 9 August 1971 internment without trial was introduced, with the army undertaking dawn raids all over Belfast and other parts of Northern Ireland. They arrested 342 people, all from nationalist

areas, although 105 were released within days. This strategy led to an upturn in violence, and the use of the Long Kesh/Maze prison outside Lisburn opened up a new space in which the struggle for state legitimacy would develop. On 3 July 1972 the army attempted to break down the barricaded 'no-go' areas that the UDA had set up in the Shankill, Woodvale and Oldpark areas. The confrontation, reported to have involved 8,000 members of the UDA, was eventually resolved partly by the army accepting the UDA's right to patrol areas and an army promise to police the boundaries with Catholic areas. On 31 July 1972 Operation Motorman was another attempt by the army to remove barricades from the streets and wrestle back control of space. In Belfast about 5,500 soldiers were used with armoured bulldozers to clear the roadblocks, this time in nationalist areas.

Between 1968 and 2005 around 1,400 people were killed and 20,000 injured by paramilitary and state violence: 85 per cent of these deaths took place within 1,000 metres of an interface, 65 per cent of those killed could be categorized as civilians, and 78 per cent of killings took place in north and west Belfast.[22]

> It is not surprising that violence encouraged political and cultural retrenchment and the physical and cognitive remapping of the city. The reorganisation of space, due to violence, increased separation and reemphasised the fundamentals of ethno-sectarian 'difference'.[23]

Aerial view of Woodvale and Ardoyne, west Belfast.

Photograph © National Museums Northern Ireland and Cecil Newman.

Boal suggests that Belfast is a polarized city, as opposed to simply a divided one. A crucial element of his description is that the governing of parts of the city takes place without consensus. 'Simple service delivery questions and planning decisions regarding the use of space are transformed into conflicts.'[24] By the 1990s 35 of Belfast's 51 local council wards contained either a 90 per cent Catholic or 90 per cent Protestant population.[25]

Violence dominated the urban landscape where many working-class people in Belfast lived in the early 1970s. It was to fundamentally change the shape of the city, particularly in working-class areas of north, east and west Belfast. While the 'no-go' areas disappeared, the reality for the forces of the state, the RUC and the army, was that their ability to work in these areas was limited and their legitimacy was challenged. The makeshift boundaries became institutionalized through the building of more permanent barriers and then fences and walls. In April 1971 an internal Government of Northern Ireland report called *Future Policy on Areas of Confrontation* recommended that the redevelopment of west Belfast, including the new 'urban motorway project', take the security situation into account. One paragraph in particular foreshadowed the approach to planning that was to dominate Belfast over the next three decades:

42. (a) As part of the overall development programme, various factories and warehouses will have to be located. Consideration should be given to the possibility of locating such accommodation along the line of confrontation, with high walls forming natural barriers […] (b) Plans for housing adjacent to the line of confrontation […] should be revised to provide more open space particularly on either side of the new natural barrier […] (c) Generally the number of open routes between the Falls and the Shankill (ie the routes which at present have to be controlled by peace-line barriers) should be substantially reduced.[26]

Meanwhile public facilities such as health and leisure centres, public services such as buses, and local businesses all had to adapt to the changed landscape. Roads were closed off and some disappeared altogether as planners and policymakers accepted the security environment.

People's experience of the city changed behaviour. The normal everyday lives of parents were altered as ordinary tasks such as shopping and looking after children were made more complicated and potentially dangerous. Begoña Aretxaga argues that the roles played by working-class women shifted significantly as political activity took place on the doorstep.[27] Schoolchildren developed knowledge of which buses to get on and which to avoid. People would move through the city avoiding certain areas. Formerly vibrant shopping streets such as Duncairn Gardens in north Belfast found themselves on boundaries and became places people were unwilling to visit. Depending on your background, areas of the city became out of bounds. A simple task such as ordering a taxi would require local knowledge since many cab firms would not

Following spread: Children's games on the streets of Belfast. Perhaps one of the defining features of the developing divisions in the city was that the conflict provided places and spaces that appeared dangerous to adults but exciting to children. Children frequently gather at interfaces that adults avoid, and they often play a role in civil disturbances.

Photograph © Alex Bowie / Hulton Archive / Getty Images.

pick up or drop off in certain areas. The damaging effect that the civil unrest had on the bus system in the 1970s led to the adoption of a distinctive mode of transport for citizens wishing to traverse the west and north of city. London-style black taxis served as buses and ran particular routes, with passengers asking to be left off or picked up anywhere along this route. The existence of this alternative transport system led the black taxi to become almost a symbol of resistance in Belfast and many of the Republican political demonstrations in the 1990s would be led by these vehicles.

The people of the city adapted to the new environment. The population of Belfast shifted. Working-class residential areas became more single identity than at any time previously. A Northern Ireland Community Relations Commission report in 1974 suggested that between August 1969 and February 1973 conclusive evidence existed for the forced movement of 8,000 families (6.6% of the population) from their homes in Greater Belfast as a result of intimidation, though it was thought the actual figure could be as high as 15,000.[28] The newly formed Northern Ireland Housing Executive developed policies that took into account the separated neighbourhoods. Separation between Protestant and Catholic became a central factor both in the allocation of housing and in decisions on new building projects. The struggle for resources was effectively polarized. More than ever, Belfast had what Murtagh and Shirlow have described as ethno-sectarian enclaves.[29]

People's perceptions of parts of the city were constructed around an ongoing use of violence. In examining the spatial formations in Belfast, Allen Feldman describes the interface/sanctuary relationship, the interface being a place of danger with areas further away feeling secure.[30] Frank Burton, who worked in west Belfast in the 1970s, described the existence of 'safe' and 'unsafe' places.

> In Belfast one generally walks round parked uninhabited cars with suspicion, casts unnerving glances at unattended parcels, scrambles to get home before it gets too dark, maps out safe and dangerous routes for journeys, all in an effort to evaluate risks which previously could be ignored.[31]

The landscape itself was not only altered by the nature of the violence but also symbolically marked through identity practices amplified by the conflict. For example, parades had always been a potential site of conflict in the city, but the intensification of the territorial divisions and the development of symbols and practices reflecting the conflicting identities magnified the role they played. Parades by the Orange Order became the particular site of confrontation since a number of 'traditional' routes moved across what had become more entrenched boundaries. In December 1970 a government commission chaired by John Taylor, then minister of state at the Ministry of Home Affairs, recommended, among other things, a 'substantial reduction in the number of parades', that members of Orange lodges in Belfast should make their way to assembly points

May 1970. 'One of the many shops on Duncairn Gardens, which was badly damaged during serious rioting on Saturday night and Sunday morning, is boarded up' (*Belfast Telegraph*). Duncairn Gardens became one of the many 'interfaces' in the north of the city.

Reproduced with the kind permission of the *Belfast Telegraph*.

as individuals and not conduct local parades, and that new legislation on parades should take into account community relations.[32] The Orange Order adapted its practices to adjust to the new landscape by curtailing small marches prior to the annual Twelfth of July parades and instead developing larger local parades.[33] In the east of the city Orange parades from Ballymacarrett would inevitably pass by the Catholic area of Short Strand. In the west the annual Whiterock parade on the last Saturday of June had a route that took it across the Falls/Shankill boundary and on to Springfield Road. In the north, parades coming from Ballysillan down to the Shankill past the predominantly Catholic Ardoyne area, and the annual Tour of the North parade, whose routes every other year included Antrim Road, close to the New Lodge, likewise became flash points. Indeed the Northern Ireland government report recommended that 'in the present circumstances Orange Parades should not be allowed to process along the Grosvenor, Springfield or Crumlin Roads, or along parts of the Antrim Road between Carlisle Circus and Duncairn Gardens'.[34]

No part of the city was unaffected by the violent struggle for legitimate control of space, but clearly some were more affected than others. The most prosperous parts of the city saw the lowest levels of political violence. The city centre, on the other hand, became a major target. The first bomb attack was at a bank on High Street on 16 July 1970, injuring 33 people. Many attacks followed using either car bombs or incendiaries. On 4 March 1972 two people were killed and 130 injured when the Abercorn restaurant was bombed. Sixteen days later six people were killed by a car bomb in lower Donegall Street. Between 1970 and 1975 300 establishments in central Belfast, a quarter of the overall retail floor space, were destroyed. The policing response to this was clearly different to that used in residential areas. This was not so much an issue of legitimacy as one of security. From 24 March 1972 two control zones were set up around the city. The inner one stopped cars parking at any time, the outer zone permitted parking only after 6 p.m., although Royal Avenue, Donegall Place, High Street and Castle Street remained open to traffic. By July a system of crude barriers was in place and pedestrians and vehicles were stopped and searched. By 1974 these had become permanent iron and steel gates with civilian searchers. The consequences for the commercial life of the city were unsurprising. At a time when many British cities were struggling economically, Belfast became a city unlikely to attract investment. Forty firms folded in 1971 and in 1972 three department stores and two hotels closed for good.

> Physical fear, the depressing bomb-scarred environment and problems of accessibility, including the lack of car parking facilities and the frequent disruptions to traffic and bus services by bomb scares and security checks, made shoppers increasingly reluctant to patronise the city centre establishments in general and evening entertainment venues in particular.[35]

On 26 March 1976 a single security zone was introduced, dubbed by some the 'Merlyn Wall', after Secretary of State for Northern Ireland Merlyn Rees. This effectively made the city centre traffic free but also led to those businesses outside the urban core suffering. Buses were allowed in but to begin with could not pick up or drop off.[36]

These drastic measures coincided with the first phase of the IRA campaign, intended to produce a quick political result by a strategy of maximum destruction. By the end of the 1970s the emphasis had switched to a 'long war' of attrition that would gradually wear down the resistance of the British government and the Unionist population.[37] Against this background some politicians as early as 1980 were suggesting a significant relaxation in city-centre security measures, but research at the time showed that shoppers preferred their retention. From September 1982, however, late-night shopping was introduced one night a week and from July 1983 buses were allowed to pick up and drop off passengers in the city centre. Searches by security staff at the edge of the zone became far more selective and searches of pedestrians were abandoned in 1984.[38] A new shopping complex was even planned for the Smithfield area of Belfast on the site of the former Grand Central Hotel. The opening in 1990 of the Castlecourt shopping centre began the recolonization of Donegall Place and Royal Avenue by a new range of retail outlets, most of them national chains.

Punk rock group The Clash pass through security gates in Belfast in October 1977. In the event the city council, responding to the moral panic that punk had provoked elsewhere in the United Kingdom, banned the group's concert. Ironically, the protest against this decision, leading to scuffles with police outside the Ulster Hall, has been credited with providing the initial impetus to the development in the period that followed of Belfast's own punk movement.

© Adrian Boot / Urbanimage.TV

No, don't trust the maps, for they avoid the moment: ramps, barricades,
diversions, Peace Lines. Though if there is an ideal map, which shows this
city as it is, it may exist in the eye of that helicopter ratcheting overhead,
its searchlight fingering and scanning the micro-chip deviations: the surge
of funerals and parades, swelling and accelerating, time-lapsed, supped
back into nothingness by the rewind button; the wired alleys and entries;
someone walking his dog when the façade of Gass's Bicycle Shop erupts in
an avalanche of glass and metal forks and tubing, rubber, rat-trap pedals,
toe-clips and repair kits.

Ciaran Carson, 'Question Time', from *Belfast Confetti*

Belfast Girl Guides, in various
uniforms from over the years,
head their float in the Lord
Mayor's Show, 1977. The
Lord Mayor's Show went
into decline in the 1970s
and 1980s with many local
companies no longer willing or
able to sponsor floats.

Reproduced with the kind
permission of the *Belfast
Telegraph*.

The changes in the city centre influenced commercial life, how people moved
through the city and the image of the city. The civic life of the city could not
remain untouched. The annual Lord Mayor's Show organized by the Junior
Chamber of Commerce took place each year in June. In the 1960s it featured
a broad spectrum of civic life including charities, major local companies and
various representations of the military. Belfast was depicted through ideas
of industry and modernity with themes such as 'Pride in Progress' (1964)
and 'Enterprise Ulster' (1965). The majority of the floats were sponsored by
businesses, from Guinness to Massey Ferguson tractors. The parades moved

down Royal Avenue past locally owned department stores Robinson and Cleaver and Anderson and McAuley. In the changed environment of the 1970s all this was hard to sustain and by the mid-1970s the city's showpiece event was struggling to get participants. By 1980 the president of the Chamber of Commerce was appealing for the big employers, who had not recently taken part in the Lord Mayor's Show, to return.[39] In 1994 the Lord Mayor's Show in Belfast had only 40 floats.[40]

Alongside the decline in the commercial and industrial heart of the city, and the significant shifts in population brought about by both ethnic conflict and economic change, the urban landscape altered through redevelopment. Regeneration in the public housing stock and the redevelopment of the transport system, particularly the roads, was to have a profound effect on how people experienced the city. The first survey by the then new Housing Executive in 1974 revealed that 24 per cent of dwellings in the core of the city were unfit.[41] Belfast was far from immune from the introduction of the prefabricated tower block. In the north of the city the Rathcoole estate, built in the 1950s, had seen a striking development which included four blocks effectively looking across Belfast harbour. Around the Divis area of west Belfast and the New Lodge in north Belfast equally dramatic changes took place. In the 1960s one tower block and a series of eight-storey decked flats were built in the lower Falls Road. These had a role in the dynamic of the conflict as they became the stage for numerous confrontations between the IRA and the British army.

The failure of these housing projects led very quickly to a second round of redevelopments that saw the removal of many of the traditional two-up, two-down dwellings but also of some redevelopment projects from the 1960s, still less than twenty years old. The style of the new developments was

Senator Joseph Kennedy (son of the assassinated Robert Kennedy) is shown around by Father Mat Wallace from St Peter's Cathedral during a visit to Divis Flats, April 1988.
Reproduced with the kind permission of Pacemaker Press International Ltd.

The Divis Complex, built between 1966 and 1972 as a high-rise solution to the housing problems of west Belfast. Most of the complex was demolished during the 1990s and replaced by more traditional housing, but the 20-storey Divis Tower remains.
Photograph © National Museums Northern Ireland and Cecil Newman.

A local resident helps clean up after about 400 nationalists and Loyalists clashed during rioting in Cluan Place and Clandeboye Gardens in east Belfast, 2005.

Reproduced with the kind permission of Pacemaker Press International Ltd.

dictated not only by the depopulation of the city and the demand for low-level single dwellings but also by the security situation and the new sectarian geography of the city. Some roads disappeared altogether while others were re-routed to take account of the interface boundaries, many now marked by walls and fences. G.M. Dawson describes one example, the development between 1980 and 1984 of Cluan Place, a small Protestant enclave on the edge of the largely Catholic Short Strand in the Ballymacarrett area of east Belfast. Here the removal of a former tram station from the Short Strand, to allow for housing redevelopment, also removed a barrier between the Short Strand and the small Protestant population in Cluan Place. Unionist politicians therefore lobbied for walls to be put up around two dozen residences in Cluan Place and plans to make it a through road were abandoned. Like so many developments in Belfast it remained a cul-de-sac to provide residents with a sense of security.[42] Security had essentially been added to a range of factors that planners in Belfast needed to consider when redeveloping roads and housing in the city.[43]

The shipyard, the mills, the factories and the skyline of red-brick chimneys were disappearing. The population of Belfast reflected these changes. Between 1951 and 1971 there had been a steady move of people from the core of the city to more suburban areas, with the urban area reaching around 600,000 in 1971. Through the 1970s and 1980s Belfast core city saw a continued decline in population and a decline in the number of households. Indeed from 1971 to 1991 the inner core of the city lost 55 per cent of its population. At the same time the outer regional area of the city grew by 39 per cent.[44]

Throughout this period the city was becoming more segregated. In 1969 59 per cent of public-sector households resided in streets that were almost completely segregated; by 1977 this had risen to 89 per cent. A rise in segregation can also be found in the private housing sector, but, interestingly, the increase, from 65 per cent to 73 per cent, was less severe.[45] The geographer Fred Boal, who over this period did more than anyone to map the changing dynamics within the city, also points out that these changes led to the increasing understanding that 'west' Belfast was Catholic and 'east' Belfast was Protestant.

Boal quotes *Northern Ireland: Regional Physical Development Strategy 1975–1979*: 'Belfast faces a combination of economic, social communal and physical development problems unparalleled in any major city in Europe.'[46] In 1982 Cowan asked the obvious question: 'What should Belfast's planners do? Should they use their position and skills to try and provide the physical form appropriate to a harmonious society? Or should they accept the existence of fear and hatred between Protestants and Catholics, and the active presence of the army and the police and merely do what they can to accommodate a state of permanent tension?'[47]

Nothin' for us in Belfast

The Pound's so old it's a pity

OK, there's the Trident in Bangor

Then walk back to the city

We ain't got nothin' but they don't really care

They don't even know you know

Just want our money

And we can take it or leave it

What we need is

An Alternative Ulster

Grab it and change it it's yours

Get an Alternative Ulster

Ignore the bores and their laws

Get an Alternative Ulster

Be an anti-security force

Alter your native Ulster

Alter your native land

'Alternative Ulster', Stiff Little Fingers/Oglvie, *Inflammable Material* 1979

Belfast punk band Stiff Little Fingers, formed in 1977, had critical and chart success in Ireland and the UK. Many of their songs, including their first two singles, 'Suspect Device' and 'Alternative Ulster', dealt with the conflict.

Photograph © Virginia Turbett / Redferns / Getty Images.

Just as significant for the landscape of Belfast was the development of the road network. Planners in 1969 produced elaborate schemes for a dual carriageway to ring the city and connect to motorways heading into counties Down and Antrim.[48] If ships and rail had defined the previous hundred years the car was destined to define the decades leading up to the twenty-first century. Only the western and northern elements of the ring roads were to be realized. The building of the M2 and Westlink dual carriageway cut a swathe through the working-class residential districts of the western inner city, while the completed highway effectively acted as a barrier between the Antrim, Shankill and Falls Road areas and the centre, with only four crossing points for vehicles. This had security implications, which by April 1971 were clear to the government,[49] as it allowed the centre of the city to become more easily secured from key working-class districts and acted to separate the largely working-class Protestant areas of Sandy Row and the Village from working-class Catholic Falls Road and Divis.

The redevelopment in the north of the city was even more dramatic. The M2 motorway eventually became eight lanes in width and cut right through the traditional docks or Sailortown district. This redevelopment rendered the York Street area almost unrecognizable and effectively destroyed it as a residential district. The working-class Protestant areas of York Road and Shore Road and the working-class Catholic areas of the New Lodge and lower Antrim Road had

The M2 motorway, 12 June 1980. The development of the motorway network in the north and west of the city effectively separated working-class residential areas from the city centre.

Reproduced with the kind permission of Pacemaker Press International Ltd.

major road junctions placed between them and the city centre. In the east of the city the three road bridges that crossed the Lagan were in the 1990s added to by a motorway bridge linking the system to the road to Bangor and a rail bridge that connected York Street railway station with Central station. But, as with the north and west of the city, working-class residential areas in the east, the predominantly Catholic Short Strand and Protestant Ballymacarrett, already separated from the city centre by the river, are now further dislocated by large road junctions. To the south the Malone and Lisburn Roads provide a lived-in and, in the case of the Lisburn Road, commercially vibrant corridor linking predominantly middle-class residential areas directly to the city centre. To the north, west and east, by contrast, the pedestrian walking to the city centre from most working-class residential areas is confronted by a desolate and intimidating combination of road junctions and empty wasteland. The *Belfast Metropolitan Plan 2015*, published in 2004, recognized this continuing problem.

> The Inner Ring Road which currently surrounds much of the city centre has left a scar on the urban fabric with large expanses of roadway inappropriate to the scale of the city, a fractured townscape and a physical and psychological barrier separating city centre from surrounding residential communities.[50]

Conflict and Consequences

While de-industrialization, road plans and rehousing provided the backdrop, it was the ongoing conflict that gave parts of this landscape particular meaning. The nature of the violence resulted in practices that changed the way that the public spaces of Belfast were used. The Ulster Workers Council strike in May

1974 brought down the power-sharing executive created by the Sunningdale Agreement of the previous December. With the UDA, which had been organizing marches in working-class Protestant areas since 1972, throwing its populist weight behind the strike, roads were blocked and the ability to control movement around the city became a key issue. Indeed, the RUC and army were often unwilling or unable to break roadblocks. The *Daily Mail* provided a particularly colourful description:

> So your wee Belfast Johnny is going to go home filthy tonight. But you can't bath him. No hot water.
> Can't read him a bed time story. No lights. Can't cheer yourself up with a fire. No coal.
> Can't make a hot drink. No electricity. Can't pop out to the pictures or bingo. They are either burned down, bombed out or closed.
> You can't catch a bus. There aren't any. Can't post a letter. It won't arrive. Can't make a local phone call without being deafened by crackles. Can't fill a carrier bag with shopping without queuing for hours. Can't use your car for pleasure. Petrol's so scarce some ingenious folk are trying to run their cars on paint thinners.
> [...] Whatever happens politically, Belfast teeters on the abyss of total administrative collapse today.[51]

This was probably to be the high point for Loyalist and Unionist groups in the widespread control of public space. The Ulster Workers Council strike was the most effective mobilization of both mainstream Unionism and Loyalism in common cause. The legitimacy of the state never looked weaker.

Violence peaked between 1971 and 1976. The stories of the victims, all briefly retold in the compilation *Lost Lives*, are a sad and brutal reminder of the nature of the conflict.[52] Some of the most notorious incidents were the work of a group from the west Belfast UVF, commonly referred to as the Shankill Butchers, who between 1975 and 1982 committed gruesome murders, estimated by some to have numbered up to 30. Most victims were grabbed from Catholic areas of the city and taken back to the Shankill Road before being brutally murdered. Other victims were Protestants from the Shankill area with whom gang members had differences. These and many other killings in the streets and back alleys of the city, particularly the working-class districts in the north and west, created a fear that altered everyday behaviour.

Another example of the relationship between violence and public space was the brief flowering of the Women's Peace Movement. On 10 August 1976 three children were killed and another fatally injured when an IRA man, Danny Lennon, was shot by the British army while driving along Finaghy Road North, so that his car careered out of control. Mairead Corrigan Maguire, sister of the children's mother Anne Maguire, along with Betty Williams and

William Craig, the former Unionist Minister for Home Affairs and later leader of the more militant Vanguard movement, with supporters during the Ulster Workers strike, 28 March 1974. The dramatic control of public space during the strike was probably the high point of resistance to political changes by working-class Loyalists.
Photograph © Keystone / Hulton Archive / Getty Images.

Ciaran McKeown, galvanized support into what became the Women's Peace Movement. For a brief period they offered a serious threat to the growing hegemony of the paramilitaries, particularly the IRA. A meeting on 14 August 1976 at Andersonstown in west Belfast attracted widespread support from Catholics and Protestants, with an estimated 10,000 people gathering for the occasion. This was probably the high point for popular, mass-participation peace movements as only on rare occasions after this was the sectarian space of working-class Belfast broken down. Despite the appearance of many peace activists in Belfast over the years, there was a dearth of popular cross-community mobilization. Williams and Corrigan won the Nobel peace prize and their movement developed into the Peace People. Sadly, Anne Maguire became the fifth victim of 10 August 1976 when in 1980 she committed suicide.

The streets of Belfast saw a different form of violent struggle when on 1 March 1981 Bobby Sands, leader of the Provisional IRA in the Maze prison, renewed Republican prisoners' demands for special category status by going on hunger strike. On 5 May he died and people in Republican areas came out on to the streets which echoed to the sound of bin lids being banged on the ground.[53] An estimated 50,000 people took to the streets for the funeral parade from St Luke's chapel to Milltown cemetery in west Belfast.

> The funeral stopped close to the Busy Bee shopping centre and Bobby's coffin was removed from the hearse and placed on trestles. Then, from among the people, emerged three IRA Volunteers armed with rifles who were called to attention in Gaelic by a fourth uniformed man. They delivered three sharp volleys over the coffin, removed their berets and bowed their heads in silence. […] Gerry Adams officiated at the graveside ceremony which began with playing the Last Post. The Tricolour was then removed from the coffin and along with the beret and gloves presented to Mrs Sands.[54]

Ten hunger strikers died before, some of their demands having been met, the campaign was called off. But the implications of such widespread popular support changed the course of Irish Republicanism in Northern Ireland.[55] While on hunger strike Sands stood successfully in a by-election for a Westminster seat, and in the aftermath key Republicans, in Belfast particularly centred around Gerry Adams and Danny Morrison, decided to contest local and national elections through the political wing of the IRA, Sinn Féin. This had a profound effect on the politics of the city. On 9 June 1983 Gerry Adams was elected as MP for West Belfast, defeating the SDLP's Joe Hendron by over 5,000 votes. Irish Republicans, while continuing an armed struggle, were also demanding to be part of the political and civic life of the city. This was to become apparent in the landscape of Belfast streets as well as in the council chamber of Belfast City Hall.

The entry of Sinn Féin into the political and civic realm was emphasized further in 1985 when seven councillors were elected to the city council. Needless to say this was to have a dramatic effect on the nature of debate as the confrontations between Unionism and Irish Republicanism, as well the contest for nationalist votes between the SDLP and Sinn Féin, now manifested itself within political institutions as well as through the security situation around the city. To begin with communication did not move beyond hostility, but as Sinn Féin's long-term position within the institutions became clear the initial Unionist strategy of refusing to acknowledge its representatives, and denying them a place on committees, became untenable. Instead the proceedings of Belfast City Council and other district councils in Northern Ireland provided a foretaste of the political engagements to come in the developing peace process of the 1990s.

A Landscape of Politics and Violence

The Belfast landscape was demarcated not only by people's experience and memory of the ongoing violence, but also through cultural manifestations such as parades, murals, flags and, particularly after the 1990s, memorials. As part of the changing tactics of Irish Republicans after the hunger strikes, and particularly their entry into politics, they began to imitate Loyalists by decorating the many gable ends of Belfast with political murals. One suggestion is that the first quasi-murals appeared in the Lenadoon area in response to the hunger strikes, with at least 100 seen within just a few months of Sands's death.[56] Many of the early Republican murals reflected the violence of the struggle, both within the prison and on the streets, with hooded gunmen depicted as symbols of resistance. But Sinn Féin's developing political and cultural agenda encouraged the appearance of more diverse messages and images.[57] Scenes from Irish history depicting the United Irishmen, the Famine and the 1916 Easter Rising, as well as murals linking the Republican struggle with those of Australian Aborigines, native Americans, the Basques and the Palestinians, and symbols of left-wing politics such as the Starry Plough, all found a place in an increasingly diverse range of murals.

In Loyalist working-class areas the painting of murals can be traced back to the early part of the twentieth century. While a variety of images of loyalty could be found, by far the most dominant was the picture of King William III (King Billy), astride his white horse, crossing the river at the Battle of the Boyne in 1690.[58] In the mid-1980s Loyalist murals also went through a transformation partially linked to opposition to the Anglo-Irish Agreement.[59] Images of King Billy began to disappear from the walls as depictions of the UVF and UDA became more prominent. The change in iconography also seemed to reflect a decline in the importance of Orangeism within the Loyalist communities. The Orange arches which would have adorned so many roads in Protestant

The Republican memorial in Twinbrook, West Belfast. Originally a Bobby Sands memorial, the inscription now reads: 'This monument has been re-dedicated by the people of Twinbrook and Poleglass in honour of those Volunteers of Oglaigh na hEireann [soldiers of Ireland] who gave their lives for Irish freedom...'

Photograph courtesy of Dominic Bryan.

UVF mural, Shankill Road west Belfast, 2010. The images create a narrative linking the struggle of contemporary Loyalists with the sacrifice made by Ulster Protestants during the First World War. Note particularly the use of the poppy.

Photograph courtesy of Dominic Bryan.

areas of Belfast started to disappear.[60] Murals became so redolent of the Belfast landscape that it became almost impossible to depict the city in news bulletins, in documentaries or through drama without using them as a backdrop.[61] Belfast and the mural became synonymous. As early as 1992 *The Rough Guide to Ireland* tourist guide gave up five pages to describing where in west Belfast the best specimens could be found.[62]

More important than the murals was the annual cycle of parades. The parades played a role in demarcating the nature of public space, not only though the routes of the marches, but also in the events and ephemera that accompanied them, such as bonfires, Orange arches, bunting, flags and painted kerb stones.[63] In Loyalist areas of the city the most significant development was the growth in 'blood and thunder' flute bands. Silver, accordion and flute bands had long accompanied Orange parades around the First and Twelfth of July, commemorating the battles of the Somme and Boyne, but the rapid growth in flute bands represented an element of the parading culture independent of the Orange Order and often, but not always, reflected the rise of paramilitarism.[64] Flutes were cheaper and easier to learn than other musical instruments and the 'rough' style of playing focused on the large bass drum was enjoyed by young men, many of whom were no longer learning skills in the shipyard. Early bands dressed simply in grey trousers with a coloured v-neck sweater and a cap, but through the 1980s and 1990s uniforms became much more elaborate and some bands started to carry flags and bannerettes referring to Loyalist paramilitary groups. Blood and thunder bands began to predominate in Orange Order events in the city, giving the parades a more assertive public face. The bands also developed their own parading repertoire, with each local band hosting an annual band parade. Some developed events that memorialized members of the UDA and UVF who had lost their lives. As with Republican murals, Loyalist bands reflected the changing political and cultural landscape in the city.

Orange Order, Sandy Row No. 5 District, on the march, 12 July 1980. The 'blood and thunder' bands that accompany many of the lodges take a central role in Orange Order celebrations. Over the years their uniforms have evolved from simple v-neck sweaters to become much more elaborate.

Reproduced with the kind permission of the *Belfast Telegraph*.

On 23 November 1985 Unionists organized a massive rally reminiscent of the signing of the Solemn League and Covenant in 1912. This was in response to the signing of the Anglo-Irish Agreement, which gave the Irish government some limited say in the running of Northern Ireland. Despite overwhelming opposition to the Agreement, and a day of action on 3 March 1986 during which roads in Belfast and elsewhere were blocked, Unionist politicians were unable to repeat the success of the Ulster Workers strike of 1974. City Hall would be adorned for many years to come with a banner proclaiming that 'Belfast Says No', but Unionism and Loyalism were unable to mobilize effectively. Following the riots and intimidation that accompanied the day of action Unionist politicians were torn between their desire to mobilize on the streets and the likelihood that this would lead to confrontation between Loyalist groups and the RUC. The potential for violence became evident in a series of confrontations that developed after 1995 as the authorities sought to prohibit or re-route Orange parades passing through contested areas. While Republicanism, despite its use of violence, was increasingly entering the civic space, Unionism and Orangeism, when allied with Loyalism, found itself in confrontation with the forces of the state. This dislocation between working-class Loyalists and mainstream Unionism in Belfast became very obvious over the twenty years that followed the signing of the Anglo-Irish Agreement.

A poignant way in which the violence impacted upon the Belfast landscape was through the numerous funerals. Many fatalities were of course buried in private family rituals but the burials both of the Maguire children and of Bobby

A banner above the entrance to the City Hall proclaims that 'Belfast' rejects the Anglo-Irish Agreement of 1985. Over the next two decades such claims to exclusive ownership of the public sphere would become increasingly untenable.

Photograph: 1986 Ulster Says No © Chris Hill, Scenic Ireland.

Sands provide examples of the potential political impact of these ritual events. Paramilitary funerals were frequently the site of contestation as security forces tried to prevent paramilitary displays or guns being fired over the coffins. Just as the other public spaces in the city were contested, so was the cemetery. Milltown cemetery off the Falls Road, in the south-west of the city, deserves particular mention. It has many historical resonances but in the modern era it is the destination for the annual Easter 1916 commemorations and has been the burial site of many Irish Republicans. As such, it has been a site of contestation between the security forces and Republicans, between Loyalist paramilitaries and Republicans, and between competing Republican groups. On 16 March 1988 Michael Stone, a member of the UDA, attacked the funerals of three IRA volunteers who had been killed by the SAS in Gibraltar ten days earlier. Television cameras recorded the events as Stone killed three people, Thomas McErlean, John Murray and Caoimhín Mac Brádaigh. At the funeral of Caoimhín Mac Brádaigh, on 19 March, two British soldiers drove a car towards the funeral cortege which was led by black taxis. The two soldiers, David Howes and Derek Wood, were pulled from the car, beaten up, then murdered by the IRA. Again, much of this was caught by television cameras, providing further powerful images of the conflict.

On 10 April 1998 in some rather unassuming buildings on the Stormont Estate in the east of the city, the Irish and British governments, the major Northern Irish political parties (with the exception of the Democratic Unionist Party), and the political parties representing both Loyalist paramilitary groups reached an agreement on the political future of Northern Ireland. This had followed a process of talks which had been boosted in 1994 by the IRA, followed by the UDA and the UVF, declaring ceasefires. Following the Agreement a referendum was held in the Republic of Ireland and in Northern Ireland on 22 May 1998. In Northern Ireland 71 per cent of those voting supported the Agreement. The city of Belfast was now potentially a capital city of a Northern Ireland that had a level of legitimacy not previously enjoyed. The level of organized violence dropped significantly. However, the legacy of the violence remained.

It is difficult to ascertain the exact nature of the social, political and economic context that created the possibility of change. Had the military strategies of the state and Republican and Loyalist paramilitaries come to a point where politics was the only way forward? Had the position of Catholics within the social structure of Northern Ireland altered enough to undermine the level of resistance? Was there just too much for Republicans to gain for them to refuse to enter the political process? And what did the slowly improving economic well-being of Belfast and Northern Ireland contribute to the process? What is more easily documented is the changes that were taking place within the city that both contributed to, and were outcomes of, the peace process.

The period of conflict from 1969 left a significant legacy for the city. Mesev, Shirlow and Downs record 1,601 victims of violence in Belfast between 1966 and 2007. Of these, the majority, 994, could be described as non-combatants, 677 of whom were Catholic, 307 Protestant and ten of other or unknown background. Of these civilians, 115 were killed by the security forces, 295 by Republican paramilitary groups (182 by the IRA), and 531 by Loyalist paramilitary groups (218 by the UVF and 248 by the UDA), with 53 victims coming under the catagory of unknown or accidental. Of the remaining dead 303 were members of the security forces or other state employees such as judges, prison officers or civil servants, and 301 were members of paramilitary groups, 130 Loyalist and 171 Republican.[65] A spatial mapping of these casualties shows that most victims were killed close to their homes, with the highest concentration in north and west Belfast, the more deprived areas of the city and close to the interfaces.[66]

These blunt statistics (and there were of course many more casualties) do not come close to capturing the effect of these deaths on family and friends and also on the way people lived in the city. The fear created was as real as the physical interface walls that now separated Protestant and Catholic working-class areas. Memories were embedded in the landscape of the city. And as

The Ballynafeigh club of the Apprentice Boys of Derry make their way to the police barrier erected to prevent them from walking along the nationalist Lower Ormeau Road on their way to the annual rally in Belfast city centre, 1999. Disputes over the routes taken by parades have been common in the city since 1969 but they became particularly acute between 1995 and 2000.

Reproduced with the kind permission of Pacemaker Press International Ltd.

people, organizations and political parties started to come to terms with the peace process, narratives of the recent past developed. Victims demanded to know and understand the particular circumstances of the loss of their loved ones and the broad role of the forces of the state and paramilitary organizations. And practices of commemoration and memorialization developed. Memorials, particularly to members of the IRA, UVF and UDA, started to appear in working-class communities throughout Belfast. Viggiani's 2006 survey showed just how extensive the range of physical memorials had become. In west Belfast alone there were 30 memorials, 21 murals with plaques attached and 26 separate plaques.[67] Another database on the Cain website recorded 279 memorials in the city by 2011, although these include some plaques inside buildings.[68] Some of the memorials are significant structures, sometimes within gardens of remembrance. Along with murals, whose themes have also developed commemorative narratives, the memorials now represent a significant part of the physical landscape of working-class Belfast. Most have no planning permission and are thus an indication that the writ of the state is still weak in many of these places.

Belfast in the first decade of the twenty-first century was as residentially divided into areas of Catholic and Protestant as at any time in its history. This was despite what appeared to be an increased movement of Catholics into more middle-class areas.[69] The lowest levels of segregation are in the middle-class areas of south Belfast while the higher levels are in working-class west

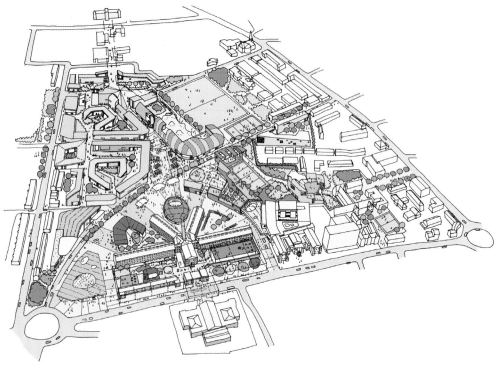

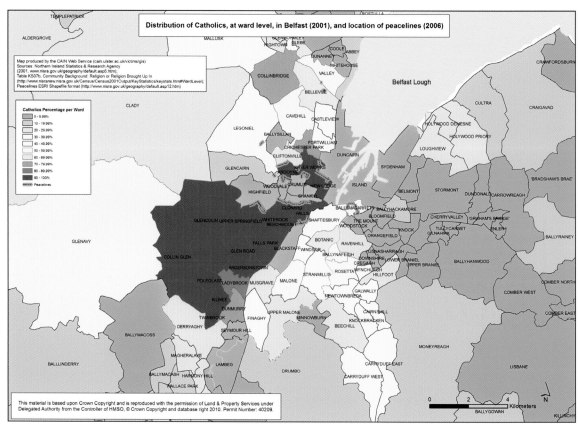

Distribution of Catholics, at ward level, in Belfast (2001), and location of peacelines (2006)

Map produced by the CAIN Web Service (cain.ulster.ac.uk/victims/gis)
Sources: Northern Ireland Statistics & Research Agency
(2001, www.nisra.gov.uk/geography/default.asp5.htm);
Table KS07b, Community Background: Religion or Religion Brought Up In
(http://www.nisranew.nisra.gov.uk/Census/Census2001Output/KeyStatistics/keystats.htm#WardLevel);
Peacelines ESRI Shapefile format (http://www.nisra.gov.uk/geography/default.asp12.htm)

Catholics Percentage per Ward

- 0 - 9.99%
- 10 - 19.99%
- 20 - 29.99%
- 30 - 39.99%
- 40 - 49.99%
- 50 - 59.99%
- 60 - 69.99%
- 70 - 79.99%
- 80 - 89.99%
- 90 - 100%
- Peacelines

This material is based upon Crown Copyright and is reproduced with the permission of Land & Property Services under Delegated Authority from the Controller of HMSO, © Crown Copyright and database right 2010. Permit Number: 40209.

Plans for the development of Girdwood barracks in north Belfast, where the practicalities of demilitarization highlight the continued fragility of the political settlement. The former army base sits empty while Unionist and nationalist politicians squabble over how the allocation of social housing proposed for the site might affect the finely balanced territorial division between Catholic and Protestant.

Reproduced with permission from the Building Design Partnership.

Residential segregation in the twenty-first century. The distribution of the Catholic population and the location of peace walls, 2001.

Source: CAIN (cain.ulster.ac.uk/victims)

© Crown copyright. Reproduced with the permission of the Controller of Her Majesty's Stationery Office and CAIN.

Belfast.[70] Between 1995 and 1998 there were very high levels of civil disorder in relation to disputes over the right of Orange parades to process through residential areas seen as predominantly Catholic. The annual Battle of the Boyne church parade to Drumcree church in Portadown, County Armagh, was the most high profile of the disputes but it had repercussions in Belfast and throughout Northern Ireland. Disputes in Belfast over Loyal Order parades on Ormeau Road, Springfield Road, Crumlin Road and Clifton Park Avenue were also highly contested. During a stand-off at Drumcree church on 7 July 1996 protests developed all over Northern Ireland. As had happened in Belfast so many times before, the tensions translated into people moving out of their houses in interface areas. This time Clifton Park Avenue in north Belfast probably suffered the worst.[71]

> I really didn't want to move out because it was my home, and I enjoyed living round there. I would have actually stayed, not in the flat, maybe in friends' or my parents' house maybe until it all blew over but I thought that if I didn't get my stuff out I'm going to come back and the flat's going to be burnt and I'm going to lose everything so I thought it was better to move out – it was very very nerve wracking.[72]

The housing on Clifton Park Avenue was vacated and later knocked down. The area adjacent, the Girdwood barracks, was, in 2011, subject to difficult negotiations over a development plan that might create more shared space.

The complexity of the territorial demarcations in the city was never more clearly exposed than by the feud between the UVF and UDA on the Shankill Road in 2000. On 19 August supporters of the leader of the UDA in the Shankill, Johnny Adair, popularly known as 'Mad Dog', unfurled the flag of the Loyalist Volunteer Forces (LVF) outside the Rex bar, a favourite venue for the UVF. The UVF, already involved in a feud with the LVF, treated this as an act of provocation. A fight ensued followed by a series of murders over the days that followed, with hundreds of families intimidated into leaving their houses by the opposing groups. The Shankill Road had a further 'interface' along Agnes Street between the UVF area at the top of the road and the UDA in the lower Shankill. And this feud itself seemed to lead to many more UVF and UDA paramilitary flags being placed on lampposts to demarcate areas controlled by the two groups.[73]

Another indicator of the continuing high level of tension that exists around interfaces was the dispute over the Holy Cross school in the Ardoyne area of north Belfast in 2001. This Catholic girls' primary school was sited at the top of the Ardoyne Road, close to the largely Protestant Glenbryn area. On 19 June 2001 confrontations arose when some men putting up UDA flags near the school were attacked. When the school year began in September, Loyalists picketed the school, protesting at what they saw as an incursion by

Children enjoying Féile an Phobail (the West Belfast Festival) on the Falls Road. The event, established in 1988, has evolved into a major international festival.

Photograph: West Belfast Festival © Chris Hill, Scenic Ireland.

Republicans. The pictures of terrified little girls being escorted by their parents while protected by a line of police officers remain among the most poignant images of the recent conflict in the city.

A Community Relations Council report in 2008 suggested there were 81 security and segregation barriers in the city.[74] A survey in 2006 counted 996 flags being displayed on the main roads of Belfast during July, with 929 still flying in September, significantly demarcating public space.[75] Together with murals, memorials and parades, Belfast at the start of the twenty-first century appears utterly divided. Segregation is not just sectarian but also based on social class. The parts of the city that are most divided are also the places of high economic deprivation. In 2006 13.3 per cent of the population of the city were claiming disability allowance, 7 per cent incapacity benefit, 15.7 per cent housing benefit, and 15.5 per cent income support.[76]

Yet there is another aspect to the story of Belfast's development through the peace process. Belfast city centre began to be used by a greater diversity of groups. On 30 November 1995 perhaps as many as 10,000 people gathered in front of City Hall to hear US President Bill Clinton give a speech and turn on the Christmas tree lights. But an apparently minor event on 8 August 1993 might be just as significant. Despite protests from Unionist councillors, a Republican Internment Commemoration parade, starting at Twinbrook in the south-west of the city, proceeded down the Falls Road and was allowed into the city centre where the president of Sinn Féin, Gerry Adams, gave a speech in front of the statue of Queen Victoria at City Hall.[77] This ended what had been throughout the twentieth century a de facto ban on Republican parades, indeed on nearly any event representing Irish nationalism, entering the city centre.

Crowds in Custom House Square enjoying St Patrick's Day 2008. The first St Patrick's Day parade in the centre of Belfast took place in 1998 and after considerable controversy it has developed into part of the civic calendar.

Photograph courtesy of Dominic Bryan.

On 17 March 1998 the first major St Patrick's Day parade took place in the centre of the city with feeder parades arriving from the nationalist areas of the Falls Road, New Lodge, Short Strand and the Markets. Máirtín Ó Muilleoir provided a vivid description:

> The tens of thousands who turned Belfast city centre black with green on Tuesday were doing more than scribbling footnotes, more than even contributing chapters to our history. They were shredding the pages of past wrongs, binning the Belfast of the pogroms and second-class citizenship, erasing the painful memory of too many Twelfths on the wrong side of the swagger stick [...] and proudly painting their own prologue: we've arrived.[78]

The next few years, however, were to see a profound change in the nature of the event. Through a complex process of negotiation, the St Patrick's Day festival was purged of overt political symbolism, and in exchange began to receive official support as a community event open to Catholics and Protestants alike. In 2006 the organization of St Patrick's Day events was taken over by the council with a carnival parade and a staged event in the newly re-opened Custom House Square.

A more long-standing event, the Lord Mayor's Show, likewise adapted to the new civic ethos. In May 1998, the day after the referendum on the Agreement, it was led by the first nationalist lord mayor of Belfast, Alban Maginness of the SDLP. Instead of the commercial floats that dominated the event from the 1950s to the 1970s the show was now styled as a 'carnival', with community groups and representatives from the increasingly diverse ethnic populations in the city taking part, making it a multicultural experience.[79] In 2002 it was led by

Belfast Pride 2011, with protestors. The annual Gay Pride event has faced protests from religious groups but has developed into a significant event in the centre of the city with floats attracting considerable sponsorship from local businesses.

Photograph courtesy of Neil Jarman.

Alex Maskey, the first Sinn Féin mayor of Belfast. In 2008 another Sinn Féin mayor, Tom Hartley, led the Lord Mayor's Carnival while a few months earlier his predecessor, the Ulster Unionist Jim Rodgers, had led the St Patrick's Day Carnival. Since 1991, meanwhile, a Gay Pride event has developed in the city. The early events attracted almost as many religious protestors as participants, but in the first decade of the new century Gay Pride grew into a well-sponsored, well-organized large carnival event.

Progress towards more equal access to civic space in central Belfast was facilitated by political developments. The 1998 Agreement, and the subsequent Northern Ireland Act, called for the creation of a more diverse cultural environment, and the same goal was recognized in the city council's Good Relations Strategy in 2003.[80] 'Our Vision in terms of this Good Relations Strategy is for a stable, tolerant, fair and pluralist society, where individuality is respected and diversity is celebrated, in an inclusive manner.' At the same time change was also promoted by economic developments. Unemployment in Belfast fell from 11 per cent in 1991 to 9.3 per cent in 1997 and to 6.5 per cent in 2009.[81] Between 2001 and 2007 manufacturing jobs in the city declined by 35 per cent, with the number of employees, 10,279, numbering less than those employed in hotels and restaurants, at 11,814, and those employed in wholesale and retail trades, at 26,557.[82] The days of the great independent Belfast stores of Robinson and Cleaver and Anderson and McAuley are long gone, but their place has been taken by a more diverse and cosmopolitan range of retail outlets. The Belfast cafe where you might once have bought a mug of tea or coffee is now a place where you can buy a cappuccino or latte. The opening in March 2008 of an impressive new shopping complex, Victoria Square, brought a

Runners in the Belfast marathon prepare to cross the peace wall at Lanark Way. The marathon, launched in 1982 and traversing both Protestant and Catholic areas, was an early success in terms of the creation of shared space. In what other event would the gates of interface walls be opened with cheering as people run through?

Reproduced with the kind permission of Press Eye Ltd.

The former shipyard and docks, now redesignated the Titanic Development Area. With a little help from James Cameron's 1997 blockbuster movie, Belfast has used the building of the ill-fated ship to market itself to tourists and big corporations.

Reproduced with the kind permission of Titanic Quarter Ltd.

further selection of the best-known multinational stores to central Belfast. The city's young people may remain defined by a Protestant or Catholic residential identification and educational upbringing, but both sides are equally keen on Hollister or Jack Wills labelled clothes.

These changes in the retail area of Belfast are matched by other developments in the built environment, set out in the *Belfast Area Urban Plan 2001* published in 1990.[83] In 1989 the Lagan Corporation was created to secure regeneration from the docks down to the gasworks off the Ormeau Road area. This saw a number of high-end residential developments, office space around the Clarendon Docks, the redevelopment of Custom House Square, the opening of the impressive Waterfront Hall in 1995 and the Odyssey entertainments complex in 2000. But there have also been attempts to utilize cultural dynamics.[84] Cultural 'quarters' have been identified. Cathedral Quarter near St Anne's Cathedral has become a hub for the arts and for nightlife while the Gaeltacht Quarter around the Cultúrlann building on the Falls Road provides a centre for Belfast's vibrant Irish-language community. There is also the Queen's Quarter around the university and the Titanic Quarter where ambitious redevelopment plans are remodelling the almost moribund Queen's Island area once dominated by the shipyard.

Titanic Town, Divided and Shared

In 2009 Belfast welcomed a record 7.6 million visitor trips. Residents of Belfast cannot help but see the irony that many tourists are attracted by two tragic stories that emanate from the city: tours of the murals and interface walls focus on echoes of a violent recent history, while a growing number of attractions commemorate the disastrous loss of the *Titanic*. The new Titanic visitors centre, opened in 2012 for the 100th anniversary of the ship's sinking, presents itself as a very distinctive part of the city landscape.

Thanks to the beginnings of a coming to terms with the violent ethno-national struggle that marked the last three decades of the twentieth century, Belfast's 'Troubles' have become marketable to the tourist and the political solutions arrived at have come to be seen as worthy of study by political scientists and students of conflict resolution all over the world. The people of Belfast have struggled with their own particular problems but they share much in common with other areas of conflict and, as such, have an interesting story to tell. Belfast has found a form of peace and started to share in some common identities but it remains ravaged by division and a violent past. However, you can now view the divisions from the top of a tour bus.

Belfast is a post-industrial city like many others in western Europe, struggling with the decline in a once-buoyant manufacturing sector. It is largely on the periphery of Europe, but in the globalized capitalist

The new Titanic Belfast exhibition centre, opened in 2012, is reflected in the memorial to those who died when the *Titanic* sank and the eight people who died building the ship. Poignantly, three of the workers' names are not even known.

Photograph courtesy of Dominic Bryan.

Tourists on a black cab tour to the west Belfast interface, 30 April 2011. It is one of the great ironies of Belfast in the twenty-first century that tourists now arrive in considerable numbers to view the interfaces and murals that are the products of a violent recent history.

Photograph courtesy of Dominic Bryan.

Following spread: The Laganside redevelopment area, 2012. In the foreground the area shown on John Adams's 1900 panorama (pp. 232–33) as a cattle market is now the centre of an ambitous scheme of urban regeneration, with the Waterfront concert hall (bottom left) and modern commercial buildings, while the east bank has become the site of upmarket apartments.

Photograph courtesy of Michael Walsh, www.pushfotografik.com

marketplace it can still benefit or suffer depending on the economic climate. On 15 September 2008 Lehman Brothers bank filed for bankruptcy in New York, sending the international money markets into turmoil and leading to major banks being bailed out in Britain and Ireland. American banking giant Citibank had moved into Belfast in 2004 and opened offices in the Titanic Quarter. On 23 November 2008 the bank required $25 billion from the US government to cover bad debts. On 4 November 2010 it announced that it would create 500 new jobs in the city.[85] As it was when it built ships, Belfast is a city intimately connected to the world around it. There is, as yet, no monument to the US taxpayer in the Titanic Quarter.

The American urban ecologist Scott Bollens has described Belfast as a polarized city where 'group identity is reinforced through ethno-nationalist expressions in the urban landscape'.[86] Yet this divided city has developed areas of sharing and has an increasingly diverse population. At the end of the first decade of the twenty-first century there is a civic culture that is intent on trying to imagine a Belfast for all its people, with parades becoming carnivals, and two traditions becoming embedded in multiculturalism. Nevertheless, the limited numbers of official forms of commemoration are overwhelmed by the multitude of plaques, memorials, murals, parades and flags that provide alternative, clashing narratives of the past. The dearth of official processes, and the cacophony of commemorative practices from the groups that did the fighting, leave most of the victims remembered only by the friends and family left behind. Belfast is a city that cannot forget its recent past but is also not quite sure how to remember it.

Notes

Chapter 1

1   *Report of the Commissioners Appointed to Enquire into the State of the Municipal Affairs of the Borough of Belfast* (BPP 1859 [2526] x.57), p. 190.

2   Below, p. 179.

3   J.A. Pilson, *History of the Rise and Progress of Belfast and Annals of the County Antrim* (Belfast: Hodgson, Greer, 1846), p. 13.

4   *BNL*, 15 October 1888.

5   Maurice James Craig, from *Some Way for Reason* (1948), in Patricia Craig (ed.), *The Belfast Anthology* (Belfast: Blackstaff, 1999), p. 197.

6   Benn, *Belfast* (1823), pp. 3–4.

7   Quoted in Raymond Gillespie, *Early Belfast: The Origins and Growth of an Ulster Town to 1750* (Belfast: Ulster Historical Foundation, 2007), p. xiv.

8   William McComb, *The Repealer Repulsed* (1841), ed. Patrick Maume (Dublin: UCD Press, 2003), pp. 193–94.

9   *BNL*, 7 June 1871.

10 Below, pp. 74–75.

11 Below, pp. 75, 101.

12 Below, p. 109.

13 Peter Clark, 'Introduction', in Peter Clark (ed.), *The Cambridge Urban History of Britain*, vol. II: *1540–1840* (Cambridge: Cambridge University Press, 2000), pp. 3–4. The precise figures are 8 per cent for England (and significantly less for Scotland and Wales) in 1500 and, for 1700, 30–33 per cent for England, 22–25 per cent for Scotland and 13–15 per cent for Wales.

14 Below, chapter 5, n. 18.

15 Hannah Barker, '"Smoke Cities": Northern Industrial Towns in Late Georgian England', *Urban History*, 31 (2004), pp. 175–90.

16 Below, p. 189.

17 W.S. Dowden (ed.), *The Journal of Thomas Moore*, vol. V: *1836–42* (Newark: University of Delaware Press, 1988), p. 2094 (16 December 1839).

18 Peter Borsay, 'The Rise and Fall of Polite Urban Space in England 1700–2000', in Andreas Fahrmeir and Elfie Rembold (eds), *Representation of British Cities: The Transformation of Urban Space 1700–2000* (Berlin: Philo, 2003), p. 34; Andy Croll, *Civilizing the Urban: Popular Culture and Public Space in Merthyr, c. 1870–1914* (Cardiff: University of Wales Press, 2000), p. 39.

19 W.A. Maguire, 'The Belfast Historic Society 1811–1835', in John Gray and Wesley McCann (eds), *An Uncommon Bookman* (Belfast: Linen Hall Library, 1996), pp. 100–18.

20 Theocritus, 'Remarks on the Belfast Historical Society', *Belfast Monthly Magazine*, xi (July 1813), p. 17. See also the earlier comments of Martha McTier in 1784: below, p. 166.

21 William Bruce and Henry Joy, *Belfast Politics* (1794) (Dublin: UCD Press, 2005), introduction by John Bew.

22 *BNL*, 6 October 1835.

23 Benn, *Belfast* (1823), pp. 65–66.

24 Benn, *Belfast* (1877), p. 666.

25 *BNL*, 2 June 1898.

26 *The Ireland of Today* (London: Times, 1913), p. 18.

27 H.D. Inglis, *A Journey Throughout Ireland during the Spring, Summer and Autumn of 1834* (London: Whittaker, 5th edn, 1838), p. 342.

28 Anna and Samuel Carter Hall, *Ireland: Its Scenery and Character* (London: Jeremiah How, 1843), III, 52–53.

29 Andy Bielenberg, *Ireland and the Industrial Revolution: The Impact of the Industrial Revolution on Irish Industry 1801–1922* (London: Routledge, 2009), p. 130.

30 *BNL*, 21 April 1862.

31 *Reports from the Consuls of the United States on the Commerce, Manufactures, Etc. of their Consular Districts for the Months of November and December 1882* (Washington, DC: Bureau of Foreign Commerce, 1883), p. 61.

32 A.G. Malcolm, 'The Influence of Factory Life on the Health of the Operative, as founded upon the Medical Statistics of this Class at Belfast', *Journal of the Statistical Society of London*, 19.2 (1856), pp. 170–81. See below, pp. 213–14.

33 R.M. Young, 'Recollections of a Nonagenarian 1906–8' (typescript in PRONI, D2930, pp. 86, 95); Inglis, *Journey through Ireland*, p. 343.

34 W.M. Thackeray, *The Irish Sketchbook 1842* (Dublin: Gill & Macmillan, 1990), pp. 304, 309.

35 *BNL*, 18 April 1851.

36 *BNL*, 6 August 1847, 5 March 1847, 1 October 1847.

37 *BNL*, 30 March 1847.

38 David Patterson, *The Provincialisms of Belfast and the Surrounding Districts Pointed out and Corrected* (Belfast: Alex Mayne, 1860).

39 *Northern Whig*, 28 July 1849.

40 S.J. Connolly, '"Like an Old Cathedral City": Belfast welcomes Queen Victoria, August 1849', *Urban History*, 39 (2012), pp. 571–89.

41 *First Report of the Commissioners for the Exhibition of 1851* (London: Spicer Brothers, 1852), pp. 102–03.

42 *BNL*, 27 August 1851.

43 *BNL*, 6 May 1853.

44 Leon Litvack, 'Exhibiting Ireland, 1851–3: Colonial Mimicry in London, Cork and Dublin', in Leon Litvack and Glenn Hooper (eds), *Ireland in the Nineteenth Century: Regional Identity* (Dublin: Four Courts Press, 2000), p. 20. Also A.C. Davies, 'The First Irish Industrial Exhibition: Cork 1852', *Irish Economic and Social History*, ii (1975), p. 46.

45 *BNL*, 7 July 1854.

46 *BNL*, 4 April 1867.

47 *BNL*, 15 January 1876.

48 *Freeman's Journal*, 29 March 1852.

49 John Sprule (ed.), *The Irish Industrial Exhibition of 1853: A Detailed Catalogue* (Dublin: James McGlashan, 1854), pp. 104, 117–18, 178–79, 186, 257, 432.

50 *Irish Industrial Exhibition, World's Fair, St. Louis, 1904. Handbook and catalogue of exhibits* (Dublin: publisher unknown, 1904), p. 8.

51 *BNL*, 6 February 1889.

52 *BNL*, 29 October 1877.

53 *M'Comb's Guide to Belfast, the Giant's Causeway and the Adjoining District* (Belfast: McComb, 1861), p. 1.

54 *Ulsterman*, 5 November 1856.

55 *BNL*, 10 February 1892.

56 *Report of Commissioners Appointed to Enquire into the Progress and Condition of the Queen's Colleges at Belfast, Cork and Galway* (BPP, 1857–8 (2413) xxi), p. 42, evidence of James M'Cosh.

57 Eileen Black, *Art in Belfast 1760–1888: Art Lovers or Philistines?* (Dublin: Irish Academic Press, 2006).

58 *Ireland of Today*, p. 165. For the place of music in middle-class culture, see Simon Gunn, *The Public Culture of the Victorian Middle Class: Ritual and Authority in the English Industrial City 1840–1914* (Manchester: Manchester University Press, 2000), chap. 6.

59 *BNL*, 5 March 1862.

60 Minutes of the town hall and improvement committee, 20 April 1874 (PRONI, LA/7/2EA/11).

61 *BNL*, 18 February 1874.

62 *BNL*, 3 April 1876.

63 *Irish News*, 2 April 1894.

64 Gillian McIntosh, *Belfast City Hall, One Hundred Years* (Belfast: Blackstaff Press, 2006), pp. 48–49.

65 Joseph McBrinn, 'Mural Painting in Ireland 1855–1959', unpublished PhD thesis, 3 vols, National College of Design, Dublin, 2007. Dr McIntosh is grateful to Dr McBrinn for generously providing her with access to his unpublished work.

66 *Northern Whig*, 1 May 1909.

67 Gillian McIntosh '"Symbolising the Civic Ideal": The Civic Portraits in Belfast Town Hall', *Urban History*, 35 (2008), pp. 363–81.

68 John Beckett, *City Status in the British Isles 1830–2002* (London: Ashgate, 2005), pp. 43–52.

69 Frank Frankfort Moore, *In Belfast by the Sea*, ed. Patrick Maume (Dublin: UCD Press, 2007), p. 86.

70 Thomas Gaffikin, *Belfast Fifty Years Ago* (Belfast: News Letter, 2nd edn, 1885), p. 21.

71 *Ireland of Today*, p. 18.

72 *BNL*, 30 September 1912.

73 *Irish News*, 30 September 1912

74 See Nuala Johnston, *Ireland, the Great War and the Geography of Remembrance* (Cambridge: Cambridge University Press, 2003).

75 *Irish Times*, 23 June 1921.

76 *BNL*, 23 June 1921.

77 *Irish News*, 23 June 1921.

78 Lady Craig's diary, 22 June 1921 (PRONI, D/1415/B/38/1–162). See also Gillian McIntosh, 'The Royal Visit to Belfast, June 1921', in D.G. Boyce and Alan O'Day (eds), *The Ulster Crisis 1885–1921* (London: Palgrave Macmillan, 2005).

79 *Irish Times*, 16 November 1932.

80 *Belfast Weekly Telegraph*, 26 November 1932.

81 Louis MacNeice, 'Northern Ireland and her People', in Alan Heuser (ed.), *Selected Prose of Louis MacNeice* (Oxford: Clarendon Press, 1990), pp. 145–46.

82 Denis Smyth, *Sailortown. The Story of a Dockside Community* (Belfast: North Belfast History Workshop, 1990), p. 22.

83 For a survey of urban government, see Jonathan Bardon, 'Governing the City', in F.W. Boal and S.A. Royle (eds), *Enduring City: Belfast in the Twentieth Century* (Belfast: Blackstaff Press, 2006), pp. 124–40. For the housing scandal, see below, pp. 281–82.

84 Diary of Miss Emma Duffin, VAD commandant at Stranmillis General Hospital, 1939–1967 (PRONI, D2109/18/9).

85 Leanne McCormack, '"Filthy Little Girls": Controlling Women in Public Spaces in Northern Ireland during the Second World War', in Gillian McIntosh and Diane Urquhart (eds), *Irish Women at War: The Twentieth Century* (Dublin: Irish Academic Press, 2011).

86 E.R.R. Green, *The Lagan Valley 1800–50: A Local History of the Industrial Revolution* (London: Faber, 1949), p. 14.

87 Patricia Craig, *Asking for Trouble. The Story of an Escapade with Disproportionate Consequences* (Belfast: Blackstaff Press, 2007), pp. 70–71.

88 *Irish News and Belfast Morning News*, 24 April 1924; *Belfast Telegraph*, 8 March 1924, 3 May 1938.

89 *Ulster* (1935). See also Sean McDougall, 'The Projection of Northern Ireland to Great Britain and Abroad, 1921–39', in Peter Catterall and Sean McDougall, *The Northern Ireland Question in British Politics* (London: Palgrave Macmillan, 1996).

90 Minutes of CEMA (Northern Ireland) Art Committee, 12 September 1950 (PRONI, COM/4/A/8).

91 'Artist's 12-Hour Day: John Luke's City Hall Mural', *Belfast Newsletter*, 13 August 1951.

92 John Hewitt, *John Luke, 1906–1975* (Belfast: Arts Council of Northern Ireland, 1978), p. 82.

93 Hewitt, *John Luke*, p. 104; Theo Snoddy, *Dictionary of Irish Artists: Twentieth Century* (Dublin: Merlin, 2002), p. 353. When the building was demolished in 2002 the mural (estimated to be worth £250,000 in 2007) remained on site for another year before being removed. Now privately owned by the salvage company, it is reported to be in storage in the Harbour Estate, Belfast; www.thegreatweeazoo.blogspot.co.uk, 'John Luke mural falls into private hands', 1 April 2007; statement on the Luke mural by Sir Reg Empey, 30 November 2007 www.niassembly.gov.uk, ref. AQW 1923/08.

94 Douglas Carson, 'A Kist o' Whistles', *Fortnight* (autumn 1990), p. 4.

95 W.R. Rodgers, *The Return Room* (Belfast: Blackstaff Press, 2010) p. 61.

96 Eamonn Hughes, 'Fiction', in Mark Carruthers and Stephen Douds (eds), *Stepping Stones, the Arts in Ulster, 1971–2001* (Belfast: Blackstaff Press, 2001), pp. 100–01.

97 See below, p. 330.

98 See Gillian McIntosh, 'Stormont's Ill-timed Jubilee: The Ulster '71 Exhibition', *New Hibernia Review*, 11 (2007), pp. 17–39.

99 W.A. Maguire, *Belfast: A History* (Lancaster: Carnegie Publishing, 2nd edn, 2009), p. 184.

100 Maguire, *Belfast*, p. 189.

101 *BNL*, 25 April 1913.

102 *Irish News*, 25 April 1913.

103 *Irish News*, 22 April 1913.

104 *BNL*, 28 April 1913.

105 Undated speech (PRONI, LA7/3B/38).

106 Lord mayor's foreword to *City of Belfast 1613–1963. Charter Celebrations. Programme of Events* (May 1963) (PRONI, LA/7/3A/193).

107 Lord mayor's foreword (PRONI, LA/7/3A/193).

108 *Irish News*, 6 May 1963.

109 Meeting of the steering committee for the 350th commemoration, 12 November 1962 (PRONI, LA7/3B/38).

110 *Irish News*, 6 May 1963.

111 John A. Young, 'Short History of Belfast and its Charters', in *City of Belfast 1613–1963*, p. 8 (PRONI, LA/7/3A/193).

1 R. Ó Baoill, *Hidden History Below Our Feet: The Archaeological Story of Belfast* (Belfast: Tandem, 2011). More detailed discussion of the archaeological periods outlined in this chapter can be found in this book on pp. 16–49 (prehistory), 50–65 (Early Christian), 66–95 (medieval) and 96–165 (post-medieval). See also the special number of *UJA*, 65 (2006).

2 P. Woodman, *Excavations at Mount Sandel 1973–77. Northern Ireland Archaeological Monographs No. 2* (Belfast: HMSO, 1984).

3 For the most recent account, see B. Hartwell, 'Prehistoric Ritual at Ballynahatty, County Down', in E. Murray and P. Logue (eds), *Battles, Boats & Bones: Archaeological Discoveries in Northern Ireland 1987–2008* (Belfast: Stationery Office, 2010), pp. 23–28.

4 I.J. Herring, 'The Forecourt, Hanging Thorn Cairn, McIlwhan's Hill, Ballyutoag, Ligoniel', *Proceedings of the Belfast Natural History and Philosophical Society*, 1 (1938), pp. 43–49.

5 S. Andrews and O. Davies, 'Prehistoric Finds at Tyrone House, Malone Road, Belfast', *UJA*, 3 (1940), pp. 152–54.

6 P. Macdonald, N. Carver and M. Yates, 'Excavations at McIlwhans Hill, Balltutoag, County Antrim', *UJA*, 62 (2005), pp. 43–61.

7 J.P. Mallory, 'The Long Stone, Ballybeen, Dundonald, County Down, County Antrim', *UJA*, 47 (1984), pp. 1–4.

8 For a fuller discussion on the annalistic dating and place-name evidence see below, chapter 3.

9 E.E. Evans, 'Rath and Souterrain at Shaneen Park, Belfast, Townland of Ballyaghagan, Co. Antrim', *UJA*, 13 (1950), pp. 6–27; B. Proudfoot, 'Further Excavations at Shaneen Park, Belfast, Ballyaghagan, Co. Antrim', *UJA*, 14 (1951), pp. 18–38.

10 B.B. Williams, 'Excavations at Ballyutoag, County Antrim', *UJA*, 47 (1984), pp. 37–49.

11 J. Ó Néill, 'A Medieval Ring Brooch and Other Nineteenth-Century Discoveries at High Street, Belfast', *UJA*, 65 (2006), p. 64.

12 P. Macdonald, 'Medieval Belfast Considered', *UJA*, 65 (2006), pp. 29–48.

13 T.E. McNeill, 'Ulster Mottes: A Checklist', *UJA*, 38 (1975), pp. 49–59.

14 E.M. Jope and W.A. Seaby, 'A Square Earthwork in North Belfast: The Site of the Ekenhead Early 14th Century Coin-Hoard', *UJA*, 22 (1959), pp. 111–14.

15 Benn, *Belfast* (1877), pp. 86–87.

16 N.F. Brannon, 'Belfast', in A. Hamlin and C. Lynn (eds), *Pieces of the Past: Archaeological Excavations by the Department of the Environment for Northern Ireland 1970–1986* (Belfast: HMSO, 1988), p. 80.

17 R. Ó Baoill, 'Digging up the Past', *Cathedral Quarter*, 1 (2003), p. 8; R. Ó Baoill, 'The Archaeology of Post-Medieval Carrickfergus and Belfast, 1550–1750', in A. Horning, R. Ó Baoill, C.J. Donnelly and P. Logue (eds), *The Post-Medieval Archaeology of Ireland 1550–1850* (Bray: Wordwell, 2007); R. Ó Baoill, 'The Urban Archaeology of Belfast: A Review of the Evidence', *UJA*, 65 (2006), pp. 8–19; R. Ó Baoill and P. Logue, 'Excavations at Gordon Street and Waring Street, Belfast', *UJA*, 64 (2005), pp. 106–39.

18 R. Ó Baoill, *Carrickfergus. The Story of the Castle and Walled Town* (Belfast: Stationery Office, 2008).

19 Benn, *Belfast* (1823), pp. 68–70; Benn, *Belfast* (1877), pp. 276–80.

20 C. McSparron, 'Excavations at Church Street, Belfast', *UJA*, 63 (2004), pp. 114–18.

21 Ó Baoill, *Hidden History*, pp. 132–35; P. Francis, *Irish Delftware: An Illustrated History* (London: Jonathan Horne, 2000), pp. 11–33.

22 M. Patton, *Central Belfast: A Historical Gazetteer* (Belfast: Ulster Architectural Heritage Society, 1993), pp. 330–31; P. Larmour, *Belfast: An Illustrated Architectural Guide* (Belfast: Ulster Architectural Heritage Society, 1987), p. 14.

23 Patton, *Central Belfast*, pp. 241–42; Larmour, *Belfast*, pp. xi, 1; R.W.M. Strain, *Belfast and its Charitable Society: A Story of Urban Development* (London: Oxford University Press, 1961).

24 P. Francis, *A Pottery by the Lagan: Irish Creamware from the Downshire Pottery, Belfast, 1787–c.1806* (Belfast: Institute of Irish Studies, 2001).

Chapter 2

25 S. Gilmore, 'The Building of Belfast: Archaeological Investigations at Annadale and Castle Espie', in Murray and Logue (eds), *Battles, Boats & Bones*, pp. 73–79.

26 M. Keery, 'Archaeological Excavations at the Ballymacarrett Glassworks, Belfast', *East Belfast Historical Society Journal*, 4.4 (2010), pp. 46–57; M. Keery, 'The Ballymacarett Glasshouses in East Belfast', in Murray and Logue (eds), *Battles, Boats & Bones*, pp. 68–73.

27 N.F. Brannon, 'Belfast, Winetavern Street', *Post-Medieval Archaeology*, 25 (1991), pp. 161–62.

28 C. Dunlop, '"An Immense Mass of Human Wretchedness and Vice": Excavating the Slums of Belfast', *Current Archaeology*, 229 (2009), pp. 32–39.

Chapter 3

1 Benn, *Belfast* (1877), p. 1.

2 P. Macdonald, 'Medieval Belfast Considered', *UJA*, 65 (2006), p. 29.

3 Raymond Gillespie, *Early Belfast: The Origins and Growth of an Ulster Town to 1750* (Belfast: Ulster Historical Foundation, 2007), pp. 37–38.

4 See W. Gray, 'Old Belfast: The Origin and Progress of the City', *Proceedings of the Belfast Natural History and Philosophical Society* (1894–95), p. 51.

5 Audrey Horning, *Ireland in the Virginian Sea: Colonialism in the British Atlantic World* (Chapel Hill, NC: University of North Carolina Press, forthcoming).

6 For example, Macdonald, 'Medieval Belfast Considered'; Gillespie, *Early Belfast*, pp. 24–52; Ruairi Ó Baoill, *Hidden History Below Our Feet: The Archaeological Story of Belfast* (Belfast: Tandem, 2011), pp. 66–95.

7 S. MacAirt and G. MacNiocaill (eds), *The Annals of Ulster (to A.D. 1131)* (Dublin: Dublin Institute for Advanced Studies, 1983), pp. 138–39.

8 K. Simms, *Medieval Gaelic Sources* (Dublin: Four Courts Press, 2009), p. 22.

9 The same notice of the battle at the Ford (*Fearsat*) is, possibly independently, also recorded in the so-called *Annals of Tigernach* as taking place in AD 665 (W. Stokes, 'The Annals of Tigernach. Third fragment. A.D. 489–766', *Revue Celtique*, 17 [1896], p. 200). The reference to the battle taking place in AD 668 within the early seventeenth-century *Annals of the Four Masters* (John O'Donovan [ed.], *Annals of the Kingdom of Ireland, by the Four Masters, from the Earliest Period to the Year 1616* [Dublin: Hodges, Smith & Co., 1856], I, 278–79) is probably derived from that in the *Annals of Ulster* (MacAirt and MacNiocaill, *Annals of Ulster*, pp. 138–39). The slight variations in the recorded date of the battle between the three annals is probably a consequence of inaccuracies introduced when their compilers converted the liturgical dating systems used in their source material to calendrical dates: see Simms, *Medieval Gaelic Sources*, p. 35.

10 F.J. Byrne, *Irish Kings and High-Kings* (London: Batsford, 1973), p. 107; J.P. Mallory and T. McNeill, *The Archaeology of Ulster: From Colonization to Plantation* (Belfast: Institute of Irish Studies, 1991), p. 177.

11 A.J. Hughes, 'Deirdre Flanagan's "Belfast and the Place-Names Therein", in Translation', *Ulster Folklife*, 38 (1992), pp. 80, 84; P. McKay, 'Belfast Place-Names and the Irish Language', in F. de Brún (ed.), *Belfast and the Irish Language* (Dublin: Four Courts Press, 2006), pp. 15–16.

12 O'Donovan (ed.), *Annals of the Four Masters*, IV, 1100–01.

13 This observation was first made in 1643 by Father Edmund MacCana; see W. Reeves, 'Irish Itinerary of Father Edmund MacCana, Translated from the Original Latin and Illustrated by Notes', *UJA*, 2 (1854), p. 57.

14 Archaeological evidence relating to the precise location of the northern bank of the lower reaches of the Blackstaff is discussed by P. Macdonald, 'Excavations within the Woolworth's and Burton Building, High Street, Belfast', *UJA*, 65 (2006), pp. 58–59.

15 See E. Getty, 'The True Position of the Ford of Belfast', *UJA*, 3 (1855), p. 311.

16 T.K. Lowry, 'The True Position of the Ford of Belfast', *UJA*, 4 (1856), p. 260.

17 R. Gillespie and S.A. Royle, *Irish Historic Towns Atlas – No. 12: Belfast to 1840* (Dublin: Royal Irish Academy, 2003), map 6.

18 Reproduced by Benn, *Belfast* (1877), opposite p. 484.

19 R.H. Bryant, *Physical Geography* (London: Heinemann, 2nd edn, 1879), p. 46.

20 S.A. Stevenson, personal communication.

21 McKay, 'Place-Names', pp. 16, 22, 27–28.

22 T. McNeill, *Anglo-Norman Ulster. The History and Archaeology of an Irish Barony, 1177–1400* (Edinburgh: John Donald, 1980), pp. 3–6.

23 Mallory and McNeill, *Archaeology of Ulster*, pp. 249–51.

24 T. McErlean, 'Later Medieval Period, 1177–1599', in T. McErlean, R. McConkey and W. Forsythe, *Strangford Lough. An Archaeological Survey of the Maritime Cultural Landscape* (Belfast: Blackstaff Press and Environment and Heritage Service, 2002), p. 91.

25 The 1262 reference was contained within the pipe roll for 46 Henry III.

26 S.J. Connolly, *Contested Island: Ireland 1460–1630* (Oxford: Oxford University Press, 2007), pp. 19–22.

27 Royal Irish Academy, MSS No.12D10. The section relating to Belfast was also translated in the nineteenth century. See T.K. Lowry (ed.), *The Hamilton Manuscripts: Containing some Account of the Settlement of the Territories of the Upper Clandeboye, Great Ardes and Dufferin, in the County of Down, by Sir James Hamilton, Knight* (Belfast: Archer & Sons, 1867), p. 51, fn. b.

28 J. O'Keeffe, 'What Lies Beneath? Medieval Components in Belfast's Urban Development', *UJA*, 65 (2006), p. 23.

29 C.J. Donnelly, personal communication.

30 McNeill, *Anglo-Norman Ulster*, pp. 68–69.

31 T. McNeill, *Castles in Ireland* (London: Routledge, 1997), p. 62.

32 R.E. Glasscock, 'Moated Sites and Deserted Boroughs and Villages: Two Neglected Aspects of Anglo-Norman Settlement in Ireland', in E. Stephens and R.E. Glasscock (eds), *Irish Geographical Studies in Honour of E. Estyn Evans* (Belfast: Department of Geography, Queen's University, 1970), p. 167.

33 T. Barry, 'The Defensive Nature of Irish Moated Sites', in J.R. Kenyon and K. O'Conor (eds), *The Medieval Castle in Ireland and Wales. Essays in Honour of Jeremy Knight* (Dublin: Four Courts Press, 2003), pp. 182–93.

34 E.M. Jope and W.A. Seaby, 'A Square Earthwork in North Belfast: The Site of the Ekenhead Early 14th Century Coin Hoard', *UJA*, 22 (1959), pp. 112–15. See also Macdonald, 'Medieval Belfast Considered', p. 32.

35 PRONI T/811/3, reproduced by Benn, *Belfast* (1877), p. 86.

36 McNeill, *Anglo-Norman Ulster*, p. 91, en. 131; Hughes, 'Deirdre Flanagan's "Belfast"', p. 81.

37 British Library, Add. MSS 6041. Both a copy of the relevant section of the calendar (PRONI T456/4; see also PRONI MIC174/1) and a questionable translation (PRONI T459/1) are held by the Public Record Office of Northern Ireland.

38 National Archives, London, C.Edw. III.File36.

39 J.E.E.S. Sharp, *Calendar of Inquisitions Post Mortem and other Analogous Documents Preserved in the Public Record Office. Vol. VII. Edward III* (London: HMSO, 1909), p. 374, no. 537; G.H. Orpen, 'The Earldom of Ulster. Part II – Inquisitions Touching Carrickfergus and Antrim', *Journal of the Royal Society of Antiquaries of Ireland* (ser. 6), 3 (1913), p. 139.

40 W. Reeves, *Ecclesiastical Antiquities of Down, Connor, and Dromore, Consisting of a Taxation of those Dioceses, Compiled in the Year MCCCVI.; with Notes and Illustrations* (Dublin: Hodges and Smith, 1847), p. 7, fn. q; Orpen, 'Earldom of Ulster, II', p. 139.

41 R. Butler (ed.), *The Annals of Ireland by Friar John Clyn, of the Convent of Friars Minors, Kilkenny; and Thady Dowling, Chancellor of Leighlin. Together with the Annals of Ross* (Dublin: Irish Archaeological Society, 1849), p. 24; B. Williams (ed.), *The Annals of Ireland by Friar John Clyn* (Dublin: Four Courts Press, 2007), pp. 210–11.

42 Orpen, 'Earldom of Ulster, II', p. 138; G.H. Orpen, 'The Earldom of Ulster, Part III – Inquisitions touching Down and Newtownards', *Journal of the Royal Society of Antiquaries of Ireland* (ser. 6), 4 (1914), pp. 60–61; G.H. Orpen, 'The Earldom of Ulster, Part IV, Inquisitions touching Coleraine and Military Tenures', *Journal of the Royal Society of Antiquaries of Ireland* (ser. 6), 5 (1915), p. 127.

43 T. McErlean, 'The Irish Townland System of Landscape Organisation', in T. Reeves-Smyth and F. Hamond (eds), *Landscape Archaeology in Ireland* (Oxford: British Archaeological Reports, 1983), p. 322.

44 Orpen, 'Earldom of Ulster, II', p. 139.

45 Orpen, 'Earldom of Ulster, II', p. 139.

46 McNeill, *Anglo-Norman Ulster*, pp. 90–91.

47 McNeill, *Anglo-Norman Ulster*, p. 91.

48 Glasscock, 'Moated Sites', pp. 171–73; McNeill, *Anglo-Norman Ulster*, p. 89.

49 Orpen, 'Earldom of Ulster, II', p. 139.

50 J. Vince, *Discovering Watermills* (Aylesbury: Shire Publications, 3rd edn, 1980), p. 3.

51 Gillespie and Royle, *Atlas*, maps 4 and 5.

52 H.S. Sweetman, *Calendar of Documents Relating to Ireland Preserved in Her Majesty's Public Record Office, London. 1171–1251* (London: Longman & Co., 1875), pp. 62–65, nos. 404–07.

53 O. Davies and D.B. Quinn, 'The Irish Pipe Roll of 14 John, 1211–1212', *UJA*, 4 (1941), supplement, pp. 53–65.

54 McNeill, *Anglo-Norman Ulster*, pp. 123–24.

55 McNeill, *Anglo-Norman Ulster*, p. 118.

56 Gillespie, *Early Belfast*, p. 37; for a detailed discussion of the decline of the earldom, see McNeill, *Anglo-Norman Ulster*, pp. 118–28.

57 K.W. Nicholls, *Gaelic and Gaelicized Ireland in the Middle Ages* (Dublin: Lilliput Press, 2nd edn, 2003), p. 159.

58 O'Donovan (ed.), *Annals of Ulster*, IV, 1100–01; see also B. MacCarthy (ed.), *Annals of Ulster, otherwise, Annals of Senat; a Chronicle of Irish Affairs A.D. 431–1131 : 1155–1541. Vol. III A.D. 1379–1541* (Dublin: HMSO, 1895), pp. 258–59.

59 MacCarthy (ed.), *Annals*, pp. 306–07.

60 O'Donovan (ed.), *Annals of Ulster*, IV, 1168–69; MacCarthy (ed.), *Annals*, pp. 340–41.

61 O'Donovan (ed.), *Annals of Ulster*, V, 1270–71.

62 A.M. Freeman, *Annála Connacht. The Annals of Connacht (A.D. 1224–1544)* (Dublin: Dublin Institute for Advanced Studies, 1944), pp. 618–19; see also O'Donovan (ed.), *Annals of Ulster*, V, 1318–19; MacCarthy (ed.), *Annals*, pp. 498–99.

63 Freeman, *Annála Connacht*, pp. 700–01; see also O'Donovan (ed.), *Annals of Ulster*, V, 1440–41.

64 *State Papers Published Under the Authority of His Majesty's Commission, Volume I: King Henry the Eighth. Part III, Correspondence Between the Governments of England and Ireland. 1515–1538* (London: His Majesty's State Paper Office, 1834), p. 100, no. XXXIV.

65 PRONI T/811/3, reproduced by Benn, *Belfast* (1877), p. 86.

66 Gillespie and Royle, *Atlas*, maps 4–6; see also Macdonald, 'Medieval Belfast Considered', figs. 1–2. See pp. 105, 126.

67 H.C. Hamilton, *Calendar of the State Papers Relating to Ireland, of the Reigns of Henry VIII., Edward VI, Mary and Elizabeth, 1509–1573, Preserved in the State Paper Department of Her Majesty's Public Record Office* (London: Longman, Green, Longman, & Roberts, 1860), p. 391, no. 5.

68 Benn, *Belfast* (1877), pp. 14–15.

69 J.S. Brewer and W. Bullen (eds), *Calendar of the Carew Manuscripts, Preserved in the Archiepiscopal Library at Lambeth, 1515–1574* (London: Longmans, Green, Reader & Dyer, 1867), p. 259, no. 207; Benn, *Belfast* (1877), p. 13, n. 1.

70 Nicholas Canny, *Making Ireland British 1580–1650* (Oxford: Oxford University Press, 2001), p. 79; Hiram Morgan, 'The Colonial Venture of Sir Thomas Smith in Ulster, 1571–1575', *Historical Journal*, 28 (1985), pp. 261–78.

71 Connolly, *Contested Island*, pp. 105–09.

72 This information is derived from an unspecified seventeenth-century manuscript which was recorded as being in private possession during the nineteenth century. See T.E. Winnington, 'Sir James Croft', *Notes and Queries* (fourth ser.), 1 (1868), p. 457.

73 See Hamilton, *Calendar 1509–73*, p. 119, no. 65.I.

74 O'Donovan (ed.), *Annals of the Four Masters*, V, 1524–25.

75 Brewer and Bullen, *Carew Mss*, p. 234, no. 198.

76 G. A. Hayes-McCoy, 'Conciliation, Coercion, and the Protestant Reformation, 1547–71', in T.W. Moody, F.X. Martin and F.J. Byrne (eds), *A New History of Ireland. III. Early Modern Ireland 1534–1691* (Oxford: Clarendon Press, 1976), p. 72.

77 Brewer and Bullen, *Carew Mss*, p. 243, no. 200.

78 Brewer and Bullen, *Carew Mss*, p. 306, no. 228.II.

79 B. Cunningham, *Calendar of State Papers. Ireland. Tudor Period, 1566–1567* (Dublin: Irish Manuscripts Commission, 2009), p. 46, no. 91; National Archives London, SP 63/17, no. 20.

80 Cunningham, *Calendar 1566–1567*, pp. 126–27, no. 277; National Archives London, SP63/19, no. 36.

81 Cunningham, *Calendar 1566–1567*, p. 257, no. 602; National Archives, London, SP 63/22, no. 69.

82 'Sir Henry Sidney's Memoir of his Government of Ireland', *UJA*, 3 (1855), p. 93.

83 B. Cunningham, *Calendar of State Papers. Ireland. Tudor Period, 1568–1571* (Dublin: Irish Manuscripts Commission, 2010), pp. 17, 22, nos. 32.1 and 39; National Archives, London SP63/23, no. 32(i); SP63/23, no. 39.

84 McErlean, 'Later Medieval Period', p. 97.

85 Cunningham, *Calendar 1568–71*, p. 22, no. 39.

86 D. Morton, 'Tuath-Divisions in the Baronies of Belfast and Massereene', *Bulletin of the Ulster Place-Name Soc.*, 4.2 (1956), p. 39; Gillespie, *Early Belfast*, pp. 37–38.

87 Cunningham, *Calendar 1568–71*, p. 40, no. 91.

88 Cunningham, *Calendar 1568–71*, pp. 60–61, no. 125.2.

89 PRONI , T/1493/41; R. Dunlop, 'Sixteenth-Century Maps of Ireland', *English Historical Review*, 20 (1905), p. 327, no. 89.

90 Cunningham, *Calendar 1568–71*, pp. 95–96, no. 226; National Archives, London, SP63/26, no. 5.

91 M. O'Dowd, *Calendar of State Papers. Ireland. Tudor Period, 1571–1575* (London: Public Record Office, 2000), pp. 48–49, no. 72.

92 Hamilton, *Calendar 1509–73*, p. 467, no. 32.i; R.M. Young (ed.), *Historical Notices of Old Belfast and its Vicinity* (Belfast: Marcus Ward & Co., 1896), pp. 24–26.

93 A.J. Butler and S.C. Lomas, *Calendar of State Papers, Foreign Series, of the Reign of Elizabeth, January–June, 1583 and Addenda. Preserved in the Public Record Office* (London: HMSO, 1913), p. 468, no. 456.

94 Brewer and Bullen, *Carew Mss*, p. 448, no. 305; see also Hamilton, *Calendar 1509–73*, p. 526, no. 66.

95 O'Dowd, *Calendar*, p. 402, no. 702.

96 A usage still common in Ulster, but now anachronistic in England. See *Oxford English Dictionary*.

97 O'Dowd, *Calendar*, p. 402, no. 702.

98 Macdonald, 'Medieval Belfast Considered', p. 38, fig. 1.

99 Benn, *Belfast* (1877), p. 48.

100 See O'Dowd, *Calendar*, pp. 572–79, nos. 960, 966–70.

101 O'Dowd, *Calendar*, p. 402, no. 702.

102 H.C. Hamilton, *Calendar of the State Papers Relating to Ireland, of the Reign of Elizabeth, 1574–1585. Preserved in Her Majesty's Public Record Office* (London: Longmans, Green, Reader & Dyer, 1867), p. 32, no. 7; Brewer and Bullen, *Carew Mss*, p. 475, no. 329.

103 O'Dowd, *Calendar*, p. 688, no. 1162.3.

104 Recounted in detail by Benn, *Belfast* (1877), pp. 51–54.

105 O'Dowd, *Calendar*, pp. 831, 845, nos. 1423, 1452.

106 O'Dowd, *Calendar*, p. 743, no. 1253.vii.

107 Hamilton, *Calendar 1574–85*, p. 585, no. 7.

108 H.C. Hamilton, *Calendar of the State Papers Relating to Ireland, of the Reign of Elizabeth, 1592, October–1596, June. Preserved in the Public Record Office* (London: HMSO, 1890), p. 228, no. 92.iv-v; E.G. Atkinson, *Calendar of State Papers Relating to Ireland, of the Reign of Elizabeth. 1599, April–1600, February. Preserved in the Public Record Office* (London: HMSO, 1899), pp. 46, 268, nos. 37.vii and 109.

109 Historical Manuscripts Commission, *Calendar of the Manuscripts of the Most Hon. The Marquis of Salisbury, K.G., &c. &c. &c. Preserved at Hatfield House, Hertfordshire. Part VII* (London: HMSO, 1899), p. 313.

110 The City of Belfast School of Music is located on the site of the former Castle High School.

111 E.M. Jope, 'Moyry, Charlemont, Castleraw, and Richhill: Fortification to Architecture in the North of Ireland', *UJA*, 23 (1960), p. 116, fig. 16; Ó Baoill, *Hidden History*, p. 92.

112 Benn, *Belfast* (1877), p. 68; Atkinson, *Calendar*, p. 326, no. 126.

113 Benn, *Belfast* (1877), p. 69; Atkinson, *Calendar*, p. 396, no. 125; W. Pinkerton, 'The "Overthrow" of Sir John Chichester at Carrickfergus, in 1597', *UJA*, 5 (1857), p. 190.

114 C. Falls, *The Birth of Ulster* (London: Methuen, 1936), p. 62; J. McCavitt, *Sir Arthur Chichester. Lord Deputy of Ireland 1605–16* (Belfast: Institute of Irish Studies, Queen's University, 1998), p. 2.

115 McCavitt, *Chichester*, pp. 222–23.

116 See R. Ó Baoill, *Carrickfergus. The Story of the Castle & Walled Town* (Belfast: Northern Ireland Environment Agency, 2008), pp. 51–53.

117 McCavitt, *Chichester*, p. 8.

118 McCavitt, *Chichester*, pp. 16–17.

119 M.S. Giuseppi, *Calendar of the Manuscripts of the Most Hon. The Marquis of Salisbury, K.G., &c. &c. &c. Preserved at Hatfield House, Hertfordshire. Part XV* (London: Historical Manuscripts Commission, 1930), p. 196.

120 Gillespie and Royle, *Atlas*, p. 1.

121 Giuseppi, *Calendar of Salisbury MSS*, pp. 196–97.

122 *Inquisitionum in Officio Rotulorum Cancellariæ Hiberniæ Asservatarum, Repertorium* (Dublin: Commissioners of the Public Records of Ireland, 1826–29), Antrim 7-Jac.I; Benn, *Belfast* (1877), pp. 746–47.

123 G. Hatchell, *Calendar of Patent Rolls of James I* (Dublin: HMSO, 1848), pp. 48–49, no. LXXIX.33.

124 Sadly, no record survives of Lord Cecil's reaction on hearing of the birth.

125 Reeves, *Ecclesiastical Antiquities*, pp. 6–7.

126 C. Bourke, 'Irish Croziers of the Eighth and Ninth Centuries', in M. Ryan (ed.), *Ireland and Insular Art A.D. 500–1200* (Dublin: Royal Irish Academy, 1987), pp. 166, 168–70, pl. II.b,d; R. Ó Floinn, 'Crozier Drop and Ferrule', in S. Youngs (ed.), *'The Work of Angels'. Masterpieces of Celtic Metalwork, 6th–9th Centuries AD* (London: British Museum Publications, 1989), pp. 152–69, no. 148.

127 The excavation was carried out by staff employed by the Parks and Cemeteries Department of the Belfast Corporation under the supervision of Dudley Waterman while work was being undertaken at the burial ground to convert it into a garden of rest. Regrettably, the excavation was not published and no plans or other records relating to the investigation survive. From correspondence preserved in the files of the Parks and Cemeteries Department (PRONI LA/7/11/BB/5) it is possible to ascertain that the excavation took place into a low mound located close to the main entrance gate to the cemetery. It was hoped that the mound represented the remains of the medieval church, but excavation demonstrated that it was formed by a pile of stones that had been thrown up over a communal grave. The excavators considered that this mass grave dated to the cholera outbreak of the 1840s and the excavation was discontinued, but not before an unrecorded amount of ferrous slag and Souterrain Ware pottery was recovered (Northern Ireland Sites and Monuments Record, SM7 File ANT 060:040). Souterrain Ware is a locally produced type of coarse ware pottery whose use dates from the seventh or eighth to the late twelfth century. Although residually deposited, its presence suggests that the Early Christian focus of activity at Shankill was close to the main entrance of the graveyard. While not datable, the ferrous slag suggests that smithing or smelting activity was once undertaken within the vicinity – such activities would not be unexpected at an Early Christian monastic centre.

128 N. Edwards, *The Archaeology of Early Medieval Ireland* (London: Batsford, 1990), pp. 99–101.

129 Gillespie, *Early Belfast*, p. 29.

130 Although local tradition ascribes a Patrician connection with the church at Shankill, there is no historical evidence to support this – the earliest reference to a dedication to St Patrick (*Ecclesia de Sancti Patricii de Vado Albo*) is contained within the *Terrier*, compiled in c.1615 which, as noted below, conflates the names of the medieval parish church and its former dependent chapel. Although it is likely that the dedication was transferred along with parochial status

from the medieval church at Shankill, it does not follow that the church at Shankill had Patrician origins. A more likely date for the dedication to St Patrick is when the church was endowed to the Benedictine Cathedral Priory in Downpatrick – an event plausibly dated to between 1183 and 1205 (Gillespie, *Early Belfast*, pp. 27–28).

131 T. Ó Carragáin, *Churches in Early Medieval Ireland* (New Haven, CT: Yale University Press, 2010), pp. 15, 110, figs. 1 and 119.

132 D. Morton, 'The Church of Shankill and the Chapel of the Ford', *Bulletin of the Ulster Place-Name Society*, 5.2 (1957), p. 35.

133 *Irish Patent Rolls of James I. Facsimile of the Irish Record Commission's Calendar Prepared Prior to 1830* (Dublin: Irish Manuscripts Commission, 1966), p. 49, no. LXXIX.

134 For details of all the early seventeenth-century variants of this name, see Morton, 'Church of Shankill'.

135 J. O'Laverty, *An Historical Account of the Diocese of Down and Connor, Ancient and Modern* (Dublin: M.H. Gill & Son, 1880), II, 403.

136 Gillespie and Royle, *Atlas*, p. 2.

137 Past surveys of the early ecclesiastical history of Belfast have noted that the evidence for the sequence outlined above is somewhat ambiguous (Benn, *Belfast* [1877], p. 368; Morton, 'Church of Shankill', p. 40; Macdonald, 'Medieval Belfast Considered', p. 40). This ambiguity arises because the inference that the *Ecclesia Alba* (White Church) at Shankill had been replaced by the *Capella de Vado* (Chapel of the Ford) as the parish church by the early seventeenth century is apparently contradicted by two separate pieces of evidence. The first of these strands of evidence is contained in an ecclesiastical document known as the *Terrier* or *Ledger Book of Down and Connor*. This compilation of the ecclesiastical possessions of the dioceses of Down and Connor is dated on internal evidence to c.1615 (Reeves, *Ecclesiastical Antiquities*, p. xxi, fn. z), but contains much detail derived from at least one lost pre-Reformation document that has been speculatively dated to c.1500 (Gillespie, *Early Belfast*, p. 27). In the section of the *Terrier* relating

to the *Ecclesia de St Patrick de Vado Albo*, it is stated that 'the church is called Shankill' (Reeves, *Ecclesiastical Antiquities*, p. 184), suggesting that the hybrid name actually signified the medieval parish church at Shankill. However, that the document fails to separately note the Chapel of the Ford, despite it containing a list of six other 'alterages' within the parish, suggests that the document's compiler was unaware that there had been a shift in the location of the parish church and in his confusion used the place-name 'Shankill', derived from the pre-Reformation source material he was using, to signify the 'new' parish church, that is, the former Chapel of the Ford. The second piece of apparently contradictory evidence is an account of the traveller Father Edmund MacCana who stated in c.1643 that there was no recollection of a sacred place in Belfast and that the parish church was still located at Shankill (Reeves, 'Irish Itinerary', p. 58). Given that the seventeenth-century church located on High Street had been built by 1622 and that the medieval church at Shankill was described as being a ruin in 1604, it is reasonable to dismiss MacCana's statement as being based upon anachronistic hearsay (Benn, *Belfast* [1877], p. 287; Morton, 'Church of Shankill', p. 40). That MacCana also noted five of the six 'chapelries' attached to Shankill that were recorded in the *Terrier* suggests that he derived his section on the churches of Belfast from this, or a closely related, outdated source, when drafting his itinerary. See Reeves, 'Irish Itinerary', p. 58.

138 For example, the early ecclesiastical site at Shankill was located upon an early routeway that led from the ford along the line of the Farset on to the Antrim plateau and inland towards Antrim (Gillespie, *Early Belfast*, pp. 15, 27).

139 O. Davies, 'Church Architecture in Ulster', *UJA*, 6 (1943), pp. 63–64; A.E. Hamlin, *The Archaeology of Early Christianity in the North of Ireland* (Oxford: Archaeopress, 2008), p. 34.

140 Gillespie and Royle, *Atlas*, p. 37, maps 4–5.

141 Gillespie and Royle, *Atlas*, map 9.

142 Reeves, *Ecclesiastical Antiquities*, p. 7, fn. r; Morton, 'Church of Shankill', p. 39.

143 Reeves, *Ecclesiastical Antiquities*, pp. 7–8, fn. s; Morton, 'Church of Shankill', p. 38. Reeves's speculative suggestion that the chapel was located within the cashel at Ballyaghagan ('Irish Itinerary', p. 58, fn. w) is not supported by the results of a recent excavation at the site. See H. Welsh, *Excavation at Ballyaghagan Cashel, Ballyaghagan, County Antrim* (Report No. 78, Centre for Archaeological Fieldwork, Queen's University Belfast, Belfast, 2011).

144 Reeves, *Ecclesiastical Antiquities*, p. xxi, fn. z; Gillespie, *Early Belfast*, p. 27.

145 See Morton, 'Church of Shankill', p. 36.

146 Reeves, *Ecclesiastical Antiquities*, pp. 184–85.

147 Morton, 'Church of Shankill', p. 38.

148 O'Laverty, *Down and Connor*, p. 406; but see Hughes, 'Deirdre Flanagan's "Belfast"', p. 91.

149 PRONI, T/1493/41. See Dunlop, 'Maps', p. 327, no. 89.

150 L. M'Keown, 'Friar's Bush', *Journal of the Down and Connor Historical Society*, 6 (1934), p. 72.

151 Morton, 'Church of Shankill', p. 39.

152 Reeves, *Ecclesiastical Antiquities*, p. 185; O'Laverty, *Down and Connor*, pp. 452–53; Morton, 'Church of Shankill', p. 38.

153 Reeves, *Ecclesiastical Antiquities*, pp. 6–7, fn. l.

154 Gillespie, *Early Belfast*, p. xiv.

155 For a detailed survey of this evidence, see Macdonald, 'Medieval Belfast Considered', pp. 42–43.

156 N.F. Brannon, 'In Search of Old Belfast', in A. Hamlin and C. Lynn (eds), *Pieces of the Past: Archaeological Excavations by the Department of the Environment for Northern Ireland 1970–1986* (Belfast: HMSO, 1988), pp. 79–80.

157 Macdonald, 'Medieval Belfast Considered', pp. 56, 58.

158 Ó Baoill, *Hidden History*, pp. 88–89.

159 J. Ó Néill, 'A Medieval Ring Brooch and other Nineteenth-Century Discoveries at High Street, Belfast', *UJA*, 65 (2006), p. 65.

160 For a summary of these excavations see Ó Baoill, *Hidden History*, pp. 171–79.

161 Contextual analysis of the sherds of transitional ware pottery recovered from excavations in St Anne's Square and Gordon Street indicates that all of the known examples are either associated with pottery of seventeenth- and eighteenth-century date or were recovered from post-medieval contexts. Although where reconstructable the sherds were derived from vessels with late medieval forms, the suggestion that they represent a fifteenth- or sixteenth-century cultural horizon remains unproven.

162 Five sherds of pottery were recovered during excavations in Queen Street and provisionally identified as being medieval in date. Comparative analysis suggests, however, that they probably date to the seventeenth century (A. Horning and N. Brannon personal communication).

1   Raymond Gillespie and Stephen A. Royle, *Irish Historic Towns Atlas – No. 12: Belfast to 1840* (Dublin: Royal Irish Academy, 2003), p. 10.

2   Robert Gavin, W.P. Kelly and Dolores O'Reilly, *Atlantic Gateway: The Port and City of Londonderry since 1700* (Dublin: Four Courts Press, 2009), p. 13.

3   PRONI, D719/77a.

4   This section of the chapter draws heavily on Raymond Gillespie, *Early Belfast: The Origins and Growth of an Ulster Town to 1750* (Belfast: Ulster Historical Foundation, 2007), where fuller discussion and references for the statements made here will be found.

5   Gillespie, *Early Belfast*, p. 93.

6   Benn, *Belfast* (1877), pp. 380–82, 475.

7   Gerald Müller and Gavin Williamson, 'Fortification of Belfast', *Irish Sword*, 19 (1994–95), pp. 306–12.

8   Gillespie, *Early Belfast*, p. 58.

9   PRONI, MIC 1P/7/2; Gillespie and Royle, *Belfast to 1840*, p. 6.

10 See below, chapter 5.

11 R.M. Young (ed.), *The Town Book of the Corporation of Belfast, 1613–1816* (Belfast, 1892), pp. 155, 186.

12 Young (ed.), *Town Book*, pp. 97, 181–82.

13 For examples see PRONI, D354/297–8, 301–2, 307–18, 325–7, 329 338–42, 346; D1950/12, 18, 19, 22.

14 PRONI, HAR/1G/1/13/1.

15 PRONI, MIC 1P/7/1.

16 PRONI, T808/227.

17 Raymond Gillespie, 'The World of Andrew Rowan: Economy and Society in Restoration Antrim', in Brenda Collins, Philip Ollerenshaw and Trevor Parkhill (eds), *Industry, Trade and People in Ireland, 1650–1950: Essays in Honour of W.H. Crawford* (Belfast: Ulster Historical Foundation, 2005), pp. 15–16, 24.

18 Gillespie, *Early Belfast*, p. 58.

19 Gillespie, *Early Belfast*, p. 80.

20 For example PRONI, MIC 1P/7/1, 12 November 1749.

21 Raymond Gillespie and Alison O'Keeffe (eds), *Register of the Parish of Shankill, Belfast, 1745–1761* (Dublin: Representative Church Body Library, 2006), p. 27.

22 Young (ed.), *Town Book*, p. 97.

23 Young (ed.), *Town Book*, pp. 16, 179, 181; Isaac Ward, 'The Black Family', *UJA* (ser. 2), 8 (1902), pp. 179–80.

24 Young (ed.), *Town Book*, pp. 7, 8, 146, 183.

25 PRONI, MIC 1P/7/2.

26 Young (ed.), *Town Book*, pp. 128, 185, 253, 265.

27 PRONI, T761/8.

28 PRONI, D 1184. The first sovereign still held land in Exeter at his death: Benn, *Belfast* (1877), p. 239.

29 Harold O'Sullivan and Raymond Gillespie, *Irish Historic Towns Atlas – No. 23: Carlingford* (Dublin: Royal Irish Academy, 2011), p. 4.

30 PRONI, D1950/5b; Ward, 'The Black Family', pp. 176–77.

31 Jean Agnew, *Belfast Merchant Families in the Seventeenth Century* (Dublin: Four Courts Press, 1996), appendix A; Edith Mary Johnston-Liik, *History of the Irish Parliament, 1692–1800* (6 vols, Belfast: Ulster Historical Foundation, 2002), IV, pp. 95–96, NAI, Prerogative Will Book, 1706–8, ff. 24–5.

32 Benn, *Belfast* (1877), p. 245; PRONI, D 719/51.

33 J.B. Leslie, *Clergy of Connor* (Belfast: Ulster Historical Foundation, 1993), pp. 118–19.

34 James McConnell, *Presbyterianism in Belfast* (Belfast: Davidson & McCormack, 1912), pp. 50–58.

35 PRONI, HAR/1G/1/13/1.

36 For one such large-scale rearrangement, see the National Archives, London, CUST 1/20, 2 November 1728.

37 Gillespie, *Early Belfast*, p. 145.

38 Gillespie and O'Keeffe (eds), *Register*, p. 25.

39 PRONI, MIC1P/7/1, January 1744, June, September 1749.

40 The National Archives, London, E157/17.

41 For examples, see the National Archives, London, PROB 11/427, f. 283v, PROB 11/485, f. 202, PROB 11/487, f. 24v, PROB 11/529, f. 146, PROB 11/867, f. 155v, PROB 11/905, f. 288.

42 PRONI, HAR/1G/1/13/1, pp. 6, 30, 34, 40, 48, 72, 88, 102, 112.

43 PRONI, HAR/1G/1/13/1, pp. 4, 24, 32, 54, 70, 136.

44 PRONI, HAR/1G/1/13/1, pp. 2, 6, 12, 18, 26, 56, 116.

45 Edited in Hugh Shields, *Narrative Singing in Ireland* (Dublin: Irish Academic Press, 1993), pp. 221–25.

46 For a Belfast reprint of a work against smuggling, see Jaspar Brett, *The Sin of Withholding Tribute by Running of Goods, Concealing Excise etc Addressed to the Trading Part of this Nation* (Belfast, 1707).

47 James Kelly, *Gallows Speeches from Eighteenth-Century Ireland* (Dublin: Four Courts Press, 2001), p. 181.

48 Gillespie and O'Keeffe (eds), *Register*, pp. 33–37.

49 PRONI, D4204/B/2/1; D 1184; D3095/B/2/4, 5.

50 Young (ed.), *Town Book*, p. 241.

51 Young (ed.), *Town Book*, pp. 130, 146. The board is reproduced in R.M.W. Strain, *Belfast and its Charitable Society* (Oxford: Oxford University Press, 1961), plate 2.

52 PRONI, D3095/B/2/5; NAI, Prerogative Will Book, 1664–84, ff. 59, 293v.

53 NAI, Prerogative Will Book, 1725–8, f. 157.

54 PRONI, D1184; NAI, Prerogative Will Book, 1728–9, f. 59v.

55 Young (ed.), *Town Book*, pp. 49, 55, 60, 67, 72, 73–74, 78, 133–34, 168.

56 Young (ed.), *Town Book*, p. 146.

57 W. H. McCaffrey, 'The Psalmody of the Old Congregation in Belfast, 1760–1840', *Transactions of the Unitarian Historical Society*, 8 (1939–42), pp. 50–52.

58 PRONI, MIC 1P/7/4.

59 Strain, *Belfast and its Charitable Society*, pp. 18–40.

60 John C. Greene, *Theatre in Belfast 1736–1800* (Bethlehem, PA: Lehigh University Press/ London: Associated University Presses, 2000), p. 60.

61 PRONI, T2420/1.

62 For examples, see Peter Seaby, *Coins and Tokens of Ireland* (London: B.A. Seaby, 1970), p. 110; Benn, *Belfast* (1877), pp. 455–65.

63 R.D. Edwards (ed.), 'Letter-book of Sir Arthur Chichester, 1612–14', *Analecta Hibernica*, 8 (1938), p. 56.

64 Agnew, *Belfast Merchant Families*, appendix D.

65 Johnston-Liik, *History of the Irish Parliament*, II, p. 168.

66 James Kirkpatrick, *An Historical Essay upon the Loyalty of Presbyterians in Great Britain and Ireland* (Belfast: James Blow, 1713), p. 287; Young (ed.), *Town Book*, pp. 44–45.

67 Young (ed.), *Town Book*, pp. 118–19.

68 William Tisdall, *Conduct of the Dissenters in Ireland* (Dublin: no publisher, 1712), p. 20.

69 Benn, *Belfast* (1877), pp. 239, 231–32.

70 Young (ed.), *Town Book*, pp. 6, 52–53, 181.

71 Agnew, *Belfast Merchant Families*, pp. 91–104.

72 Gillespie, *Early Belfast*, pp. 132–33; Gillespie and O'Keeffe (eds), *Register*, pp. 26–28.

73 PRONI, MIC 1P/7/2.

74 Phil Kilroy, *Protestant Dissent and Controversy in Ireland, 1660–1714* (Cork: Cork University Press, 1994), pp. 26, 40, 46, 55.

75 PRONI, D1759/A/2, pp. 87, 123, 130, 134.

76 Tisdall, *Conduct*, p. 25; Agnew, *Belfast Merchant Families*, pp. 33–34.

77 PRONI, D1460/1.

78 Gillespie and O'Keeffe (eds), *Register*, pp. 38–39.

79 PRONI, D395/B/2/2, 3, 5, 9, D1184; T1514/10; Benn, *Belfast* (1877), pp. 244–45; NAI, Prerogative Will Book, 1725–8, f.156v.

80 PRONI, MIC 1P/7/1.

81 PRONI, MIC 1P/7/2 'Plan of old meting house 1721'.

82 NAI, Prerogative Will Book, 1706–8, f. 24v.

83 PRONI, MIC 1P/7/2.

84 PRONI, MIC 1P/7/2.

85 PRONI, MIC 1P/7/4.

86 PRONI, D1759/2B/2.

87 Linen Hall Library, Belfast, Joy MSS 10, 21 February 1703, 22 August 1704.

88 PRONI, D1759/2B/2, f. 9v.

89 PRONI, MIC 1P/7/2.

90 PRONI, T67.

91 Young (ed.), *Town Book*, p. 57; Benn, *Belfast* (1877), pp. 445–46; William Tisdall, *An Account of the Charity School in Belfast* (n.p., 1720).

92 National Archives of Scotland, Edinburgh, E72/19/2, p. 7.

93 Benn, *Belfast* (1877), p. 448.

94 W. Innes Addison, *The Matriculation Albums of the University of Glasgow, 1728–1856* (Glasgow, 1913), pp. 4, 16, 21, 23, 29, 31, 34, 35.

95 Trinity College, Dublin, MUN/V/23/1, 2.

96 Benn, *Belfast* (1877), pp. 447–49.

97 PRONI, D 1460/1.

98 The National Archives, London, CUST 15/1.

99 National Archives of Scotland, Edinburgh, E72/19/2, p. 13; E72/19/6, 22 Dec. 1681; E72/19/8, p. 4 E72/19/11, 12 Jan. 1685; E72/19/22, 29 Apr. 1691; 26 May 1691; E72/19/19, 12 Sept. 1690.

100 Raymond Gillespie, *Reading Ireland* (Manchester: Manchester University Press, 2005), pp. 78–79.

101 Gillespie, *Reading Ireland*, p. 119.

102 John Anderson, *Catalogue of Early Belfast Printed Books, 1694–1830* (Belfast: Belfast Library and Society for Promoting Knowledge, 1890), supplemented by J.R.R. Adams, *The Printed Words and the Common Man* (Belfast: Institute of Irish Studies, 1987), appendix I.

103 Gillespie, *Reading Ireland*, pp. 13–14.

104 For the context and the role of the Belfast Society in this, see Ian McBride, *Scripture Politics: Ulster Presbyterians and Irish Radicalism in the Late Eighteenth Century* (Oxford: Oxford University Press, 1998), pp. 43–47.

105 PRONI, T3060/15; McConnell, *Presbyterianism in Belfast*, pp. 54–57.

106 Tisdall, *Conduct*, p. 68.

107 Gillespie, *Reading Ireland*, pp. 80, 89.

108 Jean Agnew (ed.), *Funeral Register of the First Presbyterian Church of Belfast, 1712–36* (Belfast: Ulster Historical Foundation, 1995), p. 10.

109 J.R.R. Adams, 'A "Directory" of Belfast c. 1740', *North Irish Roots*, 4.2 (1993), pp. 18, 20, 22.

110 Young (ed.), *Town Book*, pp. 5, 180.

111 Young (ed.), *Town Book*, pp. 183, 105.

112 National Archives of Scotland, Edinburgh, E72/10/7, 21 Feb. 1682; Benn, *Belfast* (1877), pp. 316–17.

113 Greene, *Theatre in Belfast*, pp. 20–21, 39–63.

114 Benn, *Belfast* (1877), p. 590; Adams, 'A "Directory" of Belfast', p. 19.

115 Roy Johnston, *Bunting's Messiah* (Belfast: Belfast Natural History and Philosophical Society, 2003), p. 23. On the role of music, see Raymond Gillespie, 'Music and Song in Early Eighteenth-century Belfast', in Raymond Gillespie and R.F. Foster, *Irish Provincial Culture in the Long Eighteenth Century: Making the Middle Sort. Essays for Toby Barnard* (Dublin: Four Courts Press, 2012), pp. 155–69.

116 T.G.F. Paterson (ed.), 'Belfast in 1738', *UJA* (ser. 3), 2 (1939), p. 122.

117 NAI, Prerogative Will Book, 1664–84, f. 293v.

118 Young (ed.), *Town Book*, pp. 59–60, 110–11.

119 Adams, 'A "Directory" of Belfast', p. 23; Gillespie and O'Keeffe (eds), *Register*, p. 285.

120 Gillespie, *Early Belfast*, p. 111.

121 Johnston, *Bunting's Messiah*, pp. 23–24.

122 Petri Mirala, *Freemasonry in Ulster 1733–1813* (Dublin: Four Courts Press, 2007), pp. 56–57, 70–71.

123 Strain, *Belfast and its Charitable Society*.

124 Alan Blackstock, 'Loyalist Associational Culture and Civic Identity in Belfast, 1793–1835', in Jennifer Kelly and R.V. Comerford (eds), *Associational Culture in Ireland and Abroad* (Dublin: Irish Academic Press, 2010), pp. 47–66; see below, pp. 180–86.

1 *The Letters of Lord Chief Baron Edward Willes to the Earl of Warwick 1757–62: An Account of Ireland in the Mid-Eighteenth Century*, ed. James Kelly (Aberystwyth: Boethius, 1990), p. 34.

2 George Benn, *A History of the Town of Belfast from 1799 till 1810* (London, 1880), p. 111.

3 For an overview of Belfast in the 1750s, see Raymond Gillespie, *Early Belfast: The Origins and Growth of an Ulster Town to 1750* (Belfast: Ulster Historical Foundation, 2007), ch. 5.

4 W.A. Maguire, 'A Question of Arithmetic: Arthur Chichester, Fourth Earl of Donegall', in Brenda Collins, Philip Ollerenshaw and Trevor Parkhill (eds), *Industry, Trade and People in Ireland 1650–1950* (Belfast: Ulster Historical Foundation, 2005), pp. 31–50; W.A. Maguire, 'Absentees, Architects and Agitators: The Fifth Earl of Donegall and the Building of Fisherwick Park', *Belfast Natural History and Philosophical Society, Proceedings and Reports* (ser. 2), 10 (1977–82), pp. 5–19.

5 Peter Borsay, *The English Urban Renaissance: Culture and Society in the Provincial Town 1660–1760* (Oxford: Clarendon Press, 1989).

6 *Willes Letters*, p. 34; Robert Scott, *A Breath of Fresh Air: The Story of Belfast's Parks* (Belfast: Blackstaff Press, 2000), pp. 1–3.

7 J.C. Greene, *Theatre in Belfast 1736–1800* (Bethlehem, PA: Lehigh University Press/London: Associated University Presses, 2000), p. 129.

8 Martha McTier to William Drennan, n.d. [1784], in Jean Agnew (ed.), *The Drennan–McTier Letters* (Dublin: Irish Manuscripts Commission, 1998–99), I, p. 179.

9 T.G.F. Paterson, 'Belfast in 1738', *UJA*, 2 (1939), p. 112. See above, p. 157.

10 Roy Porter, *Enlightenment: Britain and the Creation of the Modern World* (London: Penguin, 2000).

11 *The Journal of the Rev John Wesley* (London: J. Kershaw, 1827), IV, p. 123, 9 June 1778.

12 See above, p. 141.

13 R.W.M. Strain, *Belfast and its Charitable Society: A Story of Urban Social Development* (London: Oxford University Press, 1961).

14 Strain, *Charitable Society*, pp. 54–55.

15 Martha McTier to Drennan, 30 March 1801 (*Drennan–McTier Letters*, II, pp. 690–91); *BNL*, 20 January 1804.

16 R.J. Morris, 'Voluntary Societies and British Urban Elites, 1750–1850: An Analysis', *Historical Journal*, 26 (1983), pp. 95–118.

17 Charles Abbot, 'Journal of a Tour in Ireland and north Wales, September-October 1792' (PRONI T3488/1).

18 For numbers of ships and tonnage in 1723, see Arthur Dobbs, *An Essay on the Trade and Improvement of Ireland* (Dublin: A. Rhames, 1729), p. 16. Where population is concerned, Dobbs reports a total of 2,093 houses in 1725 (ibid., p. 6). This figure, however, relates to the whole parish of Belfast, and is larger than that suggested both in 1757 and in 1782 (Table 1, p. 17). On the other hand the 1,779 houses recorded in Belfast in 1757 would still have made it the sixth largest town among those listed by Dobbs, behind Dublin, Cork, Limerick, Waterford and Kilkenny.

19 W.H. Crawford, *The Impact of the Domestic Linen Industry in Ulster* (Belfast: Ulster Historical Foundation, 2005), p. 78.

20 Arthur Young, *A Tour in Ireland, with General Observations on the Present State of that Kingdom* (London: T. Cadell, 1780), I, pp. 146–47.

21 W.A. McCutcheon, *The Industrial Archaeology of Northern Ireland* (Belfast: HMSO, 1980), pp. 55–58; E.R.R. Green, *The Lagan Valley 1800–1850* (London: Faber, 1949), pp. 33–39.

22 Strain, *Charitable Society*, p. 145.

23 David Dickson, 'Aspects of the Rise and Decline of the Irish Cotton Industry', in L.M. Cullen and T.C. Smout (eds), *Comparative Aspects of Scottish and Irish Economic and Social History* (Edinburgh: John Donald, 1977), pp. 106, 113, n. 42.

24 J. Dubourdieu, *Statistical Survey of the County of Antrim* (Dublin: Dublin Society, 1812), p. 404.

25 Memorial of Cavan and Heron, 14 Nov. 1799 (NAI, Rebellion Papers 620/56/83).

26 For the population of Ballymacarrett, see Raymond Gillespie and S.A. Royle, *Irish Historic Towns Atlas – No. 12: Belfast to 1840* (Dublin: Royal Irish Academy, 2003), p. 10. For Belfast's population see Table 1, p. 17.

27 *BNL*, 23 November 1813.

28 C.E.B. Brett, *Roger Mulholland, Architect of Belfast 1740–1818* (Belfast: Ulster Architectural Heritage Society, 1976).

29 For divisions within Presbyterianism, see Ian McBride, *Scripture Politics: Ulster Presbyterians and Irish Radicalism in the Late Eighteenth Century* (Oxford: Oxford University Press, 1998).

30 *Richard Pococke's Irish Tours*, ed. John McVeagh (Dublin: Irish Academic Press, 1995), p. 38. For a suggestion that this may understate Anglican numbers somewhat see above, p. 148.

31 British Library, Liverpool Papers, Add. Mss 38368.

32 Ambrose Macauley, *William Crolly, Archbishop of Armagh 1835–49* (Dublin: Four Courts Press, 1994), p. 14. For the farewell dinner mentioned below, see pp. 41–44.

33 Martha McTier to Drennan, n.d. [1802] (*Drennan–McTier Letters*, II, p. 92). For a fuller account of the development of sectarian conflict, see below, pp. 245–55.

34 *BNL*, 2 November 1804.

35 *Third Report of His Majesty's Commissioners for Enquiring into the Condition of the Poorer Classes in Ireland, Appendix C* (BPP, 1836 (35) xxx), p. 38.

36 Martha McTier to Drennan, n.d. [1787] (*Drennan–McTier Letters*, I, p. 272); *BNL*, 2 November 1804.

37 Daniel Augustus Beaufort, 'Journal of a tour through Ireland 1787–8' (PRONI, MIC250/1).

38 Strain, *Charitable Society*, pp. 13, 43, 64, 290.

39 *Journals and Memoirs of Thomas Russell*, ed. C.J. Woods (Dublin: Irish Academic Press, 1991), p. 50; *Life of Theobald Wolfe Tone, Memoirs, Journals and Political Writings*, ed. Thomas Bartlett (Dublin: Lilliput Press, 1998), pp. 145, 147.

40 Report Book of the Belfast Special Constables (PRONI D46/1a), pp. 38, 73.

41 Martha McTier to Drennan, 12 Dec. 1797 (*Drennan–McTier Letters*, II, p. 350).

42 Report Book of the Belfast Special Constables (PRONI D46/1a), p. 89.

43 *BNL*, 1 August 1820

44 Cornwallis to Portland, 22 Oct. 1799, in Charles Ross (ed.), *Correspondence of Charles, First Marquis Cornwallis* (London: John Murray, 1859), III, p. 139.

45 Benn, *Belfast* (1877), pp. 500–03.

46 *BNL*, 16 February 1759, 12 October 1759, 21 January 1791; *Belfast Mercury*, 7 October 1783.

47 *BNL*, 25, 29 January 1771, 1 April 1791.

48 George Chambers, *Faces of Change: The Belfast and Northern Ireland Chambers of Commerce and Industry 1783–1983* (Belfast: Northern Ireland Chamber of Commerce and Industry, n.d.). For the later development of the harbour, see below, pp. 203–04.

49 McBride, *Scripture Politics*, p. 126.

50 Benn, *Belfast* (1877), p. 632.

51 Martha McTier to Drennan, n.d. [1783] (*Drennan–McTier Letters*, I, p. 125).

52 [William Bruce and Henry Joy], *Belfast Politics, Or a Collection of the Debates, Resolutions and Other Proceedings of that Town in the Years 1792 and 1793* (Belfast: H. Joy & Co., 1794), pp. 52–72.

53 Bartlett (ed.), *Life of Tone*, p. 126.

54 R.B. McDowell, *Ireland in the Age of Imperialism and Revolution 1760–1801* (Oxford: Oxford University Press, 1979), p. 572.

55 Martha McTier to Drennan, 25 Feb. 1800 (*Drennan–McTier Letters*, II, p. 580). For general accounts of Belfast's experience during and after the rebellion, see Marianne Elliott, *Partners in Revolution: The United Irishmen and France* (New Haven, CT, and London: Yale University Press, 1982); N.J. Curtin, *The United Irishmen: Popular Politics in Ulster and Dublin 1791–1798* (Oxford: Clarendon Press, 1994).

56 W.A. Maguire, *Living Like a Lord: The Second Marquis of Donegall 1769–1844* (Belfast: Ulster Historical Foundation, 1984).

57 Peel to Whitworth, 9 March 1816 (British Library, MS 40290, ff. 134–35); Whitworth to Peel, 12 March 1816 (British Library, MS40191, f. 150).

58 This discussion of the administration of the early nineteenth-century town owes much to Claire Allen, 'Urban Elites, Civil Society and Governance in Early Nineteenth-Century Belfast c. 1800–32', unpublished PhD thesis, Queen's University Belfast, 2010.

59 Minutes of Police Commissioners, 21 November 1808, 7 December 1814 (PRONI, LA7/2BA/2/1, pp. 258–59, 99).

60 Minutes of Police Commissioners, 21 November 1808 (PRONI, LA7/2BA/2/1, pp. 258–59).

61 *BNL*, 2 September 1823.

62 Brian Griffin, *The Bulkies: Police and Crime in Belfast 1800–1865* (Dublin: Irish Academic Press, 1997), chs. 3, 5.

63 For example, NAI, 620/14/188/23, 'Abstract of the contents of five letters from Belfast', June 1805; Letter signed 'A', 14 July 1806, NAI, State of the Country Papers, 1092/1.

64 *BNL*, 11 February 1820.

65 *Belfast Commercial Chronicle*, 3 May 1809.

66 W.A. Maguire, 'The Verner Rape Trial, 1813: Jane Barnes V. The Belfast Establishment', *Ulster Local Studies*, 15.1 (1993), pp. 47–57.

67 William Mitchell to Robert Tennent, 24 Nov. 1820 (PRONI, D1748/G/457/8); *BNL*, 21 November 1820; *Belfast Commercial Chronicle*, 15, 18 November 1820.

68 *Richard Pococke's Irish Tours*, p. 38.

69 *BNL*, 12 December 1828, 12 July 1833.

70 *BNL*, 3 November 1820.

71 Dubourdieu, *Statistical Survey of County Antrim*, pp. 405–07.

72 Dubourdieu, *Statistical Survey of County Antrim*, p. 519.

73 Akihiro Takei, 'The First Irish Linen Mills, 1800–1824', *Irish Economic & Social History*, 21 (1994), pp. 28–38.

74 W.A. Maguire, 'The 1822 Settlement of the Donegall Estates', *Irish Economic & Social History*, 3 (1976), pp. 17–32. See below, pp. 201–02.

1 William Makepeace Thackeray, *The Irish Sketchbook* (New York: Charles Scribner's Sons, 1904 [1842]), pp. 403–04 and p. 396.

2 Marie-Anne de Bovet, *Lettres d'Irlande* (Paris: Guillaumin et Cie, 1889); *Three Months' Tour in Ireland* (London: Chapman and Hall, 1891).

3 de Bovet, *Three Months' Tour in Ireland*, p. 302.

4 Sybil Baker, 'Orange and Green', in H.J. Dyos and Michael Wolff (eds), *The Victorian City: Images and Realities* (London: Routledge and Kegan Paul, 1973), p. 793.

5 Anthony C. Hepburn and Brenda Collins, 'Industrial Society: The Structure of Belfast, 1901', in Peter Roebuck (ed.), *Plantation to Partition: Essays in Ulster History in Honour of J.L. McCracken* (Belfast: Blackstaff Press, 1981), pp. 210–28.

6 *BNL*, 11 December 1829.

7 William M. O'Hanlon, *Walks among the Poor of Belfast and Suggestions for Their Improvement* (Belfast: Henry Greer, 1853; repr. Wakefield: S.R. Publishers, 1971), p. 101.

8 See above, pp. 37–38.

9 William A. Maguire, 'Lord Donegall and the Sale of Belfast: A Case History from the Encumbered Estates Court', *Economic History Review*, 29.4 (1976), pp. 570–84.

10 Francis Yarde Gilbert to Edward Granville, Earl of St Germans, Lord Lieutenant of Ireland, 11 February 1853, *Belfast Municipal Boundaries. Copy of Captain [Francis Y.] Gilbert's Report upon the Proposed Extension of the Boundaries of the Borough of Belfast; Together with Copies of All Documents Laid Before Him, Approving or Objecting to Such Extension* (BPP 1852–53 (958) xciv.23).

11 Sir David J. Owen, *A Short History of the Port of Belfast* (Belfast: Mayne Boyd, 1917).

12 *BNL*, 23 November 1832.

13 Jonathan Bardon, *Belfast: An Illustrated History* (Belfast: Blackstaff Press, 1982).

14 Stephen A. Royle, *Belfast Part II, 1840–1900, Irish Historic Towns Atlas*, 17 (Dublin: Royal Irish Academy, 2007).

15 Gilbert to Granville, 11 February 1853, *Belfast Municipal Boundaries*.

16 *BNL*, 4 July 1820.

17 *BNL*, 11 December 1838.

18 Michael S. Moss and John R. Hume, *Shipbuilders to the World: 125 Years of Harland and Wolff* (Belfast: Blackstaff Press, 1986).

19 *BNL*, 9 April 1847.

20 Moss and Hume, *Shipbuilders to the World*.

21 *BNL*, 28 December 1895.

22 John P. Lynch, *An Unlikely Success Story: The Belfast Shipbuilding Industry, 1880–1935* (Belfast: Belfast Society, 2001).

23 Workman, Clark Ltd, Shipbuilders and Engineers (PRONI, D2015/2/2).

24 Notes on Belfast by Thomas L'Estrange, c. 1890–1900 (PRONI, D271/15).

25 Gilbert to Granville, 11 February 1853, *Belfast Municipal Boundaries*.

26 Benn, *Belfast* (1823), p. 102.

27 *BNL*, 5 October 1824.

28 *BNL*, 1 July 1828.

29 William A. McCutcheon, *The Industrial Archaeology of Northern Ireland* (Belfast: HMSO, 1980).

30 Notes on the History of Belfast (PRONI, D1239/14).

31 James A. Beck, 'When Belfast was a Cotton Centre', *Fibres, Fabrics and Cordage* (October 1946), p. 416.

32 *BNL*, 13 October 1835.

33 Stephen A. Royle, 'The Growth and Decline of an Industrial City: Belfast from 1750', in Howard B. Clarke (ed.), *Irish Cities* (Dublin: Mercier, 1995), pp. 28–40.

34 *BNL*, 18 May 1847.

35 D.L. Armstrong, 'Social and Economic Conditions in the Belfast Linen Industry, 1850–1900', *Irish Historical Studies*, 7 (1951), pp. 235–69.

36 Annual Report of the Linen Merchants' Association (LMA) 1873 (PRONI, D2088/11/2).

37 Armstrong, 'Belfast Linen Industry'.

38 *Reports from the Consuls of the United States on the Commerce, Manufactures, Etc. of their Consular Districts for the Months of January, February, March, April and May, 1883* (Washington, DC: Bureau of Foreign Commerce, 1883), p. 75.

39 Annual Report of the LMA 1899 (PRONI, D2088/11/2).

40 Annual Report of the LMA 1915 (PRONI, D2088/11/2).

41 William Topping, 'Memoirs of the Working Life of William Topping, 1903–1956' (PRONI, D3134/1), published as *A Life in Linenopolis: The Memoirs of William Topping, Belfast Damask Weaver, 1903–1956* (Belfast: Ulster Historical Foundation, 1992).

42 Royle, *Belfast Part II*.

43 Mary Lowry, *The Story of Belfast and its Surroundings* (London: Headley, 1913).

44 Stephen A. Royle, Frederick W. Boal and Maura E. Pringle, 'New Information on the Development of Ballymacarrett: Lord Templemore's Plan of 1853', *Ulster Journal of Archaeology*, 46 (1983), pp. 137–41.

45 Friedrich Engels, *The Condition of the Working Class in England in 1844* (New York: J.W. Lovell, 1887), p. 447 (originally published as *Die Lage der Arbeitenden Klasse in England* [Leipzig: Verlag Otto Wigand, 1845]).

46 Andrew G. Malcolm, *The History of the General Hospital, Belfast, and the Other Medical Institutions of the Town* (Belfast: Agnew, 1851) (reprinted in H.G. Calwell, *Andrew Malcolm of Belfast 1818–1856, Physician and Historian* [Belfast: Brough, Cox and Dunn, 1977]).

47 Andrew G. Malcolm, *The Sanitary State of Belfast with Suggestions for its Improvement: A Paper Read before the Statistical Section of the British Association at Belfast, September 7 1852* (Belfast: Henry Greer, 1852).

48 Andrew G. Malcolm, 'The Influence of Factory Life on the Health of the Operative as Founded upon the Medical Statistics of this Class at Belfast', *Journal of the Statistical Society of London*, 19.2 (1856), p. 170.

49 John Moore, 'On the Influence of Flax Spinning on the Health of the Mill Workers of Belfast', *Transactions of the National Association for the Promotion of Social Science Meeting in Belfast*, 1867, Linen Hall Library, N13668.

50 Armstrong, 'Belfast Linen Industry'.

51 Topping, 'Memoirs of the Working Life'; Betty Messenger, *Picking up the Linen Threads: Life in Ulster's Mills* (Belfast: Blackstaff Press, 1988), p. 62.

52 Annual Report of the LMA 1892 (PRONI, D2088/11/1).

53 Samuel Browne to Francis Gilbert, 4 February 1853, *Belfast Municipal Boundaries*.

54 O'Hanlon, *Walks among the Poor*, p. 25.

55 W.A. Maguire, *Belfast* (Keele: Ryburn, 1993), p. 76.

56 John F. Bateman, *Report on the Supply of Water to the Town of Belfast* (1855), Linen Hall Library, N3283.

57 Jack Loudan, *In Search of Water, Being a History of the Belfast Water Supply* (Belfast: W. Mullan and Son, 1940).

58 Maguire, *Belfast*, p. 98.

59 de Bovet, *Three Months' Tour in Ireland*, p. 302.

60 Royle, *Belfast Part II*.

61 Belfast Corporation Minutes (BCM), 1 November 1864 (PRONI, LA/7/2EA/7).

62 *BNL*, 14 July 1846.

63 O'Hanlon, *Walks among the Poor*, p. 33.

64 *BNL*, 26, 30 April 1822.

65 Notes on Belfast by Mrs McDonnell, 1871 (PRONI, D271/12); see below, p. 239.

66 Brian Griffin, *The Bulkies: Police and Crime in Belfast, 1800–1865* (Dublin: Irish Academic Press, 1997).

67 *BNL*, 21 March 1815.

68 John Gray, *City in Revolt: James Larkin and the Belfast Dock Strike of 1907* (Belfast: Blackstaff Press, 1985), p. 209.

69 Annual Report of the LMA 1908 (PRONI, D2088/11/2).

70 Belfast Field Books, First Valuation of Ireland, 1837 (PRONI, VAL 1B 71A– VAL 1B 719A).

71 S.C. Hall, *Ireland: Its Scenery and Character* (London: How and Parsons, 1841), p. 343.

72 Stephen A. Royle, 'The Socio-spatial Structure of Belfast in 1837: Evidence from the First Valuation', *Irish Geography*, 24 (1991), p. 6.

73 *Third Report of the Commissioners for Inquiring into the Condition of the Poorer Classes in Ireland* (BPP 1836 (43) xxx.1), p. 38.

74 Hall, *Ireland*, p. 343.

75 O'Hanlon, *Walks among the Poor*, p. 50.

Chapter 6

76 Diary of Revd Anthony McIntyre (PRONI, D1558/2/3).

77 Peter Froggatt, 'Industrialisation and Health in Belfast in the Early Nineteenth Century', in David Harkness and Mary O'Dowd (eds), *The Town in Ireland* (Belfast: Appletree Press, 1981), pp. 155–85.

78 BCM, 14 October 1863 (PRONI, LA/7/2EA/6).

79 R. Timothy Campbell and Stephen A. Royle, 'East Belfast and the Suburbanization of North-West County Down in the Nineteenth Century', in Lindsay J. Proudfoot (ed.), *Down: History and Society, Interdisciplinary Essays on the History of an Irish County* (Dublin: Geography Publications, 1997), pp. 629–62.

80 *Northern Whig*, 31 December 1869.

81 BCM, 1 March 1872 (PRONI, LA/7/2EA/10).

82 Material Regarding the History of Tramways (PRONI, LA/7/26/M/1).

83 *BNL*, 30 August 1839.

84 *Report of the Commissioners Appointed to Inquire into the Municipal Corporations in Ireland* (BPP 1835 (23) XXVII.1).

85 Municipal Corporations Act (Ireland) 1840 (3 & 4 Vict. c. 108).

86 Gilbert to Granville, 11 February 1853, *Belfast Municipal Boundaries*.

87 Maguire, *Belfast*,

88 *BNL*, 9 April 1822.

89 O'Hanlon, *Walks among the Poor*, pp. 84, 88.

90 Malcolm, *Sanitary State*, p. 6.

91 Robert C. Scott, *A Breath of Fresh Air: The Story of Belfast's Parks* (Belfast: Blackstaff Press, 2000).

92 BCM, 1 January 1895 (LA/7/2/EA/19).

93 Scott, *A Breath of Fresh Air*.

94 BCM, 17 November 1886 (PRONI, LA/7/2EA/16).

95 Scott, *A Breath of Fresh Air*.

96 *BNL*, 3 November 1820.

97 BCM, 20 September 1883, 18 June 1884 (PRONI, LA/7/2EA/15).

98 Marcus Patton, *Central Belfast: An Historical Gazetteer* (Belfast: Ulster Architectural Heritage Society, 1993).

99 BCM, 10 March 1886 (PRONI, LA/7/2EA/16).

100 BCM, 1 April 1866 (PRONI, LA/7/2EA/7).

101 BCM, 16 November 1889 (PRONI, LA/7/2EA/17).

102 BCM, 1 February 1893 (PRONI, LA/7/2EA/19).

103 BCM, 1 July 1896 (PRONI, LA/7/2EA/20).

104 *Belfast Telegraph*, 25 April 1895.

105 Frederick W. Boal and Stephen A. Royle (eds), *Enduring City: Belfast in the Twentieth Century* (Belfast: Blackstaff Press, 2006).

106 John Gray, *Thomas Carnduff: Life and Writings* (Belfast: Lagan, 1994).

107 Thomas Carnduff, 'Men of Belfast', (Belfast: E.H. Thornton, 1924).

Chapter 7

1 Benn, *Belfast* (1877), pp. 593–96. For surveys of early Belfast trade unionism, see Andrew Boyd, *The Rise of the Irish Trade Unions 1729–1970* (Tralee: Anvil Books, 1972); J.J. Monaghan, 'A Social and Economic History of Belfast 1801–25', unpublished PhD thesis, Queen's University, Belfast, 1940, pp. 244–71.

2 *BNL*, 6 June 1828, 22 April 1836.

3 Vincent Geoghegan, 'Robert Owen, Cooperation and Ulster in the 1830s', in D. Ó Drisceoil and F. Lane (eds), *Politics and the Irish Working Class, 1830–1945* (Basingstoke: Palgrave Macmillan, 2005), pp. 6–26.

4 Henry Patterson, *Class Conflict and Sectarianism: The Protestant Working Class and the Belfast Labour Movement 1868–1920* (Belfast: Blackstaff Press, 1980), p. 31.

5 John Gray, *City in Revolt: James Larkin and the Belfast Dock Strike of 1907* (Belfast: Blackstaff Press, 1985).

6 Emmet O'Connor and Trevor Parkhill (eds), *Loyalism and Labour in Belfast: The Autobiography of Robert McElborough* (Cork: Cork University Press, 2002).

7 *Report of the Select Committee on Handloom Weavers' Petitions* (BPP 1835 (341) xiii), pp. 120–21.

8 Bob Purdie, 'Riotous Customs: The Breaking up of Socialist Meetings in Belfast 1893–1896', *Saothar*, 20 (1995), pp. 32–40.

9 Austen Morgan, *Labour and Partition: The Belfast Working Class 1905–23* (London: Pluto Press, 1991), pp. 269–70.

10 *The Connolly–Walker Controversy on Socialist Unity in Ireland* (Cork: Cork Workers Club, 1974).

11 O'Connor and Parkhill (eds), *Loyalty and Labour*, p. 15.

12 Betty Messenger, *Picking up the Linen Threads: Life in Ulster's Mills* (Belfast: Blackstaff Press, 1988), pp. 219–22.

13 *Times*, 13 September 1905.

14 Ian Dickson, 'Evangelical Religion and Victorian Women: The Belfast Female Mission 1859–1903', *Journal of Ecclesiastical History*, 55.4 (2004), pp. 700–25.

15 Alison Jordan, *Who Cared? Charity in Edwardian and Victorian Belfast* (Belfast: Institute of Irish Studies [1993]).

16 Janice Holmes, 'The "World Turned Upside Down": Women in the Ulster Revival of 1859', in Janice Holmes and Diane Urquhart (eds), *Coming into the Light: The Work, Politics and Religion of Women in Ulster, 1840–1940* (Belfast: Institute of Irish Studies, 1994), p. 138.

17 A.T.Q. Stewart, 'McCracken, Mary Ann (1770–1866)', *Oxford Dictionary of National Biography* (Oxford: Oxford University Press, 2004; online edn, Jan 2008 [http://www.oxforddnb.com/view/article/47301, accessed 15 March 2011]. McCracken's activism included contributions to the Belfast Ladies' Clothing Society, acting as a visitor for the Destitute Sick Poor, and advocating the prevention of the employment of climbing boys in chimney sweeping, as well as support for prison reform, the protection of animals and of course the abolition of slavery.

18 *Belfast and Province of Ulster Directory for 1852* (Belfast: James Henderson, 1852).

19 They later opened schools in Alexander Street West, Garmoyle Street, Henry Street, Earl Street as well as in Ligoniel. http://www.svp-ni.org/about_us_files/download_files/society_1850.pdf (accessed 2 May 2012).

20 *BNL*, 29 June 1829.

21 *Northern Whig*, 1, 8 September, 23 October 1849.

22 H.G. Calwell, *Andrew Malcolm of Belfast, 1818–56: Physician and Historian* (Belfast: Brough, Cox and Dunn, 1977), pp. 79–92; Sally Sheard, 'Nineteenth-Century Public Health: A Study of Liverpool, Belfast and Glasgow', unpublished PhD thesis, Liverpool, 1993, pp. 185–200.

23 Jordan, *Who Cared?*, pp. 200–01.

24 Richard Clarke, *The Royal Victoria Hospital Belfast: A History 1797–1997* (Belfast: Blackstaff Press, 1997), pp. 71–72.

25 See the opening statement of the prosecution at the subsequent criminal trial, reported in *BNL*, 13 August 1813. See also Allan Blackstock, *Loyalism in Ireland 1789–1832* (Woodbridge: Boydell, 2007), p. 166.

26 For general accounts, see Sean Farrell, *Rituals and Riots: Sectarian Violence and Political Culture in Ulster, 1784–1886* (Lexington, KY: University Press of Kentucky, 2000); Catherine Hirst, *Religion, Politics and Violence in Nineteenth-Century Belfast* (Dublin: Four Courts Press, 2002); Mark Doyle, *Fighting like the Devil for the Sake of God: Protestants, Catholics and the Origins of Violence in Victorian Belfast* (Manchester: Manchester University Press, 2009).

27 A.C. Hepburn, *A Past Apart: Studies in the History of Catholic Belfast 1850–1950* (Belfast: Ulster Historical Foundation, 1996), p. 50.

28 *BNL*, 5 September 1857.

29 Cornelius Denvir to Tobias Kirby, 12 June 1854 (Irish College, Rome, Kirby Papers, 1854/1425).

30 David Hempton and Myrtle Hill, *Evangelical Protestantism in Ulster Society 1740–1890* (London: Routledge, 1992), ch. 6.

31 S.J. Connolly, 'Paul Cullen's Other Capital: Belfast and the Devotional Revolution', in Dáire Keogh and Albert McDonnell (eds), *Cardinal Paul Cullen and his World* (Dublin: Four Courts Press, 2011), p. 304; Ambrose Macaulay, *Patrick Dorrian, Bishop of Down and Connor 1865–85* (Dublin: Irish Academic Press, 1987).

32 Hepburn, *A Past Apart*, ch. 5.

33 Hepburn, *A Past Apart*, p. 159.

34 Hirst, *Religion, Politics and Violence*, ch. 6.

35 Royal Archives, Windsor, VIC/Main/QVJ/1849, 11 August 1849.

36 *London Review*, 1 April 1865.

37 Viscount Halifax to Earl Spencer, 21 August 1872; Spencer to Halifax, 26 August 1872 (British Library, Add. Ms 76904).

38 *Northern Whig*, 12, 14 July 1849; 'County Antrim Orange Processions 1849' (NAI, Outrage Papers, Co. Antrim, 1/89).

39 *Report of the Commission of Enquiry into the Origin and Character of the Riots in Belfast in July and September 1857* (BPP 1857–8 [2309] 26), pp. 2, 24, 33, 100.

40 F. Frankfort Moore, *The Truth About Ulster* (London: Eveleigh Nash, 1914), p. 234.

41 A.F. Parkinson, *Belfast's Unholy War* (Dublin: Four Courts Press, 2004), pp. 12–13.

42 *From Dublin Castle to Stormont: The Memoirs of Andrew Philip Magill, 1913–1925*, ed. C.W. Magill (Cork: Cork University Press, 2003), p. 69. For a modern account that closely corroborates Magill's interpretation, see Tim Wilson, '"The Most Terrible Assassination that has yet Stained the Name of Belfast": The McMahon Murders in Context', *Irish Historical Studies*, 37.145 (2010), pp. 83–106.

43 Hepburn, *A Past Apart*, ch. 10.

44 Jean Agnew (ed.), *The Drennan–McTier Letters* (Dublin: Irish Manuscripts Commission, 1998–99), II, p. 136.

45 James Vernon, *Politics and the People: A Study in English Political Culture c.1815–1867* (Cambridge: Cambridge University Press, 1993), pp. 45–47.

46 Diane Urquhart, *Women in Ulster Politics 1890–1940* (Dublin: Irish Academic Press, 2000), p. 152.

47 Urquhart, *Women in Ulster Politics*, chs. 4 and 5.

48 John Lynch, *A Tale of Three Cities: Comparative Studies in Working Class Life* (Basingstoke: Macmillan, 1998), pp. 8–10.

49 See street directories for 1805, 1806, 1807, 1852, 1880.

50 *Belfast and Province of Ulster Directory for 1807* (Belfast: News Letter, 1807).

51 These examples are taken from the manuscript returns for the census of 1901, available at http://www.census.nationalarchives.ie/ (accessed 2 May 2012).

52 Alison Jordan, *Margaret Byers: A Pioneer of Women's Education and Founder of Victoria College* (Belfast: Institute of Irish Studies, 1992).

53 *BNL*, 14 November 1871, 15 May 1873.

54 *BNL*, 16 November 1887.

55 David H. Craig, 'A History of the Belfast City Hospital', *Ulster Medical Journal*, 43.1 (1974), pp. 1–14.

56 Marie Duddy, *The Call of the North: A History of the Sisters of Mercy, Down and Connor Diocese, Ireland* (Belfast: Ulster Historical Foundation, 2010), p. 126.

57 *BNL*, 12 November 1886.

58 Duddy, *Call of the North*, p. 79.

59 Eibhlin Breathnach, 'Women and Higher Education in Ireland (1879–1914)', *The Crane Bag*, 4 (1980), pp. 47–54.

60 T.W. Moody and J.C. Beckett, *Queen's, Belfast 1845–1949. The History of a University* (London: Faber and Faber, 1959), I, p. 343.

61 Alison Jordan, '"Opening the Gates of Learning": The Belfast Ladies' Institute, 1867–1897', in Holmes and Urquhart (eds), *Coming into the Light*, p. 50.

62 http://www.qub.ac.uk/schools/mdbs/AboutUs/history/ (accessed 2 May 2012).

63 Dr McIntosh is grateful to Dr Tom Clyde for access to his unpublished paper on the Hobson family.

64 Irish Architectural Archive, biographical index of Irish Architects, available at http://www.iarc.ie/biographical/ (accessed 2 May 2012).

65 For the long-overlooked importance of these considerations, see Erika Diane Rappaport, *Shopping for Pleasure: Women in the Making of London's West End* (Princeton, NJ: Princeton University Press, 2000).

66 *Irish News*, 27 February 1909.

67 *BNL*, 15 October 1858, 18 April 1888.

68 Duddy, *Call of the North*, p. 81.

69 See *BNL*, 17, 24 December 1856, 22 April 1857.

70 Jordan, *Margaret Byers*, pp. 58–61.

71 *Belfast and Province of Ulster Directory 1863–4* (Belfast: James Henderson, 1864), p. 537. For the earlier penitentiary, see Maria Luddy, *Women and Philanthropy in Nineteenth-Century Ireland* (Cambridge: Cambridge University Press, 1995) p. 109, n. 46, and for homes for fallen women generally Jordan, *Who Cared?*, pp. 168–79.

72 http://www.census.nationalarchives.ie/pages/1901/Antrim/Windsor_Ward/Brunswick_Street/974975/ (accessed 2 May 2012).

73 Duddy, *Call of the North*, pp. 35–36.

74 Leanne McCormick, *Regulating Sexuality: Women in Twentieth-Century Northern Ireland* (Manchester: Manchester University Press, 2009), pp. 14, 21.

75 *BNL*, 5 December 1882, 24 January 1893. In 1868 there were reportedly 361 prostitutes over 16 years of age, and six under 16, in Belfast (Dickson, 'Evangelical Religion', p. 710).

76 *BNL*, 24 January 1874.

77 *BNL*, 14 February 1881, 12 March 1886, 20 February 1889, 11 September 1891.

78 Sandra Burman (ed.), *Fit Work for Women* (London: Oxford Women's Series, 1979), p. 10.

79 *Street-trading Children Committee (Ireland). Report […] together with Minutes of Evidence and Appendices* (BPP 1902 [Cd.1144] xlix), p. 72.

80 Megan Doolittle, 'Fatherhood and Family Shame: Masculinity, Welfare and the Workhouse in Late Nineteenth-Century England', in L. Delap, B. Griffin and A. Willis (eds), *The Politics of Domestic Authority in Britain since 1800* (London: Methuen, 1981), p. 95. See also Maria Luddy, 'The Early Years of the NSPCC in Ireland', *Éire-Ireland*, 44.1/2 (2009), pp. 62–90.

81 Dickson, 'Evangelical Religion', pp. 700–01.

82 Luddy, *Women and Philanthropy*, p. 211.

83 Myrtle Hill, 'Ulster: Debates, Demands and Divisions: The Battle for (and against) the Vote', in Louise Ryan and Margaret Ward (eds), *Irish Women and the Vote. Becoming Citizens* (Dublin: Irish Academic Press, 2007), p. 211; Diane Urquhart, 'An Articulate and Definite Cry for Political Freedom: The Ulster Suffrage Movement', *Women's History Review*, 11.2 (2002), pp. 273–92.

84 Elizabeth Crawford, *The Women's Suffrage Movement in Britain and Ireland. A Regional Survey* (London: Routledge, 2006), p. 254.

85 *BNL*, 24 October 1893, 10 October 1894; Heloise Brown, 'An Alternative Imperialism: Isabella Tod, Internationalist and "Good Liberal Unionist"', *Gender & History*, 10.3 (1998), p. 361.

86 Brown, 'An Alternative Imperialism', p. 365.

87 *Freeman's Journal*, 16 February 1896; Catherine Morris, 'Becoming Irish? Alice Milligan and the Revival', *Irish University Review*, 33.1 (2003), pp. 79–98; Catherine Morris, 'Alice Milligan and "Fin de Siecle" Belfast', in Nicholas Allen and Aaron Kelly (eds), *The Cities of Belfast* (Dublin: Four Courts Press, 2003), p. 65. The IWA was also known as the Nationalist Association of Irishwomen, and was later renamed the Irish Women's Centenary Union. See Urquhart, *Women in Ulster Politics*, ch. 3, and Margaret Ward, *Unmanageable Revolutionaries: Women and Irish Nationalism* (London: Pluto, 1983).

88 Morris, 'Alice Milligan and "Fin de Siecle" Belfast', p. 64.

89 *Irish News and Belfast Morning News*, 8 March 1895.

90 A.C. Hepburn, *Catholic Belfast and Nationalist Ireland in the Era of Joe Devlin 1871–1934* (Oxford: Oxford University Press, 2008), pp. 9–10.

91 Gillian McIntosh, 'Ireland's First Jewish Lord Mayor: Sir Otto Jaffé and Edwardian Belfast's Civic Sphere', *Jewish Culture and History*, 11.3 (2009), pp. 1–20.

92 W.J. Harvey, *Headline: G. Heyn and Sons Ltd* (Gravesend: World Ship Society, 1990).

93 Pamela McIlveen, 'Italians in Belfast: A Case Study of Modesto Silo and Family', *Journal of the British Isles Family History Society USA*, 22 (2009), p. 1.

94 Kyle Hughes, '"We Scotsmen by the Banks o' the Lagan". The Belfast Benevolent Society of St Andrew, 1867–1917', *Irish Economic & Social History*, 37 (2010), pp. 24–52.

95 Memoir of Doagh, County Antrim (Royal Irish Academy, Ordnance Survey Memoirs, 9/III/3), p. 56.

96 Frank Frankfort Moore, *In Belfast by the Sea*, ed. Patrick Maume (Dublin: UCD Press, 2007), p. 14.

1   The names of most oral history interviewees have been altered, at their request.

2   John Young Simms, *Farewell to the Hammer: A Shankill Boyhood* (Belfast: White Row Press, 1992), pp. 177–78, 97, 27.

3   May Blood, *Watch my lips, I'm speaking* (Dublin: Gill and Macmillan, 2007), p. 26.

4   Terry O'Neill, 'Raining bombs', *Belfast Magazine*, 14, p. 13.

5   Hugh Downey, the Northern Ireland Labour Party candidate, was elected in Dock Ward in 1945 and ousted by Thomas Cole, of the Ulster Unionist Party, in 1949.

6   Interview with Kathy (born 1920), 9 January 2003.

7   F.W. Boal, 'Belfast: Walls Within', *Political Geography*, 21.5 (2002), p. 689.

8   A.C. Hepburn, *A Past Apart: Studies in the History of Catholic Belfast, 1850–1950* (Belfast: Ulster Historical Foundation, 1996), p. 72.

9   Hepburn, *A Past Apart*, pp. 76, 207.

10 http://www.census.nationalarchives.ie (accessed 5 May 2011).

11 *Irish Times*, 26 July 1921.

12 *Irish Times*, 30, 31 August 1921.

13 *Irish Times*, 16, 19 September 1921.

14 *Irish Times*, 23 November 1921.

15 Interview with Mrs Rafferty (born 1904), 10 October 2002.

16 *Irish Times*, 19 June, 2 July 1935.

17 Hepburn, *A Past Apart*, p. 187; Sam McCaughtry, *On the Outside Looking In: A Memoir* (Belfast: Blackstaff Press, 2003), p. 27.

18 Emrys Jones, *A Social Geography of Belfast* (London: Oxford University Press, 1960), p. 174; William Maguire, *Belfast: A History* (Lancaster: Carnegie Publishing, 2009), p. 158; F.W. Boal, 'Back to the River: The Lagan and Belfast in the Twentieth Century', in Frederick W. Boal and Stephen A. Royle (eds), *Enduring City: Belfast in the Twentieth Century* (Belfast: Blackstaff Press, 2006), p. 158.

19 Sam McCaughtry, *Belfast Stories* (Belfast: Blackstaff Press, 2nd edn, 1993), p. 119.

20 John Boyd, *Out of my Class* (Belfast: Blackstaff Press, 1985).

21 Blood, *Watch my lips*, p. 25.

22 Jones, *Belfast*, pp. 100, 151.

23 *Irish Times*, 12 April 1948.

24 http://www.holy-familyparish.com/global/archive.html (accessed 2 August 2011).

25 John D. Brewer et al., 'Landscape of Spires', in Boal and Royle (eds), *Enduring City*, p. 185.

26 Hepburn, *A Past Apart*, p. 240.

27 *Irish Times*, 5, 7 May 1958.

28 *Irish Times*, 22 August 1929, 15 April 1935.

29 *Irish News*, 15 January 1913.

30 *Belfast Telegraph*, 25 November 1930; S. O'Connell, 'From "Toad of Toad Hall" to the "Death Drivers" of Belfast: An Exploratory History of Joyriding', *British Journal of Criminology*, 46.3 (2006), pp. 455–69.

31 Caroline Black, *For All that I Found There* (London: Duckworth, 1973), p. 139.

32 Sam McCaughtry, *Blind Spot and Other Stories* (Belfast: Blackstaff Press, 1979), pp. 24–25.

33 Paul Larmour, 'Bricks, Stone, Concrete and Steel: The Built Fabric of Twentieth-Century Belfast', in Boal and Royle (eds), *Enduring City*, p. 42.

34 Jones, *Belfast*, pp. 264–65.

35 J.H. Johnson, 'The Geography of a Belfast Suburb', *Irish Geography*, 3 (1956), p. 150.

36 See above, p. 17.

37 Ian Budge and Cornelius O'Leary, *Belfast: Approach to Crisis. A Study of Belfast Politics, 1613–1970* (London: Macmillan, 1973), pp. 138–42.

38 Jonathan Bardon, 'Governing the City', in Boal and Royle (eds), *Enduring City*, p. 130; Maguire, *Belfast*, p. 200.

39 Hepburn, *A Past Apart*, pp. 188–89; *Irish Independent*, 1 October 1935.

40 Interview with Kathy (born 1920), 9 January 2003.

41 F.W. Boal, 'A Belfast Blitz Addendum', in Boal and Royle (eds), *Enduring City*, pp. 234–35.

42 Budge and O'Leary, *Belfast*, p. 164.

43 Jones, *Belfast*, p. 138.

44 Interview with Joan (born 1940), 14 April 2003.

45 Bill Morrison, 'Planning the City, Planning the Region', in Boal and Royle (eds), *Enduring City*, p. 146.

46 Larmour, 'Bricks, Stone, Concrete and Steel', p. 45.

47 Maguire, *Belfast*, pp. 222–23.

48 Budge and O'Leary, *Belfast*, p. 164.

49 *Irish Times*, 4 March 1969, 21 March 1968.

50 A.E.C.W. Spencer, *Ballymurphy: A Tale of Two Surveys* (Belfast: Queen's University, 1973).

51 Jones, *Belfast*, p. 146.

52 *Irish Times*, 12 November 1959.

53 Ron Weiner, *The Rape and Plunder of the Shankill* (Belfast: Farset Co-operative Press, 1978); Denis Smyth, *Sailortown: The Story of a Dockside Community* (Belfast: North Belfast History Workshop, 1990), p. 7. See also http://www.sailortown.org (accessed 3 May 2012).

54 Maguire, *Belfast*, p. 222.

55 *Belfast Telegraph*, 11 October 1967.

56 John Nagle, 'From "Ban-the-Bomb" to "Ban-the-Increase": Street Politics in Pre-Civil Rights Belfast', *Irish Political Studies*, 23.1 (2008), p. 53.

57 Budge and O'Leary, *Belfast*, p. 164.

58 Myrtle Hill, *Women in Ireland* (Belfast: Blackstaff Press, 2003), p. 127.

59 Marianne Elliott, *The Catholics of Ulster: A History* (London: Penguin Books, 2001), pp. xxxv–xxxvi.

60 Dorita E. Field and Desmond G. Neill, *A Survey of New Housing Estates in Belfast: A Social and Economic Study of the Estates Built by the Northern Ireland Housing Trust in the Belfast Area 1945–1954* (Belfast: Queen's University, 1957), pp. 15–18.

61 *Irish Times*, 4 December 1953.

62 Bardon, 'Governing the City', p. 129.

63 Dorita Field, *A Report on Unsatisfactory Tenants of Belfast Corporation in the Ballymurphy, New Barnsley and Flush Park Estates* (Belfast: Belfast Council of Social Welfare, 1960), pp. 10–11.

64 Field and Neill, *New Housing Estates in Belfast*, pp. 6–9.

65 Field and Neill, *New Housing Estates in Belfast*, pp. 42–44.

66 Field and Neill, *New Housing Estates in Belfast*, p. 55.

67 Field and Neill, *New Housing Estates in Belfast*, pp. 7, 57–59.

68 Field, *Unsatisfactory Tenants*, tables 6 and 7.

69 David Johnson, *The Interwar Economy in Ireland* (Dundalk: Economic and Social History Society of Ireland, 1989), p. 37.

70 Keith Jeffery, *Ireland and the Great War* (Cambridge: Cambridge University Press, 2000), pp. 30–32.

71 Maguire, *Belfast*, p. 195.

72 Johnson, *Interwar Economy in Ireland*, p. 34.

73 Brian Barton, *The Blitz: Belfast in the War Years* (Belfast: Blackstaff Press, 1989), p. 21.

74 Barton, *The Blitz*, p. 11.

75 Johnson, *Interwar Economy in Ireland*, p. 43.

76 *Belfast Telegraph*, 3 June 1935.

77 Maguire, *Belfast*, p. 194.

78 Johnson, *Interwar Economy in Ireland*, p. 43.

79 Interview with Bob (born 1924), 12 February 2004.

80 Hill, *Women in Ireland*, p. 119.

81 Maguire, *Belfast*, pp. 206–07; Philip Ollerenshaw, 'War, Industrial Mobilisation and Society in Northern Ireland, 1939–1945', *Contemporary European History*, 16.2 (2007), p. 173.

82 Mark Hart, 'From Smokestacks to Service Economy', in Boal and Royle (eds), *Enduring City*, p. 88.

83 Maguire, *Belfast*, pp. 208–17.

84 Graham Brownlow, 'Business and Labour in Northern Ireland since 1945', in L. Kennedy and P. Ollerenshaw (eds), *An Economic History of Ulster* (forthcoming 2012).

85 Field and Neill, *New Housing Estates*, p. 29.

86 *BNL*, 3 June 1941.

87 R.J. Lawrence, *The Government of Northern Ireland: Public Finance and Public Services, 1921–1962* (Oxford: Clarendon Press, 1965), p. 68.

88 Greta Jones, *'Captain of All These Men of Death': The History of Tuberculosis in Nineteenth- and Twentieth-Century Ireland* (Amsterdam: Rodopi, 2001), p. 192.

89 Paul Bew, Peter Gibbon and Henry Patterson, *The State in Northern Ireland, 1921–1972* (Manchester: Manchester University Press, 1996), p. 114.

90 Alun Evans, 'Health in Belfast', in Boal and Royle (eds), *Enduring City*, p. 244; Lawrence, *Government of Northern Ireland*, p. 142.

91 Interview with Ethel (born 1920), 25 September 2002.

92 Marilynn Richtarik, 'Stewart Parker at Queen's University, Belfast', *Irish Review*, 29 (2002), p. 59.

93 Elliott, *Catholics of Ulster*, p. 465.

94 Barton, *The Blitz*, p. 16.

95 *Irish Times*, 6 May 1958.

96 Hepburn, *A Past Apart*, p. 110.

97 McCaughtry, *On the Outside Looking In*, p. 43.

98 Simms, *Farewell to the Hammer*, p. 97.

99 *Irish Times*, 11 July 1958.

100 Hepburn, *A Past Apart*, pp. 110, 149.

101 *Irish Times*, 5 May 1958.

102 Sabine Wichert, *Northern Ireland since 1945* (London: Longmann, 2nd edn, 1999), p. 51.

103 Hepburn, *A Past Apart*, p. 47.

104 Jonathan Hamill, 'A Study of Female Textile Operatives in the Belfast Linen Industry, 1890–1939', unpublished PhD thesis, Queen's University, Belfast, 1999, p. 237.

105 Hill, *Women in Ireland*, p.77.

106 Interview with Harriet (born 1913), 3 November 2002.

107 F.W. Boal, 'Big Processes and Little People: The Population of Metropolitan Belfast', in Boal and Royle (eds), *Enduring City*, pp. 66–67.

108 Interview with Kathy (born 1920), 9 January 2003.

109 Interview with Lily (born 1920), 11 September 2002.

110 *Belfast Telegraph*, 3 March 1962.

111 This world is illustrated colourfully in John Campbell's novel *The Disinherited* (Belfast: Lagan Press, 2006).

112 Interview with Harriet (born 1913), 3 November 2002.

113 History of pawnbroking, ms copy extracts of a paper read to Belfast Pawnbrokers' Association by Samuel McClure, n.d. (PRONI, D2776/14);

Kenneth Hudson, *Pawnbroking: An Aspect of British Social History* (London: Bodley Head, 1982), pp. 102–03.

114 *Irish Times*, 30 March 1921.

115 Interview with Mrs Rafferty (born 1904), 10 October 2002.

116 Jonathan Bardon, 'Popular Culture', in Boal and Royle (eds), *Enduring City*, p. 276.

117 Sean O'Connell, *Credit and Community: Working Class Debt since 1880* (Oxford: Oxford University Press, 2009).

118 Larmour, 'Bricks, Stone, Concrete and Steel', p. 39.

119 *Belfast Telegraph*, 27 July 1937.

120 *Belfast Telegraph*, 7 April 1930.

121 *Belfast Telegraph*, 21 June 1935.

122 Hire purchase and credit sales agreements (order) contravention by Crawley and Quinn Ltd., Belfast (National Archives (London), BT64/5209).

123 Interview with Kathy (born 1920), 9 January 2003.

124 *Irish Times*, 10 November 1936; Bardon, 'Popular Culture', p. 285; Maguire, *Belfast*, p. 227.

125 McCaughtry, *Belfast Stories*, p. 112.

126 *Irish Times*, 23 March 1954; Bardon, 'Popular Culture', p. 286.

127 Interview with Florence (born 1915), 12 February 2003.

128 Interview with Harriet (born 1913), 3 November 2002.

129 Interview with Norman (born 1924), 18 February 2003.

130 McCaughtry, *Belfast Stories*, p. 20.

131 Leanne McCormick, 'One Yank and They're Off! Interaction between US Troops and Northern Irish Women, 1943–1945', *Journal of History of Sexuality*, 15.2 (2006), pp. 228–57; *Irish Times*, 12 August 1943; *Belfast Telegraph*, 29 May 1944.

132 *Belfast Telegraph*, 3 August 1961.

133 *Irish Times*, 16 June 1964.

134 Terri Hooley, *Hooleygan* (Belfast: Blackstaff Press, 2010), pp. 20–21; *Irish Times*, 14 December 1968.

135 Hooley, *Hooleygan*, p. 31.

136 Simms, *Farewell to the Hammer*, p. 127.

137 *Irish Times*, 5 May 1958.

138 *Irish Times*, 29 March 1956, 12 January 1959; Rex Cathcart, *The Most Contrary Region: The BBC in Northern Ireland 1924–1984* (Belfast: Blackstaff Press, 1984), p. 193.

139 *Tribune*, 16 August 1957.

140 *Independent*, 19 November 2009.

141 *Irish Times*, 5 June 1928.

142 *BNL*, 12, 19 July 1949.

143 *Belfast Telegraph*, 19 July 1955.

144 *Belfast Telegraph*, 12 August 1964.

145 *Irish Times*, 9 May, 27 September 1967.

146 *Belfast Telegraph*, 29 December 1948.

147 John Sugden, *Boxing and Society* (Manchester: Manchester University Press, 1996), p. 129.

148 Cathcart, *Most Contrary Region*, p. 182.

149 Graham Walker, *A History of the Ulster Unionist Party* (Manchester: Manchester University Press, 2004), p. 159.

1 Simon Prince, *Northern Ireland's '68: Civil Rights, Global Revolt and the Origins of the Troubles* (Dublin: Irish Academic Press, 2007).

2 Henri Lefebvre, *The Production of Space* (Oxford: Blackwell, 1991).

3 A. Boserup and C. Iversen, 'Rank Analysis of a Polarized Community: A Case Study from Northern Ireland', *Peace Research Society (International) Papers*, 7 (1967), p. 60.

4 Frederick W. Boal, *Shaping a City: Belfast in the Late Twentieth Century* (Belfast: Institute of Irish Studies, 1995), p. 47.

5 Gillian McIntosh, *Belfast City Hall: One Hundred Years* (Belfast: Blackstaff Press, 2006).

6 William Maguire, *Belfast: A History* (Lancaster: Carnegie Publishing, 2009), pp. 215–17.

7 Maguire, *Belfast*, p. 217.

8 Liam Kennedy, *The Modern Industrialisation of Ireland 1940–1988* (Dundalk: Social and Economic History Society of Ireland, 1989), p. 16.

9 Kennedy, *Modern Industrialisation*, p. 26.

10 Kennedy, *Modern Industrialisation*, p. 27.

11 Boal, *Shaping a City*, p. 41.

12 Dominic Bryan, *Orange Parades: The Politics of Ritual, Tradition and Control* (London: Pluto Press, 2000).

13 Frederick W. Boal, 'Territoriality on the Shankill–Falls Divide, Belfast', *Irish Geography*, 41.3 (2008), p. 350.

14 Bob Purdie, *Politics in the Street: The Origins of the Civil Rights Movement in Northern Ireland* (Belfast: Blackstaff Press, 1990), p. 133.

15 Simon Prince and Geoffrey Warner, *Belfast and Derry in Revolt: A New History of the Start of the Troubles* (Dublin: Irish Academic Press, 2012), p. 136.

16 Liam Kelly, 'Belfast, August 1969', unpublished PhD thesis, Queen's University, Belfast, 2012.

17 Kelly, 'Belfast, August 1969'.

18 *Belfast Telegraph*, 15 August 1969, quoted in Gordon Gillespie, *Years of Darkness: The Troubles Remembered* (Dublin: Gill and Macmillan, 2008), p. 19.

19 Colin Crawford, *Inside the UDA: Volunteers and Violence* (London: Pluto Press, 1973), p. 20.

20 *Daily Mirror*, 6 December 1971, quoted in Gillespie, *Years of Darkness*, p. 37.

21 Geoffrey Warner, 'The Falls Road Curfew Revisited', *Irish Studies Review*, 14.3 (2006), pp. 325–42.

22 Peter Shirlow and Brendan Murtagh, *Belfast: Segregation, Violence and the City* (London: Pluto Press, 2006), p. 73.

23 Shirlow and Murtagh, *Belfast*, pp. 73–74.

24 Frederick W. Boal, 'Encapsulation: Urban Dimensions of National Conflict', in Seamus Dunn (ed.), *Managing Divided Cities* (Keele: Ryburn Publishing), p. 31.

25 S.A. Bollens, *Urban Peace Building in Divided Cities: Belfast and Johannesburg* (Boulder, CO: Westview Press, 1999), p. 59.

26 Future Policy on Areas of Confrontation: Second (and final) Report of the Joint Working Party on Processions, April 1971 (PRONI, 2HD4/1634/1), pp. 19–20. See also J. Byrne, 'The Belfast Peace Walls: The Problems, Policies, and Politics of the Troubles Architecture', unpublished DPhil thesis, University of Ulster, 2011.

27 Begoña Aretxaga, *Shattering Silence: Women, Nationalism, and Political Subjectivity in Northern Ireland* (Princetown: Princetown University Press, 1997).

28 Paul Doherty and Michael Poole, *Ethnic Residential Segregation in Belfast* (Coleraine: Centre for the Study of Conflict), p. 41. Also Shirlow and Murtagh, *Belfast*, p. 70.

29 Shirlow and Murtagh, *Belfast*, p. 70.

30 Allen Feldman, *Formations of Violence: The Narrative of the Body and Political Terror in Northern Ireland* (Chicago: University of Chicago Press, 1991), p. 37.

31 Frank Burton, *The Politics of Legitimacy: Struggles in a Belfast Community* (London: Routledge and Kegan Paul, 1978), p. 20.

32 Future Policy on Processions etc: First Report of the Joint Working Party on Processions, December 1970 (PRONI, CAB4/1569/19).

33 Bryan, *Orange Parades*, pp. 88, 119–200.

34 Future Policy on Processions etc: First Report of the Joint Working Party on Processions, December 1970 (PRONI, CAB4/1569/19), p. 16.

35   Stephen Brown, 'Central Belfast Security Segment', *Area*, 17.1 (1985), p. 3.

36   Brown, 'Central Belfast Security Segment', pp. 1–3.

37   For the shift in PIRA tactics to a 'long war' of attrition, see Gillespie, *Years of Darkness*, pp. 146–47.

38   Brown, 'Central Belfast Security Segment', pp. 6–8.

39   *Irish News*, 4 December 1980.

40   *BNL*, 9 May 1994.

41   Boal, *Shaping a City*, p. 50.

42   G.M. Dawson, 'Defensive Planning in Belfast', *Irish Geography*, 17.1 (1984), pp. 27–41.

43   Dawson , 'Defensive Planning in Belfast', pp. 38–39.

44   Boal, *Shaping a City*, pp. 22–25; Paul Doherty and Michael Poole, *Ethnic Residential Segregation in Belfast* (Coleraine: Centre for the Study of Conflict, 1985), p. 98

45   Boal, *Shaping a City*, p. 28.

46   Boal, *Shaping a City*, p. 40.

47   R. Cowan, 'Belfast's Hidden Planners', *Town and Country Planning* (June 1982), p. 163.

48   Boal, *Shaping a City*, p. 101.

49   Future Policy on Areas of Confrontation: Second (and final) Report of the Joint Working Party on Processions, April 1971 (PRONI, 2HD4/1634/1).

50   Department of the Environment (2004), *Belfast Metropolitan Plan 2015*, p. 22 http://www.planningni.gov.uk/index/policy/dev_plans/devplans_az/bmap_2015.htm (accessed 20 October 2011).

51   *Daily Mail*, 28 May 1974, quoted in Gillespie, *Years of Darkness*, p. 98.

52   Chris Thornton, Seamus Kelters, Brian Feeney and David McKittrick, *Lost Lives The Stories of the Men, Women and Children Who Died as a Result of the Northern Ireland Troubles* (London: Mainstream Publishing, 1999).

53   Gillespie, *Years of Darkness*, p. 142

54   *An Phoblacht*, 9 May 1981, quoted in Gillespie, *Years of Darkness*, p. 144.

55   Richard English, *Armed Struggle: The History of the IRA* (London: Pan Macmillan 2004), pp. 206–07.

56   Bill Rolston, *Politics and Painting: Murals and Conflict in Northern Ireland* (London and Toronto: Associated University Press, 1991), p. 79.

57   Rolston, *Politics and Painting*, pp. 79–89.

58   Rolston, *Politics and Painting*, pp. 20–21.

59   Rolston, *Politics and Painting*, pp. 43–44.

60   Neil Jarman, 'The Orange Arch: Creating Tradition in Ulster', *Folklore*, 12 (2001), pp. 1–12.

61   Neil Jarman, 'Violent Men, Violent Land: Dramatising the Troubles and the Landscape of Ulster', *Journal of Material Culture*, 1.1 (1996), pp. 39–61.

62   Neil Jarman, 'The Place of Murals in the Symbolic Construction of Urban Space', in Anthony Buckley (ed.), *Symbols in Northern Ireland* (Belfast: Institute of Irish Studies, 1998), p. 91.

63   Neil Jarman, *Material Conflicts: Parades and Visual Displays in Northern Ireland* (Oxford: Berg, 1997).

64   Neil Jarman, 'For God and Ulster: Blood and Thunder Bands and Loyalist Political Culture', in T.G. Fraser (ed.), *The Irish Parading Tradition: Following the Drum* (Basingstoke: Macmillan, 2000).

65   Victor Mesev, Peter Shirlow and Joni Downs, 'The Geography of Conflict and Death in Belfast, Northern Ireland', *Annals of the Association of American Geographers*, 99.5 (2009), pp. 898–99.

66   Shirlow and Murtagh, *Belfast*; Mesev, Shirlow and Downs, 'Geography of Conflict and Death', p. 900.

67   Elisabetta Viggiani, *Public Forms of Memorialisation to the Victims of the Northern Irish "Troubles" in the City of Belfast*, database on the Cain website http://cain.ulst.ac.uk/viggiani/introduction.htm (accessed 19 October 2011).

68   Cain website memorials database, http://cain.ulst.ac.uk/victims/memorials/ (accessed 13 December 2011).

69   Shirlow and Murtagh, *Belfast*, p. 59.

70   Doherty and Poole, *Ethnic Residential Segregation in Belfast*, p. 99.

71   Neil Jarman, *On the Edge: Community Perspectives on the Civil Disturbances in North Belfast, June–September 1996* (Belfast: Community Development Centre, 1997), p. 44.

72   Resident of Clifton Park Avenue, quoted in Jarman, *On the Edge*, p. 49.

73   Dominic Bryan, Clifford Stevenson, Gordon Gillespie and John Bell, *Public Display of Flags and Emblems in Northern Ireland* (Belfast: Institute of Irish Studies, 2010), p. 8.

74   Community Relations Council, *Towards Sustainable Security: Interface Barriers and the Legacy of Separation in Belfast* (Belfast: Community Relations Council, 2008), p. 3, http://www.community-relations.org.uk/fs/doc/iwg-publication.pdf (accessed 20 October 2011).

75   Dominic Bryan and Clifford Stevenson, *Flags Monitoring Project 2006: Preliminary Findings* (Belfast: Office of the Deputy First Minister, 2007), p. 50, http://www.ofmdfmni.gov.uk/flags-monitoring.pdf (accessed 20 October 2011); Dominic Bryan and Clifford Stevenson, 'Flagging Peace: Struggles over Symbolic Landscape in the New Northern Ireland', in Marc Howard Ross (ed.), *Culture and Belonging in Divided Societies* (Philadelphia: University of Pennsylvania Press, 2009), pp. 68–84.

76   Belfast City Council, *Belfast: A Profile of the City*, p. 23, http://www.belfastcity.gov.uk/docs/BelfastProfileoftheCity2010.pdf (accessed 20 October 2011).

77   Jarman, *Material Conflicts*, p. 151; McIntosh, *Belfast City Hall*, p. 135.

78   'Glorious Green Gridlock', *Andersonstown News*, 21 March 1998.

79   John Nagel, 'The Right to Belfast City Centre: From Ethnocracy to Liberal Multiculturalism?', *Political Geography*, 30 (2009), pp. 1–10; Dominic Bryan, 'Negotiating Civic Space in Belfast, or the Tricolour: Here Today, Gone Tomorrow', *Working Paper No. 13 Conflict and Cities and the Contested State Project*, 2009, http://www.conflictincities.org/workingpapers.html (accessed 3 May 2012).

80   Belfast City Council, *Good Relations Strategy: Building Our Futures Together* (Belfast: Belfast City Council, 2003) http://www.belfastcity.gov.uk/publications/GoodRelationsStrategy.pdf (accessed 20 October 2011).

81   Belfast City Council, *Belfast: A Profile of the City*, p. 17.

82   Belfast City Council, *Belfast: A Profile of the City*, p. 16.

83 Boal, *Shaping a City*, p. 85.

84 Frank Gaffikin and Mike Morrissey,
    *City Visions: Imagining Place,
    Enfranchising People* (London: Pluto
    Press, 1999).

85 BBC News, http://www.bbc.co.uk/
    news/uk-northern-ireland-11692964
    (accessed 3 May 2012).

86 Bollens, *Urban Peace Building in Divided
    Cities*, p. 35.

Timeline

Prehistory

c.8000BC–c.7000BC

The first settlers arrive in the area around Belfast during the Mesolithic period.

c.4000BC–c.2500BC

The Neolithic period. The first permanent settlements are established at Belfast and the earliest surviving (stone) monuments, such as tombs, are erected there.

c.2500BC–c.500BC

The Bronze Age. This is probably the period during which McArt's Fort, the promontory fort on Cave Hill, was constructed.

Early and Medieval History

668 The first documentary reference to Belfast, in an annalistic entry recording a battle between the Ulaid and the Cruithin, fought at a crossing point on the River Lagan referred to as Fearsat (sandbank).

1177 John de Courcy captures Downpatrick, initiating Anglo-Norman settlement in Ulster.

1262 Ten pounds are granted to Richard de Exeter for the custody of the Castle of the Ford, marking the first documentary reference to a castle at Belfast.

1306 A Papal Taxation document lists churches at Belfast.

1333 The Inquisition Post Mortem held after the murder of the last resident earl of Ulster, William de Burgh, notes that the castle, borough town and watermill at Belfast were all destroyed, apparently in the period of unrest that followed.

1476 The castle at Belfast, now held by the O'Neills of Clandeboye, is demolished by the forces of the main O'Neill dynasty. An annalistic reference contains the earliest recorded form of the city's modern name 'Bel-feirste'.

The Sixteenth Century

1551 Belfast Castle is reputedly taken by the lord deputy, Sir James Croft.

1571 Sir Thomas Smith is granted extensive lands in eastern Ulster including Belfast.

1573 Walter Devereux, earl of Essex, is granted lands in Clandeboye and other places, including Belfast.

1574 Essex arrests Brian Mac Phelim O'Neill, lord of Clandeboye, and kills over 100 of his followers, having lured them to an entertainment at Belfast Castle. O'Neill, his wife and brother are subsequently executed in Dublin.

1594–1603 A revolt by O'Neill, O'Donnell and other Ulster Gaelic lords initiates a prolonged conflict, the Nine Years' War.

1597 Shane Mac Brian O'Neill massacres the English garrison at Belfast. The castle is quickly regained by Sir John Chichester who puts its occupants to the sword.

1603–1649

1603 Sir Arthur Chichester receives a grant for Belfast Castle and its lands. He constructs a fortified Jacobean house on the ruins of the O'Neill tower-house.

1605 Belfast is granted a charter for a market.

1608 Belfast is granted a charter for a fair.

1611 The Plantation Commissioners report that a 'bricke house' has been built and a town laid out.

1613 Belfast is constituted a corporation by charter.

1642 The first town defences are constructed.

1644 Major General Munroe seizes Belfast on behalf of parliament during the civil war.

1649 Belfast is taken by Cromwellian forces under Robert Venables.

1650–1699

1663 A new market house is constructed.

1672 A Presbyterian meeting house is recorded in Belfast.

1675 The quay is substantially enlarged.

1680 A proposal is made for the construction of Long Bridge across the Lagan. Building is completed by c.1685.

1685 The first detailed maps of Belfast are drawn up by Thomas Phillips.

1688 The Jacobite charter is issued, and cancelled after 1690.

1694 Patrick Neill, printer, of Glasgow begins printing books in Belfast.

c.1697–c.1725 The Belfast Potthouse (pottery) on Waring Street produces high-quality tin-glazed earthenwares (Delft).

1700–1749

1707 Following a disputed election, parliament confirms the exclusion of Presbyterians from the corporation of Belfast by virtue of the Act of 1704 requiring office holders to take the sacramental test. The town's second Presbyterian church is built.

1708 Belfast Castle is destroyed by fire. The Donegall family leave the town for England.

1711 Isaac McCartney lays out his Hanover Quay development.

1715 John Maclanachan maps the town. New army barracks are built in Barrack Street.

1722 Third Belfast Presbyterian church is built.

1737 The first *Belfast News Letter* is printed by Francis Joy.

1739 The Linen Hall is built in Ann Street.

Timeline

1750–1774

1752 A private Act of Parliament allows trustees of the Donegall estate to make leases for Belfast.

1752 The first meeting to initiate a Poor House is held.

1754 The Brown Linen Hall is built on Linen Hall Street (later Donegall Street).

1757 On the death of the fourth earl of Donegall (30 September), Arthur Chichester (1739–99) becomes fifth earl of Donegall, and is created marquess in 1791.

1763 The Lagan Navigation from Belfast to Lisburn is opened.

1769 The Exchange building is completed on Waring Street.

1774 The Belfast Charitable Society is incorporated.

1775–1799

1776 Assembly Rooms are added to the Exchange. St Anne's church is built on Donegall Street.

1778 The First Belfast Volunteer Company is formed.

1783 First Presbyterian church, Rosemary Street, is rebuilt. A meeting is held to establish a Chamber of Commerce. Waddell Cunningham is returned as MP for Carrickfergus.

1784 St Mary's is opened as Belfast's first Catholic place of worship.

1785 The White Linen Hall is completed. 25 George III c.64 creates the Belfast Ballast Office.

1786 Belfast Academy opens.

1787 Ballymacarrett is purchased by Donegall from Barry Yelverton, who had purchased it from the Pottinger family.

1788 The Belfast Reading Society (later Belfast Society for Promoting Knowledge, 1792) is founded. Cotton spinning begins in the Poor House.

1791 Volunteers celebrate the anniversary of the fall of the Bastille. The Society of United Irishmen is founded on 14 October.

1792 The first number of the *Northern Star* is published (4 January). The Belfast Harp Festival is held (11–14 July).

1794 The Lagan Navigation extension is formally opened (1 January).

1795 The Belfast Charitable Society takes over the town's water supply. George Augustus Chichester marries Anna May.

1797 Militia destroy the *Northern Star* printing press (19 May).

1798 United Irish risings take place in Antrim and Down (6–13 June). Henry Joy McCracken, leader of the Antrim rising, is executed in Belfast on 17 July.

1799 On the death of the first marquess of Donegall (5 January), George Augustus Chichester (1769–1844) becomes the second marquess.

1800–1849

1800 The Belfast Improvement Act (40 George III c.47) creates a partially accountable body to manage the town's affairs.

1813 A riot following the return of Orangemen from parade in Lisburn possibly marks the beginnings of Belfast's long history of sectarian conflict, although the prime motivation may have been political.

1816 Belfast town police is established.

1822 Lord Donegall commences the granting of leases in perpetuity under revised family settlement.

1823 Gas lighting is introduced.

1828 Mulholland's York Street cotton mill is destroyed by fire and rebuilt as a linen-spinning mill.

1832 The Reform Act gives Belfast two parliamentary seats and an electorate of around 1,400. The first open parliamentary elections in December return two Conservatives.

1839 William Dargan begins major improvements to the harbour. Two major cuts (1839–41 and 1847–49) create a deep-water channel. The material excavated creates Dargan's Island, renamed Queen's Island after Victoria's visit in 1849.

1842 Election of reformed corporation under the 1840 Irish Municipal Corporations Act of 1840.

1849 Queen Victoria visits Belfast on her way from Dublin to Glasgow (11 August).

1850–1899

1852   The British Association for the Advancement of Science meets in Belfast.

1853   The Harbour Commissioners provide land for iron shipbuilding on Queen's Island.

1853   The municipal boundary is extended.

1858   Edward James Harland and Company shipyard is established.

1871   The Town Hall is completed.

1872   Belfast Street Tramways Bill is passed.

1873   The gasworks is taken into municipal ownership.

1881   Royal Avenue is completed.

1887   The Blackstaff is culverted in a new channel.

1888   Belfast is awarded city status.

1888   Robinson and Cleaver's department store opens.

1893   The Belfast Water Act secures supplies from the Mourne Mountains.

1895   Electricity is first supplied to the city.

1896   Boundary extension.

1900–1949

1903   King Edward VII and Queen Alexandra visit Belfast to unveil the statue of Queen Victoria in front of the unfinished City Hall, and open the Royal Victoria Hospital.

1907   There is a major strike by dockers, carters and others.

1912   *Titanic* is launched and sinks on her maiden voyage. Ulster Protestants mobilize against Home Rule.

1920   Expulsions of Catholic and 'disloyal' Protestant workers from the shipyards initiate two years of sustained political and sectarian violence.

1921   The Northern Ireland parliament holds its first session in City Hall.

1924   The BBC commences broadcasting from Belfast.

1932   Outdoor Relief protests. Parliament Buildings at Stormont are opened.

1935   Workman, Clark and Co. shipyard closes. Ten people are killed in sectarian riots.

1941   Belfast is hit by repeated German air raids (April–May).

1943   Belfast Corporation is suspended due to financial irregularities.

1950–2011

1966   Queen Elizabeth II visits the city.

1969   Troops are deployed following serious communal violence.

1972   A multiple bomb attack by the IRA in Belfast ('Bloody Friday', 21 July) leaves nine dead and 130 injured.

1974   The power-sharing executive established under the Sunningdale Agreement collapses following a prolonged strike by the Ulster Workers Council.

1976   A rally of 20,000 people meet in Ormeau Park in support of the Women's Peace Movement (21 August).

1983   Gerry Adams wins the West Belfast seat to become an MP at Westminster.

1990   The Castlecourt centre is opened.

1994   The Provisional IRA declare an indefinite ceasefire, followed by the three main loyalist paramilitary groups.

1995   US President Clinton turns on the Christmas tree lights outside Belfast City Hall.

1997   Alban Maginness of the SDLP becomes the first Irish nationalist mayor of Belfast.

2002   Alex Maskey becomes the first Sinn Féin mayor of Belfast.

2006   Belfast City Council takes over the organization of St Patrick's Day events in the city.

Further Reading

As an attempt to provide a rounded overview of the development of Belfast this volume has two distinguished predecessors. Jonathan Bardon's *Belfast: An Illustrated History* (Belfast: Blackstaff Press, 1982), a lively narrative packed with vivid material from contemporary sources, is unfortunately now out of print. W.A. Maguire's *Belfast: A History* (Lancaster: Carnegie Publishing, 2nd edn, 2009) is a concise and authoritative survey, covering both political and social and economic developments. For those who want to look further, George Benn's substantial *A History of the Town of Belfast from the Earliest Times to the Close of the Eighteenth Century* (1877, reprinted Belfast: Blackstaff Press, 2008) contains a wealth of detail, some of it based on documentary sources since destroyed, as well as on information collected by the author from older fellow citizens.

One further classic work, again long out of print, deserves to be mentioned. Emrys Jones, *A Social Geography of Belfast* (Oxford: Oxford University Press, 1960) is both a pioneering work of historical investigation, using maps and documentary sources to trace the development of the town and city, and a snapshot of Belfast at the end of its period as a centre of heavy industry.

For a survey of the archaeological sources for Belfast, and a thorough review of the existing literature, see Ruairi Ó Baoill, *Hidden History Below Our Feet: The Archaeological Story of Belfast* (Belfast: Tandem for the Northern Ireland Environment Agency and Belfast City Council, 2011). *The Ulster Journal of Archaeology* has devoted a special issue, volume 65 (2006), to recent work on Belfast. For seventeenth- and eighteenth-century Belfast, there is now an authoritative survey in Raymond Gillespie, *Early Belfast: The Origins and Growth of an Ulster Town before 1750* (Belfast: Ulster Historical Foundation, 2007).

Writing on nineteenth-century Belfast is more extensive. Directions to the literature on specific topics can be found in the footnotes to Chapters 1, 6 and 7 above. One valuable introduction is the two remarkable fascicles of the Royal Irish Academy's Historic Towns Atlas: Raymond Gillespie and Stephen Royle, *Irish Historic Towns Atlas – No. 12: Belfast to 1840* (Dublin: Royal Irish Academy,

2003) and Stephen Royle, *Irish Historic Towns Atlas – No. 17: Belfast 1840–1901* (Dublin: Royal Irish Academy, 2007). In the wide range of writings on the town's sectarian divisions, Catherine Hirst, *Religion, Politics and Violence in Nineteenth-Century Belfast: The Pound and Sandy Row* (Dublin: Four Courts Press, 2002) stands out for its combination of a painstaking reconstruction of events and an in-depth examination of their social and political context. A.C. Hepburn, *A Past Apart: Studies in the History of Catholic Belfast 1850–1950* (Belfast: Ulster Historical Foundation, 1996) is much broader than the title suggests, and presents the results of the author's pioneering use of census records to go beyond political rhetoric and explore the real workings of religious and economic division.

For the twentieth century there is a comprehensive overview in F.W. Boal and Stephen Royle, *Enduring City: Belfast in the Twentieth Century* (Belfast: Blackstaff Press, 2006).

Notes on Contributors

Dominic Bryan was born in London and moved to Belfast in 1991 to study for a PhD in social anthropology at the University of Ulster. He joined the Institute of Irish Studies at Queen's University, Belfast, in 1999 and has been its director since 2002. His central research interest explores how public space is managed in Northern Ireland and his publications include *Orange Parades: The Politics of Ritual, Tradition and Control* (2000).

Sean Connolly has been Professor of Irish History at Queen's University, Belfast, since 1996, having previously taught at the University of Ulster. He has been editor of the journal *Irish Economic & Social History*, and was also general editor of the *Oxford Companion to Irish History* (1998). His most recent books are *Contested Ireland 1460–1630* (2007) and *Divided Kingdom: Ireland 1630–1800* (2008).

Raymond Gillespie teaches history at National University of Ireland Maynooth. He is a native of Belfast and has written extensively about the early history of the city including (with Stephen Royle) the first part of the Royal Irish Academy's *Irish Historic Towns Atlas – No. 12: Belfast to 1840* (2003), and *Early Belfast: The Origins and Growth of an Ulster Town before 1750* (2007).

Philip Macdonald is an archaeologist employed in the Centre for Archaeological Fieldwork at Queen's University, Belfast. He has directed excavations at a number of archaeological sites in Northern Ireland, including the Late Bronze Age promontory fort at Knock Dhu, the Gaelic military fort of the Nine Years' War at Inisloughlin and the post-medieval manor house at Dundrum Castle, and he has a particular research interest in the medieval history of Belfast.

Gillian McIntosh is a social and cultural historian who has worked as a research fellow at Queen's University since 1997. She has published widely on twentieth-century Northern Ireland, but has been increasingly lured into the rich urban history of nineteenth-century Belfast and its civic culture, on which she has published several articles and a book marking the centenary of Belfast City Hall. Her most recent book is (with Diane Urquhart) *Irish Women and War: The Twentieth Century* (2010).

Ruairí Ó Baoill works in the Centre for Archaeological Fieldwork, School of Geography, Archaeology and Palaeoecology, Queen's University, Belfast. He specializes in the urban archaeology of Ireland. He is the author of *Hidden History Below Our Feet: The Archaeological Story of Belfast* (2011), the first ever book-length study of the archaeology of Belfast, and *Carrickfergus: The Story of the Castle and Walled Town* (2008).

Sean O'Connell is a Senior Lecturer at Queen's University, Belfast, where he teaches modern history. He has lived in Belfast since 1999 and has learned a great deal from its rich cultural and social history. His most recent book is *Class Community and Credit: Working Class Debt since 1880* (2009).

Stephen Royle has taught at Queen's University, Belfast, since 1976 and is now Professor of Island Geography. In addition to research on islands, he has published extensively on Belfast, including two fascicles of the Royal Irish Academy's *Irish Historic Towns Atlas – No. 12: Belfast to 1840* (with Raymond Gillespie, 2003) and *No. 17: Belfast 1840–1901* (2007) and *Portrait of an Industrial City: 'Clanging Belfast', 1750–1914* (2011). He was also editor, with Fred Boal, of *Enduring City: Belfast in the Twentieth Century* (2006).

Index

Index

Subscribers to the Limited Edition

Belfast City Council

Queen's University Belfast

Adelaide Insurance Services

Alec and Joan Williams

Belfast Harbour

Byrne Looby Partners

Clearway Disposals Ltd

Crossroads Caring for Carers (NI) Ltd

Delta Print and Packaging Ltd

Dr S Peter FitzGerald CBE, Randox Laboratories Limited

Hospital Services Limited

Interfrigo Ltd, Cold Storage & Shipping Services

John Rainey, Denroy Group Limited www.denmanbrush.com www.denroy.com

Laboratory Supplies & Instruments Ltd

Michael Lagan, Lagan Construction

Pauley Business Services Limited

Professor Andrew Thompson, University of Exeter

Richard Lansdall-Welfare

RPS Group – Northern Ireland

Sangers (NI) Limited

Steven Meek, our fabulous Daddy love Zarah & Lexie

Thales, Belfast

The Linen Hall Library, Belfast

University of Ulster

W. G. Ian Ritchie and Irene C. Ritchie

WDR & RT Taggart

Wilson Gillespie & Company